Books by Daniel Hoffman

Words to Create a World
Faulkner's Country Matters
Hang-Gliding from Helicon: New and Selected Poems
Brotherly Love
The Center of Attention
Poe Poe Poe Poe Poe Poe Poe
Broken Laws
Striking the Stones
Barbarous Knowledge
The City of Satisfactions
Form and Fable in American Fiction
A Little Geste and Other Poems
The Poetry of Stephen Crane
An Armada of Thirty Whales
Paul Bunyan, Last of the Frontier Demigods

As Editor

Ezra Pound and William Carlos Williams
Harvard Guide to Contemporary American Writing
American Poetry and Poetics
The Red Badge of Courage and Other Stories

DANIEL HOFFMAN

Form and Fable

in American Fiction

'If I am overflowing with life,
am rich in experience for which I lack expression,
then nature will be my language full of poetry,
—all nature will fable, *and every natural phenomenon be a myth.'*
—Thoreau

University Press of Virginia

Charlottesville and London

THE UNIVERSITY PRESS OF VIRGINIA

This edition first published 1994

Library of Congress Cataloging-in-Publication Data

Hoffman, Daniel, 1923–
Form and fable in American fiction / Daniel Hoffman.
p. cm.
Originally published: New York : Oxford University Press, 1961. With new preface.
Includes index.
ISBN 0–8139–1525–2 (pbk.)
1. American fiction—19th century—History and criticism. 2. Literature and folklore—United States—History—19th century. 3. Folklore in literature. 4. Hawthorne, Nathaniel, 1804–1864—Knowledge—Folklore. 5. Melville, Herman, 1819–1891—Knowledge— Folklore. 6. Twain, Mark, 1835–1910—Knowledge—Folklore. I. Title.
PS374.F62H64 1994
813′.309—dc20 93–39985
CIP

Printed in the United States of America

Contents

Preface to the 1994 Edition

The republication of this book, which first appeared thirty-three years ago, invites reflection on the possible reasons for its survival over a period when the reigning assumptions of literary criticism have undergone radical changes.

I would suggest that *Form and Fable in American Fiction* was unique and has remained so in respect of its interdisciplinary critical method, a combination of close textual readings, considerations of the improvised forms required by the most significant American fictions of the nineteenth century, and interpretation of the uses made in them of myth and folklore. This synthesis resulted from my pursuit of lines of inquiry not addressed by most critics of American literature.

So-called myth criticism has long been out of fashion, but this book differed from the too-enthusiastic monomythomania of such ritualists as Joseph Campbell, Lord Raglan, and Robert Graves, as well as from the orthodoxy of Northrop Frye. Their passion to subordinate the wide ranges of human imagination to reiterations of a single pattern—not that they agreed among themselves as to the regnant archetype—resembled the ambitions of those functionalist anthropologists whose insights I adopted while rejecting their compulsions to subordinate examination of particulars to a totalizing theory of social interaction. What I did learn from my studies with Ruth Benedict and Conrad Arensberg and from my brief participation as research assistant in The Study of Culture at a Distance (a project in which social anthropologists, collecting information from survivors of the *shtetls* destroyed by the Nazis, attempted to describe a vanished culture) was that every social institution, every expression of communal identity, is interrelated to every other, and all reinforce the structure of the social group. But I had to differ with the theorists of functionalism, whose paradigms, like those of the mythographers, were largely based on the study of relatively static preliterate societies and who interpreted the interlocking of language, custom, and institutions as guarantors of the stability of culture.

My familiarity with American folklore as well as with our cultural history made inescapable consideration of the dynamics of cultural change. The rituals, myths, and folk expressions of a people in the act of defining their own identity, most often in actual or symbolic rebellions against the givens of inherited European culture, could be subversive as well as supportive of established values. Hawthorne, for instance, in 'My Kinsman, Major Molineux' used an inherited English folk festival and figure, the day of misrule with its mock king, to represent America's coming of age; but the author, a temperamental conservative alive to the indeterminacies and dangers implicit in violent change, made his prototypical American naïf, Robin, view with confusion and dismay the humiliation of his kinsman the major and his own acquiescence in the spectacle. In England the festival reinforced the society it parodied by serving as a psychological safety valve for the tensions and resentments generated by hierarchical institutions. In Hawthorne's imagination, however, the day of misrule symbolized the American Revolution, whose consequences after half a century he regarded with equivocation.

Myth criticism, like functionalist social theory, was reductive and over-deterministic; folklore, on the other hand, lacked any convincing theoretical structure. It was a field defined by its content. Still, I am glad to acknowledge the influence of several scholars upon my efforts to interpret folk materials. In his work on balladry MacEdward Leach showed how folklore texts arise from and are preserved, altered, or abandoned in response to social forces. William Fenton's studies of American Indian folklore complemented my readings in anthropology on nonliterate tribes elsewhere—studies by Malinowski, Boas, Redfield, and Margaret Mead, as well as Llewellyn and Hoebel's study of Cheyenne law. And Richard M. Dorson's many books explored the matrix of historical circumstance necessary for interpreting American folk materials.

My study presents native American folklore (and, often, folk materials inherited from Europe) in a rivalrous symbiosis with European myths. The folk materials I examine arose largely as communal expressions of responses to new conditions. Based on the motifs significantly used by the authors discussed, the folklore surveyed and interpreted here is various indeed. Superstitions, witchcraft beliefs, and providences reiterate motifs from the *Malleus Maleficarum;* remnants of pagan beliefs striate English, and hence Colonial American, folklore. Longbows, tall tales, the exaggerations of folk speech, some adapted from inherited modes, arose for the most part with the settlement of the wilderness, life on the frontier, and conflicts between denizens of the frontier and dwellers in settlements. Conceptions of regional character were defined in folk jest and anecdote, in folk song and tale, all furnishing motifs and paradigms appropriated and developed by the authors here discussed—Irving, Hawthorne, Melville, and Mark Twain.

Most folklorists are not adepts of literary criticism, and, as was observed by several reviewers of this book, critics of American literature were unfamiliar with folklore. My combining these usually separate lines of inquiry was the unexpected result of a rather wayward progress. I can truly say that I became a quandam folklorist because of being insufficiently adroit on the clarinet to play Dixieland jazz. In those years before midcentury, when jazz, scorned as vulgar and confused with popular dance music, was taken seriously only by such European critics as Robert Goffin and Hughes Panassié, I was deeply attracted to this dynamic and inventive music. For one thing, it offered a form of rebellion against the bourgeois culture in which I was raised; but the attraction, being long-lasting, went deeper than that. I speak of the music played by small groups, characterized by creative tensions between contrapuntal ensembles and the soloists' ability to transcend the musical matrix from which their parts arise—a classical style, developed by the end of the 1920s and maintained with variations for several decades. This music grew out of vocal and instrumental folk expression, combining Afro-American origins with essential elements of white musical culture; it responded complexly to the social conditions in which it was formed.

My study of this music was a personal quest—there was then no other way to learn about it than by trying to play it, attending jam sessions, collecting records, reading what was available, and analyzing such source materials as the Negro folk music recorded by Alan Lomax and the precursors of jazz recorded by Frederic Ramsay. I became perforce informed on the history of jazz and, in college, wrote a long paper on its development. This, much condensed, constituted my first professional publication ('The Folk Art of Jazz,' *Antioch Review,* Spring 1945) while I was still in the service and before graduation from college. In succeeding years I brought into my efforts to place the music in its historical circumstances a more knowledgeable analysis of its structure, with the aim of refining discrimination between individual skills and styles among instrumentalists and groups in, to use a Bix Beiderbecke title, 'Jazz as It Should Be Played.' Eleven years later I published a more sophisticated view of the music: 'Jazz, the Survival of a Folk Art,' in *Perspectives USA* (Spring 1956). This journal, funded by the Ford Foundation, appeared simultaneously in the United States and Britain and in French, Italian, and German translations; my article was subsequently translated into Polish as well. So my views of jazz were widely circulated.

I've gone into all this detail to suggest that my initial interest in folklore and my first interdisciplinary work was as an amateur of musicology. From this experience quite outside literary criticism, I learned decisively the need to consider historical and cultural as well as artistic elements in the development of a set of conventions for the expression of feeling, a style, an art form, an oeuvre. Seeing jazz as a sophisticated art form emerging from folk musical sources, themselves already highly developed, I moved on to study other folk arts and their interactions with 'high' art. As my interests were literary, I was drawn to the forms of verbal folklore—those with relatively complex structures, such as ballads and folktales, and those characterized by cultural content, such as superstitions and beliefs, jests, social folkways, and conceptions of character. To ground my understanding of both jazz and its sources, and the folklore interests that followed in their relationships to their uses in or derivations from literary works, I studied anthropology as well as literature. Columbia University had, and has, no folklore department, so I was both compelled and enabled to construct a synthesis from the disciplines I studied there.

I was early convinced that there must be a fruitful interaction between folk expressions of verbal culture and the most intense and revelatory works of literary imagination. For folklore, of the sorts I detail in this book, is itself the making manifest imaginative responses to life. To be created and perpetuated it requires the existence of a community, of shared experience over time in relative isolation—such as in a sparsely populated and homogeneous society, an occupational group (e.g., raftsmen, lumberjacks, hunters, sailors), or an ethnic group (the transplanted English villagers of Hawthorne's tales, slaves in the Old South). Men from diverse backgrounds, like the crew of the Pequod, both brought with them ancestral and racial folklore and shared other folk motifs as members of an occupation. The uses in fiction of folklore from such groups had been noted before *Form and Fable* but was described merely as contributing to local color. My enterprise was to demonstrate the thematic significance of folklore in literary works of first intensity. Careful study of ballads and folktales from oral tradition shows how their power devolves from stylistic mastery similar to that of the individual authorship of literary works. Indeed, such folk texts *are* literary works, whose authors are anonymous; their accomplishments are preserved through retellings by audiences who at their best retain the qualities in the performed texts.[1] (Of course not all folk informants are vicarious word-artists, hence the discrepant variants in collected tales and songs.)

I had developed the method of such interpretation in a book

[1] I have attempted definition of these concepts in two articles in the *Journal of American Folklore:* 'Folklore in Literature: Notes toward a Theory of Interpretation,' LXX (January–March 1957), 15–21, and 'A Theory of American Folklore,' LXXII (July–September 1959), 222–32.

previous to, and of narrower focus than, this one, investigating the folklore of American lumberjacks and its transformations in popular culture (advertising brochures, children's stories, commercially motivated adult fiction) and in literary works by Frost, Sandburg, and Auden.[2] In books subsequent to the present study I extended the approach to examine three recent British poets (Yeats, Graves, and Muir) and, as a sequel to *Form and Fable*, the uses of folk and mythic materials in several works by William Faulkner that required definition of their form.[3]

In those studies, as in this one, I combined considerations of the historical, cultural, and biographical matrix in which authors worked with close analytical readings of their texts. I readily confess my training in and practice of the methods of the New Criticism. Rigorous formal analysis seems an essential resource for literary discourse. In not only assuming—but, in the cases of well-made literary works, revealing—internal consistencies, interrelationships of diction, tone, metaphor, sound, and structure, and reliance upon or deviation from traditions of form, literary explication seemed to me analogous to functionalist anthropology's demonstrations of the mutually reinforcing linkages between social institutions and the language in which they are expressed.

The New Criticism has suffered disrepute from narrow explications by practitioners who isolated literature from its social contexts and analyzed structure and texture as though poems or novels were made of words alone and responded only to their own internal dynamics or consistencies. That the New Criticism was not intended to isolate literature from its contexts is evident in the subsequent work of its originators: Cleanth Brooks's studies of Faulkner, Robert

[2] *Paul Bunyan, Last of the Frontier Demigods* (Philadelphia, 1952; rpt. Lincoln, Neb., 1983). Richard M. Dorson cites this study as the first to give theoretical grounds for distinguishing between genuine folklore and its imitations and transformations in popular culture ('A Great Folk Hero, Perhaps,' *Yale Review*, LII [December 1952], 298–99).

[3] *Barbarous Knowledge* (New York, 1967); *Faulkner's Country Matters* (Baton Rouge, 1989).

Penn Warren's of Whittier and Dreiser, and the anthology that they, together with R. W. B. Lewis, prepared of American literature with full informative prefaces setting each work and author in relevant historical contexts. These studies should all discourage this erroneous notion that the New Criticism dogmatically excluded attention to such matters. Its method was designed to protect literature, on the one hand, from undisciplined 'appreciations' and, on the other, from criticism that subordinated literary values to political determinism, as did that of V. L. Parrington and Granville Hicks.

To the explicatory discipline absorbed from the founders of the New Criticism—I include R. P. Blackmur and Allen Tate among its exemplars—I add the cultural criticism of American literature as practiced by Richard Chase and Lionel Trilling. Not that I was so tempted, but I would scarcely have found it possible to consider a poem or work of fiction as merely a verbal construct, absent the cultural circumstances of its creation. Nor would my training and subsequent researches in anthropology, myth, and folklore and have permitted so hermetic a reading of literature.

The great works of nineteenth-century American fiction may be read in accordance with any of the various late twentieth-century critical theories, but none was written with that end in view. Speaking as one who has experienced authorship of poems as well as of critical prose, I can with conviction deny such contemporary slogans as those that decree the death of the author, or that the language writes the text, or that the poem or fiction is determined by the hegemony of the ruling class or the struggle against its rule, or by the play of economic forces, or any other extrinsic factors. These exist—as factors, not as total explanations. If the more naive practitioners of the New Criticism isolated the examined texts as constructs made solely of words, have not deconstructionists and other theoreticians committed similar reductions? The struggle that produces literary works is that of the author, using available language and available forms, which he either adapts or transforms, to respond to the pressures upon his times. The themes grasped in imagination as the most significant and importunate, and the vocabularies of texture and structure in which they are made to reveal themselves, are produced by individual effort and talent, in the context of the aforementioned and still other forces outside the language and the author.

The work of criticism is always a lesser thing than that of creation, for to what can the critic address himself but the created texts of another? In time, in permanence, and in inviolability the literary work has precedence over its interpretations. These vary with the age, one intellectual fashion succeeding another, each re-reading the same books to different ends, but the books so re-read remain. Melville, so much wiser than any of us who read or interpret him, fabled this among his many other truths, as revealed in his chapter 'The Doubloon.' As I discuss it in this book (pp. 253–56), the design on the coin Ahab nailed to the mast as reward to the first aboard who sights Moby-Dick is given in detail, the various elements in its visual vocabulary straightforwardly stated. All that we lack is comprehension of what they mean. Each member of the Pequod's crew in turn contemplates this coin, itself a symbol of the whale—and of the book, which in its first, British edition was titled *The Whale*—and what each sees excludes the vision of each of the others, since each perceptor brings to his act of interpretation his own personality, predilections, and limitations. It is only Ishmael, reporting all the versions of the other interpreters, who enables us to see how the allegories each reads are inadequate but when taken together offer the transformation of allegory's monism into the rich, various, ambiguous yet revelatory symbolism at the heart of the meaning of the entire work.

I see, as contemporary equivalents to Stubb, Flask, Starbuck, and Ahab, each locked in his own monism, the theorists—structuralist, Marxist, psychoanalytic, reader-responsive, deconstructive—whose discourse, whatever its virtues, repudiates the primacy of the author, the integrity of the author's work, and its significance as the expression of its own time. Finding ourselves at the end of our immensely disruptive century, we see that a host of political, economic, technological, and psychological revolutions have led to the abjuration of rationalism and, among the intelligentsia, a sweeping despair, the embracing of indeterminacy in place of certainties felt to be no longer attainable. In the little world of literary studies, unanchored dismay leads to the distrust of meaning and to the intellectual undermining of the authority of language as well as of social institutions. The past is dismissed save as it is read in terms of what are perceived as our own immediate needs—making the past prove our assumptions about the present.

Responsible literary discourse, however, must be based first of all on an understanding of what the works discussed were intended to mean and what meanings were achieved in them in their own time, as well as in ours. If these be ignored, we have no knowledge of our past. It is my hope that in *Form and Fable in American Fiction* my skepticism of abstractions and of totalizing theories, and the pluralist, eclectic method of analysis drawing upon hitherto neglected sources of imaginative metaphors will elucidate ten of the defining works of American fiction. What I hoped to do for Irving, Hawthorne, Melville, and Mark Twain is to demonstrate their transformations of the materials from popular and high culture, from the European past and the American present that nourished their imaginations; to replicate—or at least retrace—how each author constructed a synthesis of his experiences and his perceptions of American character in the symbolism of his writings; and to elicit interpretations not reductive of each author's intentions and achievements. The culture they struggled to express was at once stable and unstable. Among its institutions those freighted with antiquity were being challenged by those newly emergent from unprecedented conditions. Even the forms of their fictions required both observance of conventions inherited from the country of our origin and bold improvisations expressing the energies and experiences not hitherto seen in fiction.

The adventures of such figments of their imaginations as Ichabod Crane, Young Goodman Brown, Robin Molineux, Hester, Holgrave, Coverdale, Ishmael and Ahab and their shipmates, the Confidence-Man, and Huck Finn evocatively embedded in truths of history, myth, and folk expression, embody several of the central conflicts and conceptions of American life. Hence the works in which they appear have become, and remain, canonical. In *Form and Fable in American Fiction* I hope to have fairly presented the means by which they helped to form our national consciousness and to have illuminated some of the sources of our pleasure in reading them.

DANIEL HOFFMAN

Cape Rosier, Maine
August, 1993

Original Preface

In this book I am concerned to discover certain themes which have profoundly influenced the early masters of American fiction —Irving, Hawthorne, Melville, and Mark Twain—and to define the peculiar forms in which their best writings were cast. In recent years critics have acknowledged what Hawthorne and Melville had maintained all along: that they wrote not novels but romances. Yet what romances are in fact has never been satisfactorily determined. I have chosen as examples 'The Legend of Sleepy Hollow,' several of Hawthorne's best tales and his three full-length American books, Melville's *Moby-Dick* and *The Confidence-Man,* and Mark Twain's *Adventures of Huckleberry Finn.* In defining the empirical, improvised, and individual characteristics of their unique fictional forms I explore the reliance of these authors upon allegory, Gothicism, didactic, religious and travel writings, and traditions of folklore, popular culture, and mythology.

The word 'romance' may to some readers seem pejorative, connoting a trivial work of fancy where they would prefer the shaping power of imagination. 'Romance' may suggest an avoidance of 'reality,' a dependence upon fantasy, sentiment, or melodrama, an unwillingness on the author's part to face up to the real problems of his own society. Critics as disparate as V. L. Parrington, Lionel Trilling, and Erich Auerbach have found the fictional romance a less significant literary form than the novel of social realism. For valid historical reasons the assumptions of the realistic novel were to some extent unavailable to the most gifted American contemporaries of Dickens, Flaubert, and Dostoievsky. I do not propose that our romances are barren of novelistic elements; in fact they are often a curious mixture of the mimetic representation of reality and their own peculiar characteristics as romances. These latter lead the imaginations of their authors and readers not toward the treatment of society as a complex interaction of classes and forces, but instead toward an ahistorical depiction of the individual's discovery of his own identity in a world where his essential self is inviolate and independent of such involvements in history.

Thus the predilections of the form of our fiction lead us directly to consider its fables. One need not accept the subjective and unhistorical views of reality proposed by followers of Jung or by the mythographic ritual critics to acknowledge the recurrence in our culture of certain basic patterns of experience. The same conditions in American life that led our fiction-writers toward the romance instead of the novel of social documentation led them also to emphasize 'archetypal' patterns of individual experience. Such patterns of course are communally determined, preserved, and transmitted. They are clearly evident in non-literary contexts which our authors knew, and drew upon, and made the materials of their literary achievements. Their themes are already present, awaiting the authors' appropriation, in folklore, myth, and ritual.

Folklore has long been recognized in American writing, as elsewhere, as an element in the minor tradition of local color literature. My concern is to show its shaping role in ten of the most important American tales and romances. As T. S. Eliot has said of Baudelaire's imagery of city life, what is significant is not only that he used such images but that he raised them to the highest intensity. Hawthorne, Melville, and Mark Twain do not merely record local foibles in the picturesque manner of Mrs. Stowe's *Poganuc People* or Eggleston's *The Hoosier Schoolmaster*. Folk traditions contribute to their major writings at a pitch of first intensity concepts of character, of theme, of action, of language. And what is this folklore on which they draw? I find several seminal traditions transmitted both orally and in a variety of literary and non-belletristic writings from the seventeenth century onward. Conceptions of native character (first proposed by Constance Rourke) developed early and accurately reflected prevailing types. The individualism of such characters was dramatized in a rhetoric of comedy determined by native conditions, in a native idiom, and in their characteristic attitudes—independence of society, and conquest of Nature. American folklore provides also two complementary 'myths' of the land—as Eden, as Hell. The combination of an Adamic view of Man with a prelapsarian concept of Nature has had interesting consequences in our literature. So, too, has the presence of the opposite views: the defeat by an intractable wilderness of the pioneer enterprise, and the inherited Calvinist belief in Man as a fallen creature.

In a theocratic society like Colonial New England, theology is the property not only of divines and savants, nor does what we term superstition belong to the uncouth and illiterate alone. An entire populace shares the assumptions of both and interprets them as it can. Belief in witchcraft tied Cotton Mather and the humblest farmer of Salem in as tight a skein as did their common conviction of original sin. It may be objected that a learned divine can hardly be considered a folk informant; yet the dynamic transmission of folk beliefs does not observe the careful distinctions of some modern historians who would view witchcraft entirely as a branch of ecclesiastical history, nor of those who see it only as a popular delusion. Witchcraft was both at once, and although the religious basis for the belief had eroded by the nineteenth century, when our authors responded to its demonic imaginative power, it lingered potently in the folk imagination. So, too, did belief in the Remarkable Judgment, or Divine Providence, by which unnatural events spelled out the allegory of man's life. The lore of omens testified to that fascination with the mystery and terror in the wilderness and in the soul which has always been a concern of the American character complementary to its careless optimism. The folk imagination, nothing if not inconsistent, has nurtured a third supernatural tradition contradicting the convictions of witchcraft as to man's sin and of the Providence as to God's power. Relics of the unfallen pagan world survived in rituals asserting man's happy place in the cycle of Nature. These, too, have appealed to the writers of our romances.

Such traditions of native character, of comedy, of supernatural allegory, of human nature as both unfallen and demonic, have been peculiarly appropriate to the 'poetic,' nonrealistic character of the American romance. There they are often in tension with ritualistic and mythic themes from world culture as the American hero seeks to discover his own identity by rebelling against father, ruler, society, or God. Repeatedly the native hero is a metamorphic, self-reliant naïf, akin to the Yankee or Frontiersman of popular tradition. Repeatedly he must define himself in conflict with a more stable ritual-figure or society reflecting the American inheritance of European culture and its burdens of historical responsibility. First sketched in Irving's little romance of Brom Bones *vs.* Ichabod Crane, the theme emerges with clarity as Hawthorne's Robin meets his kinsman Major Molineux, as Holgrave frees himself from inherited guilt, as the settlers of Blithedale attempt to reform mankind, as Ishmael and Ahab contend for the captaincy of the former's soul, as Huck and Tom enact alternative destinies for Young America in search of self-knowledge and freedom.

Approaching ten of their works to define these authors' themes and forms, I have tried to keep continually in mind the artistic wholeness of each tale or romance. The qualities of such literary experiences—the authors' success or failure to elicit a cohesive, unified response based on the emotional logic of the materials chosen—can be justly measured only when both their intentions and the possibilities inherent in their materials are understood. Thus when Hawthorne writes of witchcraft in 'Young Goodman Brown,' when Melville tells tall tales in *Moby-Dick,* or Twain uses both witches and folk humor in *Huckleberry Finn,* we cannot claim to understand these works until we know how each author interpreted the ideas, emotions, and attitudes toward experience that he found in his folk materials, and how he tried to make those materials function in his fiction. My method in the chapters dealing with specific works is to concentrate on a close reading of each tale; I assess whatever contributions the text itself demands from folklore, myth, and ritual, or from biographical, historical, or literary antecedents.

In the opening section of this book I trace the major themes these authors found in folk traditions. The critic who takes folklore as seriously as I do cannot help being struck by the difficulties that confront his using it with discretion. On the one hand there is no general agreement even among professional scholars as to what folklore actually is. On the other, many persons have an erroneous idea of its nature, thanks to the assiduity with which popularized falsifications, undiscriminating collections, and mendacious banalities have been passed off as 'folklore' to a tradition-hungry mass audience. Responsible folklore scholarship provides a wealth of materials but an absence of interpretive conceptions which might prove useful to the reader interested in how a great author has profited from his involvement with the popular imagination of his country. The few critical works which have attempted such a study either have been impressionistic in their assimilation of folk background or have not documented their assertions sufficiently. By now, however, folklore has been collected so thoroughly that there seems no further excuse for a study involving the folk background of literature to neglect informing its readers where those folk roots may be found. In my first three chapters, it will be seen, I follow both a thematic and an historical method in surveying the several traditions referred to above.

If folklore scholarship lacks guiding critical conceptions, nothing would be further from the case when we consider mythographic criticism. Mythography has the appeal of a religion, especially in an unchurched age such as ours; and most of the critics concerned with the ritual or psychological origins of literature have been as dogmatic as Cotton Mather himself in their insistence upon a monistic and all-inclusive pattern of experience which all myth and most literature is said to exhibit. America, however, has inherited not one but many myths, and we have invented, lived through, and endured still other myths of our own. I cannot find any single myth in our writings which subsumes all others; rather our authors have responded eclectically to the premises of their culture and have made use of whatever myths from the Old World or the New seemed consistent with their own concerns. The most general statement one might make is that the hero of American folktale, legend, and romance is likely to go on a journey of self-discovery. The imagination of our romance-writers is clearly attuned to the relation between the individual and his own experience as a 'Representative Man,' to use Emerson's phrase; in his representativeness the hero experiences the concern of his culture to define its own identity as he seeks his. Far from reenacting the death and resurrection of the Corn Spirit, or the psychic childhood of the race, the hero of the American romance cuts himself off from the history of the world which bears these traditions. His dilemma is to discover the new myths which may viably take the place of those he has discarded. The discarded myths however are significantly present in the romance his actions create, for it is only in his awareness of the traditions he must not desire that he can find his own destiny.

Folklore and myth contribute not only to the materials of the romance but also to its method and its form. The aesthetic assumptions of our authors are best defined by Emerson, in whose thought the poet is the discoverer of reality, a maker of myths, an interpreter of the living metaphors by which language establishes the links between the worlds of sense and of spirit. In responding to the artistic possibilities of their mythical and folk materials our romance-writers absorbed the imaginative heritage of their culture, mastered its fragmentary achievements, and developed its incipient forms. Even when they used the materials of popular culture to reveal the inherent dangers of our unassuaged Prometheanism, to satirize the shallowness and folly of our mindless egalitarian levelling zeal, they move most deeply in the

American grain. For in such works as *The Blithedale Romance, The Confidence-Man,* and *Huckleberry Finn* they are moved by what they most love in American life—its noble promise, its capacity for moral heroism—to record with irony and savage wit the triumphs of folly in a fallible world. They find both the promise and the fallibility in our native traditions and in the working-out of the conflict between these and the heritage the American has tried to leave behind.

ACKNOWLEDGMENTS

The problems I take up in this book seem in retrospect to have been suggested by my reading F. O. Matthiessen's *American Renaissance* and Constance Rourke's *American Humor* over a dozen years ago. Later Richard Chase, in his books on Melville and on the American novel, led me further toward much of the territory I explore in mine. When I have differed with the views of these critics it is always with a sense of obligation to those whose work has been so suggestive to mine. To Mr. Chase I am indebted also for long encouragement; he and Lewis Leary knew of this study from its beginnings, foresaw better than I did what its scope would be, and most helpfully read several chapters in manuscript. Among others who have discussed the literary problems in this book to my advantage I owe most to R. P. Blackmur, Barbara M. Cross, Samuel Hynes, and Newton P. Stallknecht. Richard M. Dorson was unfailingly generous in suggesting relevant folklore sources and in giving me access to his own collection of scarce materials and field data. I am particularly grateful to Elizabeth Shepherd, formerly of the Oxford University Press, for her devoted editorial guidance. Had I been able to take advantage of all the suggestions offered by these friends this would have been a better book. Over the years I have had the assistance also of many others who answered my inquiries, led me to sources, gave me their views, listened to mine, saved me from errors, and helped me to finish this job of work by their assumption that it would be worth the doing. Some of these debts must go unnoted, but I hope all who have helped me will accept this general acknowledgment of my thanks.

I feel an obligation, as difficult to specify as it was pleasant to incur, to the challenging discussion of parts of this book by students in my American literature seminars and courses at Swarthmore College. I am similarly indebted to those in my course at the School of Letters, Indiana University, who in the summer of 1959 helped me to work out the patterns of this study.

The Faculty Research Committee of Swarthmore College generously defrayed some of my expenses in 1958-59. For making available many of the books out of which this book was made I am grateful to Howard Williams, Readers Service Librarian, and the library staff of Swarthmore College; and to the librarians at Columbia University, the Free Library of Philadelphia, the Friends Historical Society, the Historical Society of Pennsylvania, Indiana University, and the University of Pennsylvania.

The Irving chapter is reprinted with slight revisions from *PMLA* (June 1953) by permission of the Modern Language Association. The editors of *American Literature* have kindly allowed use of a passage from my article, 'Jim's Magic: Black or White?' (March 1960). Chapter 6 and part of chapter 13 first appeared in *The Sewanee Review;* these are reprinted through the courtesy of its editor, Monroe K. Spears. I thank the editors of *The Antioch Review* for permission to reprint a section of chapter 3. I should perhaps say that the recent studies of the American novel by Leslie Fiedler and of Mark Twain by Walter Blair and by Kenneth S. Lynn appeared too late for me to consult them.

My deepest gratitude I gladly inscribe here to my wife and to Kate and Macfarlane, mythmakers at my study door.

DANIEL HOFFMAN

Swarthmore, Pennsylvania
September, 1960

PART I

Fable as Reality

1

Predilections: Romance, Folklore, Myth

ONE

'When a writer calls his work a romance,' Hawthorne asserts in his preface to *The House of the Seven Gables,* 'he wishes to claim a certain latitude, both as to its fashion and material, which he would not have felt himself entitled to assume had he professed to be writing a novel.' Indeed, the more closely one scrutinizes the 'fashion' and the 'material' of Hawthorne's fiction, and of *Moby-Dick, The Confidence-Man, Huckleberry Finn,* or, in our own day, Faulkner's sagas, the more difficult it becomes to make them all conform to any set of preconceptions. It is safe only to say that whatever else they may be individually, they cannot be satisfactorily described as novels of manners. They are significantly distinguished from the work of our novelists—Cooper, Howells, and James—by their authors' structural and thematic concerns with folklore, myth, and ritual. Their uses of these cultural survivals and primitive or subconscious patterns of experience dramatize their preoccupations with the instinctual and passional forces of life, with pre-conscious and pre-Christian values, with sub-rational and often anti-rational formulations of meaning. These values of course are almost invariably found in tensest tandem with their opposites: full consciousness, directed will, reason, Christianity.

It should not be surprising that the fictional development of primitivism loomed large on a continent whose early settlement had seemed, to the *philosophes* of the Enlightenment and the poets of Romanticism, to prove the justice of Rousseau's vision of the Noble Savage and the benignity of Nature. At the same time, America was the land of emergent rationalistic democracy and of capitalistic exploitation of the land. The conflicts, therefore, between Nature and Civilization, between a prelapsarian Eden and the spoliation of Paradise necessary to the imposition of human values on an indifferent wilderness, between free will as a function of natural liberty and determinism as a result of surrender to society—these have been among the most fertile sources of tension in our national experience and our literature. In their dramatizations of these conflicts, the authors of our romances have tended to avoid the materials and forms of the conventional novel and to draw to an extraordinary degree upon folklore and myth. The social and literary situation in the American nineteenth century made the successful novel of manners a rarity and invited instead the development of fiction in another genre.

From earliest settlement onward our literary culture was dominated by Puritan and Calvinistic theology, which expounded distrust of the senses and of the arts. Particularly suspect were the arts of mimetic representation of reality. Not until the twentieth century did the drama enlist our major talents. In New England, although poetry came to be sanctioned (indeed, overvalued), Hawthorne was the only important writer of fiction to make his way against the anti-fictional prejudices of his culture. And for him the opposition of his time and place was an obsessive problem; in the end it proved a crippling one. Authors as remote from the New England tradition as Washington Irving and Melville in New York and Mark Twain in Missouri had each to contend with similar Calvinistic proscription of the arts.

Hawthorne's way, which Melville shared, was an apparent dependence upon the single mode of literary expression sanctioned by his inherited culture: allegory. The allegorical spirit is strong in all of our romance-writers, but they made allegory an instrument for the exploration of problems and the assertion of truths never suspected by the seventeenth-century divines who bequeathed them the mode. The Puritan practice of allegory was founded on the simplistic doctrines of Ramus; a mode which expressed the conviction of a literal correspondence between one set of natural objects and a separate and detachable set of spiritual truths could scarcely represent or embody very much of nineteenth-century reality. As the faith which had sustained Puritan allegory withered or was transformed, as the supernatural certainties to which allegory anchored the things of this world became dubious or obscure, the mode yet persisted and lent itself to new uses. The imaginations of Hawthorne and Melville were both committed to allegorical premises and skeptical of allegorical truths. Allegory was designed for the elucidation of certainty; they used it in the service of search and skepticism, and, at times, of comedic affirmation of human values. In the process they transformed allegorism into a symbolic method which exemplified the transcendental aesthetic of Emerson, far though either romancer was from accepting Emerson's ethics or his view of nature.

Besides this use of allegory rather than of a presumptive realism as a point of departure, the American romance-writer was in a peculiar social situation compared to his French or English contemporaries. Henry James's indictment (in his study of Hawthorne) of what America lacks is the most celebrated statement of the difficulties faced by a prospective realist. For how could one write a novel of manners in a society which would seem to have had none?

> One might enumerate the items of high civilization, as it exists in other countries, which are absent from the texture of American life, until it should become a wonder to know what was left. No State, in the European sense of the word, and indeed barely a specific national name. No sovereign, no court, no personal loyalty, no aristocracy, no church, no clergy, no army, no diplomatic service, no country gentlemen, no palaces, no castles, nor manners, nor old country houses, nor parsonages, nor thatched cottages, nor ivied

> ruins; no cathedrals, nor abbeys, nor little Norman churches; no great universities nor public schools—no Oxford, nor Eton, nor Harrow; no literature, no novels, no museums, no pictures, no political society, no sporting class—no Epsom nor Ascot! Some such list as that might be drawn up of the absent things in American life—especially in the American life of forty years ago, the effect of which, upon an English or a French imagination, would probably as a general thing be appalling. The natural remark, in the almost lurid light of such an indictment, would be that if these things are left out, everything is left out.

But James, who is justifying his own choices rather than strictly describing Hawthorne's, goes on, in his ironic way, to admit that

> The American knows that a good deal remains; what it is that remains—that is his secret, his joke, as one may say. It would be cruel, in this terrible denudation, to deny him the consolation of his national gift, that 'American humor' of which of late years we have heard so much.[1]

James's 'lurid' indictment was in fact paraphrased and expanded from Hawthorne's similar complaint in the preface to *The Marble Faun.* In yet another preface, to *The Blithedale Romance,* Hawthorne is careful to relinquish all claims to having written a novel of society, although such a case could yet be strongly made for that book. He proposes instead that his work conforms to that other genre, the romance, which, in the passage quoted at the opening of this chapter, he goes on to describe: The romance, he writes,

> while, as a work of art, it must rigidly subject itself to laws, and while it sins unpardonably so far as it may swerve aside from the truth of the human heart—has fairly a right to present that truth under circumstances, to a great extent, of the writer's own choosing or creation. . . . He will be wise . . . to mingle the marvellous rather as a slight, delicate, and evanescent flavor, than as any portion of the actual substance of the dish offered to the public. He can hardly be said, however, to commit a literary crime, even if he disregard this caution.

[1] *Hawthorne* (New York, 1879), pp. 42-3.

Such a situation is patently the result of our short history and of our egalitarian commitment. In the very decade which James describes, de Tocqueville had predicted that our cultural profession of equality would deny in theory and conceal in practice those differences between the varied stations of life which in aristocratic states are delineated and enforced by codes of manners. Egalitarian democracy would prove subversive of that distinctness of individual character at which the novelist must aim; for when everyone is equal how is anyone different from his fellows? Yet at the same time that egalitarianism denied such differences in the name of individual freedom, it cast the individual in his loneliest role in history. For he had no heritage, no tradition, no status ascribed to him by his past. He had to achieve everything he did or became, as though no man had lived on earth before him. The political and institutional emphases of this lonely individualism were reinforced by Puritan theology. Man's relation to his God was unmediated. The American had neither a class nor a history to fix his place in society, neither priest nor church to ameliorate his relation to the immensities.

Not only was our history short, but it was colonial. This circumstance produced the inevitable cultural lag between the province and the motherland; and, more important perhaps, our Puritan founders represented a minority culture in the homeland itself. With their predilection for allegory and distaste for mimesis which we have observed, the realistic fashion emerging in late eighteenth-century fiction made small impact in America. Instead our prose writers were attracted to a fictional mode which in England flourished briefly as a minor, obverse reaction to the dominant realism of Defoe and Fielding and the sentimentalized depiction of manners in Richardson.

Gothicism itself had been one of the heralds during the Age of Reason of the oncoming shift of sensibility to Romanticism. It brought together two already nascent Romantic themes—fascination with the past, and with those supernatural forces which defied the attempts of reason to comprehend and regulate experience. What is usually taken as the Gothic machinery of mystery calls for reinterpretation as the literary adaptation of supernatural folklore. In a sense the folk imagination has always been Gothic in its acceptance of the inexplicable, of the supernatural. Gothicism in its attention to the medieval past focussed on the very period when the superstitious lore of modern times was being formed. This lore is the detritus of Europe's pagan past, a past which has lingered in country customs, seasonal festivals, the lore of witchcraft, and folk belief in revenants, stregas, fairies, and other un-Christian inhabitants of the world of spirit. Much of this lore came with the settlers to the American colonies, where it survived to nourish the imaginations of our own writers of romance. Thus the elements which Hawthorne termed 'the marvellous' in his romances are at the same time 'Gothic' and folkloristic. Much of 'the marvellous' in the American romance takes advantage of folk superstition, whether actually current in oral tradition or recovered for fictional use from the writings of antiquaries and historians. Thanks to the industrious collection and classification of folklore by American scholars, it is possible to demonstrate the debt of the American romance to the varied strands of folk tradition.

Not all of our folk traditions, however, reveal fertility tokens or the dread portents of the other world. An indubitable fact of our popular culture is that 'American humor' which Henry James acknowledged in so deprecatory a way. It is not merely a trove of boisterous jokes, as Constance Rourke recognized when she called her work *American Humor, A Study of the National Character*. The most significant single comment one can make about the folk traditions of American humor is that, taken *en masse,* they propound a uniquely comic view of life and an optimistic conviction of human destiny. Although only two or three centuries old and correspondingly thin in depth and narrow in gauge, this lore has yet had time to produce a gallery of heroes who embody its values.

The American author who would use this lore may either deal with it for its own sake, accepting its creations and its values, or he may view the heroes of native folk experience as one end of a cultural tug-of-war in which the other end of the rope is grasped by the heroes of European tradition. The former option leads to regionalism, the latter to a much more powerful literature. For, if I may extend the image, the rope that is drawn taut between Ben Franklin, the Yankee, the Kentucky Screamer, and Johnny Appleseed on the one side and Adonis, Prometheus, and Christ on the other, in its very length and tension represents the continuity of culture and the struggles of history. It is the opposition of the New World to the Old. The ties that bind both together can be cut or burst asunder only by main force or reckless daring. Yet it is the American hero's destiny to try to break these ties. It is his fate to endure the consequences of their breaking.

TWO

I propose, then, that recognition of the uses of folklore and myth will enrich our responses to some of the most praiseworthy works of American fiction. It will modify received conclusions about their authors' sensibilities. And it will expose important though neglected sources of continuity linking these examples of the prose romance. The approach, however, is beset by difficulties, for both folklore and mythography may lead the unwary critic astray. Whoever explores the backwoods of folklore must find his own bearings amid the antiquarian chauvinism and the lack of intellectual focus which unhappily striate much of his source materials. The reckless penetrant of the sacred groves of ritual may be equally misled by the straightness of the path offered him by one or another monistic theory that would explain all myth. Between confusion and abstraction, how find the way?

Mr. Richard Chase, a critic conspicuously sensitive in his books on Melville, Whitman, and Dickinson to their debts to popular culture and folklore, has a salutary warning against 'myth criticism' in his latest study of the American novel. 'It is not a good idea,' he advises, 'to try to define too closely either the archetypes of the folk mind or the romance that sometimes embodies them. Neither, fortunately, is capable of being reduced to a single formula.' The fault in the method of the myth critics is that they

> will immediately and mistakenly equate romance with myth. In the critical practice of this school of thought, if not strictly in theory, there is only one myth—namely the death and rebirth of a god. This archetype is thought to constitute the essential action of tragedy especially, but also of comedy, elegy, and perhaps ultimately all valuable literary forms. It is thought, as one gathers, to be eternally recreated in man's unconscious, and also to be prescribed, in some unexplained manner, by the nature of literature itself . . . The characteristic American form of the mythic archetype is thought to be the fall from innocence and the initiation into life—an action of the soul that entails a symbolic dying and rebirth.[2]

Chase's strictures are aimed equally at the ritualistic and the psychiatric mythographers. Contemporary study of myth has developed in these two directions suggested by Frazer's *The Golden Bough* and Freud's *Totem and Taboo.* Both schools have made iconoclastic and all-inclusive claims. Among the ritualists Lord Raglan and Stanley Hyman make exactly those that Chase alleges against them. Psychoanalytic mythography, often drawing upon ritualistic works for support, proposes that all myths are one myth, and that the mythic level of consciousness as found in primitive peoples corresponds to the infantile or neurotic consciousness of modern man. These assumptions underlie the work of Otto Rank and Joseph Campbell. Still another form of mythographic dogmatism has been compounded most interestingly by Robert Graves, who uses ritualistic methods to avow euhemerism, and discovers all myth to be versions of a single pattern, itself a psychological archetype of the human soul. Although there has been increasing skepticism of these versions of monomyth—often on the grounds that the unitary vision of each monomythographer

[2] *The American Novel and Its Tradition* (New York, 1957), pp. 243-4.

differs from that of the next one—the appeal of 'myth criticism' for some literary critics has been tremendous.[3]

Recent criticism, moving from the sociology of literature in the 1930's to the close analysis of literary form by the quondam 'New Critics' in the 1940's, found the ritualistic or mythic approach congenial to its enterprise. Anthropology could be combined with aesthetic theory to provide a strong intellectual tradition which reinforced the study of artistic form with speculation on the primitive origins of art, on the mythic analogues to recent literature, and on the continuation in Western culture of archetypal patterns of organizing human experience. Now these considerations can be valuable indeed in the interpretation of modern works, and particularly of the American novel-romance. But to concentrate alone upon such mythic patterns as Hyman, Raglan, Rank, Campbell, and the Cambridge anthropologists have traced is to misread the mythic meanings of American literature.

It would seem that any consideration of historical sense, of the realities of cultural dynamics, would make this assumption self-evident. Valuable as ritualistic theory is in elucidating those areas of literature which indeed were produced under its auspices—Greek drama, epic poetry, Arthurian romance—when one turns

[3] Raglan states his position in *The Hero* (New York, 1956) and in 'Myth and Ritual,' *Myth: A Symposium*, ed. Thomas A. Sebeok (Bloomington, Indiana, 1956), pp. 76-83. Hyman gives a comprehensive survey of this approach in 'The Ritual View of Myth and Mythic,' ibid. pp. 84-94; see also his 'Myth, Ritual, and Nonsense,' *Kenyon Review*, XI (Summer 1949), 455-74, and *The Armed Vision* (New York, 1955). For psychoanalytic mythography, see Rank, *The Myth of the Birth of the Hero* (New York, 1959); and Campbell, *The Hero with a Thousand Faces* (New York, 1956). Graves's theories are set forth in *The White Goddess*, 3d ed. (London, 1952), and *The Greek Myths*, 2 vols. (Baltimore, 1955).

Criticism of the single mythic construct is given by Herbert Weisinger, 'Some Meanings of Myth,' *Comparative Literature, Proceedings of the ICLA Congress* . . . ed. W. P. Friedrich (Chapel Hill, 1959), pp. 1-10; Richard M. Dorson, 'Theories of Myth and the Folklorist,' *Daedalus*, LXXXVIII (Spring 1959), 280-90; and Stith Thompson, 'Myths and Folktales,' in Sebeok, *Myth: A Symposium*, pp. 104-10. For criticisms of Graves see Weisinger, ' "A Very Curious and Painstaking Person": Robert Graves as Mythographer,' *Midwest Folklore*, VI (Winter 1956), 235-44; and my article, 'The Unquiet Graves,' *Sewanee Review*, LXVII (Spring 1959), 305-16.

to American culture the case is rather different. The brevity of our history, our rapidly changing cultural conditions, the complex interaction of printed materials with almost all of our folk literature, the division of American religious life into scores of sects none of which dominates the national culture, the early separation of civic from religious authority, the consequent development of secular symbol systems in areas which earlier cultures identified as sacred, the lack of connection between most American forms of both high and folk art and any sacred institution—all these factors indicate that speculation as to the ritualistic origins of primitive literature and the application of ritualistic concepts to American writings will not suffice as a sole principle of elucidation.

On the other hand, to attempt an interpretation of American writings based exclusively on their uses of folklore, without considering their uses of ritual and myth, seems as unbalanced as the myth critics' slighting of folklore. Yet it is astonishing, despite its theoretical weakness, that the first serious and fruitful folk criticism of the American literary tradition, Constance Rourke's *American Humor* (1931), has until recently been so neglected. Her recognition of culturally important types of character in folk and subliterary materials is a rather impressionistic application of concepts similar to those proposed by the functionalist and culture-and-personality theories in anthropology. In her view, the significance of American folk traditions lies not so much in their origins as in their uses, and these, she shows, dramatize important concepts of human character and human fate. Rummaging through thousands of pages of musty newspapers, forgotten plays, yellowing almanacs, and the writings of scores of once-popular writers of travel journals and regional comedy, she extracted a coherent set of concepts of character widely sanctioned by continuing popular usage. In a sense the Yankee, the Frontiersman, and the Negro Minstrel are her creations; but this is only to say that she was the first to retrace their lineaments and their fortunes in the subliterary remains of early nineteenth-century American culture. Literary historians have been prone to retrace but not to venture beyond her leads to the folk roots of American writing. In literary criticism, F. O. Matthiessen showed in *American Renaissance* how valuable is an awareness of the essential connection between popular culture and literary traditions; and two provocative studies of individual authors have profited from Rourke's approach—Bernard DeVoto's *Mark Twain's America* and Richard Chase's *Herman Melville*. Yet such influential critics as Van Wyck Brooks (in *The Ordeal of Mark Twain*) and Edmund Wilson have failed to appreciate the importance to the literary imagination of the unrefined individualistic energy of popular culture—barbarous and bestial as it sometimes was—which so appals them. Itself a reality, a fact of American life, this energy found expression in metaphors of swaggering self-assertion and indomitable mastery of fate. Among its important consequences in literature was to offer a dialectical opposition to conceptions of tradition, high culture, society in its European sense. The images, symbolic acts, and even the artistic forms in which this opposition was expressed were often those of proverb, jest, folktale, journalistic sketch, and popular drama.

Although all verbal folk tradition would seem accessible to the author who would draw upon it, in fact but a few dominant folkloristic themes exert a shaping force upon the work of Irving, Hawthorne, Melville, and Mark Twain. These are, first, those which Rourke identified: comedy and character. Both dramatize man's relation to nature and to society; in the latter case, usually his independence of, or transcendence over, society. Beyond these themes, folklore also provides American literature with belief in the supernatural, a source both of mystery and of metaphoric criticism of established rationalistic values and Christian institutions. These themes are embodied in folk forms which themselves have affected the American romance. Folk comedy has in oral tradition its own rhetorical structure, its own gaudy vocabulary. Folk belief depends upon a communally sanctioned practice of allegory as a cultural cast of mind. And the fragmented annals of our folk heroes comprise a set of rituals peculiarly adapted to our preconceptions of the fate of the American character in a universe both unpredictable and benign. These are the subjects and problems which my next two chapters investigate. These folk materials penetrated American writing, sometimes on the lower levels of popular dramatics and journalism; sometimes at the highest levels of literary intensity. As well as showing this penetration, I shall try to show how our authors became aware of folk tradition, whether through antiquarian readings or through their participation in the folk life of the New England village or the whale ship or the Missouri frontier.

The myths this book examines are doubtless already familiar to the reader, and consequently do not need to be rehearsed in such detail. Initiatory rites, dead gods and resurrections, the scapegoat king and the Prince of Darkness, rebirths and the scourging of monsters—all these patterns appear and reappear. But the contexts of their presence in the works that embody them are scarcely twice alike, nor are their functions, and these are often determined by themes from folklore either analogous to or contradictory of these myths.

Mr. Chase's quarrel with the myth critics was instigated by his conviction that the one pattern they discerned in American literature led them to 'a very biased view.' 'The characteristic American form of the mythic archetype is thought to be the fall from innocence and the initiation into life—an action of the soul that entails a symbolic dying and rebirth.' Chase recognizes that the current preoccupation with 'myth' is an attempt to bulwark our age's lack of religious faith with forms of belief no longer institutionalized. Consequently he sees myth criticism as an aberrant form of religiosity, leading 'to an exaggerated opinion of works which avoid . . . involvement [with human dilemmas] and promise the immanence of grace, of final harmony and reconciliation, in a world whose contradictions it seems no longer possible to bear.' Chase's own position is exactly contrary to this one:

> Judging by our greatest novels, the American imagination, even when it wishes to assuage and reconcile the contradictions of life, has not been stirred by the possibility of catharsis or incarnation, by the tragic or Christian possibility. It has been stirred, rather, by the aesthetic possibilities of radical forms of alienation, contradiction, and disorder.[4]

This challenging formulation seems to me to point to tendencies rather than absolutes. The American imagination is indeed stirred by 'the aesthetic possibilities of radical forms of alienation, contradiction, and disorder.' But it has also been stirred by the possibilities of affiliation, resolution, and coherence. If our greatest works 'resolve contradictions . . . in oblique, morally equivocal ways,' they often do so in aching awareness of the Christian and tragic fate which it cannot be the privilege of the American imagination fully to express or of the American romance fully to embody. That the myth criticism of the past generation has asserted the contrary is the penalty which truth, in its multiplicity, exacts from a monistic method of inquiry. The tendencies defeated are as important, however, to the artistic success of these works as are the tendencies fulfilled. For in the American prose romance there is neither a single hero with a thousand faces; nor a single fable of his birth and death and resurrection; nor any such abstract structural monism. In American literature as elsewhere in the experience of human culture, myth is many, and the *archai* of the human soul are, at the least, dual, not one. Man's capacity for dialectic, rather than unity of being, is what distinguishes him from the rest of the universe; even the dreamer of unity is prepossessed by the chaos his senses reveal. For their dramatizations of the archetypes which prepossessed them, for the embodiment of the tensions which in all ecstasy, fear, and poignance their works reveal, our authors have drawn heavily upon the troves of mythic and folklore metaphors provided them by their country's traditions, and by the world's.

[4] *The American Novel and Its Tradition*, pp. 244-5, 2.

2

Longbows, Wonders, and Witchcrafts

Three strands of folklore have twined in and out of popular culture and literary tradition for the three and a half centuries of American life. These are the longbow or tall tale, the wonder or providence, and belief in witchcraft. The strains of optimistic comedy and the mystery of the supernatural provide American literature with a cast of characters; the plots of a thousand folk-tales; themes of man's relation to individual man, to society, to nature, and to those forces—both the divine and the demonic—beyond man's power, although through witchcraft he may seek to rule them. These folk traditions provide a rhetoric and vocabulary of comedy and, with the rudimentary structures of legend and myth fleshed and clothed in native conditions and local circumstance, they help to express man's deepest spiritual quests. Among our writers of first rank, Hawthorne, Melville, and Twain found in these traditions valuable patterns of a 'usable past' and, in *The Blithedale Romance, Moby-Dick,* and *The Confidence-Man,* of a 'usable present' as well.

ONE

When Benjamin Franklin hoaxed readers of a London newspaper with accounts of American sheep whose tails were so heavily laden with wool that they were trundled on wheelbarrows hitched behind, English gentlemen familiar with

Herodotus were not taken in by the joke. Although the individual motifs common in American folk humor are often of ancestry equally hoary, their particular forms and spirit are yet marked by an imaginative response to native conditions. 'I have been informed of a tulip tree that was ten feet in diameter,' wrote John Lawson in his *History of North Carolina* (1714), 'and another wherein a lusty man had got his bed and household furniture, and lived in it till his labor got him a more fashionable mansion. He afterwards became a noted man in his country for wealth and conduct.'[1] In the century following, the fertility of the soil was noted in connection not with forests so much as with crops. A contributor to the sporting journal, *The Spirit of the Times,* wrote of some settlers in 1837:

> Some were coming west because their children multiplied faster than their means of support, and Uncle Jonathan had 'writ' to 'un' that 'pumkins' grew so big out west that they made a stable for the cow out of one half, and fed her through the winter on the other half, and the only difficulty in raising garden 'sarce' was, that it grew so long that they pulled them through on the other side—and that the ground itself was so fat, that it would do very well to grease wagons and make candles, and on a pinch, it made tolerable good gravies.[2]

Good yarns die hard. This one turned up in the Ozarks in a collection made since 1920:

> A potato grew so big it couldn't be dug nohow, so they built a new cabin over it, and cut a trapdoor in the kitchen floor. Whenever the kids began hollerin' for victuals, Pogey just climbed down through the trap and shoveled up a big chunk of 'tater. Mostly the family ate the stuff boiled or fried; it was only when they hankered for 'taters baked in the jackets that it became necessary to swap provender with the neighbors. The jacket of Pogey's 'tater was three feet thick, with bark on it like a hackberry tree, not suitable for cooking. That one potato lasted the Mahone family for fourteen

[1] Quoted in Richard M. Dorson, *America Begins* (New York, 1950), p. 99.
[2] Norris W. Yates, *William T. Porter and the 'Spirit of the Times'* (Baton Rouge, 1957), p. 181.

years, and when it was all gone the hole under the house made a fine big cellar.[3]

The tale has a thousand variants, as yarns of preternatural cornstalks, turnips, tomatoes, beans, and peas proliferated over three centuries in testimony to the unbelievable beneficence of Nature in these States. If the corn grew ears as big as silos, it was only because the earth itself enjoyed a fecundity unparalleled in the universe. On the frontier, before the woods were cleared for farmland, hunters found the forests teeming with prodigious game. In the most famous hunting story before the Civil War, Thomas Bangs Thorpe's 'The Big Bear of Arkansas' (1841), the hunter speaks of the turkeys that live in his diggings:

> 'A wild turkey weighing forty pounds!' exclaimed twenty voices in the cabin at once.
>
> 'Yes, strangers, and wasn't it a whopper? You see, the thing was so fat that it couldn't fly far; and when he fell out of the tree after I shot him, on striking the ground he bust open behind, and the way the pound gobs of tallow rolled out of the opening was perfectly beautiful.'
>
> 'Where did all that happen?' asked a cynical-looking Hoosier.
>
> 'Happen! happened in Arkasaw: where else could it have happened, but in the creation state, the finishing-up country—a state where the *sile* runs down to the centre of the 'arth, and government gives you a title to every inch of it? Then its airs—just breathe them, and they will make you snort like a horse. It's a state without a fault, it is.'
>
> 'Excepting mosquitoes,' cried the Hoosier.
>
> 'Well, stranger, except for them; for it ar a fact that they are rather *enormous*. . . . But mosquitoes is natur, and I never find fault with her. If they are large, Arkasaw is large, her varmints ar large, and a small mosquito would be of no more use in Arkasaw than preaching in a cane-brake.'

In these recurrent fables of a frontier or farmland alive with marvels and gigantic in fertility, several themes of cultural significance appear. What may at first glance seem mere local

[3] Vance Randolph, *We Always Lie to Strangers* (New York, 1951), p. 83.

boosterism is in fact a reflection of a pervading American attitude toward the world of nature from which the early hunters, settlers, and farmers had to wrest a livelihood. The myth which these preposterous deadpan exaggerations project is that of the Earthly Paradise, the Land of Cockaigne, the prelapsarian Eden in the New World. Their continuing sense of wonder is based in part on fact and observation. Other motives, too, contributed to the elaboration of these yarns. Not least significant of these was the economic, for the earliest descriptions of the fabled new continent appeared in realtors' tracts designed to encourage emigration to the colonies. Only twenty-one years after John Smith's landing, Francis Higginson was writing, in *New Englands Plantation,* that 'The fertility of the soil is to be admired at . . . Yea Joseph's increase in Egypt is outstripped here with us . . . of the setting of thirteen gallons of corn [a planter] hath had increase of it fifty-two hogsheads, every hogshead holding seven bushels of London measure . . . where you may see how God blessed husbandry in this land.' Here were found lobsters, codfish, mackerel; sweet herbs, fruits, and excellent vines; abundant timber for buildings, trees for masts, berries for dyes. Best of all was firewood free for the gathering. 'Nay, all Europe is not able to afford to make so great fires as New England . . . Here is good living for those that love good fires.'[4] Such images of hospitable nature needed only a slight play of the sportive imagination to become the pumpkins as big as stables which later raconteurs would describe. The conception of the Earthly Paradise, where Nature herself is man's provider and toil is almost superfluous, caught the fancy of Coleridge and Southey. Having read Crèvecœur, they planned their departure for the New World to found a Pantisocracy where a few hours of labor a day would support their leisure spent in philosophical research. Fortunately for them, their experiment was never put to proof; otherwise they might have shared the disenchantment of those westward

[4] Dorson, *America Begins,* pp. 72-7.

pilgrims whose gullibility in the matter of big pumpkins the correspondent of the *Spirit of the Times* recorded.

In that version we already find the tale striated with irony, as it is told in a situation different from the earlier one of attracting settlers to the virgin country. Here the oldtimer tells the yarn to evince his superiority over the newcomers; *he* knows better than to be taken in by such hokum. The Big Bear of Arkansas shows us a yet more dramatic enactment of the tale in this second function: he uses it to manifest his ascendancy over an outlander, the cynical Hoosier. This is one brief skirmish in a running warfare of wits between the frontiersman and the outlander (usually a city-dweller from the East) which has been going on for two and a half centuries. In the recent Ozark version, the tale of the 'tater too big to be dug serves both of the functions just described. The raconteur, telling the yarn with 'deadpan zest' to a stranger, celebrates the virtues of Nature in his native State. At the same time he will put it over on the stranger if he can.

The tall tale thus is a form of hoax, and a hoax of course is a verbal practical joke. Whereas the actual practical joke has as its object the physical discomfiture of its victim, the tall-tale hoax has a yet more practical end. The function of the tall tale is often to serve as an initiatory rite—to apply a portentous term for a moment. 'Frontiersmen,' Mody Boatright remarks, 'prescribed the conditions under which an outsider might become a member of the group. Hoaxing and practical joking served them as a sort of initiation ceremony. . . . They had the right to know the temper of the men who were to be associated with them in such relationships that each man's survival often depended upon his fellows. . . . Hoaxing of this sort was . . . an economical means of establishing social relationships between men engaged in a common struggle.'[5] It served, also, to separate those who could not or would not adapt themselves to the needs and standards of the group.

[5] *Folk Laughter on the American Frontier* (New York, 1950), pp. 61-2.

Not only the Texas Rangers and Indian scouts whom Boatright mentions had such initiatory tall tales. Even among farmers the lines could be drawn. Hawthorne takes advantage of a subspecies of folktale, the noodle story, to delineate the scorn heaped by the real farmers of Massachusetts on the heads of the quondam agriculturists and reformers in Chapter 8 of *The Blithedale Romance:*

> They told slanderous fables about our inability to yoke our own oxen, or to drive them a-field when yoked, or to release the poor brutes from their conjugal bond at nightfall. . . . They further averred that we hoed up whole acres of Indian corn and other crops, and drew the earth carefully about the weeds; and that we raised five hundred tufts of burdock, mistaking them for cabbages; and that, by dint of unskillful planting, few of our seeds ever came up at all, or, if they did come up, it was stern-foremost; and that we spent the better part of the month of June in reversing a field of beans, which had thrust themselves out of the ground in this unseemly way. They quoted it as nothing more than an ordinary occurrence for one or other of us to crop off two or three fingers, of a morning, by our clumsy use of the hay-cutter. Finally, and as an ultimate catastrophe, these mendacious rogues circulated a report that we communitarians were exterminated, to the last man, by severing ourselves asunder with the sweep of our own scythes!—and that the world had lost nothing by this little accident.
>
> But this was pure envy and malice on the part of the neighboring farmers.

Although the Big Bear of Arkansas claimed he never found fault with Nature, the fact of course was that she was as often a merciless antagonist as a bountiful hostess to the settlers and hunters. Their need to reassure themselves of man's ineluctable victory over the indifferent or hostile elements led on the one hand to eulogizing Nature as an Earthly Paradise. On the other it could lead in exactly the opposite direction; Nature appears in a host of American folktales and songs as the Earthly Inferno, a terrain so outrageously inhospitable to all forms of life that even the Devil surrenders it. This sign was nailed to the door of a house in West Abilene when its occupant abandoned it after the drought of 1886:

One hundred miles to water
Twenty miles to wood
Six inches to hell
God bless our home
Gone to live with the wife's folks.[6]

Other settlers who remained sang songs—'Hell in Texas' or 'Starving to death on a Government claim'—but their tribulations had long since been recounted in the exaggerative yarning on earlier frontiers. *The Southern Literary Messenger* in 1840 reported that

> The dogs, in a certain county in Maryland are so poor, that they have to lean against the fence to bark. The kildees are so poor, that they have to let down the draw-bars to enable them to go into a field; and the pigs are so poor, that to prevent them from upsetting as they run down hill, they are compelled to suspend a lump of lead to their tails to balance them.[7]

New England, too, had its celebrants of Nature's preposterously inhospitable face. One wrote of Nantucket:

> Some gamesome wights will tell you that they have to plant weeds there, they don't grow naturally; that they import Canada thistles; that they have to send beyond the seas for a spile to stop a leak in an oil cask; that pieces of wood in Nantucket are carried about like bits of the true cross in Rome; that people there plant toadstools before their houses, to get under the shade in summer time; that one blade of grass makes an oasis, three blades in a day's walk a prairie; that they wear quicksand shoes, something like the Laplander snowshoes; that they are so shut up, belted about, every way inclosed, surrounded, and made an utter island of by the ocean, that to their chairs and tables small clams will sometimes be found adhering, as to the backs of sea turtles. But these extravagances only show that Nantucket is no Illinois.

[6] *Folk Laughter on the American Frontier*, p. 163.
[7] *Southern Literary Messenger*, quoted in B. A. Botkin, *A Treasury of American Folklore* (New York, 1944), p. 330.

It is with this encomium that Ishmael takes leave of land, as the Pequod heaves anchor on her fated voyage.

The comic celebration of Nature's largesse—as extreme in her deprivations as in her generosity—thus represents a rather complex intermixture of themes and motives. Genuine wonder at unexampled marvels, the zealous claims of promotional literature, the individual need for reassurance in the eternal struggle with the elements, and the social need to define the mores of the group by shared humor and hoax—all these contributed to the anecdotal comedy of dizzying exaggeration. In this strain of folklore, and in the oral art of its performance, our authors found a ready-made comic method which they could blend with other elements and put to uses of their own devising.

TWO

If the country brought forth such prodigious pumpkins, what sort of men would it grow? Among their notable qualities, surely strength commensurate with the scale of nature would be one especially prized. There's a tale told these days in Jonesport, Maine, of Barney Beal, the local strong man, who lifted a 1500-pound anchor on a bet; when 'the fellow squealed out . . . Barney carried it over to the edge of the wharf and dropped it right through the fellow's sailboat.' Perhaps he did; if so it was pretty nearly the same trick performed a century ago by Angus MacAskill in Cape Breton.[8] The feats of men as strong as oxen, or demigods, have always seemed marvellous, worth the telling and remembering.

In these times of secular depravity we merely marvel and applaud. But Cotton Mather knew what to make of a strong man when one came his way even when the Hercules was a fellow minister of the cloth:

[8] R. M. Dorson, 'Collecting Folklore in Jonesport, Maine,' *Proceedings*, American Philosophical Society, CI (June 1957), 274; James D. Gillis, *The Cape Breton Giant* (Halifax, N. S., 1926), p. 75.

> Now God had been pleased so to leave this G.B. that he had ensnared himself by several Instances, which he had formerly given of a Preternatural strength, and which were now produced against him. He was a very Puny man; yet he had often done things beyond the strength of a Giant. A Gun of about seven foot barrel, and so heavy that strong men could not steadily hold it out with both hands; there were several testimonies, given in by Persons of Credit and Honour, that he made nothing of taking up such a Gun behind the Lock, with but one hand, and holding it out like a Pistol, at Arms-end. . . . There was evidence likewise brought in, that he made nothing of Taking up whole Barrels fill'd with Malasses or Cider, in very Disadvantageous Postures, and Carrying them through the Difficultest Places out of a Canoe to the Shore.[9]

On such evidence George Burroughs was hanged for a wizard despite a lifetime of good works and Christian carriage. What seems to us arrant superstition and malicious ignorance was, for the most learned scholar in seventeenth-century America, an inevitable conclusion sanctified by ecclesiastical precedent and prescribed by dogma. The history of witchcraft and demonology lends support to the theory of cultural change, first enunciated in E. B. Tylor's *Primitive Culture*, that the sacred dogmas and kingly rituals of former times linger in degraded forms as popular superstitions, children's games, and other kinds of folklore. In the trial of 'G.B.' we encounter two forms of theologically sanctioned folklore: the wonder and the witch belief. For the moment it is the wonder or providence which concerns us. The providence is the analogue, in terms of man's relation to the supernatural world, of the tall tale in his relation to the world of nature and of men.

What is the providence? We can do no better than consult its chief chronicler, Cotton Mather's father, Increase. In *An Essay for the Recording of Illustrious Providences* (1684), Increase

[9] *Wonders of the Invisible World*, reprinted in G. L. Burr, *Narratives of the Witchcraft Cases, 1648-1706* (New York, 1946), pp. 219-20. Cf. Gillis, *The Cape Breton Giant*, pp. 52, 67 for the same prodigies.

Mather set forth the fearful record of the Lord's warnings to the people of New England, and defined the forms in which illustrious providences may be expected to manifest themselves:

> Such Divine Judgements, Tempests, Floods, Earth-quakes, Thunders as are unusual, strange Apparitions, or what ever else shall happen that is Prodigious, Witchcrafts, Diabolical Possessions, Remarkable Judgements upon noted Sinners, eminent Delivrances, and Answers of Prayer, are to be reckoned among Illustrious Providences.

'It is not easie to give an Account of things, and yet no circumstantial mistakes attend what shall be related. Nor dare I averr, that there are none such in what follows,' writes Mather, with the scrupulous concern for documentary evidence which an investigator into science should show. 'Only I have been careful to prevent them; and as to the substance of each passage, I am well assured it is according to Truth.[10]

These wonders which Mather collected from his fellow-ministers, and which entire congregations witnessed and believed, served the Puritans in precisely the same way that similar *exempla* had served the Church for a thousand years. As one might expect, popular credulity continued, long after the decline of the Puritan theocracy, to invest with supernatural power such natural phenomena as the Aurora Borealis, sudden storms, shipwrecks, or the illusion of phantom ships at sea. Stories of witches who rode horses or people by night, who curdled the cream and prevented the butter, were almost ineradicable. These materials, naturally enough, appealed to the love of the picturesque and the indigenous which was characteristic of the Romantic movement. As early as 1825 the now-forgotten Connecticut poet J. G. Brainerd rhymed accounts of place-name legends, Indian myths, and superstitions. John Greenleaf Whittier followed with *Legends of New England* in verse in 1831 and with a prose commentary on *The Supernaturalism of New England* in 1847. For them and for a host of local-colorists later in the century (like Harriet Beecher

[10] Reprinted in Burr, *Narratives*, p. 13.

Stowe, Rose Terry Cooke, and Celia Leighton Thaxter[11]) these superstitions were appealingly archaic and picturesque. But for Hawthorne and Melville they suggested more imaginative possibilities. These data from actual life, whether culled by the learned Reverend Mr. Mather or heard in the chimney corner, made concrete the allegorical mode of interpreting experience. This world, wrote Jonathan Edwards, was but 'the shadows and images of Divine things.' And among minds less platonic and erudite than his, the Divine Will was shadowed forth in the swamped boat and the falling star, the monstrous birth and the sunset cloud. The providences were proofs that our life is an allegory of the Will of God.

Here is an example of how one author reacted to an account of such a providence. We know that Hawthorne read Cotton Mather's *Magnalia Christi Americana* with great attention. In Book VII, chapter 6, he found the following portent of King Philip's War. This wonder was experienced in 1674, the year before the war began:

> Yes, and now we speak of things ominous, we may add, some time before this, in a clear, still, sunshiny morning, there were divers persons in Malden who heard in the air, on the southeast of them, a great gun go off, and presently thereupon the report of small guns like musket shot, very thick discharging, as if there had been a battle. This was at a time when there was nothing visible done in any part of the colony to occasion such noises; but that which most of all astonished them was the flying of bullets, which came singing over their heads and seemed very near to them; after which, the sound of drums passing along westward was very audible; and on the same day in Plymouth Colony in several places invisible troops of horses were heard riding to and fro. Now, reader, prepare for the event of these prodigies, but count me not struck with a Livian superstition in reporting prodigies for which I have such incontestable assurance.

[11] Many such writings are anthologized by Samuel Adams Drake in *A Book of New England Legends and Folk Lore in Prose and Poetry* (Boston, 1883).

The providence cited by Mather comprises the entire source of 'The Battle-Omen.'[12] As regards the form of the belief, Hawthorne modified it chiefly in the direction of fidelity toward oral folk tradition: he connected the spectral portent to a particular place. It is the winter of 1739, and two young men make their way through the woods, on an errand, it would appear, of raising a militia against the French. '"Is it not strange," said one . . . laughingly, "that these near commotions are foretold by none of the wild oracles which our fathers were wont to hear, on occasions of so much less interest? Their petty warfare . . . was invariably preceded by signs and omens, as if all Nature were affrighted at the prospect of an Indian campaign. Now, here we stand on the verge of a war that may chance to separate two worlds, and not so much as a trumpet in the air has sounded its approach."

'"True, the pilgrims were a favored people," said his companion. . . . "But if we had inherited the gloom of their religious faith the winds in the forest, and the meteors in the sky, would have prophesied also to us."' The travellers have now neared a certain rock where half a century earlier a fisherman had tied his boat and 'heard a sound of martial music in the air above him.' Such superstitions, Hawthorne writes,

> were the coinage of perilous and awful moments; they imbibed a desolate romance from the circumstances which formed them, and neither purification nor ornament could render them more poetical than when they issued from the hearts of our forefathers. The presage by the sound of drums and trumpet was peculiarly grand and lofty, but it would have been too cold in its magnificence, if a most singular opinion had not increased its power over human sympathies. There was a dim and indefinite idea, that the shadowy tread of the destined victims, the future slain of unfought battle-

[12] The passage for which I take Mather's account to be the probable source does not appear in Hawthorne's *Works;* it is an early sketch, published in the Salem *Gazette* (Nov. 2, 1830), and only tentatively proposed as Hawthorne's by Donald Gallup, 'On Hawthorne's Authorship of "The Battle-Omen,"' *New England Quarterly,* IX (Dec. 1936), 690-9. I am more positive than was Gallup of Hawthorne's authorship.

> fields, might be heard to accompany the prophetic music through the sky.

The men speak on in this vein until 'their talk acquired the earnestness of deep belief':

> The wind, as it howled over the snowy waste and buried itself in the forest, began to startle them by its resemblance to the spiritual minstrelsy, and the ice-crack, thundering heavily from shore to shore, rang upon their ears like the roar of cannon. And the Northern Lights . . . might readily have assumed the aspect of armed hosts and flaming towns, apparitions not unknown to the men of olden time. After a silence, which had fallen on them they knew not how, one of the travellers laid his hand upon his companion's arm.
>
> 'Surely our comrades had separated long ago,' whispered he, looking towards the village—'Why do they beat the drum at such an hour?'
>
> The church steeple, its attendant houses, and the snowy ascent upon which they stood, were distinctly visible, but there was no token of wakefulness anywhere about them. As the young men gazed, another far off and uncertain swell, like the ghost of music, just grazed upon their ears . . .
>
> A third and nearer repetition . . . now marked its origin as in the east, where the wilderness lay dark and desolate for many a mile, undisturbed from the creation till that hour by other notes than those of an Indian War Song. Again they heard it, low down towards the horizon, but ascending along the arch of the sky, alternately pealing forth as with the full breath of many instruments, and then dying away till the ear scarce caught its murmur—even in its loudest tones there was such unreality, that the listeners doubted whether all were not the echo of their own excited thoughts. . . . There was no echo from the shore and sky, but only that mysterious music, passing on in solitude. And yet, for one brief moment, the solitude seemed broken by the clash of arms, the rustle and waving of garments, the undefinable hum of a viewless multitude, journeying through the awful brightness of the night. Then came familiar voices—there were two that spoke and replied, deeming that their own bloodless lips had moved. A mighty peal of harmony broke forth, as the omen swept above their head; it died away in regular gradations till the western woods received it into their bosoms; and there its distant wail was lost.

Already, in this early treatment of New England supernatural tradition, Hawthorne had developed that 'formula of alternative possibilities,' which Yvor Winters suggests as characteristic of his method in *The Scarlet Letter*.[13] He has made it seem plausible that the music was actually heard, and that its ominous forebodings were true: the two volunteers hear the warning at the very spot where it had been before reported, and under similar conditions of military menace. The reverberating sentences describing the roll and fall of sound give reality to the apparition. Yet the tale is hedged about with skepticism in the telling; 'if we had inherited the gloom of their religious faith, the winds in the forest, and the meteors in the sky, would have prophesied also to us.' But a little later the northern lights 'might readily have assumed the aspect of armed hosts and flaming towns.' Yet again the omen is conditionally described; we are never certain whether the youths contribute to each other's illusion as 'their talk acquired the earnestness of deep belief,' or whether the ghostly music was real. The sketch succeeds better than many others Hawthorne included in *Twice-Told Tales* because of its consistent double vision. No obtrusive moral ending allegorizes the story. We are left in the ambiguity produced by the tension between the ironic, rational qualifications and the rhythmic and sensory evidence of the style. Slight as it is in content, 'The Battle-Omen' is surely a prefiguration of the method of qualified and ambiguous allegory in *The Scarlet Letter.*

Now if Hawthorne modified the content of Mather's passage by making the portent a place-legend, he made a still greater alteration in its function, while preserving—and elaborating—its original form. For Mather did not in the least doubt, first, the actuality of the occurrence, or second, the interpretation to put upon the phenomenon. For Hawthorne, however, the allegorical mode persists as an inherited disposition of intelligence and emotion, but it is cast into doubt by yet a different mode of thought and feeling. His great problem and achievement as an artist was

[13] *In Defence of Reason* (New York, 1947), p. 170.

to free himself from allegory. Living in a transcendental generation whose absolute free will he could not share, he was yet enough a product of the Enlightenment to distrust the theocratic absolutism of his seventeenth-century forebears. Far from being caught and crippled by the conflict of these two commitments, Hawthorne in his best work gained that psychological tension which characterizes his style by adopting allegory as the seeming mode of his expression, and then multiplying far beyond Cotton Mather's unitary meaning the significations which his allegory may be taken to represent. This method of alternative choices achieves fullest expression in *The Scarlet Letter;* in discussing that book, which is enriched with folklore, we shall take up this subject again.

In the folklore of providences Hawthorne found a trove of examples of his very method, for by the nineteenth century folk tradition itself no longer had the unanimity of Puritan interpretation of portents and wonders. Nor was Hawthorne the only author to take advantage of the folk providence or the wonder. The White Whale himself is *contra naturam,* believed to be a spectre, known as a spirit spout, seen simultaneously in opposite latitudes of the ocean. Melville, further removed from Calvinist certitude than was Hawthorne from Puritan absolutism, makes an even more elaborate use of allegory to demolish the monistic claims to truth of allegory itself. In doing so he, too, drew heavily upon the folklore of the supernatural, as we shall see.

THREE

It was the providence of his supernatural strength, we recall, which testified to George Burroughs' guilt. His crime was witchcraft, a theological offence carefully defined in a huge corpus of ecclesiastical literature with much of which his judge and accuser, Cotton Mather, was familiar. For the modern man, however, the conception of witchcraft has become so debased as to be merely trivial. We think condescendingly of beliefs in withered crones who ride broomsticks and play nasty tricks on neighbors who they think have insulted them. No longer believing in the power of God with the Puritans' intensity and fervor, we have lost also their capacity to believe in the power of Satan. For the same belief in spirit which raised the illustrious providences of colonial Massachusetts to the order of the miracles of Jesus went hand in hand with the conviction that the Black Man moved among the Christian Commonwealth, tempting men and women to deliver him their souls, seducing them to serve him as his witches and wizards. These beliefs the Puritans had brought with them from England. These they shared with all of Christendom.

Folk superstition thus from its beginnings comprised not the hodgepodge of ignorant and fearful supposition for which it is often dismissed, but a body of deeply felt, culturally sanctioned symbols representing profound aspects of man's relation to the supernatural. On the ultimate origins of witchcraft, as it was defined in the *Malleus Malleficarum* and allegedly practiced in all Europe and the American Colonies, there is not yet agreement. Indeed, modern investigators survey identical materials to support contradictory theories. Most probable is the view propounded by Margaret Murray and reinforced by Arne Runeberg.[14] Surveying anthropological, archaeological, theological, and folkloristic evidence, they contend that 'witchcraft' comprised the Christian reinterpretation of the surviving traces of the once-universal nature cults. Whether paganism lingered in its own right or was transformed by Christian theology and popular custom into the objectification of Satanic power, witchcraft provided mythopoetic representation of the daemonic, the naturalistic, and of the Antichrist.

American authors encountered this detritus of the pagan past in various ways. Irving, Hawthorne, and Melville all read Mather's *Magnalia* and in their fiction drew on the witch lore

[14] Murray, *The Witch Cult in Western Europe* (Oxford, 1921) and *The God of the Witches* (New York, 1952); Runeberg, *Witches, Demons and Fertility Magic* (Helsingfors, 1947).

there recorded. Irving heard with fascinated wonder the superstitions told in the chimney corner, while Mark Twain absorbed Negro lore from the slaves on his uncle's farm. Melville was a shipmate of superstitious sailors; Hawthorne had his contacts with oral tradition as well as his intense immersion in the chronicles of the trials over which his forebear had so harshly presided. Supernatural lore became a part of the imaginative furniture of the popular mind, which these authors shared. They found in that lore folk analogues to the paraphernalia of literary Gothicism. Indeed, in the Gothic writings of the early Continental and English Romantics there is a remarkable affinity for the folklore of the supernatural. In Hawthorne, Gothic devices and folk supernaturalism come together in the allegorical mode, fusing the responses to the sense of evil in 'high culture' and 'low' with incandescent intensity. Melville took warrant from the beliefs of sailors to weave a web of supernatural portents into *Moby-Dick;* of the sea itself he says, 'There is magic in it.' A generation later Mark Twain would find that ghosts, omens, spells, and witchcrafts still flourished among the folk of the Mississippi valley. There, as always before, this folklore expresses the imaginative responses of a people to the forces that shape their lives.

3

The American Hero: His Masquerade

'Something further may follow of this Masquerade.'
—Melville, *The Confidence-Man*

ONE

'What then is the American, this new man?' asked Crèvecœur in 1782,[1] posing at the birth of the Republic the question of national identity which our writers have never since ceased trying to answer. Even from the earliest settlement the conviction loomed large that human nature itself was changed by being transplanted to new circumstances. The Puritans had felt as a divine visitation the call to leave the Old World for the New and found under God's will a new Zion in the wilderness. By the middle of the eighteenth century the thoughts of emigration and the untamed land continued to sway men's minds. We have noted in the paradisal symbolism of the frontier that the wilderness becomes the fecund Garden of tall-tale fame. Melville would envisage the West as inhabited by 'the White Steed of the Prairies. . . . A most imperial and archangelical apparition of that unfallen western world, which to the eyes of the old trappers and hunters revived the glories of those primeval times when Adam walked majestic as a god, bluff-browed and fearless.' Characteristically, Melville mythicized into more heroic dimensions a con-

[1] Hector St. Jean de Crèvecœur, *Letters from an American Farmer* (New York, 1957).

viction of popular culture. The Enlightenment version of the 'bluff-browed and fearless' American settler was indeed unfallen and Adamic, but not quite as majestic or godlike as Melville proposes. This we can see in Crèvecœur's answer to his own question, 'What then is the American, this new man?'

> He is an American, who, leaving behind him all his ancient prejudices and manners, receives new ones from the new mode of life he has embraced, the new government he obeys, and the new rank he holds. . . . The American is a new man, who acts on new principles; he must therefore entertain new ideas, and form new opinions. From involuntary idleness, servile dependence, penury, and useless labour, he has passed to toils of a very different nature, rewarded by ample subsistence.—This is an American.

The character of this new man soon clearly revealed itself. At first there was the miraculous rebirth of the British serf as a freeholder in the New World; the career of one such serf, Andrew the Hebridean, was appended to the third of Crèvecœur's *Letters from an American Farmer*. But one need not be born a serf on the isle of Barra to be reborn in the American colonies. That rebirth and metamorphosis are the bywords of American life is among the lessons in Benjamin Franklin's *Autobiography*. That work and Crèvecœur's are the earliest and most influential examples of the new American character in literature. As yet the lineaments of that character are 'colonial,' the products rather of general political and social institutions than of the special culture of a particular region. Such localization was the next step in the development of popular concepts of character. Along the northeastern seaboard a well-defined type, the Yankee, developed early in folklore and, by the 1830's, appears in popular culture to have displaced the undifferentiated American of the Franklin and Crèvecœur variety. A parallel development along the frontier brought the character of the Backwoodsman into folktales, almanacs, popular fiction, theatricals, and, in the person of Davy Crockett, into national political prominence. Metamorphosis, adaptability, and indomitable self-mastery are the qualities these three types of the hero share. Whether actual men or fictitious characters, these heroes insist upon the constancy of the self behind their changing masks. Yet, as the more reflective minds of Hawthorne, Melville, and Twain used these popular stereotypes in their fiction, the question of identity could not so casually be laid to rest. Crèvecœur's question, What is the American, becomes for their characters, Who am I? Which of my masks is Me?

Andrew the Hebridean, however, felt no such ambiguity about *his* identity.

> All I wish to delineate [Crèvecœur writes] is, the progressive steps of a poor man, advancing from indigence to ease; from oppression to freedom; from obscurity and contumely to some degree of consequence—not by virtue of any freaks of fortune, but by the gradual operation of sobriety, honesty, and emigration.

To succeed, Andrew must cast off his ancient heritage as though it were a chrysalis. Only then can the real man within come forth in all his human power, sustained by the laws; for 'we are the most perfect society now existing in the world.' Arriving in Philadelphia, Andrew is befriended by the benevolent American Farmer who assures him that 'Your future success will depend entirely upon your own conduct; if you are a sober man . . . laborious, and honest, there is no fear that you will do well.' No less than twelve times do these adjectives, the apices of bourgeois virtue, come together in Crèvecœur's discourse on Andrew. It is true that the Hebridean does not know how to handle a hoe or an axe, and that his wife must be apprenticed in a friendly kitchen to learn the rudiments of pioneer housekeeping. These skills being soon acquired, Crèvecœur and a friend stake Andrew to a hundred acres of land. The ever benevolent farmer invites the neighborhood to a frolic; amid the convivial folk festival of house-raising a new American is born:

> When the work was finished the company made the woods resound with the noise of their three cheers, and the honest wishes they formed for Andrew's prosperity. . . . Thus from the first day he

> had landed, Andrew marched towards this important event: this memorable day made the sun shine on that land on which he was to sow wheat and other grain. . . . Soon after, further settlements were made on that road, and Andrew, instead of being the last man towards the wilderness, found himself in a few years in the middle of a numerous society. He helped others as generously as others had helped him. . . . he was made overseer of the road, and served on two petty juries, performing as a citizen all the duties required of him.

The combination of his own sobriety, industry, and honesty with 'our customs, which indeed are those of nature' and our laws, which derive 'from the original genius and strong desire of the people,' leads ineluctably toward the triumphant transformation of Andrew. By Crèvecœur's time, deistic optimism had for many colonists quite replaced the earlier Puritan emphasis on original sin. Man, in accordance with the new philosophy of the age, is inherently good, and America, being free from the inherited evils and injustices of Europe, offers him the unprecedented opportunity to be reborn to a brighter destiny. Although neither Crèvecœur nor his age held credence in such superstitions as witchcraft or wonders, surely this transformation of a peasant into a free American is as miraculous an instance of shape-shifting as anything reported at Salem. The power of transformation, of self-transformation, is no longer seen as malevolent. It partakes of the same beneficent energy that populates the forests and the farmyards with prodigious plenitude of game and fecundity of crops. Already the American character is defined as the exercise of metamorphic power.

Crèvecœur's ingenuous account of Andrew is the prototype of the Horatio Alger story. It is the new fairy tale of the new man on the new continent. He begins life in Europe, in the state of subjection to which history has condemned him. But by emigrating to the New World,

> He begins to feel the effects of a sort of resurrection; hitherto he had not lived but simply vegetated; he now feels himself a man, because he is treated as such.

His symbolic gesture is to discover his own humanity in a land where all men hold the highest and equal rank of citizens.

In time the American hero developed a more sophisticated character. The next representative hero adapted himself to almost all of the human possibilities of thought and action in his time. Benjamin Franklin begins his dizzying progress in much the same vein that Crèvecœur had begun Andrew's adventures:

> Having emerged from the poverty and obscurity in which I was born and bred, to a state of affluence and some degree of reputation in the world, and having gone so far through life with a considerable share of felicity, the conducing means I made use of, which with the blessing of God so well succeeded, my posterity may like to know, as they may find some of them suitable to their own situations, and therefore fit to be imitated.

It is worth recalling that Franklin formed the plan of his life upon his reading of Cotton Mather's *Essays To Do Good.* Although the didacticism of his purpose perpetuates the Puritan emphasis on studying the example of a holy life, his goal is not holiness. It is success. The simple bourgeois formula of honesty, sobriety, and industry which brought about Andrew's resurrection is elaborated in Franklin's famous table of virtues, as well as in a hundred examples drawn from his own life. One cannot gainsay D. H. Lawrence's mockery of Benjamin for his denial that 'The soul of man is a dark vast forest, with wild life in it. Think of Benjamin fencing it off! . . . He made himself a list of virtues, which he trotted inside like a gray nag in a paddock.' This charge, or at least its spirit, was anticipated by Melville. As one who dived deep into the recesses of the self, he could not help but find Franklin's character a shallow show of outward versatility lacking inner conviction. Thoreau was more in tune with the popular culture of the time when he wrote, 'Franklin —there may be a line for him in the future classical dictionary, recording what that demigod did, and referring him to some new genealogy. "Son of —— and ——. He aided the Americans to gain their independence, instructed mankind in economy, and drew down lightning from the clouds."'[2] It was his role as rebel rather than as conciliator, and his hardheaded virtues and practical approach to the mastery of life which made the hero of the *Autobiography* seem a prototypical figure among his countrymen. Quite consistent with these qualities was his rationalistic derision of the superstitions of Puritan times in his bagatelle, 'A Witch Trial at Mount Holly.'

In the midst of so much that is admirable in Franklin's career, what seems to have most appealed to the popular mind were the ingredients of a stock figure, half wily savant, half homely philosopher. The emergent Yankee trickster was already limned in Ben's burning his light later than his rival's, pushing a wheelbarrow down Main Street to promote his own reputation for industry, rising in the world by the heft of his own cunning till at last he dines with kings. Allied with this emphasis on the too-clever side of Ben is the popular confusion of Franklin himself with Poor Richard, his fictitious gaffer who paved *The Way to Wealth* with proverbs. 'Love your neighbor; yet don't pull down your hedge'; 'Write with the learned, pronounce with the vulgar'; 'Fish and visitors stink after three days'; 'If you would be wealthy, think of saving as well as getting.' These apothegms of bourgeois caution could, like his tricksy maneuvers to get ahead, be regarded as somewhat incompatible with the other Franklin of popular tradition—the wise statesman, the original scientist, the patriarchal patriot. Mark Twain, in a sketch at Franklin's expense, complained that 'His maxims were full of animosity toward boys. Nowadays a boy cannot follow out a single natural instinct without tumbling over some of those everlasting aphorisms and hearing from Franklin on the spot.' Franklin, pretending industriousness, might say 'Procrastination is the thief of time,' but Mark Twain knows better: 'In order to get a chance to fly his kite on Sunday he used to hang a key on the string and let on to be fishing for lightning.'

[2] Quoted by F. O. Matthiessen, *American Renaissance* (New York, 1941), p. 636.

> He was always proud of telling how he entered Philadelphia for the first time, with nothing in the world but two shillings in his pocket and four rolls of bread under his arm. But really, when you come to examine it critically, it was nothing. Anybody could have done it.[3]

In a trenchant satirical sketch of Franklin, Melville presents the sententious, calculating sage at Passy, in whom 'The diplomatist and the shepherd are blended; a union not without warrant; the apostolic serpent and dove.' This portrait, in *Israel Potter,* is perhaps as shrewd an assessment of Franklin's virtues and as striking an indictment of his faults as the narrator of the *Autobiography* has ever received. Melville ranks him with Jacob in the Bible, and Hobbes, as 'labyrinth-minded, but plain-spoken Broad-brims . . . keen observers of the main chance; prudent courtiers; practical Magians in linsey-woolsey.' The dualism of his personality, the contrast between his humble beginnings and the worldly, sophisticated, and cunning old soothsayer Israel Potter meets in Paris, makes Franklin suspect:

> Having carefully weighed the world, Franklin could act any part in it. By nature turned to knowledge, his mind was often grave, but never serious. At times he had seriousness—extreme seriousness—for others, but never for himself. . . . This philosophical levity of tranquility, so to speak, is shown in his easy variety of pursuits. Printer, postmaster, almanac maker, essayist, chemist, orator, tinker, statesman, humorist, philosopher, parlour man, political economist, professor of housewifery, ambassador, projector, maxim-monger, herb-doctor, wit: Jack of all trades, master of each and mastered by none—the type and genius of his land. Franklin was everything but a poet.

In his protean and hydra-headed versatility the metamorphic Franklin seemed a moral chameleon. Who and what is he, ultimately, underneath all these rebirths and resurrections? Franklin's own character exhibited in its most highly developed form that versatility which frontier conditions and a limited popula-

[3] 'The Late Benjamin Franklin,' in *Sketches New and Old; Writings of Mark Twain* (New York, 1917), XXIII, 188-92.

tion made necessary in a new country. De Tocqueville had noticed the premium placed in America on the Jack-of-all-trades, at the expense of the master-craftsman who was useless beyond his one specialty. If this prized versatility did not long outlast the division of labor brought about by post-bellum industrialization, it was characteristic of American life in the early nineteenth century. This was true on every level of society, from the farmer-mechanic-peddler to the likes of George Washington and Thomas Jefferson, both of whom were quondam philosophers, scientists, architects, statesmen, politicians, and farmers. That the plebeian Franklin should have been the most successful citizen of this universe suggests the remarkable degree of social and intellectual mobility possible even before the establishment of the Republic.

Franklin's philosophy was too self-confident for us to view his life as a search for values, although he so viewed his early years. He soon enough found the set of values—respectability and probity in business, an accommodating deism in religion, a faith of serving God through service to man in public life—which he followed throughout the rest of his long career. His intellectual energy was equalled only by his curiosity, and his theoretical interests never far outran his pragmatism in applying new concepts. No sooner had he discovered the electric nature of lightning than he patented a lightning-rod! Here was Yankee science at its birth, in which intuitive hunches lead to the discovery of great principles, and those discoveries to immediate applications.

But if Franklin had no doubt about his own identity, we cannot say the same for every young man who emulated him by trying half a dozen careers. Washington Irving and Walt Whitman taught school and edited newspapers and entered politics before discovering their essential selves. Melville of course was teacher, clerk, sailor, whaler, captive of cannibals, and Polynesian beachcomber until he found by the accident of writing his adventures that literature was his true career. Mark Twain started out as cub pilot, miner, and itinerant journalist, before making the literary strike that uncovered his richest ore. What a man does determines in the long run what he is. These writers did not know who they were until they found their right vocations. Yet their writings are populated with American characters who, true to the expansive spirit of the age, move from one identity to another with neither effort, preparation, nor reflection. At the same time, however, the problem of identity, of discovering the essential self, has been a particularly acute one in American literature. With so many selves to choose from, anyone who does have deeper commitments to the life of the spirit than Melville detected in Ben Franklin must discover which of his own masks is made of the flesh and skin of the face that wears it.

The metamorphic variety of American life and the impetus it gave toward self-determined transformation is thus made spectacularly apparent in Ben Franklin's career. Franklin, with his universality, fairly represents the nascent American character. In popular culture and our early literature, however, native characters did not have Franklin's easy movement through all the conditions of life. They began as local characters whose idiosyncrasies were typical of their regions. From the first the colonies had been differentiated by their several creeds, methods of settlement, and systems of government. These differences, to which was added the greatest difference of all—that between the life of the settled seaboard and the harsh existence of the frontier—are already visible in the earliest depictions of indigenous character. As befits a national literature in its primitive beginnings, these earliest depictions often appear in theatricals. They were, in fact, ritualistic portraits in which the several identities of the American were enacted and revealed. Whether as Yankee peddler or Kentucky boatman, metamorphosis, on a humbler level than Franklin's yet just as self-determined and as optimistic, was at the core of their nature.

TWO

One evening in Boston, in 1838, a crowd in a theatre gasped with awe and terror as Dan Marble, the famous Yankee actor, deliberately leaped over Niagara Falls—from the very roof of the theatre, seventy feet above the stage—to reappear, ebulliently, in a pool of foam. The piece of which this leap was the climax was *Sam Patch: or, The Daring Yankee.* Many in the audience had already seen, or would soon see, the renowned James Hackett, another actor, in his famous impersonation of Nimrod Wildfire, 'The Lion of the West.' This remarkable hero of *The Kentuckian; or, A Trip to New York,* in his buckskin and powder-horn, characteristically admonished an English fop,

> If you think to get rid of me without exchanging a shot, you might as well try to scull a potash kettle up the falls of Niagara with a crowbar for an oar.

Defying the falls of the Niagara, as Carlyle observed at about this time, was a proverbial expression of the American Spirit. And so were the two rodomontade braggarts on the stage. The Yankee and the Frontiersman had come out of the country village and the virgin timber, shouting their boasts, revelling in their own rusticity. These two plays were but selected instances in a flood of stage pieces, journalistic sketches, almanac characters, humorous collections, folk-told yarns, ballads, doggerel verses, and songs which limned their collective portraits in the early nineteenth century. Not only did they body forth the types already long familiar to the popular mind; their adventures, as sung, written, read, and enacted in crude though symbolic gestures, exemplified the attitudes toward character and destiny of the popular culture whose creatures they became.

The impulse which launched these rustic heroes on their impudent careers reverberated too in the aphoristic profundity of a voice much more couth than theirs. While Nimrod Wildfire and Sam Patch cavorted on their respective stages, in a nearby lecture hall another crowd leaned forward in hushed attention to a seer's admonishment:

> There is a time in every man's education when he arrives at the conviction that envy is ignorance; that imitation is suicide; that he must take himself for better or for worse as his portion . . . The power which resides in him is new in nature, and none but he knows what that is which he can do, nor does he know until he has tried. . . .
>
> Whoso would be a man must be a nonconformist. . . . No law can be sacred to me but that of my own nature. Good and bad are but names very readily transferable to that or this; the only right is what is after my constitution, the only wrong what is against it.

The evening's lecture was 'Self-Reliance'; the lecturer, an accomplished impersonator who, on other nights, would be billed as 'The Hero,' 'The Poet,' 'The Philosopher,' 'The American Scholar,' 'The Man of the World,' 'The Reformer,' 'The Transcendentalist.' A decade later he would be characterized in Lowell's 'A Fable for Critics' as

> A Greek head on right Yankee shoulders, whose range
> Has Olympus for one pole, for t'other, the Exchange.

These lines on Emerson, from the pen which in that same year (1848) immortalized the Yankee type in the homely guise of Hosea Biglow, suggest the kinship of the Sage of Concord with the rude and rustic stereotype of regional popular character. The same contradictions that Lowell finds in Emerson he sees in the Yankee at large—'A strange hybrid, indeed, did circumstance beget, here in the New World, upon the old Puritan stock, and the earth never before saw such mystic-practicalism, such niggard geniality, such calculating-fanaticism, such cast-iron enthusiasm, such sour-faced humor, such close-fisted generosity.' [4]

Emerson's transcendental counsel has its affinities with the self-assertive folk spirit of both the Yankee and the Kentuckian. Half mystical though his vision of the world might be, in his attempts

[4] 'Introduction' to *The Biglow Papers,* first series; *Works* (Boston and New York, 1890), VIII, 35.

to ground the perception of the spirit in the experience of the senses he even leaned toward the folk vocabulary of the time.[5] Yet these affinities with popular culture in Emerson's essays were but fragmentary, compared with the effect the popular stereotypes of character would have on the fiction of his contemporaries, Hawthorne and Melville, and after them, Mark Twain.

What were these images? How did they evolve?

The origin of the very name *Yankee* is a mystery, a secular mystery. *The Dictionary of American English* discovers the term to be no older than the French and Indian War, when it was apparently the cognomen of certain regiments from Connecticut. In any case, we owe to the British redcoats of the Revolution the distinctive sobriquet, for it was they who used it to deride their homespun foes. If we knew who first coined the term we might also be able to know the original author of the song, 'Yankee Doodle.' This catchy fife tune soon enough passed into folk provenience. Its verses recapitulated the adventures of a nascent folk hero —the young man from the provinces who comes to town to enlist in the Continentals and make his way in the world. In the decades after the Revolution this high-stepping, wide-eyed naïf underwent some interesting transmogrifications and enjoyed some adventures as yet unsuspected by the Down East seamen, merchants, and farmers who rallied to Paul Revere's harried cry. 'Yankee Doodle' became a stock property of the Yankee drama which emerged just after the Revolution—the rustic Jonathans, Jedediahs, and Ichabods of a score of plays announced their independence as they whistled, sang or recited the famous song. Even before the song got into plays—the Yankee first walks onstage as the rustic servant Jonathan in Royall Tyler's famous comedy,

[5] See John Q. Anderson, 'Emerson and the Language of the Folk,' in Mody C. Boatright, et al., ed., *Folk Travelers* (Dallas, 1953), pp. 152-9; and C. Grant Loomis, 'Emerson's Proverbs,' *Western Folklore*, XVII (Oct. 1958), 257-62.

The Contrast (1787)—it had inspired many a stanza depicting rustic life in original poems which took their rhythm and refrain from its well-nigh universal popularity. Among the most popular of these was a broadside written in 1795 by Thomas Green Fessenden, 'Jonathan's Courtship,' known also as 'The Country Lovers':

> A merry tale will I rehearse,
>   As ever you did hear, sir,
> How Jonathan set out so fierce
>   To see his dearest dear, sir.
>
> Yankee doodle, keep it up,
>   Yankee doodle dandy,
> Mind the musick—mind the step,
>   And with the girls be handy. . . .
>
> 'Miss Sal, I's going to say, as how
>   'We'll spark it here tonight,
> 'I kind of love you, Sal, I vow,
>   'And Mother said I might.' . . .
>   Yankee doodle &c. . . .
>
> 'Are you the lad who went to town,
>   'Put on your streaked *trowses,*
> 'Then vow'd you could not see the town,
>   'There were so many houses?'
>   Yankee doodle, &c. . . .

Here was Jonathan Jolthead, rustic swain: circumlocutious, head abulge with gossip and afire with witchcraft superstition, bashful, tongue-tied, and afraid for his life of sparking. A more amusing picture of a farm boy's discomfiture in romance was not rhymed again for half a century, until Lowell wrote 'The Courtin'.' Fessenden's broadside was at once reprinted, anthologized, and republished in his *Original Poems* (London, 1805; Philadelphia, 1806). Its comic portrayal of the New England rustic represents the first stage in the emergence of the Yankee as a character type.[6]

The second stage is his appearance in plays. The earliest stage Yankees, like Jonathan in *The Contrast*, were usually bumpkin servants on their first trip to town; but soon the Yankee end-man became the center of the show. By the 1820's such character actors as Dan Marble and Yankee Hill were commissioning plays in which to exhibit their mastery of the stereotyped comic character. To the original qualities of rusticity, boastfulness, inquisitiveness, and independence, played off against the mores of a more highly polished urban society, the Yankee as hero added a bracing bravery, downright honesty, and upstanding moral certitude. These sterling qualities were often exhibited in plots of treacle which involved the attempt of a villain to seduce or abduct the heroine—dastardly knavery foiled by the indomitable Jonathan. In Richard M. Dorson's detailed study of these early plays, at least eleven examples of stock Yankee characters appear before 1819. Since these all conform to a single type rather than exhibit individual characteristics, Dorson concludes that 'it is more probable that a permanent Yankee folk type existed apart from [Tyler's] dramatic imagination and was adopted, and not created, by the playwrights.' The facts that the playwrights sometimes used the Yankee traits as a disguise for other characters and that these plays have repeated references to the Yankee as 'an original,' 'a perfect natural,' 'a real live Yankee,' indicate the 'existence of a mythical Yankee who was properly the property of the folk.' Further evidence is the 'tendency to give individual

[6] In the preface to his London edition Fessenden wrote, 'My allusions and metaphors are mostly taken from objects which I saw in America around me. My nymphs and swains are not of Arcadian breed. My Jonathans and my Tabithas are more like the Cloddipoles and Blouzelindas of Gay than the Damons and Daphnes of Pope; and I will not assert, that I have not, in some instances, *caricatured* the manners of the New England rusticks. Still, however, the peasantry of New England, as described in my poems, will be found to bear some semblance to what they are in real life.' (p. xi.)

examples of the genus a common name, Jonathan.'[7] Tyler's play stated the theme which most of the later stage Yankees repeated: the contrast between the polished manners of the English dandy (aped by his obsequious butler), who proves to be both a villain and a fraud, and the dashing honesty and manliness of the American swain, aided by his oafish, naïve, and bungling Yankee servant, Jonathan, who has a heart of gold beneath a comically unsophisticated exterior.

On stage the Yankee had been the country clown in the city. A smart Down East editor, Seba Smith of Portland, hit upon the notion of rusticating the now-familiar Yankee character, and exhibiting him against the background of his native village. Happily, Smith was able to elaborate this conception, having an unusual ear for the cadences and vocabulary of actual New England country speech and a sense of humor which delighted in comic portraiture as well as in political satire. Once Jonathan is recast as Major Jack Downing of Downingville, Away Down East in the State of Maine, he suddenly ceases to be the oafish victim of his own unfamiliarity with the decorum of the city. The Yankee as countryman reverses the role. He now plays a version of Pastoral, in which he possesses the limitless wisdom of his motherwit. It is the complexities of an overweening sophistication, both social and political, which get the short end of the axe handle when measured against his horse sense, honesty, and shrewdness in appraising human motives. Smith could take advantage, in the Major Jack Downing papers, of the satirical possibilities offered him by a character both naïve and clairvoyant. Thus Major Downing, as a political commentator, acts on the presumption that in a democracy the common citizen can address the head of the State (he writes directly to General Jackson), since the Government cares as much about each of the people as the people care about the Government. His native village is named for his grandfather, a doddering gaffer who de-

[7] 'The Yankee on the Stage—A Folk Hero of American Drama,' *New England Quarterly*, XII (Sept. 1940), 467-93, esp. pp. 468, 472, 480-82.

tains every passerby with his endless account of the 'fatigue of Burgwine.' The old soldier's discursive garrulity, first published in 1833, would not be matched in print until Mark Twain wrote down 'His Grandfather's Old Ram' in *Roughing It* (1871). The Major's grandfather was not only a Revolutionary soldier, but also a pioneer. It is curious how his settling as far Down East as he could go prefigures the western treks of so many later veterans and folk heroes. When Major Downing first appears, then, he is seen in the settlement his own family had founded and lived in for three generations. This roots him to a place in a way that most Yankee characters are not rooted in popular lore; at the same time Downingville prefigures the Jalaam of Lowell's *Biglow Papers*, the Poganuc and Oldtown of Mrs. Stowe's novels, the Deep Haven of Miss Jewett's stories, the Tilbury Town of Robinson's poems, and so represents a large forward step in the development of New England's regional literature.

On the 18th of January, 1830, readers of the Portland, Maine, *Daily Courier* first made the acquaintance of Jack Downing. In a letter to his cousin Ephraim Downing, 'up in Downingville,' Jack declared as how he had come to Portland to 'sell my load of axe handles, and mother's cheese, and cousin Nabby's bundle of footings.' While in town he has 'been to meeting, and to the museum, and to both Legislaters, the one they call the House, and the one they call the Sinnet.' Of course this village boy is the yokel of Yankee jokelore, who doesn't get the point at all of the political wrangling he sees. But as a matter of fact the parliamentary wranglers look pretty venal and stupid when measured against his clear notions of how a democratic legislature ought to conduct itself. This simple pattern of using the good life of the bumpkin village to measure the devious city takes full advantage of the nostalgia for a golden age of simplicity. The rural village appears constantly in American literature, oratory, and thought as an almost-contemporary symbol of the Golden Age. Associated with this concept are several other equally seminal notions: Rousseau's ideal of the Noble Natural Man, Crèvecœur's idealization of the farmer, Jefferson's of the artisan and farmer class; and the opposite but complementary conceptions about the city as the place of evil. The usual pattern of one numerous genre of the American novel is to move an innocent character from his country home into the temptations and evils of city life. This pattern conforms not only to that found in the 'young man from the province' class of novels, but also to the movement of populations in the American nineteenth and twentieth centuries.

With the Rural Village as the locus of a paradisal symbolism in folklore and popular culture, we may well expect to find secular analogues to the Fall. Seba Smith achieved a delicate balance in Jack Downing between innocence and knowledge; his Major—his whole village of Downingville—has a knowledge which does not cost them their Down East paradise because it is instinctual knowledge, not the hard, mean knowledge gained by experience. Their innate good natures and their birthright of Yankee wisdom make such characters as Major Downing inviolable against chicanery. (The stage Yankee, too, had been a towering pine tree of natural goodness and virtue.) But when the Yankee character is uprooted from the stabilizing influences of village life, and, in accordance with the mercantile temper of the times, takes to the roads with a pack of notions, clocks, and nutmegs, the moral quality of our delight in the folk character is perceptibly altered. President Timothy Dwight of Yale College, 'whose experience with the peddlers of Connecticut must have been extensive,' inveighed against their effect upon mercantile morality in New England:

> Men, who begin life with bargaining for small wares, will almost invariably become sharpers. The commanding aim of every such man will soon be to make a good bargain: and he will speedily consider every gainful bargain as a good one. The tricks of fraud will assume, in his mind, the same place, which commercial skill and an honourable system of dealing hold in the mind of a merchant. Often employed in disputes, he becomes noisy, pertinacious,

> and impudent. . . . I believe this unfortunate employment to have had an unhappy influence on both the morals and manners, of the people.[8]

Doubtless there were honest peddlers, but nobody told stories about *them*. In folk anecdote and jokelore the itinerant Yankee peddler came into focus. The sketches featured his pack of notions and his sharp bargaining ways. They told of the Connecticut peddler who tried to sell brooms to the merchants of Providence. (This one was recorded in 1852, three decades after President Dwight's jeremiad.) Having no luck, at last he found a dealer who 'would put his goods at cost price, for the sake of trading.' After long negotiations they agreed to terms: payment for the brooms to be half in cash and half in goods. The brooms unloaded and cash payment made, the merchant asked, 'Now, what will you have for the remainder of your bill?'

> The peddler scratched his head . . . walked the floor, whistled, drummed with his fingers on the head of a barrel. By and by, his reply came—slowly and deliberately.
>
> 'You Providence fellers are cute, you sell at cost . . . and make money. I don't see how 'tis done. Now I don't know about your goods, barrin' one article, and, ef I take anything else, I may be cheated. So, seein' as t'won't make any odds with you, I guess I'll take brooms. I know them like a book, and can swear to what you paid for 'em.'

Note that this sharp deal was driven because both merchant and peddler pitted wits for the sake of trading. There were countless stories of similar shrewdness.[9]

[8] *Travels in New-England and New-York* (1821), quoted by G. L. Kittredge, *The Old Farmer and His Almanack* (Cambridge, 1904), p. 145.

[9] On the development of the Yankee peddler see Rourke, *American Humor*, pp. 3-32; Walter Blair, *Native American Humor* (New York, 1937), pp. 17-62; Richardson Wright, *Hawkers & Walkers in Early America* (Philadelphia, 1927). The broom story is from the *Yankee Blade* (Boston, 24 Jan. 1852), reprinted in R. M. Dorson, *Jonathan Draws the Long Bow* (Cambridge, 1946), pp. 81-2. P. T. Barnum told the same yarn a different way, with the merchant outwitting the peddler, in *Struggles and Triumphs*, ed. G. S. Bryan (New York, 1927), pp. 48-50; reprinted in Botkin, *A Treasury of American Folklore*, pp. 394-5. For other

The heroes of folklore and of popular culture inevitably display those qualities of character which their celebrants admire. Since the recorded anecdotes of the nineteenth century contain so many yarns of this type, we may well ask ourselves what indeed is the significance of the popularity of the Yankee peddler as a roguish picaro. In an interesting discussion of the relation between mythical concepts and personal identity, Jerome S. Bruner remarks on two basic mythic plots:

> the plot of innocence and the plot of cleverness—the former being a kind of Arcadian ideal, requiring the eschewal of complexity and awareness, the latter requiring the cultivation of competence almost to the point of guile. The happy childhood, the good man as the child of God, the simple plowman, the Rousseauian ideal of natural nobility—these are the creatures of the plot of innocence. At the other extreme there are Penelope, the suitors, and Odysseus. . . . New versions arise to reflect the ritual and practice of each era—the modifications of the happiness of innocence and the satisfaction of competence.[10]

For early nineteenth-century America, the Yankee villager is one expression of the myth of innocence, the Yankee peddler of the myth of competence. But our native trickster hero has of course sold his soul for knowledge—not that he ever thinks about his soul in the crafty jokelore that preserves the shards from which his *Odyssey* might have been written. Even in the most ambitious attempts to give the peddler a name, a face, a personality, he remains rather the shifty, sparring, crafty side of a man than does he become a personality nearly as well-rounded as Major Downing.

It was a Nova Scotian judge named Thomas Chandler Haliburton who took up Seba Smith's idea of a series of satirical newspaper sketches about a single regional character, and substituted for the village yokel of Downingville a master of shifts and disguises in the itinerant profession. By 1837 Haliburton had

yarns see Dorson, *Jonathan*, pp. 78-94; Botkin, *A Treasury of New England Folklore* (New York, 1947), pp. 2-63.

[10] 'Myth and Identity,' *Daedalus* (Spring 1959), pp. 353-4.

published in book form his first collection, *The Clockmaker, or the Sayings and Doings of Samuel Slick.* His Sam Slick is admirable, as tricksters are, without being exactly *likeable.* He peddles his clocks and opinions up and down New England, Canada, the West, and even visits England and the Continent in a series of books that spanned the next twenty years. Fencing wits with whoever crosses his path, he assumes changes of costume (Easterner's broadcloth or Westerner's leggings), temperament, or opinion as the occasion warranted. Like the Connecticut broom peddler, he trades just for the sake of trading; he goes the broom peddler one better, trading not for profit but for pure pride:

> I met a man this morning, said the clockmaker, from Halifax, a real conceited lookin' critter as you een a most ever seed, all shines and didos. He looked as if he had picked up his airs arter some officer of the regulars had worn 'em and cast 'em off. . . .
>
> Well, says he to me, with the air of a man that chucks a cent into a beggar's hat, a fine day this sir. Do you actily think so said I? and I gave it the real Connecticut drawl. Why, said he, quite short, if I didn't think so, I wouldn't say so. Well says I, I don't know, but if I did think so, I guess I wouldn't say so. Why not? says he— Because, I expect, says I, any fool could see that as well as me; and then I stared at him, as much as to say, now if you like that are swap, I am ready to trade with you agin as soon as you like.[11]

Now the yokel comes out on top against the city slicker, a further reversal of the earlier Yankee role.

By the Civil War the Yankee stereotype had divided in the popular mind, as journalists and dramatists spawned two varieties of Yankee creatures to catch the public fancy. His shrewd, narrow-nosed commercialism and self-seeking aspects, joined to his impervious egotism and colossal self-satisfaction, made for a caricature of the already proverbial type. Sam Slick was the most popular expression of this side of the Yankee—albeit Lowell accused him of being a slander against the regional character.

[11] T. C. Haliburton, 'A Yankee Handle for a Halifax Blade,' *The Clockmaker* (Philadelphia, 1837), pp. 101-2.

To the South, in Alabama, another rogue's adventures were laughingly devoured in the newspapers where Johnson J. Hooper first published his *Adventures of Simon Suggs* (reprinted in book form, 1845). Hooper's hero, whose motto proclaimed 'IT IS GOOD TO BE SHIFTY IN A NEW COUNTRY,' is the most fully developed American picaro before Melville's *The Confidence-Man.* In this introductory passage his creator allows us a glimpse behind the comic mask Simon usually wore:

> The shifty Captain Suggs is a miracle of shrewdness. He possesses in an eminent degree, that tact which enables man to detect *the soft spots* in his fellow, and to assimilate himself to whatever company he may fall in with. Besides, he has a quick, ready wit, which has extricated him from many an unpleasant predicament, and which makes him whenever he chooses to be so—and that is always—very companionable. In short, nature gave the Captain the precise intellectual outfit most to be desired by a man of his propensities. She sent him into the world a sort of he-Pallas, ready to cope with his kind from infancy, in all the art by which men '*get along*' in the world; if she made him in respect to his moral conformation, a beast of prey, she did not refine the cruelty by denying him the fangs and the claws.[12]

One instance of his avarice and shifty deception is already familiar in Mark Twain's borrowing from 'Simon Suggs Attends a Camp Meeting' for his description of the spiritual and literal piracy of the King in *Huckleberry Finn* (chap. 20).

Yet the native picaro had admirable qualities too—his enterprise, his adaptability, and his peddler's mission (whatever the motive) of bringing the comforts of civilization to every cabin on the farthest frontier. In the 1840's a folk hero embodying these qualities appeared. First in cabins and farms along the Muskingum valley, then in the pages of Henry Howe's *Historical Collections of Ohio,* and eventually in the folklore and fiction of the entire country, the adventures of Johnny Appleseed grew even more miraculously than did the orchards he had planted. Paddling down the Ohio to Marietta at the mouth of the Muskin-

[12] *Adventures of Captain Simon Suggs* (Philadelphia, 1845), pp. 12-13.

gum, then up that stream to its tributaries' tributaries, John Chapman set out apple seeds to make ready the earth for populations yet unborn. He also left behind him books, which he split into sections and passed out to lonely settlers on one trip, circulating the fragments from cabin to cabin on his return. Beloved by the Indians, he was immune to their ferocities during the War of 1812; in fact he saved many settlers from their vengeance. He befriended the animals; if he saw one abused by its master he would buy it and give it away to a more humane pioneer. Johnny Appleseed spoke frequently with angels.

It does not matter that a painstaking biography of John Chapman shows him to have been a Yankee trader after all. Born in Leominster, Massachusetts, in 1774, he appeared, during his travels in Ohio, to be as representative a Yankee type in his 'mystic-practicalism' as any friend of Hosea Biglow in Jalaam. First, his mysticism. Robert Price has shown how theologically sophisticated was this early disciple of Swedenborg and how important his role in spreading the doctrine of the New Jerusalem on the unpromisingly hard terrain of the Ohio frontier. He even offered to trade some of his land to the New Church in return for shipments of Swedenborg's tracts, which he would disseminate on his journeys. This offer points to the conclusion that Johnny Appleseed was no 'pauper philanthropist'—actually he owned hundreds of acres of choice Ohio land and based his seemingly eccentric life on a sound principle of economics. 'The one unique thing about John's seedling tree business . . . was his scheme for moving it with the frontier.'[13] These facts, which Price spent years tracking down, were obliterated by the popular image of Johnny Appleseed, as it was embellished and romanticized in succeeding decades. To become this humble image of the Hero as Civilizer, Sam Slick had to cast off all his characteristics but his garments

[13] Robert Price, *Johnny Appleseed: Man and Myth* (Bloomington, Ind., 1954), p. 38. A popular romanticized account, from which the foregoing details are drawn, is W. D. Haley, 'Johnny Appleseed: A Pioneer Hero,' *Harper's New Monthly Magazine,* XLIII (Nov. 1871), 830-36; reprinted in Botkin, *A Treasury of American Folklore,* pp. 261-70.

and his peripatetic ways. Gone are the shiftiness, the cunning, the insidious sophistry, the trade for the sake of trading. To bring religion and reading to the trappers and woodsmen in their lonely cabins, to enrich the hillsides with orchards for the sake of mankind yet to come, this peddler all but denies his Yankee lineage.

Yankee self-assertion—the impulse of self-definition through symbolic action—appears most dramatically in the figure of Sam Patch. Like Johnny Appleseed, Patch was an actual person, a textile worker in Pawtucket, Rhode Island, who attracted local attention by plunging, feet first, from the roof of a shed into the river beneath. Spurred on to seek fortune and national fame by spectacular leaps, Sam Patch abandoned his loom for a grand tour of waterfalls. Heralded by handbills proclaiming his motto, 'Some things may be done as well as others,' he climbed to flimsy platforms and plunged into the swirling froth. Sam conquered the great Niagara, but the Falls of Genesee at last proved his undoing. Attempting his feat after one too many drinks of whiskey, he lost his poise about twenty feet from the water and landed sideways. As often happens, a mysterious death may catapult a poseur into legendary fame. Sam's body didn't come to the surface for six months. By then it was far too late to prove that he was dead. He had jumped through the bowels of the world and turned up alive in the South Seas.[14] He was also knocking about the American West, as alleged by many travellers. While some might scoff, none could deny that he had been on the stage of many a theatre. As Nature imitates Art, so men are tempted

[14] In an amusing sidelight by one folk hero on another, Sam Slick tells Edward Everett of Congress about Patch: 'The last dive he took was off the falls of Niagara [sic] and he was never heered of again till tother day, when Captain Enoch Wentworth, of the Susy Ann Whaler, saw him in the South Sea. Why, says Captain Enoch to him, why Sam, says he, how on airth did you get here? I thought you was drowned at the Canadian line. Why, says he, I didn't get *on* airth here at all, but I came right slap *through* it. . . . If I don't take the shine off the Sea Serpent, when I get back to Boston, then my name's not Sam Patch.' Haliburton, *The Clockmaker,* p. 46.

to assume the role of the heroes in their myths: Dan Marble leaped from the height of the theatre into a trap in the floor, behind the pool of water, where a bedspring padded with shavings cushioned his fall. Even more significant than professional theatricals, however, 'the jumping mania affected audiences. Clerks jumped counters, farmers jumped fences, boys and old folks vied in "doing" Sam Patch.'[15]

Here was a natural subject for celebration by these very clerks and farmers. Sam's common origin, his braggadocio, and senseless defiance of danger—not to mention his showmanship—objectified in one symbolic act the qualities of self-assertive independence, rebellion against convention and authority, and, above all, self-reliance no matter what the stakes or the odds. These attributes had long been rooted in the American grain, in the Yankee character, and the boys and oldsters jumping fences to 'do' Sam Patch were in a sense performing a ritual by which they asserted that for them, too, 'Some things may be done as well as others.' Those things included plunging from the security of seaboard cities into the unfathomed perils of the wilderness.

THREE

The settlers of the West developed images of their indigenous traits too. In the period before the Civil War the prototypical frontiersman, like his Yankee counterpart, provided a multiple image. At first, as Backwoodsman, he is a type of the Natural Man, inherently superior to civilized decadence, his egalitarian goodfellowship not quite disguised by his shaggy exterior and helliferocious manner of speech. Backwoods brawlers must have formed an unofficial fraternity throughout the sparsely settled districts of the young Republic, for early travellers' journals re-

[15] The fragments of this curious saga are assembled in R. M. Dorson, 'Sam Patch, Jumping Hero,' *New York Folklore Quarterly*, I (Aug. 1945), pp. 132-51. The latest literary recrudescence of Sam Patch is to appear as one of the aspects of the hero of William Carlos Williams's epic poem *Paterson* (New York, 1948), pp. 24-7, 48f.

port countless instances of their ear-chewing, cheek-ripping, eye-gouging battles. Augustus Baldwin Longstreet gives vivid descriptions of such fights, and of a lone plowboy's rehearsal of one, in his *Georgia Scenes, Characters, Incidents, &c. in the First Half Century of the Republic,* a work which in 1835 marks the inception of a Frontier literature comparable to the Yankee regional writings discussed above. But Longstreet's 'The Fight' and 'Georgia Theatrics' were no exaggeration of the real thing; if elaborated with tall talk and touched with fantasy, they were yet based on life.

The frontiersman, it is well to remember, was not always a Westerner, but he was usually farther west than the seaboard Yankee. In the early days of the republic the frontier was often just a few miles inshore or a few hundred yards from the inland village or town. In her study, 'The Rise of Theatricals,' Constance Rourke identifies the first frontiersman intended for the American stage as 'A minor character called Raccoon or Coony in the early comic opera *The Disappointment* [who] seems to have been a frontiersman, but the piece was never performed . . . though it was twice printed, in 1787 and 1796, and so must have had some sort of circulation.' By a curious coincidence Royall Tyler's Jonathan emerged on the stage at the same time (1787), and our two principal character types have been in tandem almost ever since. In her tantalizingly unspecific way Miss Rourke adds that 'With his braggadocio and half-Indian way he was pictured in a few stories of the War of 1812.' Just which stories, whether drama or fiction, she does not say, but she does remark that 'Cockalorum . . . the lively typical figure with his . . . gaudy hunting costume was not to emerge noticeably in the theater until 1822, when he appeared with a rush—to music, gusty music, a song, "The Hunters of Kentucky," which celebrated those backwoods Kentuckians, "half horse, half alligator," who had helped Jackson win the Battle of New Orleans.' [16]

[16] Rourke, *The Roots of American Culture* (New York, 1942), pp. 125-6. The song is reprinted from Samuel Woodward's *Melodies, Duets, Trios* . . . (1826) in Botkin, *A Treasury of American Folklore,* pp. 9-10.

The frontiersman's earliest full-dress appearance in fiction is, surprisingly, in a famous sketch by our first gentleman of polished letters. Brom Bones, in Washington Irving's 'The Legend of Sleepy Hollow,' demonstrates already in 1819 that the Dutch rowdies of the upper Hudson Valley were frontiersmen of the same stamp as the Ohio riverboatmen and Missouri trappers. Lacking the stories of the War of 1812 mentioned by Rourke, however, it would seem that the first frontiersman actually to appear in a stage play is the character Opossum in Alphonso Wetmore's three-act farce, *The Pedlar*, 'Written for the St. Louis Thespians, By Whom It Was Performed with Great Applause' in early 1821. In the final curtain speech Opossum reveals the original on whom his character was doubtless based: 'If you'll let me live single, till after the dog days, Mike Fink and I will go and catch a barr, and we'll have a barbecue, for wedding supper, any how.'[17] In earlier speeches Opossum reproduces the boisterous brag of the backwoods bully:

> *I'm half sea horse & half sea serpent.* Did you ever see my coon dog, stranger? (*Whistles.*) Which eye shall I take out, Mary? . . . I'll tell you, stranger, my name is Opossum—I'm a 'wild-cat'—I've got the swiftest horse, the sharpest shooting rifle, and the prettiest sister—so if you offer to wrestle with her again, you must run faster than the yankee pedlar did, or my coon dog will tree you.

There is, inevitably, a 'yankee pedlar' in the piece:

> *Nutmeg:* Halloo the house! I suppose the old cogger is not up yet. He little thinks the greatest genius in the universe, now stands before his door, ready to cheat him out of half he is worth. (*Window opens, old Prairie puts his head and the muzzle of a rifle out.*)
>
> *Old Prairie.* Who the devil are you, Mr. Impudence?
>
> *Nutmeg.* A travelling merchant, sir—all the way over the mountains, from the town of New Haven, with a cart load of very useful, very desirable and very pretty notions: such as, tin cups and nutmegs, candlesticks and onion seeds, wooden clocks, flax seed and

[17] Alphonso Wetmore, *The Pedlar* (St. Louis, 1821), facsimile reprint edited by Scott C. Osborn (Lexington, Ky., 1955), p. 34.

lanterns, Japanned coffee pots, and tea *sarvers*, together with a variety of cordage and other dry goods.

By the end of Act I, Nutmeg has sold a lantern to every member of Old Prairie's household and has cheated the sailor Harry Emigrant in a horse-swap.

Contrasted to his shrewdness with its smack of the counting-house is the energetic activism of the frontiersman. A drunken boatman enters, singing:

Boatman. Quarter less twain. (*Opossum rises, and advances.*)
Opossum. Who are you, stranger?
Boatman. A steam boat, damn your eyes.
Opossum. Then I'm a Missouri snag—I'm into you.
Boatman. I'm full of chain pumps—come on—I'm a five horse team.
Opossum. Then I'll blaze your leader. (*Strikes him in the face . . .*)
Boatman. No gouging?
Opossum. And no ear biting . . .

It is obvious that these three characters, who so closely resemble the Yankee peddlers and ring-tailed roarers of the Jacksonian newspaper sketches a decade later, are based on the already widely known stock figures of oral tradition. Yet *The Pedlar* is not lacking in literary derivations. As Scott C. Osborn's preface to the recent reprint observes, Wetmore's piece is 'A crude mixture of melodrama, farce, low comedy, Restoration comedy, and intrigue play . . .' *The Pedlar* is 'derivative almost throughout,' based entirely on stock devices—'disguises, mistaken identities, assignations, the fortuitous discovery of a long-lost son and a will, the eloping couples.' The characters too are dramatic conventions: the female wit, the clever servant, the discomfited father, the old man in love with a young girl; 'Pecanne is a Lydia Languish, Opossum a Tony Lumpkin, Harry Emigrant an imitation of salty-spoken sailors from Wycherly on.' Two scenes are adapted from *She Stoops To Conquer*, while 'Nutmeg's lament for the loss of his wares is a burlesque of Wolsey's farewell to his greatness.' The playwright who combined dependence upon all of these eighteenth-century staples with realistic observations of frontier life and the adaptation of native stereotypes from oral tradition was a Connecticut-born soldier, merchant, lawyer, publisher, and sometime author. Osborn concludes that '*The Pedlar* has no literary value,' and that its only merit 'lies in its Western characters and local color.' Part of its historical value, however, is to remind us of the complexity of the literary matrix into which characters, themes, and settings from folklore were introduced. Even so crude a production as *The Pedlar* (the only play by a man who was after all a literary amateur) demonstrates the cultural background—richly cosmopolitan, by folk standards—of the earliest drama on the American frontier.

The Pedlar illustrates one of the knottiest problems involved in understanding the absorption of folk materials into literature. The transformation to which folklore is necessarily subjected by the literary imagination complicates its identification. Even when the author retells verbatim stories from oral tradition, he is never a folk redactor. The literary context in which he places such tales is itself a change worked upon them. He may enclose the folk motifs in a more elaborate literary structure or contrast them to a different frame of reference than would a folk raconteur telling the same story. Further, he may extend and develop germinal plots or characters. One of the most important functions of folk materials in literature is to offer contrasts to the materials drawn from traditions other than the folk. The interplay of native folklore and European literary traditions is one of the important sources of tension in much American writing. Mark Twain, for instance, made Tom Sawyer a repository of chivalric notions from *Don Quixote* and Sir Walter Scott, while Huck Finn, with his protean disguises, superstitions, innocence, and closeness to nature, is a figure embodying many themes, traits, and motifs of American folklore.

Wetmore's frontiersman had alluded to Mike Fink, the original on whom his own braggart prowess was modelled, almost a decade before Fink himself became the hero of a cult of popular literature which lasted into the 1880's. Walter Blair and Franklin Meine, who reconstructed Fink's biography and reprinted the literature about him, find considerable evidence that in the decade of the 1820's Mike Fink had already become a hero of oral folklore.[18] Like Sam Patch and Johnny Appleseed, Mike was at first just a real man, born in Fort Pitt (Pittsburgh) around 1770 when that rowdy and endangered settlement comprised twenty cabins. Life there hardened the men and boys who lived it, and Mike, as a settler who knew him records, became a prodigy of physical strength, appetites, and endurance. He was soon a supermarksman and a famous hunter.

Mike was bred as an Indian fighter. He had an appetite for that business, which was his first career. Later, when Pittsburgh had grown and the Indians retreated, he became a keelboatman. When the steamboats encroached on the keel- and flat-boats he went west of the rivers and began his third career as a trapper. In each of his manifestations he retreated from society to preserve his own savage nature from change. During his lifetime Fink was the hero and scourge of towns along the Ohio and the Mississippi. In time he became the archetype of his breed. 'He was in fact a Mississippi river-god, one of those minor deities whom men create in their own image and magnify to magnify themselves,' Miss Rourke claims for him.[19] Whether fact or legend, the stories told about him typified popular attitudes toward the men who first rid the wilderness of Indians and split the silence of the waters with their boathorns and ballads of Shawneetown.

Who could have foretold that the first scribe to record the rough saga of this shaggy boatman would be a contributor to a

[18] *Half Horse Half Alligator: The Growth of the Mike Fink Legend* (Chicago, 1956), pp. 43-55, 260. All of the ensuing accounts of Fink are taken from this collection with the exception of Mike's setting a woman's hair afire, from Henry Howe, *The Great West* (New York, 1857), pp. 277-8, reprinted in Botkin, *A Treasury of American Folklore*, pp. 34-5.

[19] *American Humor*, p. 54.

satin-bound ladies' annual? True, *The Western Souvenir, A Christmas and New Year's Gift for 1829,* was published in Cincinnati, and its editor, James Hall, declared independence from Eastern originals, saying, 'It is written and published in the Western country . . . and is chiefly confined to subjects connected with the history and character of the country which gives it birth.' Although Hall, a leading early writer of the Ohio Valley, wrote much of the contents, his work was overshadowed by 'The Last of the Boatmen,' contributed by Morgan Neville. This author had actually known Mike Fink during his own Pittsburgh boyhood. Just as Longstreet in *Georgia Scenes* and Hooper, in *Adventures of Simon Suggs* would describe the outrageous barbarity and guile of frontiersmen from the viewpoint of an observer from a higher culture, so did Neville present his uncouth Achilles as a picturesque specimen of an already vanishing phase of Western life. Unlike the later writers from the South, Neville does not abandon his own hifalutin' style to reproduce the barbaric yawp of his subject. He tells of meeting Mike, while on a riverboat, and witnessing Mike's feat of shooting a tin cup from his brother's head—the William Tell motif in buckskins; recounts Mike's prowess at killing an Indian; alludes to 'a thousand legends [that] illustrate the fearlessness of his character'; and reports that his hero died when, performing his tin cup shoot, he aimed too low, and a friend of the victim, 'suspecting foul play, shot Mike through the heart before he had time to re-load his rifle.'

In addition to these simple motifs Neville contributes a picturesque description of his hero and a set of ennobling comparisons:

> With a figure cast in a mold that added much of the symmetry of an Apollo to the limbs of a Hercules, he possessed gigantic strength. . . . At the court of Charlemagne he might have been a Roland; with the Crusaders he would have been the favorite of the Knight of the Lion-heart; and in our revolution, he would have ranked with the Morgans and Putnams of the day. He was the hero of a

> hundred fights, and the leader in a thousand daring adventures. . . . Wherever he was an enemy, like his great prototype, Rob Roy, he levied the contribution of Black Mail for the use of his boat. . . . On the Ohio, he was known among his companions by the appellation of the 'Snapping Turtle'; and on the Mississippi, he was called 'The Snag.'

Within the next two decades Fink's adventures were retold and elaborated in such repositories of Western local color as the Cincinnati *Western Monthly Review,* the St. Louis *Reveille,* and the nationally admired *Spirit of the Times;* the authors were such then-prominent litterateurs of the West as Timothy Flint, Thomas Bangs Thorpe, John S. Robb, and Emerson Bennett. Briefer, more vigorous sketches than theirs appeared in the Davy Crockett Almanacks for 1837, 1839, and 1850-53. None of these writings is in itself of first quality, but taken together they form a strong subliterary tradition which defines the anarchic frontiersman's character with a clarity that helps us understand the significance of the type in the writings of Melville and Twain.

The Mike Fink sketches present an unwitting mixture of sentimentality and barbarism. When looking for a fight, Mike Fink announces himself in Emerson Bennett's version of the ring-tailed roarer's brag:

> Hurray for me, you scapegoats! I'm a land-screamer—I'm a watch-dog—I'm a snapping turckle—I can lick five times my own weight in wildcats. I can use up Injuns by the cord. I can swallow niggers whole, raw, or cooked. I can out-lick, out-dance, out-jump, out-dive, out-drink, out-holler, and out-lick any white thing in the shape o' human that's put foot within two thousand miles o' the big Massassip . . .

John S. Robb improved upon the original tale of Mike's marksmanship. He has Mike take up the taunt, 'Why, you couldn't hit the hinder part of that nigger's heel up thar on the bluff, 'thout damagin' the bone.' Dead-eye Fink fired in jest; when the local magistrate tried to arrest him for the prank, Mike quipped, 'I want you to pay me for trimmin' the heel of one of your town niggers! I've just altered his breed, and arter this his posterity kin warr the neatest kind of a boot!' To cure 'a woman who passed for his wife' of winking at another man, Mike made her lie down in a bed of leaves which he then set afire. He kept her there till her hair blazed; this was quite a joke.

Thomas Bangs Thorpe, the author of 'The Big Bear of Arkansas,' wrote of Mike in 'The Disgraced Scalp Lock' (1842). His Fink gives a brave Indian the mortal insult of plucking a feather from his headdress; he pursues Mike a thousand miles down the river but Fink's rifle cheats the Indian of a deserved revenge. Mike's philosophy is dualistic in this sophisticated adventure story: on the one hand he gives us the ruthless wilderness code which Uncle Ben, in Arthur Miller's *Death of a Salesman,* will preach in mid-twentieth-century: 'I was never particular about what's called a fair fight. . . . It's natur that the big fish should eat the little ones.' But speaking in a different voice, Thorpe's Mike transcends his time in this lament:

> What's the use of improvements? When did cutting down trees make deer more plenty? Who ever found wild buffalo or a brave Indian in a city? Where's the fun, the frolicking, the fighting? Gone! Gone! The rifle won't make a man a living now—he must turn nigger and work.

The woodsman who makes possible the coming of civilization cries out in nostalgia and bitterness against the things he has wrought. Mike Fink, the retrograde bully and roustabout, is here made to mouth the ambivalent feelings of a more polite public regarding the destruction of the wilderness Eden—in which his cruelties were never called to account—by the oncome of civilization, law, and restraint.

However savage such men as Mike Fink were in fact, their unknowing roles as harbingers of civilization justified an idealization of the frontiersman's character:

> Though held in sort a barbarian, the backwoodsman would seem to America what Alexander was to Asia—captain in the vanguard of conquering civilization. Whatever the nation's growing opulence

> or power, does it not lackey his heels? Pathfinder, provider of security to those who come after him, for himself he asks nothing but hardship. Worthy to be compared with Moses in Exodus, or the Emperor Julian in Gaul, who on foot, and bare-browed, at the head of covered or mounted legions, marched so through the elements, day after day. The tide of emigration, let it roll as it will, never overwhelms the backwoodsman into itself; he rides upon advance, as the Polynesian upon the comb of the spray.

This is Melville, eulogizing the frontiersman in *The Confidence-Man* (1857). Melville's woodsman is not Mike Fink but another Ohio Valley character first drawn by James Hall, who had published Neville's sketch of Fink in 1829. Three years later Hall, in his *Legends of the West,* outlined the career of one Colonel Moredock, a monomaniacal Indian-hater. Although Moredock's passion invests his character with a tragic dignity lacking in Fink, it is noteworthy that Melville's treatment of the woodsman, whom he presents ideally and then in the grimness of his barbarous fixation, parallels the dualistic popular conceptions of frontier character.

A decade after *The Pedlar* appeared, the poets William Cullen Bryant and Fitz-Greene Halleck served, with Prosper Wetmore, as judges of a contest offering a three hundred dollar prize for 'an original comedy whereof an American should be the leading character.' The winner was James Kirke Paulding with his farce, *The Lion of the West.* The play was produced the following year (1831), but in the course of its theatrical history it was twice rewritten—the second time, for its London run in 1833, by William Bayle Bernard who retitled it *The Kentuckian, or A Trip to New York.* Bernard's, presumably, is the version in which James H. Hackett, the actor-producer who offered the original prize, continued to appear in America as Nimrod Wildfire for over two decades. Yet with the exception of a single speech of backwoods braggadocio quoted in the *Daily Louisville Public Advertiser* for October 17, 1831, the text of Paulding's play disappeared and *The Lion of the West* has been known only by reputation for 125 years. Now, thanks to the resourceful literary detection of James N. Tidwell, the text of Bernard's adaptation has been recovered from the British Museum.[20] There is some doubt as to how closely the Bernard text resembles Paulding's original, yet a comparison of the condensed newspaper extract, the backwoodsman's brag, with the corresponding passage in Tidwell's edition shows only minor discrepancies. I quote the entire speech to show, among other things, the development of rhetorical bragging over the rough-and-ready brawling of Wetmore's Opossum. Nimrod Wildfire tells the following yarn to illustrate to an English merchant the fighting customs of his native region:

> Well, I'll tell you how it was. I was riding along the Mississippi one day when I came across a fellow floating down the stream sitting cock'd up in the starn of his boat fast asleep. Well, I hadn't had a fight for as much as ten days—felt as though I must kiver myself up in a salt bin to keep—'so wolfy' about the head and shoulders. So, says I, hullo, stranger, if you don't take keer your boat will run away wi'you. So he looked up at me 'slantindicular,' and I looked down on him 'slanchwise.' He took out a chaw of tobacco from his mouth and, says he, I don't value you tantamount to that, and then he flopp'd his wings and crowed like a cock. I ris up, shook my mane, crooked my neck, and neighed like a horse. Well, he run his boat foremost ashore. I stopped my waggon and set me triggers. Mister, says he, I'm the best man—if I ain't, I wish I may be tetotaciously exflunctified! I can whip my weight in wild cats and ride strait through a crab apple orchard on a flash of lightning—clear meat axe disposition! And what's more, I once back'd a bull off a bridge. Poh, says I, what do I keer for that? I can tote a steam boat up the Mississippi and over the Alleghany mountains. My father can whip the best man in old Kaintuck, and

[20] By a coincidence the Bernard text was discovered at the same time by Nils Erik Enkvist, *American Humour in England before Mark Twain* (Abo, Finland, 1953), p. 22. The condensation of Nimrod's brag appears in M. M. Mathews, *The Beginnings of American English* (Chicago, 1931), pp. 116-17; and in Botkin, *A Treasury of American Folklore,* pp. 13-14. The full text appears in *The Lion of the West,* ed. James N. Tidwell (Stanford, 1954), pp. 54-5.

> I can whip my father. When I'm good natured I weigh about a hundred and seventy, but when I'm mad, I weigh a *ton.* With that I fetched him the regular Ingen war-whoop. Out he jumped from his boat, and down I tumbled from my waggon—and, I say, we came together like two steam boats going sixty mile an hour. He was a pretty severe colt, but no part of a priming to such a feller as me. I put it to him mighty droll—tickled the varmint till he squealed like a young colt, bellowed 'enough' and swore I was a 'rip staver.' Says I, *ain't* I a horse? Says he, stranger, you're a *beauty* anyhow, and if you'd stand for Congress I'd vote for you next *lection.* Says I, would you? My name's Nimrod Wildfire. Why, I'm the yaller flower of the forest. I'm all *brimstone but* the *head,* and that's *aky fortis.*

In the literary development of cockalorum bragging, Paulding's version stands midway between Wetmore's crude reduction of the real thing and Mark Twain's still more rhetorical grandiloquence in the raftsmen's fight in the third chapter of *Life on the Mississippi.* The vogue of *The Lion of the West,* and its influence upon later characterizations of the frontiersman, may be inferred from the popularity of this one speech. We can assume that the Louisville paper was, like most other journals of the time, widely exchanged, and that Nimrod Wildfire's boast was widely read by editors and journalists elsewhere on the frontier. It was also much copied and plagiarized. A Paulding scholar has made two interesting discoveries about this fight anecdote: first, Paulding himself had written a similar sketch fourteen years earlier in *Letters from the South* about a battle between a bateaux-man and a wagoner; and second, the much superior version from his play was lifted by the author of *The Sketches and Eccentricities of Col. David Crockett of West Tennessee* (1833), who changed little beside the name of the candidate in the next election.[21] This, however, was fair enough, since Paulding had modelled Nimrod Wildfire on Davy Crockett in the first place. When, according to one observer, 'at Crockett's request Hackett gave the play in Washington,' and came on stage in the character of

[21] Floyd C. Watkins, 'James Kirke Paulding's Early Ring-Tailed Roarer,' *Southern Folklore Quarterly,* XV (Sept. 1951), 183-7.

Wildfire, he 'bowed first to the audience and then to Crockett. The redoubtable Davy returned the compliment to the amusement and gratification of the spectators.'[22]

The pattern of humor in *The Lion of the West* devolves upon the contrast between Nimrod Wildfire and one Mrs. Wollope, an English lady bearing an unmistakable resemblance to the author of the recently published *Domestic Manners of the Americans.* Arriving in America, she remarks,

> At length I've reached the scene of my experiment. To ameliorate the barbarism of manners in America has been the ruling wish of my life . . . the plan I have concerted is founded, I conceive, on a true knowledge of the national character. The root of all the evils of this country is familiarity—where every one is equal, every one is familiar; and this is linked with another barbarism—the women here like those of Turkey are treated as domestic slaves. Now my system is to raise my own sex to its proper dignity, to give them the command and so refine the men.

It is curious to see how this sententious and self-righteous Englishwoman (as Paulding depicts her) offers, as the butt of the satire, two opinions which other American authors would find in the native grain. James Fenimore Cooper and Herman Melville (in *The Confidence-Man*) would have no quarrel with her suspicion of the evils of egalitarian dogma; while Hawthorne, in *The Blithedale Romance* and Henry James in *The Bostonians* would show the passion for feminist agitation to be, as James observes in his notebook, 'the most salient and peculiar point in our social life.' As a dramatic work *The Lion of the West* is slapdash; its humor is rudimentary, its situations stock, and Paulding's opinions pretty chauvinistic. The comedy runs along these lines:

> *Caesar*. Gemman at de bar send you his card.
> *Mrs. Wollope*. His card—the king of clubs? (*Turns it over and reads*) Colonel Wildfire. Is he a gentleman?
> *Caesar*. Don't know, marm—said he was a horse. (*Exit*)

[22] Tidwell, 'Introduction' to *The Lion of the West,* p. 8.

Mrs. Wollope. A horse! Oh, of the horse—a cavalry officer—the very thing I wished to see. Now for a specimen of an American gentleman.

Wildfire enters, brings forward two chairs, sits in one and puts his feet on the other. Mrs. Wollope inquires where he is from:

Wildfire. Old Kaintuck's the spot. There the world's made upon a large scale.

Mrs. Wollope. A region of superior cultivation—in what branch of science do its gentlemen excel?

Wildfire. Why, madam, of all the fellers either side the Alleghany hills, I myself can jump higher—squat lower—dive deeper—stay longer under and come out drier.

A moment later he tells her the yarn of the hat floating in the swamp—when he lifted it with his whip, 'a feller sung out from under it, Hallo stranger, who told you to knock my hat off? . . . I'm doing beautifully—got one of the best horses under me that ever burrowed—claws like a mole.' 'This,' says Mrs. Wollope, 'shall be the first well authenticated anecdote in my perusal.'[23] If the Englishwoman is an overbearing snob, the backwoodsman is likewise a caricature, although of course a kindly one. His integrity as one of Nature's noblemen makes a manly contrast to the cowardice of another character, a fraudulent English lord. The Flower of the Forest always shows his virtues best when played off against the decadence and the moral decay which our popular mythology viewed as the inevitable burdens of complex social organization and of the aristocratic past.

The figure of Nimrod Wildfire in Paulding's play lends support to Mody Boatright's contention that 'tall talk . . . is a notification of the repudiation of the values of the outsiders, that is, of gentility. . . . The frontier braggart assumed the role expected of

[23] This yarn became, or had already become, one of the most popular tall tales on the frontier. Paulding's is the earliest version I have found, but others appear in Thoreau's *Walden* (1854); in *The Spirit of the Times* (1856); in Rourke, *American Humor*, pp. 37-8 (printed without attribution); in Vance Randolph, *We Always Lie to Strangers* (New York, 1951), pp. 253-4.

him; but in exaggerating it to comic epic proportions, he satirized it.'[24] The difficulty with this argument is that on occasion the satire becomes the thing itself. This we may observe in the case of Davy Crockett, the real-life original of Paulding's Nimrod Wildfire.

FOUR

Colonel Crockett has but lately died another death. For almost a century, only folklorists studying the heroes of nineteenth-century tall tales or historians interpreting the Age of Jackson concerned themselves with the life and supposed writings of David Crockett or with the fragmentary yarns and apocryphal legends which became attached to his name. The resurrection of Davy Crockett as a temporary hero of contemporary culture is a sociological phenomenon of great interest. Why should this all-but-forgotten congressman from the canebrakes, this picturesque bear-killing, yarn-spinning, hard-drinking Indian fighter with no qualification for public life other than his gregarious manner and ready tongue, suddenly become a national infatuation whose fame was celebrated in every medium of mass communication, whose name endorsed a hundred and one products in the market place?

In considering Crockett's recent resurrection it is well to remember that he had had two earlier careers as a figure in the popular imagination. The first corresponds more or less to the events of his own lifetime, as they are recounted in his 'autobiography.' This is the Crockett whom V. L. Parrington attacks in *Main Currents of American Thought*—the ignoramus who buys his constituents drinks to win their votes, the wise-cracking hick whose folksy jokes distract the crowd from the serious speeches of his better-qualified opponents. This is the Crockett who boasts that 'at the age of fifteen, I did not know the first letter in the

[24] *Folk Laughter on the American Frontier*, p. 22.

book,' and that when appointed a magistrate he could scarcely sign his name but 'relied on natural born sense, and not on law to guide me; for I had never read a page of a law book in all my life.' [25] The popular appeal of this Crockett is easy to assess, even though the book to which a friend more literate than he signed his name (*A Narrative of the Life of David Crockett* . . . [1834]) is one of the most pedestrian and circumstantial of American biographies. Crockett's amanuensis (the evidence compiled by James A. Shackford [26] indicates that he was Thomas Chilton) was not an able writer. Only in the accounts of the Colonel's electioneering does his style approach the vividness of a well-told yarn; this, despite the opportunities many Indian fights and bear hunts afforded him to draw the long bow. Despite its flatness, however, this life of Crockett had popular appeal because his career confirmed a stereotyped pattern of American life. It tells 'how I worked along to rise from a canebrake to my present station in life,' [27] and gives jocular intimations that a seat in Congress is only a way-station on the road to the White House. This is not merely a success story, a rags-to-riches fable; it is an incarnation of the democratic dogma at its lowest level. The Crockett of *A Narrative* professes to love his parents, to share his meat with the hungry, to be a brave fighter and a skilled hunter, to stand on his principles against even President Jackson; but what makes him a success is none of these virtues. It is his ability to feel out the meanest level of approach in dealing with his constituents, to conceal from them his ignorance of the matters on which he will have to deliberate, and to undercut his opponents in stumping the district. The appeal of Crockett as politician is dangerous and demagogic. As Randall Jarrell has remarked in quite another connection, 'When you defeat me in

[25] *The Autobiography of David Crockett*, ed. Hamlin Garland (New York, 1923), pp. 36, 90.

[26] *David Crockett, The Man and the Legend* (Chapel Hill, 1956), pp. 89-90.

[27] *Autobiography*, ed. Garland, p. 111.

an election simply because you were, as I was not, born and bred in a log cabin, it is only a question of time until you are beaten by someone whom the pigs brought up out in the yard.'

But Crockett as politician fades from the popular memory even during his own lifetime, and the outlines of the second phase of his renown begin to emerge. Now, in *Colonel Crockett's Exploits and Adventures in Texas* (1836) the magnetism of Crockett the frontiersman already attracts incident and anecdote from free-floating comic tradition, both oral and journalistic, and his adventures verge on the fabulous. The climax of course is the apocryphal account of his heroic death at the Alamo. Thereafter, as Constance Rourke observes in her biography of Crockett, the popular imagination took license to make of Crockett what it would. The best indication of what his second image became is found in the anecdotes from the Crockett almanacs collected in Richard M. Dorson's *Davy Crockett: American Comic Legend.* Here is a genre of popular literature—the yarn—scarcely removed from oral tradition; the best of these almanac stories derive their rhetorical structure, their vividly animistic imagery, and their compelling combination of the humorous, the grotesque, the heroic, and the horrible from the art of the folk raconteur.[28] Here we find Crockett supernaturally hideous, Crockett entering the animal world, Crockett displaying Jovian and Promethean prowess, Crockett screaming his brag, Crockett snapping fire and lightning from his knuckles, Crockett climbing Niagara, Crockett saving the earth from extinction with a kick and a daub of bear-oil when the sun freezes fast on its axis.

The diction of these fantasies is as remarkable as their situations; the yarns abound in such prodigies of the language as 'tetotatious,' 'exfluncate,' 'absquatulate,' 'slantindicular.' Where the

[28] I have analyzed the narrative craft of some of these stories in *Paul Bunyan, Last of the Frontier Demigods* (Philadelphia, 1952), pp. 41-3. See Howard Mumford Jones's introduction to Dorson's collection; and, for bibliographical references, Dorson's article, 'The Sources of *Davy Crockett: American Comic Legend,*' *Midwest Folklore,* VIII (1958), 143-9.

Crockett of the autobiographies congratulated himself on his own illiteracy, these etymological sideshows are obviously parodies of the Latinate vocabulary and rhetorical fustian of the high oratorical style of the time. To have invented or understood the point of such words as these, one would have to be capable of comprehending Mr. Henry Clay, and perhaps of declining Latin nouns oneself.

'Popular declamation of the '30's and '40's has often been considered as bombast when it should be taken as comic mythology,' Miss Rourke observes.[29] This mythology, like every other, must embody widely shared convictions about man's place in the universe. When Crockett appears as a virtual demigod he does indeed represent communal values colored by folk fantasy. He symbolizes man's uneasy relation to nature on the frontier. His aggressions against bears and his command of lightning and waterspouts are surely imaginative reactions to peril. If this second Crockett is mythological, the myth is that man can easily conquer nature and control it. In the most Promethean of his exploits—his rescuing the world from icy darkness by freeing the earth and sun from the frozen machinery of the universe—his reward is not the vulture and the rock, but this:

> The sun walked up beautiful, salutin' me with sich a wind o' gratitude that it made me sneeze. I lit my pipe by the light o' his topknot, shouldered my bear, an' walked home, introducin' people to the fresh daylight with a piece of sunrise in my pocket.

There is not even the recognition of tragic possibility, much less of tragic fate, in these ebullient assertions of man's superhuman powers. The frontiersman knew tragedy enough in the life he lived and the deaths he died, but his folktales and popular writings transformed the materials of tragic life into either melodrama or farce. The folk imagination dealt with such realities as death and decomposition by affirming their existence in terms so

[29] *American Humor,* p. 64.

outrageously revolting as to deny the mere realities themselves their due in human feeling.

It is apparent that this phase of Crockett's fame corresponds to a passing phase of American history. With the settlement of the frontier, the supplanting of the clearing by the village, the dominance of industry over a handcraft and agrarian economy, and especially the accelerating effects of the Civil War upon social change, the fantasies of Crockett from the ante-bellum frontier faded from the popular mind. Except in Texas, where the Alamo and its traditions have always been revered, Crockett was all but forgotten.

Why, then, was Davy Crockett revived on a nation-wide scale in the 1950's? Did his most recent image draw on either the demagogy of his first popular appearance or the folk fantasy of the second? It is obvious that the third Crockett is an artifact not of folklore but of contemporary popular culture. There was no current oral tradition of folktales to be tapped by the authors of television and radio scripts, comic strips, juvenile storybooks, songs, and jingles. Both the historical Crockett and the almanac folk hero had been so long dead that the new Crockett could be made—would have to be made—to fit contemporary needs and to dramatize contemporary concepts of character.

We can relate the Crockett fad to the increasing antiquarian interest in certain folkloristic materials from the American past. Stanley Hyman, among others, has commented on the growing vogue for 'the folksy' in the theatre, the dance, painting, and other arts.[30] The art forms of popular culture are among the most potent of 'technicways' (to use Howard Odum's term), ready at a moment's notice to create new images to satiate the hungers of the popular imagination. The manufactured heroes of mass media thus fulfill an important function in maintaining the stability of certain values in contemporary society. One such

[30] Stanley Edgar Hyman, 'The American Folksy,' *Theatre Arts,* XXXIII (April 1949), 42-5.

value is the illusion of continuity with the historical past. As many observers have remarked, the need for cultural roots seems to be proportionately greater as the rate of social change increases. The disruptive effects on the sense of personal identity of rapid technological change, the high rate of social and spatial mobility, and the insecurities inevitable in a culture where status is (or is thought to be) achieved rather than ascribed—all these factors make attractive the common sharing of references to the national past. This complex of factors applies to the appeal of Davy Crockett even though the majority of the American population is descended from forebears who came to this country after Crockett had died. But since the vision of the national past shared in popular culture is created and presented by the technicways, what is shared is the past that the present desires, not the actual traditions (folkways) of the past as it really was.

Again, if we consider Crockett with the other heroes of juvenile popular culture, we observe that the fantasies they offer of escape from the present are conceived in terms of two contrary simplifications of life. One—the category to which Crockett belongs—presents an idealized past in which technology and science are absent; the other looks forward to a future still more technological and scientific than the present. The alternation between these two juvenile utopias has, I suspect, been going on for quite a time. One would need precise information on the respective reigns of such figures as Tom Swift, Tom Mix, Buck Rogers, the Lone Ranger, and Superman, as well as Davy Crockett. Underlying the variations of these heroes' fantasy-worlds there is of course a basic pattern of similarity. They all not only invite their audiences to escape into the remoteness of the Vanished American West or of the Supercity of the Future; they also reinforce certain values in the world from which they offer escape. The morality of their fantasy-worlds is absolute—no gradations of innocence or guilt. Consequently their decisiveness is never hedged about by such deterrents to immediate action as the complex circumstances of actual life usually and painfully provide.

The security they offer is that of absolute rightness combined with force. This is obviously a dangerous simplification, but an attractive one. Crockett, whose motto, as everyone knows, was '*Be sure you're right, then Go Ahead!*' fits well into this pattern of superconfident, self-righteous individualism.

While alternation between the Western Folk Hero and the Future Spaceman (or perhaps their simultaneous appeal) seems to characterize popular culture, we may wonder why the recent version of the Westerner was not the usual cowboy but a long-forgotten backwoods politician. Surely the identity of the heroes of juvenile popular culture bears some relation to the preoccupations of the adult world. Is there some possible connection between the rise of the resurrected Crockett and the going-ahead of Senator McCarthy? Although some observers felt that the Crockett boom ended because the hero had been 'oversold' and his youthful public simply tired of him, it may not be irrelevant to note that Crockett faded from the airwaves a little after McCarthyism ceased to be the most sensational feature of the political scene.

Among the literary manifestations of the recent Crockett fad were two reprintings of his supposed autobiographies.[31] Both run together the three narratives of 1834, 1835, and 1836 without indicating where one ends and the other begins, and they make many unacknowledged deletions from Hamlin Garland's already condensed text. For instance in the new editions we find the following passage:

> I let the people know as early as then, that I wouldn't take a collar around my neck.
>
> (Citadel edition, p. 130; Signet edition, p. 87)

In the Garland edition this passage occurs on page 111, Chapter XIII of *A Narrative of the Life of David Crockett . . .* (1834), and reads:

[31] *The Life of Davy Crockett* (New York, Citadel Press and Signet Books, 1955).

I let people know as early as then, that I wouldn't take a collar around my neck with the letters engraved on it,

> MY DOG.
> ANDREW JACKSON

Why is the legend on Davy's collar inadmissible now? Because Andy Jackson too is a hero of consequence who stands in the popular mind for the same values imputed to Crockett: coonskin democracy, the triumph of the common man. Crockett's opposition to Jackson's western land policy no longer interests us. In the pantheon of our popular culture we cannot have such a repudiation of one hero by another who represents the same values, for how then could we affirm those values? Accordingly, the new editions of Crockett's life do not make much sense, for the embarrassing fact of his opposition to Jackson is so intrinsic to the political part of the text that it cannot be eliminated by an editor's shears.

Half a century ago Frank Norris in an eloquent polemic declaimed:

> The plain truth of the matter is that we have neglected our epic . . . no contemporaneous poet or chronicler thought it worth his while to sing the song or tell the tale of the West because literature in the day when the West was being won was a cult indulged in by certain well-bred gentlemen in New England who looked eastward to the Old World, to the legends of England and Norway and Germany and Italy for their inspiration, and left the great, strong, honest, fearless, resolute deeds of their own contemporaries to be defamed and defaced by the nameless hacks of the 'yellow back' libraries. . . .
>
> And the Alamo! . . . the very histories slight the deed . . . Yet Thermopylae was less glorious, and in comparison with that siege the investment of Troy was mere wanton riot. . . . Young men are taught to consider the 'Iliad,' with its butcheries, its glorification of inordinate selfishness and vanity, as a classic. Achilles, murderer, egoist, ruffian, and liar, is a hero. But the name of Bowie, the name of the man who gave his life to his flag at the Alamo, is perpetu-

> ated only in the designation of a knife. Crockett is the hero only of a 'funny story' about a sagacious coon.[32]

We can no longer blame the gentility of Eastern writers for our failure to have created an epic of the Alamo or to have supplanted Achilles with Colonel Crockett. Although the age of epic literature would seem to be long since over, such a literature may yet come from the winning of the West. It will first require our recognition as a national culture that Prometheus chained to the rock is not only myth but reality, while the image of Davy Crockett striding over the hills, exempt from sacrifice for the piece of sunlight in his pocket, is our nation's self-defeating dream.

FIVE

The American folk hero is startlingly different from most of the great heroes of myths or of Märchen. Unlike them, the American has no parents. He has no past, no patrimony, no siblings, no family, and no life cycle, because he never marries or has children. He seldom dies. If death does overtake him, it proves to be merely a stage in his transformation to still another identity. No one has cursed his birth or set him afloat on the sea; neither was he suckled by a beast nor rescued by a cowherd from the fierce elements to which a tyrannous father had condemned him. Although he may wear many disguises, it cannot be usually said that he returns incognito to his homeland, rids his country of scourges, and is recognized as the throne's true heir. The pattern of action of the hero tale, as outlined by Lord Raglan in *The Hero,* does not fit very well the adventures of our plebeian peddlers, brawlers, and emergent capitalists. Nor can we apply to them with much confidence Otto Rank's view that myths of the hero are created 'by means of retrograde childhood fantasies' in which the Oedipal 'family romance of neurotics' become univer-

[32] Frank Norris, 'Essays on Authorship,' in *Complete Works* (New York, 1903), IV, 280-81.

salized as the life histories of mythical heroes.[33] Our folk heroes have no family romances. Among our group of heroes only the careers of Franklin and Crockett begin to approach the fullness of the human life cycle in their respective autobiographies. In popular culture we have seen how Franklin is reduced to the get-ahead Poor Richard while Crockett becomes the go-ahead woodsman whose varied exploits in guile, hunting, and conquest of nature are entirely discontinuous, a collection of motifs rather than a coherent story. Other men who became folk heroes—Fink, Patch, Johnny Appleseed—left behind a still more fragmentary basis for their reputations. Each lived in the minds of his celebrants and emulators as an instance of metamorphosis culminating in a single dramatic gesture. From Andrew the Hebridean onward, that gesture was the annunciation of their own destinies as self-made men, their abandoning an old self for rebirth in a new. But after Andrew the old self that was let die was not that of a European peasant; it was simply an earlier incarnation of a character whose essence was not radically altered by his assumption of successive roles.

The American folk hero appears as a generic expression of the youthful culture which produced him. His characteristic virtues are the qualities of youth: indomitable self-confidence, and a courage in his adaptation to the world which proves almost an heroic denial that tragedy can be possible for *him*. But from another perspective the virtues of youth are the defects of immaturity. In his easy progress from one role to another without ever being compelled to accept the full commitment of spirit to any, the ever-popular image of the American folk hero exists on a psychological plane comparable to that of adolescent or pre-adolescent fantasy. In every culture the concept of maturity implies a full commitment to fixed values; until modern times these values were sacred. Their fixity had been established by supernatural powers, and the passage from childhood to maturity was marked

[33] *The Myth of the Birth of the Hero* (New York, 1959), pp. 69, 84.

by initiatory rites in which the sacred knowledge that came to the present from the beginning of time was passed on to the initiate. To be worthy of this knowledge the child in him had to die; his soul had to seek its sources in the power that created the world; and he had then to be reborn into his responsibilities and his grace. Before the submission to this immutable pattern, however, the child-spirit can envisage any or all fulfillments of the potentialities of its psychic energies. In the American folk hero the transformations are metamorphoses without being rebirths. The concentration of psychic energy necessary for spiritual commitment and spiritual change is not apparent in either the bourgeois get-ahead values of Ben Franklin-Poor Richard or in the sly or boisterous go-ahead values of Sam Slick-Davy Crockett. Only in the person of the American Literatus Walt Whitman does the power of self-determined metamorphosis approach the transcendent heroism of those myths of the Old World from which all our folk images attempted to liberate us. For only in Whitman is the assertion of selfhood made with such all-encompassing passion as to become in itself an escape from selfhood. The 'self' Walt sings is, as Richard Chase observes,[34] a metaphor with the power of myth, linking the ego to the entire world of apprehended sense and transforming all that it encompasses into 'a knit of identity.'

Identity, as de Tocqueville foresaw, would prove an elusive and prepossessive concern for an egalitarian society. The American temperament has always favored activism over meditation; the typical self-discovery of the American character has been conceived as an immersion in experience, rather than as contemplative withdrawal. It is as though the more reality one's experiences could encompass or be touched by, the nearer one could come to self-definition. Consequently, the metamorphic pattern of American life and of the American folk hero's career sets its exemplars in linear motion through as many conditions of 'real-

[34] In *Walt Whitman Reconsidered* (New York, 1955).

ity' as possible. These metamorphoses, as we have seen, are only outwardly comparable to the rebirths achieved by initiatory rites in cultures or institutions of sacred orientation. Their function, nonetheless, is a ritualistic one: not a *rite de passage* but a ritual of intensification, in which the powers of the self are affirmed, reinforced, and glorified by each demonstration of their successful use. These powers prove the self spiritually indomitable and adaptable to the wildest vicissitudes of fortune or nature. The historical and folk examples we have traced prove not only these considerable positive powers, but also the limitations of the American notion of selfhood. The self-determinative hero turns out to have as his goals a set of concepts more characteristic of the culture of the early American republic than of human history at large. His character is aggressive, competitive, shrewd. He seeks mastery over nature. With respect to society, he seeks to demonstrate superiority over other individuals but not ordinarily does he recognize society as an organic structure, in which power can be exercised for extra-personal ends.

Since the exposition of character is both an aim and method of fiction, what could American authors make of the fragmentary folk sagas which outlined the folk concepts of heroic personality? These sketches could be taken uncritically, accepted in the same spirit of resilience in which they were offered by the popular mind. Hawthorne's peddler Dominicus Pike, his Holgrave in *The House of the Seven Gables,* Melville's Ishmael, Twain's Huck Finn, all reflect both the metamorphoses and the self-reliance of the folk models we have examined. But these authors could use the same folk concepts to create characters whose qualities they viewed with the gravest reservations. Often these characters, critically examined by their authors, are presented in situations which define their fates as representative of the national destiny. Hawthorne's Robin in 'My Kinsman, Major Molineux,' Melville's Captain Delano in 'Benito Cereno,' his Ahab and the whole cast of *The Confidence-Man,* Twain's Duke and Dauphin, all project elements of the American folk hero into situations with which his spiritual immaturity and his lack of human depth make him inadequate to deal. Further, the literary enlargement of the native folk heroes is often drawn against a contrasting set of heroic values, those of the world-mythical heroes whose fates and powers are so different from their own. Thus Hawthorne contrasts his Yankee Robin against the ancient ritualistic figure of the Dying King; Ishmael presents himself as a Yankee, both bumpkin dupe and trickster; while Ahab, though in part a frontiersman—an 'Arkansas duellist'—also subsumes the attributes of a Slayer of the Beast (Perseus, St. George), a shaman, and a Christ. Huck Finn, as I have mentioned, represents the triumphantly moral American imagination in contrast to the decadent European chivalric romanticism of Tom Sawyer. The patterns seem as capable of variation as the imaginations of their authors could make them. The depictions of native character, whether sympathetic or critical, and tensions between them and representatives of the older heroic traditions in world mythology, contribute much to the sense of largeness, of archetypal representativeness, which we find in the American prose romance. This representativeness is certainly not the function of surface realism. It inheres in the romance because the characters themselves are so often modelled on half-legendary archetypes projected fragmentarily by the folk imagination.

4

Prefigurations: 'The Legend of Sleepy Hollow'

ONE

The first important literary statement of the themes of native folk character and superstition was made, fittingly enough, in the first literary work by an American to win world-wide acclaim. When *The Sketch Book of Geoffrey Crayon, Gent.* appeared in London in 1819, its author became the first of a long series of expatriate Americans who found their native roots all the more poignant for viewing them from a distance.

Washington Irving was fortunate, granted his special though restricted gifts, to be alive and in England at that moment in the history of literature. He sought out, and was taken up by, Sir Walter Scott, who was showing how the sentiment of nostalgia for the past could infuse fiction and become its informing principle. In his novels Scott projected that sense of historical continuity which formed a curious undercurrent of sensibility even before the Romantic movement began. Little though the Augustans attended the medieval or more recent past, there were important eighteenth-century successors to such early antiquarian works as Sir Thomas Browne's collection of *Vulgar Errors* (1648) and Samuel Pepys' collection of broadside ballads. Bishop Percy's *Reliques of Ancient English Poetry* (1765) and John Brand's *Observations on the Popular Antiquities of Great Britain* (1795) laid the groundwork for the two directions British folklore study has followed ever since. Scott took his prominent place in both with his ballad collection, *The Minstrelsy of the Scottish Border* (1802) and his comprehensive *Letters on Demonology and Witchcraft* (1830). Much more influential, however, than these formal studies in introducing a whole generation of readers—and authors—to such materials was his use of folklore in his own fiction. One of Scott's earliest and most popular disciples along this line was a young American *littérateur*, the London representative of P. E. Irving & Co., New York dealers in hardware.

Washington Irving was already something of an antiquary. His early *Knickerbocker's History of New York* reveals him to be enchanted with the very past he satirized. In *The Sketch Book* Irving used several themes to which he would again and again recur: the Gothic tale in the German manner of 'The Spectre Bridegroom,' the antiquarian nostalgia of the four sketches on English Christmas customs, the character sketch of 'The Village Angler.' The two selections destined for most enduring fame, however, were careful reconstructions of the scenes of Irving's own boyhood in the Dutch communities of the Hudson Valley. One of these retells a German folktale in this American setting, in which Rip Van Winkle sleeps away his twenty years after a heady game of bowls with the ghostly crew of the Half-Moon. In the other tale, 'The Legend of Sleepy Hollow,' Irving brought into belles-lettres for the first time the comic mythology and folk beliefs of his native region. In Ichabod Crane and Brom Bones he dramatized that clash of regional characters—the Yankee versus the Backwoodsman—which would soon become a major theme in our literature, as well as a continuing motif in a century and a half of folktales, and in our national history.

It is surprising that the extent to which Irving drew upon native folklore has scarcely been acknowledged. The chief reason for this seems to be Henry A. Pochmann's convincing demonstration, in 1930, of the extent of Irving's indebtedness to his German contemporaries. Stanley T. Williams, in his definitive biography, gives us a further exploration of Irving's methods of composition.[1] When we see the extent to which Irving depended on other men's books, often translating without acknowledgment, we can understand why recent critics are reluctant to grant him credit for originality in interpreting American themes.

The foremost students of American humor have strangely overlooked 'The Legend of Sleepy Hollow.' Walter Blair does call it 'a characteristic piece of American humor,' but his remark is relegated to a footnote. And Constance Rourke, writing with her usual felicity, remarks that 'in the Knickerbocker History and in Rip Van Winkle Irving created a comic mythology as though comic myth-making were a native habit, formed early . . . But his Dutch people were of the past, joining only at a distance with current portrayals of native character.' [2] Why did Miss Rourke not mention 'Sleepy Hollow'? I do not know; but I hope to show that in Ichabod and Brom Bones, Irving gave us portrayals of *current* native character projected backwards in time, rather than merely historical types unrooted in contemporary folklore.

There are of course good reasons why Brom and Ichabod have not been so recognized. For one thing, Irving's style is hardly what we expect in a folk document. For another, the Hudson

[1] Irving's use of folk traditions of piracy is noted by W. H. Bonner, *Pirate Laureate: The Life & Legends of Captain Kidd* (New Brunswick, N. J., 1947), pp. 151-65; Leonard Beach discusses Irving's use of American themes and recognizes Ichabod as 'Irving's judgment of Puritanism': 'Washington Irving,' *University of Kansas City Review*, XIV (1948), 259-66. Pochmann notes 'Irving's German Sources in The Sketch Book,' *Studies in Philology*, XXVII (July 1930), 477-507; see also 'Irving's German Tour and Its Influence on His Tales,' *PMLA*, XLV (Dec. 1930), 1150-87. Pochmann shows, with parallel texts, that in 'Rip Van Winkle' Irving translated and expanded the story of Peter Klaus, a German goatherd who fell asleep for years, which he found in the *Volkssagen* of Othmar; and in 'The Legend of Sleepy Hollow,' he demonstrates Irving's indebtedness to the Rübezahl legends in *Volksmärchen der Deutschen*, by Musaeus. See also Williams, *The Life of Washington Irving* (New York, 1935), I, 177-86.

[2] Blair, *Native American Humor*, p. 16, n. 3. Basing his judgment of Irving as a native humorist on the *Knickerbocker's History of New York*, Blair considers Irving as primarily 'a disciple of neoclassicism,' and concludes (p. 14) that 'he employed a technique which, admirable though it was, differed from that of typical American humor.' Rourke, *American Humor*, p. 77.

Valley Dutch have long been thought an alien people by the Anglo-Saxons who conquered, surrounded, and outnumbered them. But the third and principal reason is Irving's own treatment of his Dutch materials. Almost everywhere *except* in 'The Legend of Sleepy Hollow' he deliberately altered the traditional characteristics of the Dutch for the purposes of his own fiction. As a consequence of Irving's popularity and of widespread ignorance of what the Dutch were really like, his caricatures were widely accepted as portraits of the Dutch-Americans. Paulding, writing *The Dutchman's Fireside* twenty-two years after the *Knickerbocker History,* imitated his friend in attributing chuckle-headedness and indolence to the brothers Vancour. In Cooper's *Satanstoe* (1845), however, we get a more realistic picture of the Dutch; his Guert Ten Eyck amply fulfills the historian Janvier's description: the Dutch 'were tough and they were sturdy, and they were as plucky as men could be.'[3] Only in 'The Legend of Sleepy Hollow' did Irving give a Dutchman these attributes; everywhere else he made them fat, foolish, pompous, and pleasure-loving. Here his usual Dutchman does appear (Van Tassel), but only in the background. Brom Bones is his realistic Dutch frontiersman, who meets and bests a Yankee in the traditional conflict of our native folk humor. Why did Irving choose this theme, so different from his usual preoccupations?

When we admit his dependence upon books, we must look at the kinds of authors on whom he depended. Othmar and Musaeus were collectors and redactors of folktales and märchen. Irving knew personally a third folklorist, Dr. Karl Böttiger, 'who undoubtedly was able to give him expert advice on his folklore studies.'[4] Wherever Irving went he collected popular sayings and beliefs; he was prepossessed by a sense of the past, and recognized

[3] Thomas A. Janvier, *The Dutch Founding of New York* (New York, 1903), p. 4; Janvier takes issue with Irving's characterization of the Dutch on pp. 1-3, 9, 14, 46, 105, and 131-2.

[4] Pochmann, 'Irving's German Tour,' *PMLA,* XLV, 1153-4.

the power—and the usefulness to a creative artist—of popular antiquities. Brom and Ichabod had their beginnings in local characters he had known as a boy; [5] what made them take their singular form, however, was the direction in which Irving's imagination impelled them. And that direction was toward the fabulous. The fabulous was Irving's milieu.

In a reminiscence twenty years after *The Sketch Book*, Irving revealed that Diedrich Knickerbocker had learned the legend of Sleepy Hollow from an old Negro who gave him 'that invaluable kind of information, never to be acquired from books,' and from 'the precious revelations of the good dame at the spinning wheel.' [6] Of Musaeus' *Volksmärchen* he says nothing. But he may well indeed have heard such stories in the old Dutch chimney corners. H. W. Thompson recounts similar motifs in York State folklore: nightly visitations by a shrieking woman 'tied to the tail of a giant horse with fiery eyes'; and 'a curious phantom . . . uttering unearthly laughter, lights shining from her finger tips.' There were revenants aplenty in Catskills. Still another important part of Dutch folk culture was the lusty practical joking [7] which Cooper used in some of the most spirited pages in *Satanstoe*. Both aspects of Dutch folk life—the villagers' superstitions and their humor—are immortalized in 'The Legend of Sleepy Hollow.'

[5] Brom Bones was identified by Pierre M. Irving as a wag of Tarrytown who 'boasted of once having met the devil . . . and run a race with him for a bowl of milk' (*Life and Letters of Washington Irving*, London, 1892, I, 282). See Williams, *Life*, I, 429, n. 90, for a similar account; on p. 430, n. 91, he names Brom Van Allstyne of Kinderhook as the original of Irving's character. Ichabod Crane, Williams finds (p. 109), was modelled upon 'Jesse Merwin, the homespun wit' and village schoolmaster, as well as upon Fielding's Partridge and the schoolmaster in Goldsmith's *Deserted Village*.

[6] 'Sleepy Hollow,' in *Biographies and Miscellanies*, ed. Pierre M. Irving (New York, 1866), pp. 514-16.

[7] Thompson, *Body Boots & Britches* (Philadelphia, 1939), pp. 119-21; Carl Carmer, *The Hudson* (New York and Toronto, 1939), p. 35, lists some typical pranks.

TWO

Irving sets his story in a folk society: 'It is in such little retired Dutch villages . . . that population, manners, and customs remain fixed; while the great torrent of migration and improvement, which is making such incessant changes in other parts of this restless country, sweeps by them unobserved.' And again: 'The neighborhood is rich in legendary lore . . . Local tales and superstitions thrive best in these sheltered long-settled retreats.' Into this community comes Ichabod Crane, 'a native of Connecticut, a State which supplied the Union with pioneers for the mind as well as for the forest.' Ichabod is Irving's Connecticut Yankee, the fictional ancestor of Mark Twain's Hartford mechanic. But his nearer descendants are Sam Slick, Jack Downing, Hosea Biglow. Before any of these was born in print Ichabod had already been a country teacher, a singing master, a sometime farmer; later he is to undergo still further metamorphoses which link him still more closely to these heroes of popular legend and literature. Like Ben Franklin, like Hawthorne's Holgrave, like the schoolmaster in *Snow-Bound* and Melville's marvelous Confidence Man, he was a jack of all trades. Metamorphosis is always magical, but now, in an egalitarian society, the magic is the power of self-reliance, not of Satan.

Ichabod's native shrewdness and perseverance are somewhat compromised by his credulity. 'No tale was too gross or monstrous for his capacious swallow.' Ichabod devoutly believed in all the remarkable prodigies retailed in Cotton Mather's *History of New England Witchcraft* (that is, the *Magnalia Christi Americana*). There he found spectral ships manned by ghostly women, heretics giving birth to monsters, revenants pursuing the innocent with invisible instruments of torture. But of all the ghostly tales in the valley, the one Ichabod Crane most liked to hear was that of the Headless Horseman.

Meanwhile, we remember, Ichabod falls in love with Katrina

Van Tassel; more exactly, seeing her father's prosperous farm, he envisages 'every roasting pig running about with a pudding in his belly, and an apple in his mouth.' Considerations of this sort lead Ichabod into a most interesting reverie: he imagines 'the blooming Katrina, with a whole family of children, mounted on the top of a wagon loaded with household trumpery, with pots and kettles dangling beneath; and he beheld himself bestriding a pacing mare, with a colt at her heels, setting out for Kentucky, Tennessee, or Lord knows where.' Here we have Ichabod Boone—Connecticut's pioneer of the wilderness as well as of the mind. Traditionally the American frontiersman has resented the mercantile civilizer; in a thousand folktales the shaggy woodsman frightens the Yankee clear out of the district.

Ichabod's fatuous dream of pioneering prepares the way for his rival's entrance: 'a burly, roaring, roistering blade . . . Brom Van Brunt, the hero of the country round, which rang with his feats of strength and hardihood.' He had 'a mingled air of fun and arrogance,' and was 'always ready for either a fight or a frolic; but had more mischief than ill-will in his composition.' Famous for horsemanship, 'foremost at all races and cockfights' was Brom; 'and when any madcap prank, or rustic brawl, occurred in the vicinity, [the neighbors] always shook their heads, and warranted Brom Bones was at the bottom of it.'

Making allowances for Irving's smoothly flowing style, what we have here described is a Catskill Mike Fink, a Ring-Tailed Roarer from Kinderhook. While Irving was writing these lines in London, the real Mike Fink was somewhere west of Pittsburgh, shooting the heel off a nigger to make his foot fit the shoe, scalping Indians for the pure hell of it, roistering in towns along the Ohio. In Brom Bones's good-natured mischief there is a tinge of Mike Fink's brutality, if not of his sadism. That other favorite frontiersman, Davy Crockett, had not by 1819 become a national figure; yet the type—the swaggering frontier braggart, the prodigious hunter and strong man, the daredevil, the mischief-maker—was already well established in oral tradition. Irving's depiction of Brom Bones certainly gave these characteristics new clarity as they are combined for the first time in a fictional portrait of the *genus* frontiersman.

Irving now pits his rival suitors against each other. Ichabod, the Yankee, 'had a happy mixture of pliability and perseverance in his nature.' Although he is caricatured unmercifully, he is not entirely unworthy of our grudging admiration; a thoroughly self-reliant citizen, he adapts his strategy to meet the case. 'To have taken the field openly against his rival would have been madness,' so Ichabod insinuates himself into Katrina's notice while masquerading as her singing-master. Here he outwits Big Brom in the contest, perennially fresh in American comic lore, between wit and strength. But Ichabod forces Brom Bones to draw upon his own resources—the rough fancy of the frontiersman—as well as upon brute strength. This proves a dangerous combination for the scholar.

At Van Tassel's quilting frolic, when the old Negro tunes the fiddle and rosins the bow, Ichabod finds his métier, fair grounds whereon he can excel Brom Bones. The ungainly form of the pedagogue achieves animation if not grace, for he is from Down East in Connecticut and is sufficiently sophisticated to know how to dance with a lady. Brom, the bumpkin, 'sorely smitten with love and jealousy, sat brooding by himself in one corner.'

The dancing over, talk now turns to the recently concluded Revolutionary War. Old soldiers' exploits become more heroic at each telling, as Irving skillfully moves us from the reality of the dance to mildly comic exaggerations of heroic truth, then to the supernatural itself. We are near Sleepy Hollow, and 'there was a contagion in the very air that blew from that haunted region.' The mythology of war blends with that of the otherworld, lending credence to the supernatural, as we learn that 'mourning cries and wailings [were] heard and seen about the great tree where the unfortunate Major André was taken'; and we hear of 'the woman in white, that haunted the dark glen at Raven Rock,' who 'was often heard to shriek on winter nights before a storm, having perished there in the snow.' But the presiding spirit at this haunted conference was the Headless Horseman, who tethers his horse in the graveyard, haunts the church, and chases travellers. Brom Bones has met him. Riding his horse, Daredevil, Brom challenged the ghost to race for a bowl of punch—'and should have won it too, for Daredevil beat the goblin horse all hollow, but, just as they came to the church-bridge, the Hessian bolted, and vanished in a flash of fire.'

Here is the bravado of the American hero, so confident of his own powers that he will risk everything for nothing, as Sam Patch did when he jumped Niagara just to prove that 'Some things can be done as well as others.' Such reckless daring makes the Faustus legend seem native in this land; Irving tried his hand at that in 'The Devil and Tom Walker' a generation before Hawthorne gave the devil's compact more sombre treatment, a century before Stephen Vincent Benét outdid him in this comic mode.

But Ichabod reasserts the dominance of evil over American self-reliance: he quotes Mather on witches, and describes the ghosts he has seen himself. The homely Puritan cannot accept the bravado of the backwoods Natural Man; Ichabod and Brom inhabit different worlds although they live in the same village. When Ichabod bids Katrina good night, he is chagrined to find that his hopes for a prosperous match have somehow gone awry. Perhaps, having observed her rival swains' reactions to supernatural perils, she has decided not to be a Puritan's bride, however nimbly he may dance the quadrille. Ichabod steals away heavy at heart.

Now, in the best-known part of the story, comes Irving's debt to Musaeus. But the stylistic control of the atmosphere shows Irving's own talent at its best, while the conclusion of the story is of signal importance in the literary development of an American myth. The darkness deepens; all the tales of ghosts and witches crowd into Ichabod's brain. Now he crosses the stream where André was captured, a haunted brook. Ichabod is appalled to find he no longer rides alone. A silent horseman plashes beside him. Coming out of the valley, Ichabod gets a look at his companion and discovers, in terror, that he carries his head in his hands! Crane rushes toward the church-bridge, where the Hessian, pursuing Brom, had disappeared. Reaching the bridge, Ichabod turns 'to see if his pursuer should vanish, according to rule'—a fine pedantic touch!—but sees instead 'the goblin rising in his stirrups . . . hurling his head at him. Ichabod endeavored to dodge the horrible missile, but too late.' He falls from his horse, 'and the black steed, and the goblin rider, passed by like a whirlwind.'

Ichabod was never seen again in Sleepy Hollow. His landlord burns his copy of Mather's *Witchcraft* and determines to keep his own children from school, 'observing that he never knew of any good come of this same reading and writing.'

THREE

Here in this York State valley, Irving's Dutch braggart concocts the perfect backwoodsman's revenge on the Yankee.[8] This first statement of the theme is among the most memorable it has ever received in our literature; it is with us yet and ever has been, in Davy Crockett outwitting peddlers, in a thousand dime novels and popular magazines in which the yokel gets the best of the city slicker.[9]

[8] The perfection of Irving's 'Legend' becomes even more apparent by comparison with 'Cobus Yerks,' Paulding's imitation of 'Sleepy Hollow.' Instead of Yankee vs. backwoodsman, we find a stupid, superstitious Dutchman frightened by a ghostly dog, otherwise Tim Canty, a merry Englishman. Now the story is reduced to its supernatural motif only; the richness which Irving's 'Legend of Sleepy Hollow' holds for us, its reverberations on the themes of national and regional character, are entirely lacking in Paulding's caricature. *Tales of The Good Woman*, ed. W. I. Paulding (New York, 1867), pp. 285-99.

[9] Mark Twain's first newspaper sketch was a version of this motif, called 'The Dandy Frightening the Squatter,' reprinted in *Tall Tales of the Southwest*, ed. F. J. Meine (New York, 1930), pp. 447-8; discussed by Bernard DeVoto in *Mark Twain's America* (Boston, 1932), pp. 90-91.

The rustic hero may be naïve and honest, with only his common sense to help him make his way in the world; so he appears as Jack Downing, as Hosea Biglow, as Robin in Hawthorne's *My Kinsman, Major Molineux,* as Huckleberry Finn. Or he may be a swashbuckling braggart, half horse, half alligator, like all the ring-tailed roarers and Thorpe's Big Bear of Arkansas. No matter; in either form he represents the American élan, the pioneer, the Natural Man rebelling against the burden of guilt of the ages. It was he who cut the cords that bound him to the English throne, to all king-ridden Europe. Naked he stands in the wilderness, bereft of the past, confident that all human history begins—with *him.*

Who is his adversary? Perhaps an insufferable fop from the city to the East—traditions, culture, lineage, class distinctions always come from the East in American mythology: from New England, from Europe. Perhaps he is a shrewd, narrow-nosed Yankee peddler. No matter; in either form he stands for that ancient heritage of useless learning and inherited guilt against which the American, in each succeeding generation, must rebel.

Such are the roles in this ever-recurring fable of the American destiny. Washington Irving, whose birth coincided with that of the Republic, formulated a theme of its national literature with his dramatization of the Republic's dominant myth. Even Henry James is in his debt.

But what of Ichabod Crane? Did the pumpkin kill him? Of course not! Our folk heroes never die. Wearing the magic cloak of metamorphosis, they stave off death forever by simply changing their occupations. The ungainly pedagogue is no more—long live the New York City lawyer! For that is what Ichabod becomes after he makes his way from Sleepy Hollow. And onward and upward he goes: from the bar into politics, from his office to the press, thence to the bench. Far be it from Washington Irving to analyze or criticize the great American myth; where he finds a mythology of humor, he improves it on its own grounds. Responding instinctively to his fabulous materials, he makes Ichabod unforgettable in a stunning caricature. Brom, who is much more like life, is not so memorable, even though Americans always love a winner.

Yet Ichabod is not ultimately the loser in this legend. All he has lost is a farm girl's love and a measure of self-respect; the former was no real passion, the latter can be repaired. Ichabod Crane is a sorry symbol of learning, of culture, of sophistication, of a decayed religious faith, of an outworn order in the world. His very name suggests decrepitude: 'And she named him Ichabod, saying, The glory is departed from Israel' (I Sam. iv. 21). But Ichabod Crane is no Israelite; although an anachronism in all other respects, he is yet an American. And therefore he is immortal. Back to the city he goes, to find success.

Brom Bones stays in the village and gets the girl. He deserved her more than Ichabod did, for while the scholar danced and counted his stuffed pigs, Brom experienced two human emotions: jealousy and love.

Ichabod also knew two emotions, and two only. His were fear and ambition. He is not the loser, because he leads a full and prosperous life, experiencing to the brim the two emotions which give meaning to his existence: fear, in Sleepy Hollow, and ambition, in New York City. For it is the same ambition which led him to court Katrina Van Tassel that takes him later to the bar and the polls, to the editor's chair and the judge's bench. Ambition of this magnitude requires for its satisfaction a culture sufficiently complex to be capable of corruption. It cannot be gratified in the folk society of Sleepy Hollow Village, where the good people are as pure as the air.

Fear and ambition are Ichabod's, but not love. That is because Ichabod Crane is not wholly human. A sterile intellectual, his head aswim with worthless anachronisms, his heart set on material gain, Ichabod is gracelessly devoid of the natural human affections. He is the bumpkin's caricature of what life in the seat of a corrupt civilization can make of a man.

When one compares 'The Legend of Sleepy Hollow' to the bulk

of Irving's work it seems anomalous that he could have mustered the imaginative power to enrich us so greatly, for most of Irving's writing betrays a lack of creative energy, a paucity of invention. Irving, after all, was never able successfully to transcend the limited aims of a 'sketch,' and he continued to rework his old themes in new disguises,[10] telling a tale now set in old Dutch New York, now in Germany, now in England, now in Spain. *Bracebridge Hall, Tales of a Traveller,* most of *Wolfert's Roost* and *The Sketch Book* itself make tedious reading today. They show all too plainly Irving's faults: his dependence upon secondary sources, and the restricted range of emotional experience from which he was able to create fiction. But in the characters of Ichabod and Brom Bones, Irving found archetypal figures already half-created by the popular imagination. Among all of Irving's characters only Rip Van Winkle has as great a power to move us; and Rip, too, is what the highly developed but narrow gift of a storyteller whose milieu was the fabulous has made of a character from folklore. Although the original Peter Klaus was German, the themes of Rip Van Winkle are universal: the pathos of change, the barely-averted tragedy of loss of personal identity. And, as Louis LeFevre has pointed out,[11] Rip is indeed close to an aspect of the American national character—that yearning for escape from work and respon-

[10] Much later Irving was to return to the frontier materials he used for Brom Bones in 'The Early Experiences of Ralph Ringwood,' a fictionalized biography of Governor Duval of Florida (*Wolfert's Roost,* New York, 1865. pp. 294-341). Some of the supernatural lore from 'The Legend of Sleepy Hollow' turns up here too, notably an apparition of a horse as a devil (pp. 298-9). Of his late frontier sketches Beach notes, 'Strange that Irving should have come so close to Longstreet's and Craddock's property! Strange too that he should not have known what to make of it' ('Washington Irving,' *University of Kansas City Review,* XIV, 266). Perhaps the key to this puzzle is that Ralph Ringwood, a Kentuckian, meets only Westerners and hence there is no opportunity for Irving to give this sketch the dramatic power which the conflict of regional characters made possible in 'The Legend of Sleepy Hollow.' In view of the popularity, as well as the artistic success, of the earlier sketch, it is indeed surprising that Irving should have followed it with so poor an effort.

[11] 'Paul Bunyan and Rip Van Winkle,' *Yale Review,* XXXVI (Autumn 1946), 66-76.

sibility which is exemplified by a host of gadgets and the day-dream dramas of contemporary popular culture. Irving's Knickerbocker Dutchmen were, as Miss Rourke observed, remote caricatures resurrected from a distant past. But when Irving dramatized the homely comic figures he found in native American folk traditions, his Ichabod and Brom pass so readily into the reader's own imagination that they seem to be persons we have always known. 'The Legend of Sleepy Hollow' sketches the conflict of cultures which the rest of our literature has adumbrated ever since. One could predict *that* from Irving's story; both Ichabod Crane and Brom Bones lived lustily ever after. They are rivals yet.

PART II

Hawthorne

'The tradition is just as good as truth.'
—Hawthorne, *American Notebooks*

'Tradition . . . the wild babble of the time . . . is responsible for all contrary averments.'
—*The House of the Seven Gables*

5

Folklore and the Moral Picturesque

ONE

Nathaniel Hawthorne led so uneventful a life that one is tempted to consider its most significant incident to be his withdrawal from the world during the ten years following his graduation from Bowdoin College in 1825. 'I sat down by the wayside of life, like a man under enchantment, and a shrubbery sprung up around me, and the bushes grew to be saplings, and the saplings became trees, until no exit appeared possible through the entangling depths of my obscurity,' he writes in the preface to *The Snow-Image.* He felt himself somehow isolated from the life around him; his *Twice-Told Tales* he thought had 'blossomed in too retired a shade.' Hawthorne would seem hardly fitted by temperament or inclination to respond with sympathy, as Irving had, to the bumptious fantasy of the comic popular tradition; nor, with his skeptical detachment from life, to find much imaginative use for the supernatural lore which had so frightened Ichabod Crane.

But this is to overlook the fact that his home town of Salem is renowned as the one place in America where folk superstition was taken as dogma. Hawthorne's great-great-grandfather, a magistrate, had had a hand in that tragic business in 1692. The conduct of that ancestor who had 'made himself so conspicuous in the martyrdom of the witches,' gave him one of his predestined themes. Witchcraft, however, was of the past; as Hawthorne looked about him in the bustling port of Salem he could resurrect the Black Man and his orgiastic covenanters only by a concentrated act of the historical imagination. The supernatural folklore of his present-day New England seemed lacking, to Hawthorne, in the very qualities which made the dark traditions of the past available to his imagination. 'A New England ghost does not elevate us into a spiritual region; he hints at no mysteries beyond the grave. . . . If he indeed comes from the spiritual world, it is because he has been ejected with disgrace, on account of the essential and inveterate earthiness of his substance.' So Hawthorne remarked in reviewing Whittier's *Supernaturalism of New England* with obvious disappointment that so promising a title should produce such meagre results. 'We should naturally look for something duskier and grander in the ghostly legends of a wild country, than could be expected in a state of society where even dreams are covered with the dust of old conventionalisms,' he writes. 'But, if there be any peculiarity, it is, that our superstitions have a more sordid, grimy, and material aspect, than they bore in the clime from which they were transplanted.'[1]

In his best supernatural tales Hawthorne would resurrect this richer transplanted English lore among the first two generations of Puritans. But although his best-known stories are of the past, three of his four long romances are set in contemporary time, and even in his early book, *Twice-Told Tales,* about one-fourth of the thirty-nine sketches deal with his own day. In many of these—e.g. 'Rills from a Town Pump' and 'The Toll-Gatherer's Day'—the thinness of content and texture would seem to corroborate Henry James's comments on Hawthorne's *American Notebooks.* James was struck by the paucity of incident upon which the prospective romancer was able to gaze in the simple, almost classless society of his small New England village. Among the observations which James found trivial are many evidences

[1] Hawthorne's review appeared in the *Literary World,* I (April 17, 1847), 247-8; it is reprinted by Randall Stewart in 'Two Uncollected Reviews by Hawthorne,' *New England Quarterly,* IX (Sept. 1936), 505-7.

of Hawthorne's contacts with contemporary folk traditions. Indeed, for a man so retiring, Hawthorne shows an unusual curiosity about, and receptivity to, the fantasies of character and belief of the common people he met on his rambles. Since he kept his notebooks with a view to gathering material for his fiction, he apparently thought to make tales and sketches of the observations I am about to extract from his pages. Although it has often been remarked that his fictions correspond very little to the realistic and homely details of the journals, I hope to show a larger degree of consonance between his folkloristic raw materials and certain of his writings than has been observed.

Character, of course, is always a fiction-writer's concern, and Hawthorne had ample opportunities to observe the peculiarities of local and regional types. He was naturally aware of the Yankee as a type, or stereotype, and seems pleased at his opportunities of observing live originals of that famous breed. We find a detailed observation of a peddler 'Setting off his wares with the most extravagant eulogies' at the Williams College commencement in 1838; other Yankee characters wander in and out of the notebooks as Hawthorne describes 'a dry jester, a sharp shrewd Yankee, with a Yankee's license of honesty'; the 'wild, ruined, and desperate talk' of a one-armed soap-maker; and a jolly blacksmith whose 'conversation has much strong, unlettered sense, imbued with humor, as everybody's talk is, in New England.' He writes of a cattle-drover of 'wild scriptural-styled eloquence' who so 'strangely mingled humor with his enthusiasm, and enthusiasm with his humor' that one could not tell 'whether he were in jest or earnest.' On a visit to the Isle of Shoals, Hawthorne noted the inquisitive prying and rustic crudities of two Yankee bumpkins. And on that island he listened for hours while Levi Thaxter, whose wife (Celia Leighton Thaxter) would years later write local-color fiction, expounded the beliefs of fisherfolk in a ghost that guarded Captain Kidd's buried loot, and recounted local legends of a murder and of a rock that was 'rent asunder at the time of the crucifixion.' Hawthorne learned from another islander how to use a divining-rod in search for buried treasure, and from the Thaxters he heard of a ghost recently seen in their own home by an Irish nurse. Hawthorne in turn 'taught them how to discover the hidden sentiments of letters, by suspending a gold ring over them.' [2]

Hawthorne, then, was something of an amateur antiquary, in whose works, as in Irving's, we might well look for imaginative treatments of superstitious beliefs and regional characters. He was certainly aware of the fictional possibilities of such oral stories as came his way. He cannot leave the Custom House, in the introduction to *The Scarlet Letter,* without reflecting that:

> I might . . . have contented myself with writing out the narratives of a veteran shipmaster, one of the Inspectors. . . . scarcely a day passed that he did not stir me to laughter and admiration by his marvellous gifts as a story-teller. Could I have preserved the picturesque force of his style, and the humorous colouring which nature taught him how to throw over his descriptions, the result, I honestly believe, would have been something new in literature.

This novelty it would be left for Hawthorne's friend, the former fo'castle hand Herman Melville, to provide. Hawthorne himself recognized the captain's yarns as 'a different order of composition' from his own. By 1850 he could be sure that this was so, for he had earlier tried to use the stuff of sailors' yarns and fisherfolks' beliefs in his sketches. He had found that this was not the true direction of his own genius. A glance at 'The Village Uncle,' [3] his principal failure in this line, will show us how difficult Hawthorne found it to write directly about the very folk

[2] *American Notebooks,* ed. Randall Stewart (New Haven, 1932); Yankee characters, pp. 47, 45, 36-8, 55, 257-60; pirates, ghosts, and divinations, pp. 261-73, *passim.*

[3] Richard M. Dorson has called attention to some of the folklore motifs in Hawthorne's notebooks and in this sketch in 'Five Directions in American Folklore,' *Midwest Folklore,* I (Fall 1951), 149-65. Ray B. Browne notes farflung analogues in folk literature to Hawthorne in 'The Oft-Told *Twice-Told Tales:* Their Folklore Motifs,' *Southern Folklore Quarterly,* XXII (June 1958), 69-85.

character and beliefs in his own New England which he found so interesting.

> [Uncle Parker] looked like . . . a shipmate of the Flying Dutchman. . . . One of [his] eyes had been blown out with gunpowder, and the other did but glimmer in its socket. Turning it upward as he spoke, it was his delight to tell of cruises against the French, and battles with his own shipmates, when he and an antagonist used to be seated astride of a sailor's chest, each fastened down by a spike nail through his trousers, and there to fight it out. Sometimes he expatiated on the delicious flavor of the hagden, a greasy and goose-like fowl, which the sailors catch with hook and line on the Grand Banks. He dwelt with rapture on an interminable winter at the Isle of Sables, where he had gladdened himself amid polar snows, with the rum and sugar saved from the wreck of a West India schooner. And wrathfully did he shake his fist, as he related how a party of Cape Cod men had robbed him and his companion of their lawful spoil, and sailed away with every keg of old Jamaica . . . Villains they were, and of that wicked brotherhood who are said to tie lanterns to horses' tails, to mislead the mariner along the dangerous shores of the cape.

In one journalistic paragraph Hawthorne throws away yarns of battle and sailors' duels, tall tales of the hunt and plunder, and the deception of mariners by land pirates. His village uncle rambles on:

> Like Uncle Parker . . . I am a spinner of long yarns. . . . I overflow with talk. . . .
>
> If melancholy accidents be the theme . . . I tell how a friend of mine was taken out of his boat by an enormous shark; and the sad, true tale of a young man on the eve of his marriage, who had been nine days missing, when his drowned body floated into the very pathway, on Marblehead Neck, that had often led him to the dwelling of his bride,—as if the dripping corpse would have come where the mourner was. With such awful fidelity did that lover return to fulfill his vows! Another favorite story is of a crazy maiden who conversed with angels and had the gift of prophecy, and whom all the village loved and pitied, though she went from door to door accusing us of sin, exhorting to repentance, and foretelling our de-

> struction by flood or earthquake. If the young men boast their knowledge of the ledges and sunken rocks, I speak of pilots who knew the wind by its scent and the wave by its taste, and could have steered blindfold to any port between Boston and Mount Desert, guided only by the rote of the shore,—the peculiar sound of the surf on each island, beach, and line of rocks, along the coast. Thus do I talk. . . .

Talk, talk, talk, a garrulous profusion of motifs each of which might well be the theme of an entire sketch. The man-eating shark suggests Melville, while the skilled pilots—whose keen sense many a New England folktale records—remind us of Twain's Captain Bixby some thousand miles inland on another waterway. None of these motifs, however, becomes anything in 'The Village Uncle,' although the yarn of the melodramatically drowned bridegroom [4] may have led Hawthorne to the conjunction of bride and shroud in 'The Wedding Knell.' The prophesying Millerite—most characteristically Hawthornian of these folk character-sketches—does not appear again either. And neither Uncle Parker nor the old gaffer who talks thus ever become characters at all.

In such sketches as 'The Village Uncle' Hawthorne's attempt to use folk materials pictorially led toward the still-nascent genre of local color, a direction which never interested him in its own right. Hawthorne would leave such realistic regionalism to Harriet Beecher Stowe (in *Oldtown Folks* and *Poganuc People*), to Celia Leighton Thaxter and Sarah Orne Jewett, to Rowland Robinson and George S. Wasson. As he tells us in 'The Old Apple Dealer,' Hawthorne was a 'lover of the moral picturesque.' On the whole he found such folk traditions as those just enumerated amply picturesque but insufficiently moral. The raw materials

[4] For a pilot in oral tradition who steered by the taste of the brine see George Wheeler, *History of Castine, Penobscot & Brooksville, Maine* (Cornwall, N. Y., 1923), p. 389 (1st ed., Bangor, Me., 1875). A drowned lover floating past his or her beloved's door is a commonplace in New England lumberjack balladry. This occurs, for instance, in their most widely distributed song, 'The Jam at Gerry's Rocks,' in Roland Palmer Gray, *Songs and Ballads of the Maine Lumberjacks* (Cambridge, Mass., 1925), pp. 3-9, and in William Main Doerflinger, *Shantymen and Shantyboys* (New York, 1951), pp. 238-9; see also 'Mary on the Silver Tide,' Doerflinger, p. 282.

from folklore—whether the yarn be of piracy or plunder, seamanship or murder,—seemed, like Whittier's labored ghost stories, to present only 'the earthy surface of the Yankee character.' Such materials, and the Yankee character itself, would be amplified in Hawthorne's work only when he had reinterpreted them in the terms required for moral romance.

TWO

What Hawthorne, as an author of moral romances, found attractive in folklore was its projection of 'the Marvellous,' that imaginative element so essential to his revealing 'the truth of the human heart.' But 'the Marvellous' was difficult to manage in the rationalistic light of contemporary life. 'It will be very long,' writes Hawthorne, 'before romance-writers may find congenial and easily-handled themes, either in the annals of our stalwart republic, or in any characteristic and probable events of our individual lives. Romance and poetry, ivy, lichens, and wall-flowers, need ruin to make them grow.' So reads his apology for having set *The Marble Faun* in Italy, where these advantages of cultural desuetude are available. Even when Hawthorne presents contemporary life, as in *The House of the Seven Gables,* he does so against a constant reflection of the past. When the present appears unsupported by a long background, as in *The Blithedale Romance,* the elements of 'the Marvellous' seem an imposition upon our credulity. They are set in a society in which supernaturalism has degenerated to a theatrical spectacle put on by a charlatan mesmerist. But by setting his tales in the past, in a theocratic society in which belief in superstition, witchcraft, and satanism was as 'real' as belief in God, Hawthorne could take full advantage of the romancer's prerogative of presenting the truths of the human heart 'under circumstances, to a great extent, of the writer's own choosing or creation.' Before we trace these demonic images in Hawthorne's Puritan romances, however, there is yet another aspect of contemporary life which did lend itself to the uses of his imagination.

In the metamorphic quality of American society, Hawthorne, despite his plaint to the contrary, did find a congenial theme in the 'characteristic and probable events of our individual lives.' We have seen some of his notebook observations of the persons who played in life the Yankee roles as typified by the popular mind. The ubiquitous peddler had caught Hawthorne's fancy even before he set down the bantering palaver of the one who drummed his trade to the commencement crowd at Williamstown. Two years earlier his notebook suggests the familiar figure as a moral emblem—'Fortune to come like a pedlar with his goods . . . selling them, but asking for them the sacrifice of health, of integrity, perhaps of life in the battlefield, and of the real pleasures of existence. Who would buy, if the price were to be paid down?' [5] Chill though this suggestion is, at Williamstown Hawthorne had enjoyed the peddler's fun: 'I could have stood and listened to him all day long.' But in 1834, before either of these entries, Hawthorne had already written a tale around a peddler who 'drove a smart little mare, and was . . . keen at a bargain, but none the worse liked by the Yankees; who, as I have heard them say, would rather be shaved with a sharp razor than a dull one.' There is foreboding in the title of 'Mr. Higginbotham's Catastrophe,' but the catastrophe never takes place, and the tone of the tale is that of the folk humor on which it is based:

> '. . . if Squire Higginbotham was murdered night before last, I drank a glass of bitters with his ghost this morning. . . . He didn't seem to know any more about his own murder than I did.'
>
> 'Why, then, it can't be a fact!' exclaimed Dominicus Pike.
>
> 'I guess he'd have mentioned it, if it was,' said the old farmer.

The language is, for Hawthorne, surprisingly close to folk speech —the cider-tart speech of the go-ahead Yankee: 'a crusty old

[5] *Complete Works of Nathaniel Hawthorne*, ed. G. P. Lathrop, 13 vols. (Boston and New York, 1882), IX, 35. All quotations from Hawthorne are based on this edition, hereafter cited as *Works*.

fellow, as close as a vice'; 'Ill news flies fast, but this beats railroads.'

We do not often think of Hawthorne as a comic author, yet he had his moments of comedic grace. His peddler Dominicus Pike is an early and masterful representation of the Sam Slick tradition, with his provincialism, inquisitiveness, resourcefulness, and insouciance. Dominicus Pike was 'always itching to hear the news and anxious to tell it again'; after 'lighting his cigar with a sun-glass,' he meets a traveller who tells him that old Mr. Higginbotham of Kimballton was murdered last night. Pike spreads this news from town to town, improvising upon the bare report. But as we have seen, his account is devastatingly challenged, and 'The pedlar had no heart to mingle in the conversation any more.' His spirits revive the next morning, though, when he meets another traveller who again tells him that Mr. Higginbotham had been murdered the preceding night. Once more the peddler is harbinger of sensational tidings, and enjoys a hero's welcome for his exciting news. But yet again the tale proves false: the victim's niece arrives to report her uncle alive that morning. Nothing daunted by the villagers' derisive barrage of 'filthy missiles,' Pike muses on the niece's charms until he comes at length to Kimballton. There he decides to see for himself whether or not Higginbotham is hanging from his pear tree, as both travellers had reported. Dominicus finds the old man at that instant being hoisted aloft by an Irishman—whose fellow-conspirators had each defected and fled in the two days past. The peddler saves old Higginbotham's life, marries his niece, inherits his fortune, and sets up 'a large tobacco manufactory.' Such is the easy rise in a capricious world of this lucky, gregarious fellow.[6]

[6] Tales based on the exaggeration or misinterpretation of news must have had considerable circulation in the early nineteenth century, before railroads linked the scattered New England communities together. C. Grant Loomis found an account in Thoreau's *Journal* for Nov. 29, 1857 (X, 215), almost a quarter century later, which amusingly chronicles the widespread repercussions of the following remark: 'Miss Emeline Barnett told a little

The connection of this ebullient tale with yet another popular tradition is indicated in 'Passages from a Relinquished Work.' There the narrator appears as 'the celebrated Story Teller,' star of a village theatrical. His career is to 'recite his famous tale of Mr. Higginbotham's Catastrophe,' a piece which 'afforded good scope for mimicry and buffoonery.' But although his recitation is a huge success, the crowd laughed at the wrong places in the story. It seems they were laughing at *him,* for he was unaware of 'a stiff cue of horsehair' which a joker had attached to his collar, and did not see its gestures mocking his own. This Story Teller (whose plight anticipates that of the teacher in *Tom Sawyer*), is the ward of a stern Parson from whom he had run away to write novels and go on the stage. 'I seemed to see the Puritanic figure of my guardian standing among the fripperies of the theatre and pointing to the players . . . with solemn ridicule, and eyeing me with stern rebuke. His image was a type of the austere duty, and they of the vanities of life.' This conjunction of the Puritanic 'type' of austere duty and the costumed mummers who emblemize vanity would be most dramatically developed in 'The Maypole of Merry Mount.' Here Hawthorne cannot assume the gestures of the Yankee raconteur or the vain disguises of the theatre without feeling the reproach of his guardian-spirit. In *The Scarlet Letter* this fictive Puritan is replaced by Hawthorne's own ancestors; the story teller there can brave their censure, for his tale then was indeed a moral

boy who boards with her, and who was playing with an open knife in his hand, that he must be careful not to fall down and cut himself with it, for once Mr. David Loring, when he was a little boy, fell down with a knife in his hand and cut his throat badly.' Before long news was out that David Loring, grandson of the afore-mentioned, had cut his throat in an accident; that the grandfather had committed suicide (this death was received with appropriate remarks on his character); word reached his family in Framingham from the mother of a schoolmate of the grandson, who had written it in a letter. Loring's nephew made the trip post-haste, arriving to find his uncle entirely alive, his throat uncut. ('Thoreau as Folklorist,' *Western Folklore,* XVI [April 1957], 92.) Although the plot is not quite the same as in Hawthorne's tale, Thoreau's report of a real occurrence shows a similar humor based on the same kinds of possibilities for misunderstanding.

romance, not merely the fortuitous rise of a Yankee peddler in a world unstained by sin.

Other folk characters too caught Hawthorne's eye. Viewing the Falls of the Genesee, he muses on the legend of Sam Patch, already 'poetical . . . to me as I pictured the catastrophe out of dusk and solitude.' But it is not the daredeviltry of Patch which takes Hawthorne's imagination. 'How stern a moral may be drawn from the story of Sam Patch!' he ponders. 'Was the leaper of cataracts more mad or foolish than other men who throw away life, or misspend it in pursuit of empty fame, and seldom so triumphantly as he? That which he won is as invaluable as any except the unsought glory, spreading like the rich perfume of richer fruit from various and useful deeds'—a stern moral indeed to draw from Sam's last failure to prove that 'Some things may be done as well as others.'

Hawthorne's sketch of 'Rochester' concludes with an observation of an 'idle man' who 'carried a rifle on his shoulder and a powder-horn across his breast, and appeared to stare about him with confused wonder, as if, while he was listening to the wind among the forest boughs, the hum and bustle of an instantaneous city had surrounded him.' This is the only depiction of a contemporary frontiersman in Hawthorne's work.[7] His woodsman is as isolated and bewildered in the bustling city as was Irving's Rip Van Winkle after his twenty years' slumber.

Yet when Hawthorne, during the Civil War, had an audience with President Lincoln, he drew upon the stereotypes of both Yankee and woodsman to describe him: 'Unquestionably, Western man though he be, and Kentuckian by birth, President Lincoln is the essential representative of all Yankees, and the veritable specimen, physically, of what the world seems determined to regard as our characteristic qualities.' He presumes that when

[7] It would seem that Hawthorne's only use of the popular designation for the backwoodsman occurs when he speaks of 'the physical prowess of our half-horse and half-alligator giants of Kentucky' in a paragraph for *The American Magazine*, May 1836, p. 386; reprinted by Arlin Turner in *Hawthorne as Magazine Editor* (University, Louisiana, 1941), p. 245.

'Uncle Abe' flung 'his lank personality into the chair of state . . . it was his first impulse to throw his legs on the council-table, and tell the Cabinet Ministers a story.' His yarns are afloat in Washington, 'and are certainly the aptest, pithiest, and funniest little things imaginable; though, to be sure, they smack of the frontier freedom and would not always bear repetition . . . on the immaculate pages of the Atlantic.'[8] The President's expression seemed to him 'weighted with rich results of village experience':

> A great deal of native sense; no bookish cultivation, no refinement; honest at heart, and thoroughly so, and yet, in some sort, sly,—at least, endowed with a sort of tact and wisdom that are akin to craft, and would impel him, I think, to take an antagonist in flank, rather than to make a bull-run at him right in front.

His characteristic quality is 'Yankee aptness and not-to-be caughtness'; 'I should have taken him for a country schoolmaster. . . . If he came to Washington a backwoods humorist, he has already transformed himself into as good a statesman (to speak moderately) as his prime minister.'

As Hawthorne observed the American character, it did not seem inevitable that its metamorphic propensities need always be fused with Yankee shrewdness. In other biographical sketches he shows his sensitivity to metamorphosis as a principle since Colonial times defining the characteristic American career. Of Sir William Phips he remarks that 'The contrast between the commencement and the close of his life was the effect of casual circumstances,' for here was an utterly commonplace and boorish man elevated to wealth, knighthood, and a governorship by the fortuitous accident of discovering a treasure-laden galleon in the Indies. Sir William Pepperell 'may be taken as the representative of a class of warriors, who diversified a life of commerce or agriculture by the episode of a city sacked, or a battle

[8] Indeed they did not bear repetition in the *Atlantic,* whose queasy editor suppressed half of Hawthorne's description of the President. The entire sketch, 'Chiefly About War Matters,' appears in *Works,* XII, 299-345; Lincoln is described on pp. 309-14.

won, and, having stamped their names on the page of history, went back to the routine of peaceful occupation.' But the most interesting of Hawthorne's lives of eminent past Americans is his sketch of his late friend and landlord, Thomas Green Fessenden (1771-1837).

Here was a would-be Franklin, a man of virtually unlimited abilities, a universal genius of the age. He began as a Yankee poet who 'had caught the rare art of sketching familiar manners, and of throwing into verse the very spirit of society as it existed around him,' but he was not content to rest on such laurels and so became successively a lawyer, a patent agent, an inventor, an investor; essaying verse again, a satirist; the satirist was succeeded by the editor, who found time to serve in the state legislature and, occasionally, 'to elicit some old-fashioned tune of soothing potency' from a bass viol. Metamorphosis was the very root of his restless nature. Visiting Fessenden in his last illness, Hawthorne found the old man 'talking, with a youthful glow of fancy, about emigrating to Illinois . . . and picturing a new life for both of us in that Western region.' The portrait is kindly, even affectionate, yet it is everywhere touched with reservations. 'Mr. Fessenden was ill-qualified to succeed in the profession of law, by his simplicity of character, and his utter inability to acquire an ordinary share of shrewdness and worldly wisdom.' As a patent agent, 'Mr. Fessenden had been lured from his country by as empty a bubble as that of perpetual motion.' His interest in law was succeeded by 'a taste for scientific pursuits,' but his invention of a pneumatic pump for coal mines, though original and ingenious, proved too expensive to be patented. As investor he was taken in by a confidence man. Reduced to earning a living by his pen, 'A subject was offered him, in which no other poet would have found a theme for the Muse': Fessenden, 'as might be expected, was a believer' in the latest form of medical quackery—a metallic 'tractor' which alleviated inflammatory diseases by removal of superfluous electricity—and wrote a poetical opus defending this humanitarian device against its detractors.

Hawthorne remarks that Fessenden was the real butt of his own satire. His works abound with 'grotesque ideas aptly expressed.' In a life of perpetual instability and metamorphosis the only successful stages were the first and last. As Yankee poet and as editor of a journal of 'rural economy' he made real contributions to his culture. One must not omit to mention his 'Patent Steam and Hot-Water Stove,' which whistled while it heated the room, 'thereby making the fireside more cheerful.'

Hawthorne forebears to judge this eccentric genius, other than to say,

> On my part, I loved the old man because his heart was as transparent as a fountain; and I could see nothing in it but integrity and purity, and simple faith in his fellow-men, and good-will towards all the world. . . . a man indeed in intellect and achievement, but, in guileless simplicity, a child.

A Ben Franklin *sans* Poor Richard, Fessenden was a child indeed, most childlike in his inclination rather 'to form prospects for the future than to dwell upon the past.' Among the *personae* of Hawthorne's fiction, the ineluctable threshold which must be crossed between youth and maturity, between innocence and moral responsibility, is the acceptance and understanding of one's past. With this stern view of initiation into life, Hawthorne, we may expect, in his fiction throws the most ironic scrutiny upon the free and easy, ever-changing self-determinism of the unencumbered American career.

6

Yankee Bumpkin and Scapegoat King

ONE

'In youth, men are apt to write more wisely than they really know or feel; and the remainder of life may be not idly spent in realizing and convincing themselves of the wisdom which they uttered long ago.' This reflection occurred to Hawthorne as he gathered his fugitive writings of two decades for *The Snow-Image, and Other Twice-Told Tales.* The very last of these, whether so placed as a capstone or an afterthought, proves to be his earliest full success and one of the most durable and contemporary fictions of his entire career. 'My Kinsman, Major Molineux' is unusual among Hawthorne's writings in its overt treatment of the most important political and cultural problem of the American republic: self-determination and its consequences. The tale is striking, too, in its bold and direct appropriation from folk traditions and popular culture of the representative traits of the New England character. Hawthorne would use these humorously in 'Mr. Higginbotham's Catastrophe,' ironically in portraying Holgrave in *The House of the Seven Gables,* and descriptively in his war-time account of President Lincoln. But now, in 1832, he anticipates by a quarter-century Melville's use of similar materials and themes in 'Benito Cereno' and *The Confidence-Man* to attack the popular doctrines of optimism and self-reliance which those traditions themselves exemplify. In 'My Kinsman, Major Molineux' these folk themes are placed in dramatic opposition to an eighteenth-century Colonial reenactment of the ancient ritual of the deposition of the Scapegoat King. This ritual occurs in the story as the fulfillment of the hero's quest for his influential kinsman; its function, in terms of his own development, is to provide a ceremony of initiation. What is revealed to him is self-knowledge far deeper than his callow folk-character had hitherto anticipated.

In Hawthorne's tale, a youth named Robin, now eighteen and thinking it 'high time to begin the world,' sets out from his father's farm on his 'first visit to town.' There, with the help of Major Molineux, his father's cousin, he expects to make his fortune. Thus Robin is on the threshold of metamorphosis, like young Ben Franklin walking up Market Street with a loaf of bread under his arm. Committed to upward mobility, he is as yet dependent upon benevolent, paternalistic authority. As he becomes 'entangled in a succession of crooked and narrow streets' his quest for his kinsman brings him only bafflement and mocking laughter from every quarter: from a ridiculously solemn old man, from a barber, an innkeeper, a demoniac fiery-eyed patron at the inn, a trollop in a scarlet petticoat, a watchman. Parties of men approach, speak to him in gibberish, and when he cannot answer curse him in plain English. In desperation Robin accosts a muffled burly stranger with his cudgel and demands to be directed to his kinsmen. Instead of forcing his passage the man says, 'Watch here an hour, and Major Molineux will pass by.' With a start Robin recognizes the demoniac of the inn. 'One side of the face blazed an intense red, while the other was black as midnight . . . as if two individual devils, a fiend of fire and a fiend of darkness, had united themselves to form this infernal visage.' Now, waiting by moonlight on the church steps, Robin thinks of the home he has left. In a reverie he sees his father giving the family blessings: 'Then he saw them go in at the door; and when Robin would have entered also, the latch tinkled into place, and he was excluded from his home.' He dreams —or wakes—to see his kinsman's face regarding him from a nearby window. Waking in truth, he asks a passing stranger whether he must wait all night for Major Molineux. The stranger, a mature, prepossessing man, 'perceiving a country youth, apparently homeless and without friends . . . accosted him in a tone of real kindness.' When Robin tells his mission the gentleman replies, 'I have a singular curiosity to witness your meeting,' and sits beside him. Soon sounds of a Saturnalia approach, then a wild procession headed by the double-faced man, who watches Robin the while, swirls past by torch-light, drawing a cart. 'There, in tar-and-feathery dignity, sat his kinsman, Major Molineux!'

> He was an elderly man, of large and majestic person, and strong, square features, betokening a steady soul; but steady as it was, his enemies had found means to shake it. . . . But perhaps the bitterest pang of all was when his eyes met those of Robin; for he evidently knew him on the instant, as the youth stood witnessing the foul disgrace of head grown grey in honor. They stared at each other in silence, and Robin's knees shook, and his hair bristled, with a mixture of pity and terror.

Then, one by one, the laughing mockers of his night-long adventure add their derisive voices to the din. 'The contagion . . . all at once seized upon Robin . . . Robin's shout was the loudest there.' At the leader's signal, 'On they went, like fiends that throng in mockery around some dead potentate, mighty no more, but majestic still in his agony . . . and left a silent street behind.' Robin's companion lays a hand on his shoulder. 'Well, Robin are you dreaming?' Robin, 'his eye not quite as lively as in the earlier part of the evening,' replies by asking to be shown the way to the ferry. 'I grow weary of town life, sir.' But this friendly stranger declines to oblige him, suggesting that 'If you prefer to remain with us, perhaps, as you are a shrewd youth, you may rise in the world without the help of your kinsman, Major Molineux.'

From even this crude précis of the plot it is hard to take seriously Parrington's strictures against Hawthorne as a mere romancer of the murky past who avoided dealing with the problems and issues of Jacksonian democracy. One of the two chief interpretations of 'My Kinsman, Major Molineux,' that of Q. D. Leavis,[1] suggests how deeply involved Hawthorne was with the basic problems of American self-realization. She sees this tale as 'a symbolic action which . . . takes the form of something between a pageant and a ritual drama, disguised in the emotional logic of a dream.' She suggests that the tale be subtitled 'America Comes of Age,' and reads it as an historic parable in which Robin 'represents the young America' who has come to town, 'that is, the contemporary scene where the historic future will be decided.' The opening paragraphs of the tale establish that popular insurrections and violent deaths of the governors were characteristic of the history of the colonies.

A quite different reading is suggested by Hyatt H. Waggoner and elaborated by Roy R. Male.[2] Waggoner emphasizes the dreamlike manipulation of incident, sound, and color in the tale, and reads its primary meaning as a revelation of an Oedipal conflict. The tale reveals 'man's image of himself as the destroyer of the father—because he has wished the destruction—a destroyer bathed in guilt yet somehow justified. . . . Passing through the stages of initial identification with the father image, rejection, and shame, Robin at last emerges with the help of the stranger into maturity.' Male's elaboration of this Freudian reading suggests 'that visions of the father figure may commonly be split into two or more images.' The pompous old man and the watchman then 'are shapes of what Robin is attempting to leave behind.' Other figures are 'various forms of the cultured kinsman he is seeking.'

> Thus as he verges upon maturity the young man's yearnings for freedom from authority and for a worldly patrimony take on exag-

[1] 'Hawthorne as Poet' [Part I], *Sewanee Review*, LIX (Spring 1951), 198-205.

[2] Waggoner, *Hawthorne, A Critical Study* (Cambridge, 1955), pp. 47-53; Male, *Hawthorne's Tragic Vision* (Austin, Tex., 1957), pp. 48-53.

> gerated proportions. The dual aspect of this psychic conflict can be seen in the 'infernal visage' of the 'double-faced fellow,' whose complexions are split. . . . The grotesque fusion of the two forms is a distorted father image in which youthful misrepresentation of both the real father and the real uncle are combined.

Robin's real father appears in his dream of home, and again as the kindly stranger who stays by his side during the imaged destruction of Major Molineux. The kinsman, of course, is the most potent father-image in the story.

TWO

The truth of the tale includes both these theories and more. Hawthorne's most successful fictions may be described by a phrase from one of his least effective stories: 'I can never separate the idea from the symbol in which it manifests itself.' [3] In his best tales, simple arrangements of objects, persons, or actions are the symbols, but these are so economically chosen as to represent complex constellations of ideas. Certainly the pattern of action in 'My Kinsman, Major Molineux' is at the same time a journey, a search, an initiation. Robin is indeed a representative American, first as witness, then as participant, in a cultural-political experience of archetypal significance to our national identity. He is also a representative young man who must come to terms with his feelings about his father, about the past, about authority, in order to pass from adolescence into maturity.

In psychological terms, Male is probably right that all the men in the story are displacements or substitutions for the father, in his several aspects: as authority (to be feared, courted, or ridiculed), and as paternity (to be loved, escaped from, and depended upon). But there are other implications necessary to a full involvement with the tale. Major Molineux is not only the Father as Authority, he is also the Past which must be rejected. Specifically, he represents British rule—in political terms he is

[3] 'The Antique Ring,' *Works*, XII, 67.

the representative of the Crown. If psychologically the Major displaces Robin's father, politically and culturally he actually displaces the King. As authority figure, whether patristic or regal, he represents Order, Tradition, Stability. But as the Father-King in a cart whose 'tar-and-feathery dignity' inspire the tragic emotions of pity and terror, Major Molineux takes on yet further dimensions. He is the Sacrificed King, the Royal Scapegoat, the 'dead potentate . . . majestic still in his agony' around whom the townsfolk 'throng in mockery.' Frazer analyzes the Scapegoat King as a ritual role invested with two functions, the expulsion of evil and the sacrificial death of the divine ruler whose declining potency is renewed in his young successor. One can hardly suggest that this modern anthropological theory was available to Hawthorne in 1832, but from his tale we can infer his intuitive understanding of the primitive ritual which he used metaphorically in describing the downfall of Major Molineux. The rebellion in the tale, although dated vaguely around 1730, is clearly a 'type' of the American Revolution. This was indeed the supercession of an old order by a new, from which ensued a revitalization of the energies of American society. Hawthorne remarks that the colonists had frequently attacked the person of their royal governors, however suppliant to their demands the governors, as individuals, had been. In this there is the inference that in tarring and feathering Major Molineux the conspirators are symbolically ridding the colony of a symbol of the chief evil that prepossessed their consciousness as a culture. Further warrant for inferring Major Molineux to represent a Scapegoat King is suggested by one of the identities of his antagonist, the man with the double visage.

This character may be, as Male proposes, a double father-image combining 'youthful misrepresentation of both the real father and the real uncle.' Yet we must also take him more literally than this; or, if we take him in metaphors, let the metaphors be Hawthorne's own. He is described as both 'a fiend of fire and a fiend of darkness,' and, when he rides on horseback at the head of the ceremonial procession, 'his fierce and variegated countenance appeared like war personified; the red of one cheek was an emblem of fire and sword; the blackness of the other betokened the mourning that attends them.' He is War, Death, and Destruction, and again he is the Devil, with 'his train [of] wild figures in Indian dress,' his 'infernal visage,' and his eyes that glowed 'like fire in a cave.' He is well chosen to play the part of Riot, of Disorder, of the Lord of Misrule, in the pageant it is Robin's destiny to behold. He is in charge of the procession of 'fiends' and of their lurid rites, the 'counterfeited pomp,' the 'senseless uproar' in which the tumultuous multitude lead Major Molineux to his humiliation.

And Robin joins this yelling mob! His mocking laughter is the loudest there! Not even the shame, the agony of his kinsman, not even his own emotions of pity and terror, can hold him from making their 'frenzied merriment' his own. There are buffetings of passion, there are possibilities of evil and of guilt, which Robin's callow rationalism cannot fathom. Setting out merely to make his way in the world, he has wandered unknowingly toward an appointed rendezvous, a ceremony which seems to have been prepared specifically for his benefit. It is his initiation.

But an initiation into what? The sensitive suggestions of Mrs. Leavis, Waggoner, and Male may be supplemented by a closer scrutiny of Robin himself. When we have seen who he is and what he represents up to the moment of his initiation, we can better understand the significance of that ritual for him.

Seven times in this tale Robin is characterized as 'a shrewd youth.' Like his antecedent bumpkins in popular tradition—Brother Jonathan, the peddlers of folk anecdote, Jack Downing, Sam Slick—he is nothing if not shrewd. But Robin is shrewd only by his own report. 'I'm not the fool you take me for,' he warns the double-faced demon, yet that is exactly what he is. Although mystified at every turn, denied the common civilities by those he meets, taunted and mocked by strangers at the mention of his kinsman's name, he never once loses confidence in his own shrewdness. Rebuffed by the pompous old man and the innkeeper, fleeing the temptations of the prostitute, his response to their jeering laughter is thrice again to account himself 'a shrewd youth.' Even in his last encounter with the stranger who proves to be kindly, Robin is still depending on his motherwit to carry him through all situations. 'For I have the name of being a shrewd youth,' Robin tells his older friend. 'I doubt not that you deserve it,' the friend replies. Yet at the beginning of his night of misadventure Robin had stepped jauntily off the ferry without realizing that he had no idea where he was going. 'It would have been wise to inquire my way of the ferryman,' he muses, 'But the next man I meet will do as well.' This, however, is not at all the case. Everyone he meets is, unknown to him, involved in the conspiracy to overthrow his kinsman the royal governor. When Robin cannot give their password, parties of conspirators curse him in plain language. When he obstinately inquires for the Major the people in the inn and the barbershop hoot at him. When he tries the door of the pretty little prostitute she tells him that she knows his kinsman well. 'But Robin, being of the household of a New England clergyman, was a good youth, as well as a shrewd one; so he resisted temptation, and fled away.' He cannot yet face the knowledge that Major Molineux, his kinsman (and father), has had carnal knowledge of a woman, just as Young Goodman Brown will be dismayed to learn that his father had followed the Devil to the witches' carnal Sabbath before him.

It is characteristic of Robin that he always accepts the most simplistic rationalizations of the most baffling and ominous experiences. One would think him affrighted by the demoniac double-faced man he accosts before the church. We recognize this portentous apparition as ringleader of the uprising, but Robin merely muses, 'Strange things we travellers see!" and sits down to await the Major. 'A few moments were consumed in philosophical speculations upon the species of man who had just left him; but having settled this point shrewdly, rationally, and satisfactorily, he was compelled to look elsewhere for his amusement'! Now the moonlight plays over the commonplace scene 'like the imaginative power,' and Robin cannot define the forms of distant objects which turn ghostly and indistinct 'just as his eye appeared to grasp them.' His dream of home is more real than the actual things he is now among, and when he wakes 'his mind kept vibrating between fancy and reality' as shapes lengthen and dwindle before him. Despite all these physical sensations of confusion and the constant evidence of his noncomprehension of what is happening, Robin trusts to his 'name of being a shrewd youth.' This is Yankee self-reliance with a vengeance! His 'bright, cheerful eyes were nature's gifts,' and he would seem to think he needs no others. Robin, the shrewd youth from the backwoods, proves to be the Great American Boob, the naïf whose odyssey leads him, all uncomprehending, into the dark center of experience.

When the tale opens, Robin has just made a crossing of the water and entered the city. He has left behind him the security as well as the simplicity of his rural birthplace—in his reverie before the church his country home seemed an Arcadian bower of 'venerable shade' and 'golden light.' But in his dream of returning home the door closes before him. Like Wakefield, Robin has left his home and cannot return. It is true that, as opposed to Wakefield's perverse impulse, he had good reasons (Robin is a younger son and won't inherit the farm), but nonetheless by leaving his appointed place and station to participate in the fluidity of egalitarian city life he too has made himself an exile. Just how egalitarian that city life will prove Robin must learn with dismay. The change to which he has committed himself is not only one of place and status but involves also the breaking of human ties, as every act of independence does to some degree. Much as Robin resembles the folk characters of Yankee yarn and jokelore, the difference—and it is tremendous—is that such characters had no human ties to break.

Robin's journey toward independence is magnified a thousandfold by the throes of the town itself on the evening of his arrival. In their quest for self-determination the urban conspirators of the town are far in advance of the country-bred youth whom they mock. Until the very end of the tale Robin still counts on his kinsman's preferment; the independence he seeks is therefore qualified, not absolute. The townsfolk no longer accept the limited independence granted by royal governors, even those who 'in softening their instructions from beyond the sea . . . incurred the reprehension' of the Crown. They have cast their die for total disseverance of their bonds. Hawthorne's imagery puts them in league with the Devil to do so.

Thus an ironic tension underlies all of Robin's misadventures. Those who deride him are really his mentors, and he, invoking the patronage of their enemy his kinsman, is actually their ally, since both they and he are seeking independence. After his dismay at beholding his kinsman's degradation, Robin's sudden shout of laughter may seem to the reader inexplicable. So it is, from a point of view as rational and 'shrewd' as his own. But the emotional logic that produced his outburst is inescapable. It is an emotional not a rational logic, for in that instant, with neither premeditation nor understanding, Robin has cast off the remaining dependence of his immaturity.

Then, at the Devil's behest, the frenzied procession moves on, leaving Robin behind in the silent street. What has he learned from his initiation?

His lessons must be inferred from the tale, for when it ends Robin is still in a state of shock. 'I begin to grow weary of town life,' he says. He wants to go home. But, as his dream has already told him, he has no home now. He must stay. What he might muse on is his new knowledge of the demonic depths from which the impulse to self-determination leaped up in the torchlight. He might give 'a few moments' in 'philosophical speculations' upon the Saturnalian passions which shook him as he, like the populace, dethroned Order and rejected Tradition while under the aegis of the Lord of Misrule. In their act of revolt they have all thrown down the old king of Stability and crowned the new prince of War and Destruction.

To judge from the effect upon Robin of his experiences hitherto, there is little chance of his learning much from these reflections. Although devoted to the dogma of Yankee self-reliance, he had learned nothing from anything that had touched him. We are, however, told that his faith in himself is rather shaken, for 'nature's gift,' his 'bright, cheerful eyes,' are now 'not quite as lively as in the earlier part of the evening.'

One source of hope for Robin is the continued interest of the gentleman who had befriended him. This nameless figure, as we have seen, represents the viable influence of his father upon his soul: the manly guidance of a non-possessive, non-inhibiting paternal love. The tale ends with the steadying voice of this personage, whose interested detachment from the pillorying of Major Molineux hints that he has seen all this before. In his experience he knows that this ritual, like all *rites de passage,* is ever again repeated for the benefit of each initiate. Even his irony at the end is indulgent without being patronizing, for he suggests that Robin will have to make up his own mind, 'as you are a shrewd youth,' whether to stay in town and 'perhaps . . . rise in the world without the help of your kinsman, Major Molineux,' even though he surely knows that Robin cannot return to his pastoral home. This means that Robin now is free of the past, and has the power of self-determination. But this power comes to him inextricable from the terrifying and tragic emotions that have involved him.

And what of the Colony? Is it truly free, or has it exchanged the rule of a benevolent governor for the tyranny of riot and chaos? On the political level Hawthorne's fable is less reassuring than on the personal. There is no double of Major Molineux who represents in the realm of power what Robin's friend stands for as an aspect of the parent. Yet so closely has Hawthorne intertwined the cultural with the psychological implications in this tale that we cannot help taking Robin's friend as representing also the viable aspects of Major Molineux. What his patient and tolerant advice to Robin suggests, then, is that this ordeal has been performed before by society as well as by the self. The implication is that the forces of Order and Stability do in the end prove stronger than those of Destruction and Misrule which dethrone them. Harrowing though these disruptive forces be, in Hawthorne's vision of American history they do serve the end of re-establishing a stable order based on institutions more just than those overthrown. (This was in fact the case, as the fire-brained Committees of Correspondence were superseded, after the reign of War and Death, by the framers of the Constitution and the *Federalist Papers.*[4]) Still another indication that the reign of Riot will be but brief lies in the carnival atmosphere which suggests that Major Molineux's successor, the two-faced man, is the Lord of Misrule. His reign is but a mock reign, a temporary season of emotional debauch necessary to the purification and rebirth of society. At its conclusion Order is imposed again upon the rampaging passions of the Saturnalia. On this succession the continuity of culture itself depends. In 'My Kinsman,' then, there is a qualified, half-skeptical hope that when the town wakes up from its collective nightmare, tradition will be re-established in accordance with the new dispensation of absolute liberty which the Devil's league had won in the darkness.

But as in the case of Robin's personal fate, the consequences of these public actions are not affirmed, not even proposed. All consequences are but inferences from this fable. Our inferences must be guided by the probabilities which the characterization of Robin in terms of the traditional figure of the Yankee naïf sug-

[4] If the spirit of revolt is in this tale a Devil, he appears elsewhere in Hawthorne as 'The Gray Champion,' the regicide Goffe who signed King Charles's death warrant. 'His hour is one of darkness, and adversity, and peril. But should domestic tyranny oppress us . . . still may the Gray Champion come, for he is the type of New England's hereditary spirit.' There, as in 'Legends of the Province House' and 'Endicott and the Red Cross,' rebellion is the divine right of an oppressed people.

gests. There is no clearer statement in our literature than 'My Kinsman, Major Molineux' of the psychological and cultural burdens of personal freedom and of national independence. Hawthorne's Robin allows us no undue confidence in the degree of understanding with which the American character will bear them.

7

'The Maypole of Merry Mount' and the Folklore of Love

ONE

One of Hawthorne's most interesting tales is 'The Maypole of Merry Mount.' Here, as in 'The Gray Champion,' 'Legends of the Province House,' 'My Kinsman, Major Molineux,' and a dozen other stories to be written later, he was guided by the aesthetic instinct that had led him to project as his earliest work a volume to be called *Seven Tales of My Native Land.* The original stories, he reports in 'The Devil in Manuscript,' were so disappointingly inadequate that he burned them. But the labor of their writing taught him a lesson he could learn from no one else in America at that time: how to mingle the imaginary with the actual American past so that folk traditions have the appearance of history, and history gains the heightened grandeur of legend.

'The Maypole' takes place during the final hours of the dissident colony at Mt. Wollaston, Massachusetts, where in historic fact one Thomas Morton, an anti-Puritan High-Churchman and Royalist, had established a trading-post with the Indians. 'The facts, recorded on the grave pages of our New England Annalists, have wrought themselves, almost spontaneously, into a sort of allegory,' writes Hawthorne in his prefatory note. But, as G. H. Orians has shown, he played rather freely with those grave pages in making Morton's dissolute band into a hedonistic cult whose object of worship is the Maypole. Q. D. Leavis and John B. Vickery have recently interpreted the tale from rather different points of view; Mrs. Leavis finds Hawthorne here to be a ritual dramatist concerned with cultural history, while Vickery takes him as a ritual anthropologist tracing religious evolution.[1] There seem plausible grounds for both views; yet neither does full justice to Hawthorne's intentions or achievement.

His story begins with a description of Merry Mount, where 'May, or her mirthful spirit, dwelt all the year round. . . . Through a world of toil and care she flitted with a dreamlike smile.' The communicants of the Maypole, 'should their banner be triumphant, were to pour sunshine over New England's rugged hills, and scatter flower seeds throughout the soil.' But we are never permitted to forget that this colony is imperilled by the surrounding Puritans. The incipient struggle is defined in the third sentence: 'Jollity and gloom were contending for an empire.' After the Maypole and the mummers in animal garb dancing around it are described, these protagonists appear: 'A youth in glistering apparel' has his arm about 'a fair maiden, not less gaily decorated than himself.' They are surrounded and crowned by roses. As we meet them they are being joined 'in holy matrimony' by Blackstone, 'a clerk of Oxford and high priest of Merry Mount.' The ceremony has the aspect of a masquerade, although we are told that 'This wedlock was more serious than most affairs of Merry Mount, where jest and delusion, trick and fantasy, kept up a continual carnival.' The couple are actually participating in a double ceremony: not only are they marrying

[1] Orians, 'Hawthorne and "The Maypole of Merry Mount,"' *Modern Language Notes,* LIII (March 1938), 159-67; Leavis, 'Hawthorne as Poet,' op. cit. pp. 179-95; Vickery, 'The Golden Bough at Merry Mount,' *Nineteenth-Century Fiction,* XII (Dec. 1957), 203-14. The most perceptive reading of the tale is that of Richard Harter Fogle, *Hawthorne's Fiction: The Light and the Dark* (Norman, Okla., 1952), pp. 59-69. 'The core of the story lies in a conflict between abstractions, and the outcome is determined in accordance with an assumption about the world and reality. The dour Puritan triumphs because he is in tune with the nature of things.'

one another, but they are also Lord and Lady of the May. This is both a personal and a ritual wedlock.

At just this moment, as the 'dim light' of sunset is 'withdrawn' from 'the whole domain of Merry Mount,' some 'black shadows have rushed forth in human shape' from the 'black surrounding woods'

> The Puritans had played a characteristic part in the Maypole mummeries. Their darksome figures were intermixed with the wild shapes of their foes, and made the scene a picture of the moment, when waking thoughts start up amid the scattered fantasies of a dream.

Their leader, Endicott, is 'the Puritan of Puritans,' whose very 'frame and soul seemed wrought of iron,' in contrast to the 'silken' revellers who now cower about him 'like evil spirits in the presence of a dread magician.' With his own sword he hews down the Maypole, orders stripes, stocks, branding, and cropping of ears for its captured votaries, and then turns to the newly wedded couple. 'I am minded that ye shall both have a token to remember your wedding day,' he threatens them. The youth, Edgar, whom Hawthorne still calls the May Lord, replies with manly fortitude:

> 'Stern man, how can I move thee? Were the means at hand, I would resist to the death. Being powerless, I entreat! Do with me as thou wilt, but let Edith go untouched!'

None of this courtly charity from the pitiless Puritan: '"Not so,' replied the immitigable zealot. 'We are not wont to show an idle courtesy to that sex, which requireth the stricter discipline."' Yet even this 'iron man was softened . . . at the fair spectacle of early love.' Although he decrees that Edgar's 'dark and glossy curls' be cropped 'forthwith' he admits that 'There be qualities in the youth, which may make him valiant to fight, and sober to toil, and pious to pray; and in the maiden, that may fit her to become a mother in our Israel.' And so it was Endicott, 'the severest Puritan of all,' who crowned their marriage with 'the wreath of roses from the ruin of the Maypole, and threw it, with his own gauntleted hand, over the heads of the Lord and Lady of the May.' No more did they return to 'their home of wild mirth . . . made desolate amid the staid forest,' for 'the moral gloom of the world overpowers all systematic gaiety.' Yet, as their garland 'was wreathed of the brightest roses that had grown there, so in the tie that united them, were intertwined all of the purest and best of their earthly joys. They went heavenward, supporting each other along the difficult path which it was their lot to tread, and never wasted one regretful thought on the vanities of Merry Mount.'

TWO

The special quality of this tale is its uncompromising equivocality of vision. Everything in it is presented from a double perspective, hence none of its statements are assertions and all have the power of imaginative reverberation. The initial presentation of the Merrymounters is as sympathetic to their enterprise as can be, yet by the end of the second paragraph their way of life has been called 'dreamlike,' and the invocation, 'O, people of the Golden Age, the chief of your husbandry was to raise flowers!' points ambiguously toward condemnation for frivolity. The opening rhapsody soon gives way to increasing qualification, and finally to censure. The dancers at the Maypole are masqued as animals. They are in perfect sympathy with Nature, and Nature with them. 'A real bear of the dark forest' joins their ring, and 'His inferior nature rose half way, to meet his companions as they stooped.' They are introduced as a 'wild throng' of 'Gothic monsters, though perhaps of Grecian ancestry'; 'It could not be that the fauns and nymphs, when driven from their classic groves and homes of ancient fable, had sought refuge as all the persecuted did, in the fresh woods of the West.' How ambiguous the implications! The masquers are allied with 'the persecuted'—not only with Quakers and Antinomians like Roger Williams and Anne Hutchinson but with the Puritans themselves—who seek refuge in 'the fresh woods of the West.' But to the Puritans, later in the story, these same woods are the abode of 'the fiend, and his bond slaves'—the votaries of Merry Mount. Although these 'could not be' pagan spirits of the ancient world, later, when their Bacchic priest unites the Lord and Lady of the May, 'a prelude of pipe, cithern, and viol, touched with practised minstrelsy, began to play from a neighboring thicket,' quivering the Maypole itself with the sound. These are the antique instruments of Arcady, not those of Mt. Wollaston, Massachusetts.

How, then, are we to react to these masquers? Here they are associated with the age-old heritage of civilization itself, just as their Maypole is bedecked with a bridal wreath of roses, 'some that had been gathered in the sunniest spots of the forest, and others, of still richer blush, which the colonists had reared from English seed.' This wreath, the intermixture of ancient cultivation with the nurture of this new wild place, is about to be thrown over the lovers by Blackstone when the Puritans invade the scene; instead it is Endicott who so crowns their union. Sympathetically as we may tend to view the Merrymounters, we have yet to contend with their characters from another view, that of the 'one stern band' who came to the New World 'to pray.' In a passage reminiscent of the *Anatomie of Abuse* (1583), an attack by the Puritan pamphleteer Philip Stubbes upon Maypoles, idleness, and papistry (excerpts from which Hawthorne read in the books he consulted for background), the Merry Mount contingent is described as 'minstrels . . . wandering players . . . mummers, rope-dancers, and mountebanks, who would long be missed at wakes, church ales, and fairs. . . . Sworn triflers of a lifetime, they would not venture among the sober truths of life not even to be truly blest.' With them came 'All the hereditary pastimes of Old England': crowning the King of Christmas and the Lord of Misrule, huge bonfires on St. John's Eve. And 'At harvest time . . . they made an image with the sheaves of Indian corn, and wreathed it with autumnal garlands, and bore it home triumphantly. But what chiefly characterized the colonists of Merry Mount was their veneration for the Maypole. It has made their true history a poet's tale.'

Before we investigate their veneration for the Maypole we must acknowledge the opposite aspect of this 'poet's tale': the Puritans. They are first introduced as 'most dismal wretches,' who toil with their weapons 'always at hand,' and come together only to hear interminable sermons and 'to proclaim bounties on the heads of wolves and the scalps of Indians,' both of which were members of the Merry Mount masquerade. The Puritans' whipping post is their Maypole.

Adamantine though these men 'of a sterner faith' are shown, punitive though their actions be, we cannot, after such a qualification of the claims to our sympathy of the opposite faction, consider them merely as hateful. Although 'their festivals were fast days, and their chief pastime the singing of psalms,' they are yet dedicated to the ennobling conception of a moral life. Their virtues Endicott names in granting pardon to Edgar and Edith: courage, sobriety, piety. But if the Merrymounters, 'sworn triflers of a lifetime,' lacked the moral energy of Puritanism, the Puritans as surely lacked the spirit of love in which the Maypole had its roots. Because neither of these rival factions of mankind has the virtues of the other to compensate for its own defects, Hawthorne does not permit us to accept wholeheartedly the partial truth which either side represents. That is why the 'grim Puritans, . . . each with a horseload of armor to burden his footsteps' appear just as shadowy, insubstantial, and monstrous as the masquers of Merry Mount, in whose 'Maypole mummeries' they 'had played a characteristic part.' And that is why, in the resolution of this crisis, Hawthorne allows the heart of the ironclad Endicott to be touched by beholding love in others, and to complete the wedding begun by the priest who wore 'pagan decorations' on 'his holy garb.' But the Puritan's heart can melt only so much: he can unbend from righteousness only to admit the newly wedded pair into Puritan life. To feel the heart's tug further earthward is beneath him; he has abjured all recognition of man's animal nature, and so, confronted by a bear who would rise to mankind, 'the energetic Puritan' decrees 'shoot him through the head! I suspect witchcraft in the beast.' As Edgar and Edith leave the ruined Maypole forever behind them, 'it was their lot to tread' a 'difficult path.' We are told, true, that 'They went heavenward,' which is to say that they sought Christian salvation within the terms laid down to them by Endicott, the terms of Puritan society. The parallel to Milton's Puritan epic of the expulsion from Eden is unmistakable:

> They, hand in hand, with wandering steps and slow,
> Through Eden took their solitary way.
> [PL, XII, 648-9]

THREE

So essential to this tale are religious imagery and ritual action that the suggestion was perhaps inevitable that the story be read in the terms proposed by Frazer's *The Golden Bough.* John B. Vickery—the suggestion is his—discovers that Frazer's anthropology and Hawthorne's fiction have the same theme: the 'logic of religious evolution.' In the Maypole story he finds 'the transmutation of the phallic worship of the Maypole and the mimetic Sacred Marriage of fertility rituals into obeisance to the whipping-post, the "Puritan Maypole," and respect for the sacramental union of Christian marriage.' This may seem plausible but ritual criticism has its dangers, as we see when Vickery goes on to propose that

> the 'Gothic monsters' with 'Grecian ancestry' are theriomorphic equivalents of the spirits of vegetation. The wolf, the goat, and the bear, all are emblems of the corn-spirit: while the stag, which on occasion symbolized longevity, hints perhaps at the god's ability to return to the world and to live on despite the vicissitudes to which he must necessarily be subject.

These creatures at Hawthorne's Maypole may be three corn-spirits and one longevity mummer, but curiously the first three occur together in Milton's *Comus*, which we know Hawthorne to have read. There the evil potion of the lord of lust can change the human countenance

> Into some brutish form of wolf or bear,
> Or, ounce or tiger, hog [i.e. boar] or bearded goat,
> All other parts remaining as they were.
> [lines 70-72]

Hawthorne, a stickler for verisimilitude, omits the beasts not native to his North American forest. His parallels in 'The Maypole' are frequent enough to make credible this debt to *Comus*. The 'English priest' is twice described as 'the very Comus of the Crew,' and Norris Yates has proposed that Milton's stage direction before Comus's first speech suggests the revels at Merry Mount, while the later directions for the break-up of his crew and the smashing of his glass may be the prototype for Endicott's destruction of the Maypole.[2] Despite these debts to Milton where Vickery proposes anticipations of *The Golden Bough*, it is yet true that many of the elements Hawthorne took from descriptions he had read of the English folk observance of May Day do have in his tale a cultural significance similar to that which Frazer finds for them in a context of world folklore. But to apply so simplistically a scientific theory to a work of art is subversive of the tensions in Hawthorne's tale that give it dramatic power. The tale itself is designed to present something other than 'the logic of religious evolution.' That was one of Frazer's aims, but it is only of secondary interest to Hawthorne.

Several correspondences between 'The Maypole of Merry Mount' and Frazer's second volume, *The Magic Art*, can in fact be made for the simple reason that both authors consulted the same source book for the traditions celebrating the May folk festival. All readers are familiar with Hawthorne's attribution, 'The masques, mummeries and festive customs, described in the

[2] 'Ritual and Reality: Mask and Dance Motifs in Hawthorne's Fiction,' *Philological Quarterly*, XXXIV (Jan. 1955), 60.

text, are in accordance with the manners of the age. Authority on these points may be found in Strutt's Book of English Sports and Pastimes.' Frazer, as it happens, did not consult Strutt. But what has not been observed of Hawthorne is that in preparing 'The Maypole of Merry Mount' he actually read another work on British antiquities besides Strutt's, and this one proves to be among Frazer's most frequently cited British references: *The Every Day Book* by William Hone.[8]

Why did not Hawthorne acknowledge Hone as well as Strutt? It is true that for specific details of the May mummeries, masques, and customs, Strutt is his primary source. As Orians has noted, the stag and goat appear in the 1801 edition of *Sports and Pastimes,* as do also the salvage man with his girdle of green leaves, the grinning match, the horse collar, fool's cap and bells, the employment of the Maypole for year-round activity, and the sunset abrogation of lordly rights. Taking all these specific points from Strutt's synoptic and orderly collection, what use then did Hawthorne make of Hone?

The Every Day Book is a triple-volume product of the crazy-quilt school of antiquarian collecting, an assemblage of traditional materials of every sort in calendrical order, since almost every day was sacred to some saint or celebrated by folk observance somewhere in the British Isles. The three volumes together present seventy-five pages on May Day, its customs and its celebration in literature. Here are accounts of the setting-up of Maypoles, descriptions of the marriage of the Lord and Lady of May, the costumes of mummers and of Jack-o'-the-Green, the construction of May garlands and lovers' knots, and disquisitions on the pagan origins of May Day going back to the Roman festival of Flora. Hone quotes liberally from verses celebrating the May,

[8] (London, 1826). Hawthorne borrowed Strutt from the Salem Athenaeum from Jan. 9-29, 1835, and later supplemented this material by borrowing Hone from Sept. 5-12 and Oct. 17-Nov. 13, 1835 and again from Feb. 25-March 9, 1836. 'The Maypole of Merry Mount' first appeared in *Twice-Told Tales,* 1837.

for the poets 'have made the day especially their own; they are its annalists.' He reprints May Day selections from Browne's 'Pastorals,' Spenser's *Eclogues,* Langhorne's 'Buchanan,' Lady Craven, Lydgate, and Herrick's 'Corinna's Going A-Maying'. His second volume anthologizes from Chaucer (Arcite's observance to May, *Knight's Tale,* 1491-1515) and Dryden's paraphrase; a sonnet of Sannazaro; stanzas from Gay, Matthew Prior's 'The Garland,' the nymphs' song from *Pan's Anniversary* by Ben Jonson, and May Day sentiments by poets of lesser moment.[4]

Besides these literary poems there are many versions of traditional Maying carols. One in particular may have attracted Hawthorne's eye, since it mentions the flower which gave his family its name. Certainly the author who in 'Rappaccini's Daughter' translated his own name into 'Monsieur de l'Aubépine' would have noted the carol which Hone remarks was sung 'by him who has the honour to crown his lass the "May-day queen"':

> O then, my love, from me receive
> This beauteous hawthorn spray,
> A garland for thy head I'll weave,
> Be thou my queen of May.
>
> Love and fragrant as these flowers,
> Live pure as thou wert born,
> And ne'er may sin's destructive powers,
> Assail thee with its thorn.

These sentiments are appropriate enough for a May Lord who is destined to become a Puritan husband.

Prose selections include a nostalgic excerpt from Washington Irving's 'May-Day Customs,' a picturesque account of a sumptuous fifteenth-century Robin Hood May pageant, and a quotation from Leigh Hunt:

> All this worship of May is over now. There is no issuing forth in glad companies to gather boughs; no adorning of houses with 'the

[4] Hone, *Every-Day Book,* I, 545, 536-54; II, 37-63, 557-618. (Numbers indicate columns, two to a page.)

flowery spoils'; no songs, no dances, no village sports and coronations, no courtly-poetries, no sense and acknowledgment of the quiet presence of nature, in grove or glade.

Hunt's melancholy sounds again in an excerpt from Pasquil's *Palinodia* (1634):

> Happy the age, and harmlesse were the dayes,
>   (For then true love and amity was found)
> When every village did a May Pole raise
>   And Whitsun-ales and MAY-GAMES did abound:
> And all the lusty yonkers, in a rout,
> With merry lasses daunced the rod about,
> Then Friendship to their banquets bid the guests,
> And poore men far'd the better for their feasts.
>
> . . . .
>
> But since the SUMMER POLES *were overthrown*
>   And all good sports and merriments decay'd
> How times and men are chang'd, so well is known. . . .

Throughout Hone's volumes appear many laments for the severity of the Puritans, who in their fanatical zeal destroyed the innocent May Day merriment of Old England. Hone prints the Puritan order of 6 April 1644 which decreed the abolition of Maypoles:

> The lords and commons do further order and ordain, that all and singular *May-poles*, that are or shall be erected, shall be taken down, and removed by the constables, bossholders, tithing-men, petty constables, and church-wardens of the parishes, where the same be, and that no May-pole be hereafter set up, or suffered to be set up within this kingdom of England, or dominion of Wales; the said officers to be fined five shillings weekly till the said May-pole be taken down.

In his third volume he remarks,

> That the excesses and lawless misrule attributed to this *Floralian* festival, by the fanatic enthusiasts of the Cromwellian age, ever existed, is indeed greatly to be doubted. It was celebrated as a national festival, an universal expression of joy and adoration, at the commencement of a season, when nature developes her beauties,

dispenses her bounties, and wafts her 'spicy gales,' rich with voluptuous fragrance, to exhilarate man, and enliven the scenes around him.

The selection in Hone perhaps equally pregnant with suggestion for Hawthorne was a reprinting of a scarce tract by Thomas Hall, *Funebria Florae, the Downfall of May-games* (1661). This takes the form of a dialogue in which Flora, goddess of flowers, is tried by jury. Holy Scriptures, Pliny, Lactantius, Synodus Francica, Charles II, Ordinances of Parliament, Solemn League and Covenant, Order of the Council of State, Messrs. Elton and Ames, Bishop Babington, Bishop Andrews, and Ovid comprise the twelve eclectic jurors. 'These,' says the Crier, 'with all the godly in the land, do call for justice against this turbulent malefactor.'

> Judge: Flora, thou has here been indicted for bringing in abundance of misrule and disorder into church and state; thou hast been found guilty, and art condemned both by God and man,—by scriptures, fathers, councils,—by learned and pious divines,—and therefore I adjudge thee to
>
> PERPETUAL BANISHMENT
>
> that thou no more disturb this church and state, lest justice do arrest thee.

Thus concludes this Puritan bagatelle; its opening—the charge against Flora—is also apropos of Hawthorne's Merry Mount:

> Flora, hold up thy hand, thou art here indicted . . . for that thou, contrary to the peace of our sovereign lord, his crown and dignity, hast brought in a pack of practical fanatics, viz.,—ignorants, atheists, papists, drunkards, swearers, swashbucklers, maid-marians, morrice-dancers, maskers, mummers, May-pole stealers, health-drinkers, together with a rascallion rout of fiddlers, fools, fighters, gamesters, lewd-women, light-women, contemners of magistracy, affronters of ministry, rebellious to masters, disobedient to parents, misspenders of time, and abusers of the creature, &c.[5]

[5] Hone, III, 542, 545-51. The author, Hall, prefaced his dialogue in the perfect Puritan spirit, feeling obliged to justify his exercise of fancy as 'the most facile and fruitfullest way of teaching.' In a metaphor whose irony Hawthorne may have marked, Hall avows that 'a pleasant allusion may do

Thus Hawthorne's probable debts to Hone are three. First is the aura attaching to the May-day customs of olden times, which the nostalgic antiquarian presents in a glow of retrospection as a golden age of carefree dance, of joy and love. This is in direct contrast to the attitude of the Puritan annalists of New England, such as Governor Bradford, who described Morton's settlement as a place of 'great licentiousness . . . dissolute life . . . riotous prodigality . . . profuse excess.' [6] The idealization of the worship of the Maypole was absolutely essential to the thematic tension of Hawthorne's tale. While Strutt obliged him with descriptive accuracy, Hone's selections—especially those quoted above and Herrick's 'Corrina's Going A-Maying'—gave him a richly documented sense of a golden age with a long lineage in literature and in civilization itself.

Second is Hone's association of the spirit of the May with that of poetry, not only in his eclectic anthologizing but in his statement that the poets 'have made this day especially their own' and 'they are its annalists.' Hawthorne too would write of the Merrymounters that their 'veneration for the Maypole . . . has made their true history a poet's tale.' There is a special sense in which this is true of Hawthorne's story, a sense I shall explore below.

More obvious perhaps is Hawthorne's third presumed debt to Hone. In *The Every Day Book* he found abundant evidence to intensify his sense of the conflict, during Puritan times, between the forces of 'jollity' and those of 'gloom.' This conflict was of far greater importance there than in the single New England incident at Merry Mount. Not only does Hone present the Puritans as fanatical executioners of all pleasure, but his selections reveal the long tenacity of folk observance through the twenty centuries since Roman times. They show, too, the perseverance of Maypole festivals despite the Puritans' severe punitive meas-

that which a solid argument cannot do; as, in some cases, iron may do that which gold cannot.' [III, 545.]

[6] *Of Plymouth Plantation*, ed. S. E. Morison (New York, 1952), 205-6.

ures. Thus Hawthorne found a far greater warrant of probability than his Colonial sources provided for making the opposition between Maypole worship and the faith of the Puritans a central metaphor in his tale.

If we compare Hawthorne's story with the account he read in Governor Bradford's journal we can see to what extent 'the facts . . . wrought themselves, almost spontaneously, into a sort of allegory':

> And Morton became Lord of Misrule, and maintained (as it were) a School of Atheism. . . . They also set up a maypole, drinking and dancing about it many days together, inviting the Indian women for their consorts, dancing and frisking together like so many fairies, or furies, rather; and worse practices. As if they had anew revived and celebrated the feasts of the Roman goddess Flora, or the beastly practices of the mad Bacchanalians. Morton, likewise, to show his poetry composed sundry rhymes and verses, some tending to lasciviousness . . . which he afficed to this idle or idol maypole. They changed also the name of their place, and instead of calling it Mount Wollaston they called it Merry-mount, as if this jollity would have lasted for ever. But this continued not long, for . . . shortly after came the worthy gentleman Mr. John Endecott . . . Who visiting these parts, caused that maypole to be cut down and rebuked them for their profaneness and admonished them to look there should be better walking.

It is apparent that what interposed between these facts and Hawthorne's allegory—his 'almost spontaneity'—was a subtilization of tone, a sympathetic rendering of cultural values which 'the grave pages of our New England annalists' regarded as utterly depraved. This subtilization, this sympathy with the folk customs of an antique festival of love, was in all probability suggested to Hawthorne by his reading of Hone. But Hawthorne was no antiquarian sentimentalist. He could use such suggestions for the purposes of his 'moral romance' without accepting them. His own soul is in both camps, and he uses the nostalgic charm of Hone's popular traditions and romantic poetry to make more poignant his American retelling of the Puritan myth of the Fortunate Fall.

FOUR

What, on the other hand, did Frazer draw from Hone? In *The Magic Art* he cites from Hone descriptions of May garlands; testimony that Maypoles stood the year-round; depiction of a Maypole hung with fresh garlands and topped by a birch; and description of Jack-o'-the-Green, the mummer in a wicker cage of leafy boughs.[7] This evidence, in conjunction with customs culled from Celtic Britain, Scandinavia, Estonia, France, Russia, and Germany, contributes to the pattern Frazer elucidates of vestigial tree-worship ultimately deriving from the mating of the Lord and Lady of May, the ritualistic union of the spirits of vegetation through whose fruitful juncture the fertility of the world is ensured.

Some of the images Hawthorne appropriated from the antiquaries were obviously vestigial symbols of ancient fertility belief. How else can one interpret the harvest doll mentioned above? Yet it will not do to ritualize everything in the story. Mr. Vickery, for instance, observes:

> [An] image of death that contributes to the midsummer symbolism of the defeated god is the figure of the 'flower-decked corpse.' This figure is accompanied 'with merriment and festive music, to his grave. But did the dead man laugh?' The laughter and rejoicing of the Merrymounters stem from their conviction that the corpse, like the dead Adonis, would return to life. . . . In effect, the question casts doubt on the whole concept of rejoicing and resurrection. The dead man does not laugh precisely because he is a *dead man,* that is, not a man-god capable of reviving. The associations with Adonis and his Gardens of flowers are ironic and designed to underscore a contrast of major significance, that between man and divinity, mortality and immortality.

[7] *The Golden Bough: The Magic Art and the Evolution of Kings* (New York, 1935), II, 61, 70, 71, 82.

This dead man in Hawthorne's story turns up in a paragraph enumerating the frivolities of perpetual May at Merry Mount. Just after the introduction of the Puritans and their whipping-post, the tone is most critical of Merry Mount. The sentence immediately preceding mention of the corpse reads:

> Often, the whole colony were playing at blindman's buff, magistrates and all, with their eyes bandaged, except a single scapegoat, whom the blinded sinners pursued by the tinkling of the bells at his garments.

In this context a dead Adonis is gratuitous. Plainly the 'flower-decked corpse' is to those who followed him 'with merriment and festive music, to his grave' as the open-eyed scapegoat was to the 'blinded sinners,' who also followed the sound of music—'the tinkling of the bells at his garments.' 'Scapegoat' is an extraordinarily harsh word in the first context of a mere game; but it transfers its implications to the second procession, where the dead man, unlaughing, alone has the somber knowledge the revellers at Merry Mount deny. They do not acknowledge death; for them, life, as their priest advises, is 'a dance.'

Acquaintance with calendar customs reveals that the folk—especially in the Celtic regions of Britain—have for centuries confused the celebration of May Day (the Celtic Beltane) with Midsummer. Both were seasonal festivals marking the return or propitiation of fecundity, and both were celebrated with ritual marriages and bonfires.[8] Yet Vickery suggests that Hawthorne's hold-

[8] For example, the materials assembled by G. L. Gomme in *Popular Superstitions*, vol. III, (London, 1884), from *The Gentleman's Magazine Library* ('being a classified collection of the chief contents of *The Gentleman's Magazine* from 1731 to 1868'). Beltane fires are reported on both 1 May and 23 June; dances and garlands are observed on both May Day and St. John's Eve. A poem by Googe (1570) avows the latter custom (pp. 46-62).

The British folklorist Charles Thomas observes, 'There can be little doubt that confusion took place between May-Day and Midsummer, the former, perhaps under influence from Iron Age Gaul and the Romans, becoming primarily a spring festival on the base of the original Beltane [April 30th/ May 1st], the mid-year fires of the Samhain half-year being amalgamated with those at the later mid-summer solstice.' Further confusion was en-ing of the Maypole ritual at Midsummer 'is a covert way of indicating the death of fertility cults as well as of the vegetative deity,' since on the following day 'the sun begins to decline in intensity and power.' The succession of Puritans to Maypole votaries bears this out, since 'the radically different character of [Puritan] worship suggests the destruction of [the Merrymounter's] phallic practices.'

It is sufficient to the aesthetic intentions of this tale to regard Hawthorne's choice of Midsummer's Eve instead of May Eve as his recognition of the tragedy of life's transience. This recognition is not shared by the roisterers around the Maypole. To them, as we have seen, 'May, or her mirthful spirit, dwelt all year round.' They are living as though in the Golden Age, when time was not, or before time was. Even when death comes they do not recognize him. Hawthorne must have felt that the vernal equinox was the most poignant moment to dramatize this conflict between the ethos of Merry Mount—out of time but living a *carpe diem* hedonism—and that of the Puritans, whose thoughts dwelt on eternity but who lived this life without wasting a minute in idleness. (One thinks of the time-eternity tension in 'The Artist of the Beautiful,' the artist of eternity confined to a clockshop.)

Hawthorne nowhere denies that the paganism of Merry Mount can be an efficacious faith. It does place men in sympathetic relation to Nature:

> Spring decked the hallowed emblem with young blossoms and fresh green boughs; Summer brought roses of the deepest blush, and the perfected foliage of the forest; Autumn enriched it with that red and yellow gorgeousness which converts each wildwood leaf into a painted flower; and Winter silvered it with sleet, and hung it round with icicles, till it flashed in the cold sunshine, itself a frozen sun-

couraged by the adoption, in 1752, of the Calendar Act (New Style), which eliminated eleven days in order to co-ordinate the Church year with the solar year. *The Sacrifice* (Studies in the Folk-Lore of Cornwall, No. 2, n. p., 1952), pp. 33-8.

> beam. Thus each alternate season did homage to the Maypole, and paid it a tribute of its own richest splendor.

Nature *is* the realm of those powers attributed to the Maypole, and time, in the realm of Nature, being continuous, is endless. What is in question here is not the actuality of the vegetative power the Maypole symbolizes, but the possibility of human lovers living long under its aegis. When we meet the May Lord and Lady, 'Bright roses . . . were scattered round their feet, or had spontaneously grown there': they actually have the magical power of inducing fecundity in the earth with which ritual endows them. Although Merry Mount is 'a continuous carnival,' this ritual couple is also to be joined in actual marriage. Thus they are assuming mutual responsibilities in a community of two, the minimal society. 'O, Edith, this is our golden time,' cries Edgar, '. . . it may be that nothing of futurity will be brighter than the mere remembrance of what is now passing.' And this is true, as it was true of Adam and Eve:

> Alas, for the young lovers! No sooner had their hearts glowed with real passion than they were sensible of something vague and unsubstantial in their former pleasures, and felt a dreary presentiment of inevitable change. From the moment that they truly loved, they had subjected themselves to earth's doom of care and sorrow, and troubled joy, and had no more a home at Merry Mount.

Then human love dooms them to time's vicissitudes, and exiles them from the merry rout.

We have seen that the marriage ceremony—as well as the ritual coupling—is performed by Blackstone, whom Hawthorne casts (unhistorically) as a bacchic renegade priest. Note that when Endicott discovers them he does not doubt the efficacy of the pagan wedding ceremony; indeed, he completes its final gesture himself, crowning them with the wreath of flowers grown from the forest's sunny floor and from richer English seeds. In the final paragraph, as the wreath drops around their heads, Hawthorne still calls them 'the Lord and Lady of the May.' They retain their ritual identities as well as their own. 'But as their flowery garland was wreathed of the brightest roses that had grown there [at Merry Mount], so, in the tie that united them, were intertwined all the purest and best of their early joys.' Their marriage, though consecrated by a stern Christian hand, was made in their 'golden time,' in their unfallen Eden, and if they 'never wasted one regretful thought' on its 'vanities,' they preserved, in their heavenward journey, through 'the moral gloom of the world' all that was visible of their primal innocence. Though it lead at last to heaven, the origin of love is rooted in the pagan past. The roots of love are so deeply planted in the rites that glorified the world's fecundity, the fructifying power of Nature herself, that to the very end the Christian wife and husband remain the Lady and Lord of the May. Or, to drop Hawthorne's consistent metaphor, the psychological origins of love lie too deep for the Puritan moral sense to thwart or supersede; morality may control love, but love does not originate in the denials which morality requires.

Now I have been speaking not of 'phallic cults' but of love. The focus of the tale is neither exclusively the advent of a new religious dispensation, nor, as Mrs. Leavis avers, the power struggle between the Puritans and the votaries of pleasure. Obviously there *is* a succession, on the level of force, of pagan Maypole worship by Puritan piety. But, as I have just suggested, in no sense does Endicott's band succeed in hewing the roses of their May Day out of the souls of Edgar and Edith. Hawthorne's major theme is neither the supersession of religions nor of cultures; what he does here dramatize is the evolution of self-knowledge in the human soul. In 'The Maypole of Merry Mount' he uses a reconstruction of an improbable historical episode to image forth a perfect objectification for the soul's progress from innocence and delight through recognition of mutability and responsibility to submission to law in order to live in the human community. The law is not perfect, the community is fallen, and though love look not back to its origins it yet bears up to heaven itself the garland that was grown in the 'fresh forest.' The Lord and Lady of May are much nearer grace than is ironclad Endicott, for they never cast out of their souls their kinship with Nature, their capacity to love.

The focus of 'The Maypole of Merry Mount' is then on the love of Edgar and Edith, on the fate of the Lord and Lady of May who are exiled from Paradise by the 'real passion' which makes them subject to time; exiled by the mutual responsibility which makes necessary the assumption of a moral life. This is a love story, and the couple is being married on a day ever famous in folklore, in song, and in verse as a time propitious for love.

Originally this propitiousness to love did derive from the refertilization of the earth through the sacred—and impersonal—marriage of Male and Female principles. In the period with which Hawthorne and we are concerned, however, these anthropomorphic origins had long since undergone a humanization in the folk observance of the holiday. An almost universal rule of cultural change which the ritualistic critics of literature do not often remember is that forms outlast their original functions; forms persist while functions change. By the late Renaissance, although some of the forms of these ancient ceremonies remained in use among the peasantry of Europe, their significations had largely altered from the invocation of tribal or national fecundity to the casting of charms for both harvest and for love. Folklore, more flexible than its ritual origins, is ever responsive to the shaping pressures of cultural change. The traditions collected in Hone's *Every Day Book* show the direction of vestigial pagan ceremonial forms, still retained after centuries of Christianity, toward these ends: ensurance of good harvests, and love on the level of individual fulfillment.[9] This humanization of

[9] Perhaps it is worth remarking that neither Hone nor Strutt—nor their contributors—had Frazer's awareness of the connection between folk customs and the pagan cults of Northern Europe; their ascriptions of paganism are almost invariably to the Roman past, supported by quotations from Ovid and other authors. Contributors to the *Gentleman's Magazine* a few

pagan cult materials is certainly apparent in Hone's poetry selections, particularly in the Maying carol of the hawthorn and in 'Corinna's Going A-Maying,' which Hawthorne could have read there did he not already know Herrick's ceremonial poem of love.

FIVE

There is yet one further dimension in which 'The Maypole of Merry Mount' must be taken. Fogle has remarked that, although the Puritans are closer to reality, and all that Merry Mount possesses is but a dream,

> this dream is not merely one of coarse revelry; it is the dream of play, of art, of imagination. It is fallacious in that the dreamers leave out too much of their whole experience. . . . They imitate and abstract from life without living.

The Puritans, of course, make the opposite error, mistaking 'the burden of life . . . for the whole of reality.'[10]

If I have shunted aside somewhat Mrs. Leavis's interpretation of this tale it is only because I find it more rewarding to approach 'The Maypole' within other contexts in the Hawthorne canon than the political. Among these is the double context which we may term (a) his criticism of the Puritan ethic, and (b) the problem of the artist. Their combination here gives us the problem of the artist in Puritan culture, and applies as well to Hawthorne himself as to his merry mummers. The opposition of Endicott's band to the Maypole crew, it is plain, represents the punitive, repressive Puritan ethos. This spirit always attacks the imaginative freedom which attempts to participate in the aesthetic order of Nature and to imitate, reproduce, or enhance that order in masquerade, mummery, music, song, and dance.

years later in the century began to cite Druidic customs and Scandinavian practices, shoring up a foundation for the Cambridge school to build on. Hawthorne wrote too early to have absorbed ritual theory from the antiquaries available to him.

[10] Fogle, *Hawthorne's Fiction*, pp. 64-5.

The conflict between Puritan repression of the senses and the artist's spiritual freedom is often framed by Hawthorne in these terms. The rebuke of the author's ancestors in 'The Custom House' is but the climactic rendering of an obsessive theme. Their charge against the life of art is the same as that in 'The Maypole': it is an imitation of life, not life itself. Hawthorne's Puritans recognize the daimonic power in art, and confuse it with demonism. They are especially inimical to the artist's freedom to imitate the identity of another moral being without, it would seem, assuming the moral burdens of his model. Now Hawthorne himself was empiricist enough to know the fallacy of this Platonic moralism. His own aesthetic partakes of Aristotle's theory of artistic kinesis even while sending the artist on a transmigratory flight toward the Ideal Butterfly in a realm of Platonic Forms more pure than those in Nature. The achievement of art is itself the fulfillment of an ideal, and, as we learn in 'The Artist of the Beautiful,' once the transcendental ideal of perfection has been clasped, the artist is proof against the time-serving mockers of his enterprise, proof against the violent destruction of his handiwork.

In 'The Maypole of Merry Mount' the votaries of the golden age, as we have seen, dwell, like Owen Warland, among the values of eternity, not those of time. From the romantic idealizations of the May by the poets and antiquaries cited in Hone, and from Governor Bradford's assertions that Morton wrote licentious verses and named his Maypole 'Merry-Mount, as if this jollity would have lasted for ever,' Hawthorne could see the conjunction of all the arts with a long-past time when 'true love and amity was found.' This is a time out of time, an unfallen time when the ideal and the real were one. Although the May Lord and his bride must be expelled from this Eden—although the Eden be destroyed—its roses are imperishably woven into the garland that unites them. The source of the dream of art, like the source of life which the votaries of the Maypole worship, is love. It is true that Merry Mount is insubstantial, a dream.

But that much of Merry Mount as was not mere vanity—the dream of love, of fecundity, of the unity of man and Nature, which in their masquerades and mummings, in their songs and dances, they actually possessed—remains theirs forever. It is true that that possession was incomplete, denying as it did the necessary human obligations on which the Puritans insist. Lucky that Lord and Lady of the May, for theirs was a perfect knowledge, the sum of the two imperfections in which they lived. For them, at least, duty could be superimposed upon the artist's dream of love. They could be doubly joined in ritual and in love, doubly wedded by Bacchus and the iron Puritan, doubly rewarded by their revel at Merry Mount and by their destination in a Christian Heaven.

The folklore of love and the poetic traditions of the May which Hawthorne found in Hone and Strutt must have assumed a lasting and personal significance in his imagination. This dream of perfect love in the artist's eternity was not exhausted by its elaboration in his tale. Perhaps he liked to think of himself as the 'village sport' whose honor it was 'to crown his lass the May-day queen' with a hawthorn wreath. It is certain, at any rate, that when, six years later, he wrote into his journal an encomium of his wife, he called her a 'twin-sister of the Spring,' for 'both have the power to renew and re-create the weary spirit. I have married the Spring!—I am husband to the month of May.'

8

Just Married!—In the Village of Witches

ONE

Another of Hawthorne's newly married couples never had known carefree bliss as Lord and Lady of the May. For Young Goodman Brown, after a proper Puritan upbringing by his father, the deacon, the minister, and Goodwife Cloyse who taught him the catechism, was wedded in Salem village to pretty Faith, with pink ribbons on her cap. Young Goodman has a rendezvous to keep with a stranger in the forest, and although Faith importunes him to 'tarry with me this night . . . of all nights in the year,' he leaves her behind, dissembling his 'evil purpose.' Goodman's 'covenant' is kept with a dark-clad stranger whose staff 'might almost be seen to twist and wriggle itself like a living serpent.' Walking together, they 'might have been taken for father and son.' Reluctantly the youth penetrates the dreary forest where, though 'It was all as lonely as could be . . . the traveller knows not who may be concealed . . . he may yet be passing through an unseen multitude.'

They overtake old Goody Cloyse, who greets the stranger familiarly: 'And is it your worship indeed . . . in the very image of my old gossip, Goodman Brown, the grandfather of the silly fellow that now is.' Her broomstick has been stolen but she's off to the meeting afoot, 'for they tell me there is a nice young man to be taken into communion tonight.' She disappears on the stranger's 'writhing stick,' and a moment later the deacon and minister ride by. 'There is a goodly young woman to be taken into communion,' says the deacon; the minister urges him to 'Spur up,' for 'Nothing can be done, you know, until I get on the ground.' Goodman Brown begins to understand toward what he is 'journeying so deep into the heathen wilderness.'

The rest of the story I shall discuss below, with closer attention to certain details. Brown's destination is a Witches' Sabbath —'of all nights in the year' this must be October 31, All Saints' Eve, and he finds, at a rock altar flanked by blazing pines, all the worthies of Salem in the coven of the Prince of Darkness. At the call, 'Bring forth the converts!' Brown steps forward—'he was himself the chief horror of the scene, and shrank not from its other horrors.' 'Thither came also the slender form of a veiled female.' The Devil addresses them: 'Depending upon one another's hearts, ye still had hoped that virtue were not all a dream. Now are ye undeceived. Evil is the nature of mankind. Evil must be your only happiness. Welcome again, my children, to the communion of your race.' At a natural basin in the rock, 'the shape of evil' dipped his hand and prepared 'to lay the mark of baptism upon their foreheads, that they might be partakers of the mystery of sin.' At this eleventh hour Young Goodman Brown cries in agony and terror, 'Faith! Faith! look up to heaven, and resist the wicked one.'

Young Goodman Brown never knew whether Faith obeyed him. The phantasmagoric tableau vanishes, and he finds himself alone in the dark forest. 'A hanging twig, that had been all on fire, besprinkled his cheek with the coldest dew.' Hawthorne's control of his powerfully ambivalent structural metaphors in this story—the synoptic *enjambement* of journey, initiation, and witchcraft—gives him the authority to ask at the end, without diminution of intensity, 'Had Goodman Brown fallen asleep in the forest and only dreamed a wild dream of a witch-meeting?' The author can even say, 'Be it so if you will; but alas! it was a dream of evil omen for young Goodman Brown.' His life henceforth leads not, like Edgar the May Lord's, toward heaven by a difficult path; his heart has been blighted by this initiation into the coven of evil that binds mankind. 'They carved no hopeful verse upon his tombstone, for his dying hour was gloom.'

This tale is one of Hawthorne's masterpieces, and it has received its share of appreciative comment. Fogle sensitively explicates the delicate balance Hawthorne achieved between ambiguity of implication and clarity of form, while Roy R. Male finds the center of meaning in 'the fact that Faith's ambiguity is the ambiguity of womanhood and . . . the dark night in the forest is essentially a sexual experience, though it is also much more.'[1] My concern is to discover what imaginative possibilities Hawthorne found in his ancestral *donnée* of Salem witchcraft and how he realized them in 'Young Goodman Brown.'

All readers of course acknowledge that the Witches' Sabbath is one of Hawthorne's most memorable dramatizations of man's recognition of evil, and it is often remarked that Hawthorne did not forget that his own great-great-grandfather 'made himself so conspicuous in the martyrdom of the witches, that their blood may fairly be said to have left a stain upon him.' To do justice to Hawthorne's achievement we will do well to take as seriously as he did, for artistic purposes, the role of his Salem forebears in 1692. Speaking of the witch-condemning magistrate and of an earlier Hathorne who had scourged the Quakers, Hawthorne writes in the introductory chapter of *The Scarlet Letter*, 'I, the present writer, as their representative, hereby take shame upon myself for their sakes, and pray that any curse incurred by them —as I have heard, and as the dreary and unprosperous condition of the race, for many a long year back, would argue to exist— may now and henceforth be removed.'

Such a curse was in fact pronounced on Judge Hathorne. 'That God would take vengeance' was the cry of Goodwife Cary's husband, who had been forced to see her tortured and taunted by accusers whose cruelties that magistrate abetted in the names

[1] Fogle, *Hawthorne's Fiction*, pp. 15-32; Male, *Hawthorne's Tragic Vision*, pp. 76-80.

of piety and justice.[2] The curse on the one hand identifies these antecedent Hathornes with the Pyncheons in *The House of the Seven Gables;* but on the other it identifies Nathaniel Hawthorne's sense of inherited guilt, of original sin, with their inhumanities.[3]

When a writer is truly prepossessed by the guilt of his pious ancestors in such affairs, we cannot dismiss the involvement of his fictional characters with curses and witchcraft as merely the Gothic machinery of romance, nor as artistic devices for producing ambiguities. Hawthorne *was* thus prepossessed by the part of his paternal forebears in Salem's season of horror. The zeal of those Puritans to discover satanism in their neighbors became for their descendant an emblem, an allegorical 'type,' of their particular tragic flaw—hypocritical pride. Endicott would serve as 'the Puritan of Puritans' in 'The Maypole,' but his iron rigidity would be manifested elsewhere in Hawthorne's work in contexts yet more destructive of man's capacity for bliss. When the Puritans had dealt with Morton's one dissident colony on the neighboring hill and turned instead upon each other, the consequences of their iron rule blighted both themselves and their posterity. In his historical sketch 'Main Street' Hawthorne without ambiguity presents their triumphs against the heretics and witches who threatened the Puritan commonwealth, and concludes,

> It was impossible for the succeeding race to grow up, in heaven's freedom, beneath the discipline which their gloomy energy of character had established; nor, it may be, have we even yet thrown off all the unfavorable influences, which, among many good ones, were bequeathed us by our Puritan forefathers. Let us thank God for

[2] Nathaniel Cary's letter was printed by Robert Calef in *More Wonders of the Invisible World* (1692), reprinted in Burr, *Narratives of the Witchcraft Cases,* p. 351.

[3] The actual curse pronounced upon the Pyncheons, 'God will give you blood to drink,' were the dying words of Sarah Good to the Rev. Nicholas Noyes of Salem who was present at her execution. Judge Hathorne had committed Sarah Good's four-year-old child to prison, where she was fettered in irons. See Calef in *Narratives,* pp. 345, 358.

having given us such ancestors; and let each successive generation thank Him, not less fervently, for being one step further from them in the march of ages.

The source of that balance between Hawthorne's clarity of design and ambiguity of meaning, which Fogle justly proposes as the key to his achievement, lies in his capacity to present the world of his Puritan forebears through a simultaneous double-exposure. We see old Salem both as they saw it, accepting their values, and as it appears from Hawthorne's very different view. Thus the Puritan values function both as absolutes (to the characters) and as one of several possible choices offered to the reader. Hawthorne so manages this doubleness that he can criticize Puritanism without destroying our suspension of disbelief in its premises. One of these which served his purposes especially well was witchcraft.

'It has also been made a doubt by some,' four New England clergymen wrote in 1689, introducing a book by Cotton Mather which Nathaniel Hawthorne would read, 'whether there are any such things as Witches, *i.e.*, such as by Contract or Explicit Covenant with the Devil, improve, or rather are improved by him to the doing of things strange in themselves and besides their natural Course. But (besides that the Word of God assures us that there have been such, and gives order about them) no Age passes without some apparent Demonstration of it.'[4] Puritanism was perhaps as close to the Manichean as any Christian sect has come; the Power of Evil was acknowledged with the same fervor as the Power of Light. Indeed, it was a faith more pessimistic than that of the ancient dualists, for it made no provision for the goodness of man. The terrifying insecurity of each soul that it was not among the Elect produced those psychological tensions in Puritan culture which set the New England background apart from the heritage of the other colonies. One of those tensions reached the breaking-point in Salem,

[4] *Memorable Providences, Relating to Witchcrafts and Possessions*, reprinted in *Narratives*, p. 95.

where upright, pious citizens like John Hathorne condemned their neighbors to death on evidence no stronger than this:

> These ten . . . did vehemently accuse [Goodwife Cory] of Afflicting them, by Biting, Pinching, Strangling, etc. And they said, they did in their Fits see her likeness coming to them, and bringing a Book for them to Sign; Mr. Hathorne, a Magistrate of Salem, asked her, why she Afflicted those Children? she said, she did not Afflict them; he asked her, who did then? she said, 'I don't know, how should I know?' she said, they were Poor Distracted Creatures, and no heed to be given to what they said; Mr. Hathorn and Mr. Noyes replied that it was the Judgement of all that were there present, that they were bewitched, and only she (the Accused) said they were Distracted; She was Accused by them, that the Black Man whispered to her in her Ear now (while she was upon Examination) and that she had a Yellow Bird, that did use to Suck between her fingers. . . . When the Accused had any motion of their Body, Hands or Mouth, the Accusers would cry out, as when she bit her Lip, they would cry out of being bitten . . . if she stirred her Feet, they would stamp and cry out of Pain there. After the Hearing the said Cory was committed to Salem Prison, and then their crying out of her abated.

The passage is from Calef's *More Wonders of the Invisible World* (1692), a book bitterly critical of the trials.[5] This same woman appears in 'Young Goodman Brown'; Goody Cloyse complains to the Black Man that her broomstick 'hath strangely disappeared, stolen, as I suspect, by that unhanged witch Goody Cory.' (Goody Cloyse, herself indicted for witchcraft, was the sister of two other witches, one whom Mr. Hathorne examined, the other whom he committed.[6])

Hawthorne found two means of taking witchcraft seriously as a way of revealing 'the truths of the human heart.' Accepting the reality of witchcraft as a sin, he would share the Puritans' abhorrence, as unredeemedly damned souls, of all who trafficked

[5] Calef, in *Narratives,* p. 344. That Hawthorne read it we infer from the victims named in 'Main Street, whose sufferings are reported by Calef alone among the chroniclers of Salem.

[6] Ibid. pp. 346-7.

in sortilege and necromancy. In his early story, 'The Hollow of the Three Hills,' a young woman meets a withered witch by such a spot, 'so gray tradition tells,' as was 'once the resort of the Power of Evil and his plighted subjects. . . . in the performance of an impious baptismal rite.' But this woman has long since received the Devil's baptism, and the role of the old witch is to bring to life before her the parents she has dishonored, the husband she has driven mad, the child she has killed. In her crimes against the human heart she, like Ethan Brand, is guilty of the Unpardonable Sin; still capable of remorse, she dies, the final victim of her own enormities. Some of the materials for 'Young Goodman Brown' are touched on here, but by the time Hawthorne conceived the later tale he had devised a far more radical means of employing them.

Suppose Hawthorne, for artistic purposes, to have taken witchcraft at exactly the value his great-great-grandsire put upon it; suppose him to have been able to believe that Goody Cory and others like her had really made covenants with the Black Man; suppose such Accusers as Abigail Williams were factually correct in reporting 'That she saw a great number of Persons in the Village at the Administration of a Mock Sacrament.'[7] What were the logical moral consequences of beliefs such as those Judge Hathorne had acted upon? It is obvious that no one was exempt from suspicion, that the hysterical seizures of the accusers might be produced by the 'spirit' of any member of the colony. Mistress Ann Hibbens, the sister of Governor Bellingham himself, had been executed for a witch in 1656. When the line between the damned witches and the accusing Christians became too fine to draw with certainty, even the avid Cotton Mather had to concede 'that some of those that were concerned grew amazed at the number and condition of those that were accused, and feared that Satan, by his wiles, had entrapped innocent persons under the imputation of that crime; and at last, as

[7] Calef, in *Narratives*, pp. 345-6.

was evidently seen, there must be a stop put, or the generation of the kingdom of God would fall under condemnation.'[8]

Suppose, then, that an innocent young Puritan, newly married, as yet unaware of his taint of original sin, should leave his faith just long enough, on one night, to follow the dark stranger into the forest—and find there the Witches' Sabbath where those who took the Devil's communion were all the members of his daylight world of piety. Hawthorne takes witchcraft more seriously, in fact, than had John Hathorne or Cotton Mather, for unlike them he does not flinch to acknowledge the covenant of the fallen nature of all mankind. Magistrate Hathorne seems not to have recanted or repented after the general amnesty, as did a more distinguished judge, Samuel Sewall. John Hathorne would seem to have made no connection between the state of his own soul in God's sight and his responsibility, say, for the sufferings of Giles Cory, whose wife he had committed for witchcraft. Cory, also accused and seeing that none had been cleared by trial, 'chose to undergo what Death they would put him to . . . [The sentence was pressing, *peine forte et dure*]. His Tongue being prest out of his Mouth, the Sheriff with his Cane forced it in again when he was dying.'[9] No, Nathaniel Hawthorne could accept the guilt of alleged witches only as their individual share of the guilt of mankind. He must accept also the guilt of their accusers and tormentors. 'Young Goodman Brown' is one of his expiations for John Hathorne's guilt, as well as for his own.

Not only an expiation but a judgment upon his fathers, too. For what Young Goodman Brown learns at the Witches' Sabbath, while it is a knowledge more profound than that of the zealots who did the devil's work in 1692, is still but a partial knowledge. It is too incomplete to win him wisdom or happiness. He is so blinded by perception of evil that his life is ever after blighted. In this he is true to the Puritan past, as Haw-

[8] Mather, *Magnalia Christi Americana*, Book VI, chap. lxxxii.
[9] Calef, in *Narratives*, p. 367.

thorne envisaged it. In the struggle between jollity and gloom, Young Goodman Brown would seem to have had no choice. On his return to Salem he finds his wife Faith 'gazing anxiously forth, and bursting into such joy at the sight of him that she skipped along the street and almost kissed her husband before the whole village.' This would have been, for Brown, but to deepen their 'stain of guilt' in the eyes of their fellow-hypocrites. 'Goodman Brown looked sternly and sadly into her face, and passed on without a greeting.'

This tale, like 'The Maypole of Merry Mount,' presents the symbolistic development of details elaborated from within a frame of allegory. The names of the couple are as allegorical as any in Bunyan: The Puritan Everyman is the husband of Christian Faith. By the end of the tale he proves more Puritan than Christian, renouncing her larger vision for the 'distrustful,' 'desperate,' 'gloom' of his life and death. Faith, too, had been at the Witches' Sabbath; she can accept man even with full knowledge of his evil nature. But Goodman lacks her largesse, her charity, her balance. 'Often, awaking suddenly at midnight, he shrank from the bosom of Faith; . . . when the family knelt down at prayer, he scowled and muttered to himself, and gazed sternly at his wife, and turned away.' Faith remains true to him —she follows his 'hoary corpse' to the grave, but he has indeed been damned by his night among the witches.

TWO

The singular quality of Young Goodman Brown's adventure is the intensity with which the dramatic, theological, psychological, and cultural dimensions of the tale are fused together in the single structural metaphor of his journey into the dark forest and his return to the daylight world. Traditions of witchcraft served Hawthorne's complex purposes with extraordinary precision in each of these dimensions of meaning. If 'Young Goodman Brown' is the most profound work of fiction drawing on those traditions in American writing,[10] one reason for this is that Hawthorne knew better than any author of his century what the traditions signified or could be made to signify. The interest in Salem withcraft of James Russell Lowell, for instance, or of Professor Kittredge, proves to be merely preliminary to an attempt to exculpate their Puritan ancestors from the opprobrium of history.[11] Hawthorne, as we have seen, had the courage to recognize the cosmic irony of the situation in which innocent, charitable Christians were tortured to death by the ministers and magistrates of God's chosen people. But it is not only his tragic sense of the family connection that makes witchcraft a masterful metaphor in Hawthorne's tale. From his wide study of witchcraft and of the witchcraft trials came the materials he fused into the multiplex pattern of 'Young Goodman Brown': from the self-righteous accounts by zealots like Increase and Cotton Mather, the caustic attack upon them by Robert Calef, the records in the Essex County Courthouse, as well as from Hawthorne's awareness of oral traditions concerning witchcraft and of treatments of the subject in literature by Cervantes, Goethe, and Irving. The peculiar significances of this story are

[10] For a survey of 'New England Witchcraft in Fiction' see G. H. Orians, *American Literature,* II (March 1930), 54-71.

[11] Lowell, in his essay 'Witchcraft,' occasioned by the publication in 1867 of *Salem Witchcraft* by Charles W. Upham, echoes that historian in averring that 'The proceedings of the Salem trials are sometimes spoken of as though they were exceptionally cruel. But, in fact, if compared with others of the same kind, they were exceptionally humane . . . it is rather wonderful that no mode of torture other than mental was tried at Salem. . . . all died protesting their innocence. . . . though an acknowledgment of guilt would have saved the lives of all [sic]. This martyr proof of the efficacy of Puritanism in the character and conscience may be allowed to outweigh a great many sneers at Puritan fanaticism.' Lowell cites the case of Goody Cary to prove that 'The accused . . . were not abandoned by their friends. In all the trials of this kind there is nothing so pathetic as the picture of [Nathaniel] Cary holding up the weary arms of his wife . . . and wiping away the sweat from her brow and the tears from her face.' Of Mr. Hathorne's retort he says nothing. *Among My Books* (Boston, 1882), pp. 146-7.

See G. L. Kittredge, *Witchcraft in Old and New England* (Cambridge, Mass., 1922), pp. 362-5.

rooted in the cultural significances of witchcraft itself. This we can see by examining a schematic statement of the way his structural metaphor served Hawthorne. We can trace the elaboration in his tale of the several kinds of meaning associated by long tradition with witchcraft and the Witches' Sabbath.

Hawthorne's protagonist takes a journey, away from daylight, reality, piety, and Faith. Traveling through darkness he is guided by the Satanic image of his own father (and grandfather) toward an initiation into both forbidden knowledge and a secret cult. The ceremony of initiation is a ritual representing the spiritual inversion of Christianity (the rock 'altar,' the trees ablaze like both 'hell-kindled torches' and 'candles' at an evening meeting,' and the 'mark of baptism' which the Devil is about to place on their foreheads). The forbidden knowledge in whose name the Devil-Father welcomes Brown and Faith 'to the communion of your race' is not only knowledge of man's evil nature generally, but knowledge specifically of original sin, represented by the welcoming spirit of Brown's father among the fiends as well as by the Devil's having assumed his father's form. It is also carnal knowledge, sexual sin. As we have seen, however, Faith is in the forest too; in one sense she *is* the forest, and Brown has qualified for admission to the witches' orgy by having carnal knowledge of her. (In another sense, however, which is ever equally valid in the tale, Faith transcends Brown's knowledge of evil with all-encompassing love.) In rejecting her love after his initiation, Brown is guilty of that Manichean prepossession with the dark side of man's nature which Hawthorne presents as the special sin of the Puritans. Each of these suggestions is a characteristic feature of the traditional attitudes toward witchcraft.

In the Salem trial records it is apparent that belief in witches was held on two different levels of conception by the seventeenth-century Puritans in New England.[12]

[12] An acquaintance with the British and Continental literature on the subject shows that these two types of belief were characteristic of Christian

On the one hand there is the belief of the Accusers. What, in fact, did such witnesses as those who testified against Goody Cory offer as evidence of her guilt? That she afflicted them, made them sick, caused them to itch or to vomit, afflicted their livestock, caused shipwrecks at sea, wrought havoc with their silverware, invisibly caused solid objects to move, had intercourse with devils, suckled her familiar at a hidden teat on her body. Such charges as these recur innumerably in the long annals of witchcraft. They led Professor Kittredge to regard as the basis of witchcraft the belief that human beings can with supernatural powers wreak harm and destruction on their enemies.

The second type of belief in witches is of a different sort. The Black Sabbath in 'Young Goodman Brown' may stand as representative of the more highly organized, conceptual regard for witchcraft as the involvement of the witches in a religious cult which rivals Christianity. Indeed, it is a sect which threatens the Christian commonwealth with destruction. Consequently the witches are not content with the expression of personal malice; nor are they merely individuals who have made solitary compacts with the Devil. They are organized into covens, the Devil or one of his minions is their acknowledged priest and leader, they hold services which are horrible and blasphemous parodies of the Christian Mass, and the working of their will is one of the trials with which God in His Almighty Wisdom has decreed that the Faith of the Christian Commonwealth shall be tried on earth.

This sophisticated intellectual conception is in fact a development of medieval theology, which took for granted the identity of the sorcerers and necromancers mentioned in the Bible with the witches discovered in contemporary Christendom. The

attitudes toward witchcraft since the Middle Ages. In no way was the experience of Salem uniquely a Colonial American phenomenon; indeed, much has been made by Kittredge and other writers of the comparative mildness of the American epidemic when seen in the context of English, Scottish, French, German, or Scandinavian experience.

prodigious learning of Increase and Cotton Mather, both of whose works on witchcraft Hawthorne studied, reflects their intimate familiarity with a large corpus of theological literature on witchcraft. The authoritative compendium of orthodox theological opinion on this subject is the *Malleus Maleficarum* of Henricus Institoris (1489). The arguments quoted above in favor of belief in witchcraft, offered exactly two centuries later by Cotton Mather and his four sponsors, are contained in the answer to the first Question in *Malleus.* Kittredge, whose *Witchcraft in Old and New England* lists the prolific theological discussion of the problem on both sides of the Atlantic, concludes that

> the orgies of the Witches' Sabbath [were] systematized in the fourteenth and fifteenth centuries by the scholastic ingenuity of devout theologians and described in confessions innumerable wrung by torture from ignorant and superstitious defendants in response to leading questions framed by inquisitors who had the whole system in mind before the trial began.[13]

To support this theory Kittredge suggests that the Church, from its first concern with witchcraft, regarded the practice as heretical. Since the Church had had long experience with the perpetration of other heresies—Manichaean, Paulician, Catharian, Waldensian—in each instance of which there was a rival religious organization, when the medieval theologians turned their attention to witchcraft their speculation followed long-established dogmatic practice.[14]

In 'Young Goodman Brown' Hawthorne makes effective use

[13] Op. cit., p. 243.

[14] 'In the course of the fourteenth century the papal inquisitors discovered (so they thought) a new heretical sect—the sect of devil-worshipping witches. These, it logically followed, must hold meetings, and such meetings must resemble those of other heretics. . . . The idea of a Sabbath of Witches was neither ancient nor of popular origin. It was a mere transference. What was already established in the inquisitorial mind with regard to the Satanic Synagogue of the Cathari was shifted, as a matter of logical course, to the alleged assemblies of the new heretical sect, the devotees of witchcraft.' *Witchcraft in Old and New England,* p. 246.

of both sets of beliefs. He employs the theological conceptualization of witchcraft as the cult of the Antichrist for the architecture of his tale, and he uses several folk beliefs (not necessarily dependent upon the foregoing) for verisimilitude of detail and for the evocation of wonder, awe, and terror. The compact with the Black Man, the Devil's shape-shifting and his serpentine staff, the transportation of witches by means of magical ointments and broomsticks, their existence as disembodied spirits, the withering of living things at the witches' or Devil's touch, are motifs of folk belief often encountered independently of the Witches' Sabbath. Yet the theological construct had by the late seventeenth century passed into popular tradition, since such notorious cases as the trials of the Lancashire witches in 1612 had been celebrated in unnumbered chapbooks, black-letter ballads, popular narratives, and literary works. Consequently some of the informants (like Abigail Williams) averred that they had witnessed Black Masses and the ceremonial partaking of the evil sacrament by the neighbors they accused.

Hawthorne thus is able to take advantage of the idea—by Puritan times both theological and popular—that witchcraft represents forbidden knowledge, and that its attainment takes the form of an initiatory ceremonial, a Witches' Sabbath. In folklore the two strains of witchcraft and demonology merged in this ceremony, where the witch sold his soul to the Devil. Hawthorne quotes almost verbatim from Cotton Mather's *Wonders of the Invisible World* when he tells us that Faith stepped forward to receive the Devil's baptism beside 'Martha Carrier, who had received the devil's promise to be queen of hell.'[15]

The theological level of 'Young Goodman Brown' is greatly strengthened by the youth's horrified recognition that the form of his father seems to beckon him toward the unholy communion. This is itself a dreamlike duplication of the first appearance of the Black Man in the forest, for when Goodman walked

[15] Burr, *Narratives*, p. 144.

beside him 'they might have been taken for father and son.' The paternal image is reduplicated yet again when Goody Cloyse greets 'The devil! . . . Yes, truly it is, and in the very image of my old gossip, Goodman Brown, the grandfather of the silly fellow that now is.' She of course is using *gossip* in its original sense of *God-sib*—'A person spiritually related to another through being a sponsor at a baptism.' This is to say that Goodman Brown's grandfather had taken Goody Cloyse to her first witch meeting. The tripling of generations in Brown's family who have taken the Devil's Mass reinforces the theological conception of witchcraft as one of Satan's entrapments of the human soul. Our original sin makes us vulnerable.

The inference is unmistakeable that Old Brown had had carnal knowledge of Goody Cloyse, and that it was through such carnal knowledge that her initiation was completed. Young Goodman's bitter rejection of Faith after his return to the 'real' world supports the inference that it was through his knowledge of her that he made acquaintance with the Black Man in the first place. He is reliving the Puritan allegory of the Fall, in which woman, as Governor Endicott warned the May Lord, is 'that sex which requireth the stricter discipline.' But if woman is the agent of the Fall, for Young Goodman Brown that Fall is anything but fortunate, for it fails to prepare the way for his salvation.

The forbidden knowledge, then, is sexual knowledge and its attendant guilt. Its possession forces Brown to recognize that all the antecedent generations of his name have also sinned as he has sinned. If the procreative act is sinful, then all mankind is indeed knit together in the Devil's skein: 'Evil is the nature of mankind. Evil must be your only happiness.'

The association of witchcraft itself with sexuality, debauchery, and carnal abandon is an aspect of popular tradition of which Hawthorne shows his empathetic understanding. The evidence of modern anthropological scholarship strongly suggests that witchcraft perpetuated the same fertility cult religion which survived also in the folk rituals observing the seasonal festivals. 'The only essential difference between these two kinds of rites is that, while the popular fertility rites were carried out publicly with the whole village participating, the witches' sabbaths were carried out in secret, at night, and were participated in only by witches and wizards who were initiated into the secret art.'[16] In the *Malleus Maleficarum* witches are said to copulate with devils, to impair the power of generation, and to deprive man of his virile member. Such ecclesiastical negation of their influence on fecundity argues that the witches themselves claimed exactly the contrary power.

Since the association of witchcraft with fertility is rooted in the rites performed to invoke increase, the connection is maintained most strongly where witches are thought of as members of a sect performing communal rituals. Contrarily, when popular belief regards the witch as merely an individual malefactor, the connection with sexual abundance withers in the popular mind. The latter is the stage in which New England tradition for the most part conceived of the witches. Although there is sporadic mention of witch meetings among travellers' accounts of the seventeenth century[17] and although some of the Salem Accusers spoke of witch meetings, the notion of the witch most generally held was that of the malicious woman who uses the limitless infernal powers bestowed on her by the Prince of Darkness—to

[16] Runeberg, *Witches, Demons, and Fertility Magic*, p. 241. Runeberg suggests that witchcraft in its modern form emerged when the pagan magicians and the Catharian cultists were driven to join forces by inquisitorial persecution.

[17] For example, John Josselyn (1675) reported how Mr. Foxwell, sailing a shallop off Cape Ann at night, heard 'loud voices from the shore, calling Foxwell, Foxwell, come a shore . . . upon the Sands they saw a great fire, and Men and Women hand in hand dancing about it in a ring, after an hour or two they vanished . . .' Landing by daylight 'he found the footing of Men, Women and Children shod with shoes; and an infinite number of brand-ends thrown up by the water but neither *Indian* nor *English* could be met with on the shore, nor in the woods. . . . *There are many stranger things in the world, than are to be seen between London and Stanes.*' Quoted in Dorson, *Jonathan Draws the Long Bow* (Cambridge, 1946), pp. 26-7.

prevent the farmer's butter or annoy her neighbors' cows.[18] By the end of the eighteenth century the idea of the coven drops out of recorded beliefs; oral traditions, as Hawthorne heard them, would elaborate the simple motifs of transformation, malice, the magic weapon, and the afflicted crone which he knew from a poem he praised—'The Country Lovers' (1795) by his friend Thomas Green Fessenden:

> . . . a witch, in shape of owl,
>   Did steal her neighbor's geese, sir,
> And turkeys too, and other fowl,
>   When people did not please her.
>
> And how a man, one dismal night,
>   Shot her with silver bullet,
> And then she flew straight out of sight
>   As fast as she could pull it.
>
> How Widow Wunks was sick next day,
>   The parson went to view her,
> And saw the very place, they say,
>   Where forsaid ball went through her! [19]

Nonetheless in 'Young Goodman Brown' the projection of witchcraft as sexual knowledge is arrestingly clear. It is true that much of the traditional imagery of witchcraft is easily susceptible of carnal interpretation—the serpentine staff, flying, the leaping flames—but Hawthorne manages his descriptions so skillfully that the phallic and psychosexual associations are made

[18] Dorson gives some sixty instances of such witchcraft beliefs in nineteenth-century New England, *Jonathan Draws the Long Bow,* pp. 33-47. See also Clifton Johnson, *What They Say in New England* (Boston, 1896), pp. 235-60; John Greenleaf Whittier, *The Supernaturalism of New England* (London, 1847), pp. 49-55, 62-3.

[19] For folk provenience of the belief that only a silver bullet can kill a witch, see Whittier, *Supernaturalism of New England,* p. 49; Johnson, *What They Say in New England,* p. 240; Dorson, pp. 40-41; for the transference of the wound from the witch's animal to her human form, see Whittier, pp. 52, 63; Johnson, pp. 238, 239, 260; Dorson, pp. 35-6. These references span the entire nineteenth century.

intrinsic to the thematic development of his story. The Puritan focus of the tale brings out with special clarity the inherent sexual character of Young Goodman's quest. Brown's whole experience is described as the penetration of a dark and lonely way through a branched forest—to the Puritans, the Devil's domain. At journey's end is the orgiastic communion amidst the leaping flames. Along the way, when Young Goodman abandons himself to the Devil, he 'grasp[ed] his staff and . . . seemed to fly along the forest path . . . rushing onward with the instinct that guides mortal man to evil.' Where, if in neither the Salem trial records nor in contemporary traditions of witch lore, did Hawthorne find the connection between witchcraft and sexuality that becomes one of the important cruces of his story?

The answer can only be in Hawthorne's reading of European writings which presented witchcraft in a different aspect from his American sources. We know that he was intimately familiar with Goethe's *Faust*,[20] and that he had read *El colloquio de los perros* of Cervantes in the Spanish. These works include two of the most important imaginative treatments of witchcraft. In *Faust*, Part I, after witnessing the disgusting orgies of Walpurgisnacht, Faust is given the witches' potion by Mephistopheles and immediately turns into a goatish lecher. In Cervantes he found a detailed enumeration of witch beliefs that extended the moral and theological implications of Goethe's treatment. The witch Canizares, mistaking one of the dogs for the son of another witch, pours out to him a long monologue revealing her own witchcraft. We know Hawthorne to have read this one of *Los novelas ejemplares*, for when, in 'Young Goodman Brown,' Goody Cloyse meets the Devil, they exchange a recipe for flying ointment: an application of 'juice of smallage, and cinquefoil, and wolf's bane—Mingled with fine wheat and the fat of a newborn babe' gives the witch the gift of flight. It has been observed

[20] Hawthorne mentions Goethe in 'A Virtuoso's Collection.' His dependence on Goethe for the theme of the Devil's Compact is proposed by William Bysshe Stein, *Hawthorne's Faust* (Gainesville, Fla., 1953).

that Hawthorne used this identical recipe a year later (July 1836) in a magazine he edited, and here he added a comment which shows that he knew exactly what he was doing with his witches in 'Young Goodman Brown':

> Cervantes, in one of his tales, seems of the opinion that the ointment cast them into a trance, during which they merely dreamt of holding intercourse with Satan. If so, witchcraft differs little from nightmare.[21]

But Cervantes provided Hawthorne with more than the recipe for flying salve and the equating of witchcraft with nightmare, important as these are in 'Young Goodman Brown.' The old witch in *El colloquio de los perros* tells the dog,

> We go to meet [our lord and master] in a large field that is a long way from here. There we find a huge throng of people, made up of witches and wizards . . . we gorge ourselves with food, and other things happen which . . . I should not dare tell you as they are so filthy and loathesome that they would be an offense to your chaste ears . . . Vice becomes second nature and witchcraft is something that enters into our blood and bones. It is marked by a great ardor, and at the same time it lays such a chill upon the soul as to benumb its faith and cause it to forget its own well-being, so that it no longer remembers the terrors with which God threatens it nor the glories of Heaven that he holds out to it.
>
> In short, seeing that it is a sin that is concerned with carnal pleasure, it must of necessity deaden, stupefy, and absorb the senses . . . I see and understand everything, but carnal pleasure keeps my will enchained, and I always have been and always shall be evil.[22]

21 'Witch Ointment,' from *The American Magazine*, reprinted in Arlin Turner, *Hawthorne as Editor* (University, La., 1941), p. 253. See Fanny N. Cherry, 'The Sources of Hawthorne's "Young Goodman Brown,"' *American Literature*, V (Jan. 1934), 342-8. Another source of the formula was Bacon, *Sylva Sylvarum* X, 975. Hawthorne's recipe corresponds roughly to the first of three formulae in Margaret Murray, *The Witch Cult of Western Europe* (Oxford, 1921), with the addition of baby fat from the third. Miss Murray had these tested by A. J. Clark, an analytical chemist, who reported that aconite (wolf's bane) and hemlock (smallage) would in fact produce the illusion of flight (pp. 100-105, 279-80).

22 Cervantes, *Three Exemplary Novels*, transl. by Samuel Putnam (New York, 1950), pp. 186, 189.

Hawthorne, too, would send his Goodman Brown to a nightmare-meeting of carnal pleasure and universal sexual guilt. The youth's acceptance of fleshly ardor lays a chill upon his soul, benumbs his faith, and alienates him from the glories of Heaven. When the Devil welcomes Goodman and his bride to the communion of the damned, he endows them with the power to know the secret sins of 'all whom ye have reverenced from youth'; and these are sins of sexual passion—adultery, murder of mates, of babes born out of wedlock. To know such sins as these, the Devil tells them, is 'your nature and your destiny.'

The lore of witchcraft thus served Hawthorne well, connecting 'the communion of the race' superstitiously with the Devil's Compact, psychologically with sexual knowledge and guilt, theologically with evil and original sin, and culturally with acceptance of the past. Young Goodman's journey resembles Robin's search for his kinsman, but the fertility rites he celebrates are a bitter parody not only of the Christian sacraments but of the pagan paradise of 'The Maypole of Merry Mount.' His Fall from innocence is unredeemed, as we have seen, by his incapacity to return Faith's love. Like Aylmer in 'The Birthmark,' he had to have perfection—or nothing. In his sense of his own sin, then, Young Goodman is self-deceived. For it is not his implication in sexual sin which damns him, but his Puritan misanthropy, his unforgiving lovelessness, his lack of faith in Faith. She, as both his mortal wife and his *ange blanche,* had, like him, appeared before the Font of Evil. She is in fact the Devil's only antagonist in this tale, for are not all the Puritans—preachers, teachers, catechists and all—roaring about in the orgiastic coven? They have all taken the Black Man's black bread; Faith alone has such faith in man that she can transcend the revelation that he is fallen. But Young Goodman Brown, like his own fathers, like Goody Cloyse and all of Salem, like Hawthorne's distinguished ancestors too, really believed in witches, rather than in men. And so he joylessly became one.

9

Hester's Double Providence: The Scarlet Letter and the Green

ONE

Hawthorne seems never to mention the imagination without invoking images of supernatural power. In 'Feathertop' the imagination is compared to witchcraft, in 'The Snow Image' to magic, in 'The Devil in Manuscript' to demonism. Although invocation of the Muse was out of fashion when Hawthorne wrote his romances, in his prefaces he performed a somewhat similar rite. In each he attempts to define the nature of his imaginative faculty. And in each he sets forth the difficulties in the way of its exercise upon the materials of reality. These difficulties he felt to be especially acute in his American climate of rationality, skepticism, and literal-mindedness. The preface to *The Scarlet Letter* is no brief foreword, but the fifty-page sketch of 'The Custom-House.' Its primary reason for being is to lead the reader backwards in time, away from the dull commonplaceness of the present toward the past in which the imagination can illuminate reality with a glow like moonlight or firelight. What Hawthorne seeks is 'a neutral territory, somewhere between the real world and fairy-land, where the Actual and the Imaginary may meet, and each imbue itself with the nature of the other.' There, he says, 'Ghosts might enter . . . without affrighting us.'

Only by the exercise of psychological distance from fact could Hawthorne create his neutral territory. While in the Custom

House, his imagination was but 'a tarnished mirror.' In bringing to life 'the figures with which I did my best to people it' he found the intermixture of the supernatural with the real an artistic necessity. For the very reason that the contemporary attitude toward art and its essential myths seemed typified by the scorn of Peter Hovendon (in 'The Artist of the Beautiful') or by the unfeeling insensitivity of the hardware merchant (in 'The Snow Image'), the creation of myth seemed all the more urgent to Hawthorne. One must question F. O. Matthiessen's judgment that 'Hawthorne . . . did not conceive of his work in any relation to myth. He did not seek for universal analogies, but gained his moral profundity by remaining strictly a provincial and digging where he was.'[1] At the lower levels of imaginative intensity his predilection towards myth is apparent enough. Granting that such juvenile books as *Tanglewood Tales, A Wonder Book,* and *Grandfather's Chair* were but hack work, we nonetheless observe that Hawthorne chose as his subjects the making plausible of Greek myths and, as in his early tales, the making mythical of Colonial history.

When we turn to Hawthorne's American romances we shall find that they are indeed conceived in relation to myths. Some of the mythic elements will be those which we have already discovered in his tales. In the romances as in the shorter fiction, his images of unfallen paganism, of the universal community of witchcraft, of the self-transforming native character, are combined with other elements not the results of provincial experience. Where these three themes had often furnished Hawthorne with the major concepts for his tales, in the romances they are more often used as ancillaries to the dominant tensions. They provide him with three culturally sanctioned traditions upon which to draw in delineating his characters and their symbolic roles.

In *The Scarlet Letter* the folklore of the supernatural is peculiarly appropriate to the development of Hawthorne's con-

[1] *American Renaissance,* pp. 630-31.

flicts. The romance itself may be said to be based upon yet another myth, if we may consider as myth the Puritan doctrine which it is the fate of Hester, Dimmesdale, and Chillingworth to test. In his re-creation of Puritan society in this book, Hawthorne, as we have already observed, takes pains to include superstition and witchcraft among the articles of popular belief. In fact the moral universe of *The Scarlet Letter* contains both the diabolical otherworld of 'Young Goodman Brown' and the pagan paradise of Merry Mount. These supernatural realms are metaphorically and inferentially significant, but the locale of the action, unlike that in these shorter tales, is literally the life of this world. Merry Mount was an Eden before the Fall, the Witches' Sabbath seemed a dream, but Governor Bellingham's Boston, with jail and scaffold at its very center, represents the actual world. It is just such a world through which the lovers expelled from Merry Mount would have to follow a 'difficult path,' though heaven be their destination.

The May-day paradise of Hester Prynne and Arthur Dimmesdale has been blasted and they expelled before the story of *The Scarlet Letter* begins. When we revisit the scene of what the Puritans called their sin but what the author terms their 'crime,' we are again in the forest. This was the site of both the Maypole and the witches' revels. The imagery of paganism and of witchcraft picks up these supernatural associations in *The Scarlet Letter*. Among a people to whom 'religion and law were almost identical,' superstition proves surprisingly nearer than dogma to spiritual truth.

While these uses of pagan and witchcraft belief are allusive and imagistic, there is yet a further role played by superstition in *The Scarlet Letter*. For his most characteristic device of style —which is to say, his way of looking at experience—Hawthorne took advantage of the folk tradition of the wonder. He makes the letter itself a supernatural providence; yet instead of evoking allegorical certitude it produces ambiguity on every side. Its significance is established by the conflicting testimony of several eye-witnesses. Popular tradition believes them all. Hawthorne's reliance upon the alternative interpretations which oral tradition gives to supernatural wonders proves to be a structural principle essential to his conception of *The Scarlet Letter.*

TWO

In Hawthorne's romance the scarlet letter itself serves as the controlling symbol of our thought, continually raising and defining problems which its inflicters did not acknowledge to exist. Those Puritan judges, sincerely pious but tragically restricted in their understanding of the soul, are unwittingly guilty of a sin more grievous than Hester's own. For they have taken it into their prideful hearts to pass absolute judgment upon a fellow-being, and to construct, for the supposed benefit of their own holy community, a man-made remarkable providence in imitation of God's wonders. Recalling Increase Mather's definition of the genre, we recognize Hester's 'A' as among the 'Remarkable Judgements upon noted Sinners' which comprised one of the varieties of his *Illustrious Providences.*

But if the Puritans in Hawthorne's romance are unaware of their own pride in presuming to judge Hester as God judges her, we are enabled to see their inadequacies as the letter works its influence in ways they had not dreamed. Not only that, but God Himself has passed a 'Remarkable Judgement' upon Hester. This judgment His zealous communicants are too blind to recognize, although it is just as plainly visible as the ignominy with which they brand her. For the actual 'Remarkable Providence' which God has brought about as a living emblem of Hester's sin is revealed in the same opening scene in which we first see the scarlet letter. Hester appears on the scaffold bearing her child in her arms: it is soon manifest that in the allegorical scheme of this romance, Pearl = 'A.'

It is through its similitude with Pearl that the scarlet letter can become endowed with life. Indeed, it seems to have a life of its own, as we shall see, in which the letter changes its relationship to the other characters as well as its meanings in itself.

But such a fluidity of meaning is of course intolerable in allegory. Hawthorne's artistic method is to use allegory to destroy the absolute certitude of the allegorical mind: by offering several certainties which any given phenomenon, wonder, or providence may be believed to represent, and by attributing to each of these alternatives a tenable claim to absolute belief, Hawthorne undermines the dogmatic monism of allegory itself. His reliance upon the folklore of providences as well as the theological absolutes of Puritanism made available to him the resources of this 'formula of alternative possibilities,' as Yvor Winters has termed it. Its first occurrence in *The Scarlet Letter* concerns the interpretation of a wild rose which has sprouted at the threshold of the first structure erected by the Puritans in the new colony—a prison:

> This rose-bush, by a strange chance, has been kept alive in history; but whether it had merely survived out of a stern old wilderness, so long after the fall of the gigantic pines and oaks that originally overshadowed it,—or whether, as there is fair authority for believing, it had sprung up under the footsteps of the sainted Ann Hutchinson, as she entered the prison-door,—we shall not take upon us to determine.

We note that the choice is unresolved between a botanical happenstance and a Divine providence—ironically, from the Puritan view, linking Hester to the heretical Mrs. Hutchinson and connecting both with a saint's legend.

This style seems indubitably Hawthorne's own. Its salient feature is the skeptical offering of the multiple meanings, each borne aloft by the clause of a rather formal periodic sentence. The tone of this style is curiously both detached and committed, both amused and serious, both dubious and affirmative. Its commitment, seriousness, and affirmation, however, all point to something other than the literal content of its assertions; toward *that* the style indicates detachment, amused tolerance, dubiety. What is seriously affirmed is that *something* was signified by the rose-bush. But the very presence, uncontradicted, of both alternatives quite compromises our willingness to believe unreservedly in either. Yet again, the fact that both are possible deters us from dismissing either one. Hawthorne uses his device of multiple choices to affirm neither the absolute claims of Puritan dogma nor the absolute claims of right reason. What it does affirm is, as one would expect of Hawthorne, a multiple truth larger than either of the partial truths offered by its alternatives: the world of fact *is* an hieroglyph of the spirit, and the language of the spirit is beyond the capacity of either unassisted belief or unassisted reason to read aright. Perhaps its reading requires the collaboration of both the intellect and the passions.

How did Hawthorne invent, or where derive, his most characteristic stylistic device? Here is another instance of the alternative possibilities offered the reader to explain a supernatural event. The subject of this passage is Sir William Phips, Royal Governor of Massachusetts during the witchcraft trials in 1692, who rose to wealth through the discovery of buried treasure:

> It was reported, that he had dreamed where the galleon was laid. Whether his extraordinary spirit of enterprise, led him to undertake the search of the wreck, and taking advantage of the delusive spirit of the times, he pretended to the favour of a vision which he never had, in order to procure assistance in an undertaking which a rational calculation might not render worthy of the hazard attending it; or whether having placed his imagination upon the scheme, his mind embraced the object in an agreeable manner when he was asleep, or whether there was a divine special influence in his favour, is not yet detached.

Hawthorne twice wrote of Phips [2] but the passage just quoted is not by him. It was published nine years before his birth in a book from which he mentions having taken the motif of 'The Great Carbuncle' (1837). The account of that Indian legend is skeptically dismissed, as a chimaera practised upon the gullible

[2] *Works,* XII, 227-34; IV, 484-92.

Puritans, on the page immediately preceding the account of Sir William's treasure-laden dream. James Sullivan, in his *History of the District of Maine* (Boston, 1795), reflects the rationalism of his time in the presentation of all such wonders of the invisible world. As for witchcraft, he is proud to avow that the sensible settlers of Maine had no use for that delusion which so painfully afflicted their brethren in Massachusetts. And yet for all his liberality and rationality, Sullivan cannot bring himself wholly to dismiss the possibilities of religious supernaturalism, although he is openly scornful of what he takes to be mere superstition.

I do not suggest that Hawthorne modelled his style on Sullivan's, but that the similarities in their treatment of marvels indicate a like cast of mind. Hawthorne, too, inclines toward rational skepticism; yet even more than the historian of Maine, he is unwilling to give all to reason and so deny the supernatural portent whose existence proves for him the reality of the world of spiritual truths. Indeed, in his presentation of wonders Hawthorne made them as plausible as possible, as though to emphasize the partial claims of both reason and belief. Just as he studied the wonders reported by the Puritan chroniclers, he did research too on the scientific explanations of extraordinary phenomena. In September 1837 he had borrowed Sir David Brewster's *Letters on Natural Magic* (London, 1832) from the Salem Athenaeum. This study gave explanations from the sciences of acoustics, optics, mechanics, chemistry, and medicine of such illusions as ghostly apparitions, spectral sounds, phantom ships, etc. —the very sorts of phenomena which Increase and Cotton Mather had so diligently collected from eye-witnesses a century and a half earlier. It may have been Brewster's dedication to Sir Walter Scott and his mention of Scott's *Letters on Demonology and Witchcraft* which led Hawthorne a week later to borrow that book, the most comprehensive and interpretive history of superstititon he had read.

The final and definitive use in *The Scarlet Letter* of this treatment of the illustrious providence offers no less than four alternatives to the meaning of the most remarkable wonder in the book. The passage is so important that it must be quoted at some length; Dimmesdale has just mounted the scaffold, confessed himself Hester's love, and torn the ministerial garment from his breast.

> Most of the spectators testified to having seen, on the breast of the unhappy minister, a SCARLET LETTER—the very semblance of that worn by Hester Prynne—imprinted in the flesh. As regarded its origin, there were various explanations, all of which must necessarily have been conjectural. Some affirmed that the Reverend Mr. Dimmesdale, on the very day when Hester Prynne first wore her ignominious badge, had begun a course of penance . . . by inflicting a hideous torture on himself. Others contended that the stigma had not been produced until a long time subsequent, when old Roger Chillingworth, being a potent necromancer, had caused it to appear, through the agency of magic and poisonous drugs. Others, again—and those best able to appreciate the minister's peculiar sensibility, and the wonderful operation of his spirit upon the body,—whispered their belief, that the awful symbol was the effect of the ever active tooth of remorse, gnawing from the inmost heart outwardly, and at last manifesting Heaven's dreadful judgment by the visible presence of the letter. The reader may choose among these theories.

What is yet more remarkable, however, is the testimony of still further eye-witnesses who 'denied that there was any mark whatever on his breast, more than on a new-born infant's.' Such an infant of course is Pearl, who is everywhere equivalent to the scarlet letter itself. But before we follow that unmarked babe, let us note the interpretation of Dimmesdale's death proposed by those who saw no mark on him. They denied that he had 'even remotely implied . . . the slightest connection, on his part' to Hester's guilt.

> According to these highly respectable witnesses, the minister, conscious that he was dying,—conscious, also, that the reverence of the multitude placed him already among saints and angels,—had desired, by yielding up his breath in the arms of that fallen woman, to

> express to the world how utterly nugatory is the choicest of man's own righteousness . . . He had made the manner of his death a parable, in order to impress on his admirers the mighty and mournful lesson, that, in the view of Infinite Purity, we are sinners all alike.

Now a parable is just as much an allegory as is a providence, whether the latter be the result of a wizard's black magic or Heaven's dreadful judgment. Lest we be too prone to accept this parable, Hawthorne immediately qualified the testimony of his 'highly respectable witnesses':

> Without disputing a truth so momentous, we must be allowed to consider this version . . . as only an instance of that stubborn fidelity with which a man's friends . . . will sometimes uphold his character, when proofs, clear as the midday sunshine on the scarlet letter, establish him a false and sin-stained creature of the dust.

There are ironies within the ironies of Hawthorne's style; the very disclaimer of the parable of Dimmesdale's death supports the lesson which that death was said to be meant to teach.

Among all these versions, where, indeed, is the truth? We, as well as the onlookers, have been given evidence throughout the book to uphold each of the four alternatives. The final choice, however, based on the denial that Dimmesdale was either marked or guilty, is yet a deeper revelation of spiritual truth than the three which found on Dimmesdale's flesh a manifestation of his suffering spirit.

THREE

It is apparent that the Puritans badly bungled the case of Hester Prynne. The scarlet letter they condemned her to wear was a self-evident judgment: A for Adultery. 'Giving up her individuality, she would become the general symbol at which the preacher and moralist might point, and in which they might vivify and embody their images of woman's frailty and sinful passion.' Hester would cease to be a woman, and be henceforth a living emblem in a morality play: guilt without redemption, suffering without end.

Yet in her first appearance the child at her breast made her, 'A' and all, resemble 'the image of Divine Maternity.' By mid-point in the tale we can be told that 'The scarlet letter had not done its office,' for her 'A' has taken on significations unintended by the judges. After some years of tending the sick as a 'self-ordained Sister of Mercy,' it was said that 'The letter was the symbol of her calling. . . . They said it meant Able, so strong was Hester Prynne, with a woman's strength.' Stranger still, it 'had the effect of the cross on a nun's bosom,' endowing Hester with 'a kind of sacredness.' Yet she herself tells Pearl that the 'A' is 'The Black Man's mark,' and when, in her forest rendezvous with Dimmesdale, she removed the scarlet letter, and shook loose her hair, she was at once transformed. 'Her sex, her youth, and the whole richness of her beauty, came back,' as sunshine flooded down in token of the sympathy of Nature—'that wild, heathen Nature of the forest, never subjugated by human law, or illumined by higher truth.'

But now Pearl does not recognize her mother.

Many modern readers find Hester's elf-child intolerably arch, with her pranks and preternatural knowledge. She is indeed a remarkable infant, distinguished as much for her fidelity to the actual psychology of a three-year-old child as for the allegorism with which Hawthorne manipulates her strange behavior. Her fixation upon the 'A' might seem completely arbitrary, yet children of that age do indeed become attached to familiar objects in just such a fashion. Pearl was closely modelled on Hawthorne's own little daughter Una. And if Una was named for Spenser's allegorical heroine, Pearl, as Mr. Male remarks, takes her name from the passage in Matthew which signifies truth and grace.[3] When Hester strips herself of the scarlet letter she regains her pagan sexuality in the heathen world of Nature, beyond human

[3] Cf. 'the Pearl of Great Price' in 'The Intelligence Office,' *Work*, II, 370.

law and divine truth. She has also taken off a token familiar to Pearl since earliest infancy. Both literally and figuratively, her child must resent her changed appearance until the familiar badge of discipline is resumed.

At one point Pearl amuses herself by mimicking her mother. She has been gazing into a pool in the woods, 'seeking a passage for herself into its [reflected] sphere of impalpable earth and unattainable sky.' Her attempt to merge herself into the elements is unavailing, and she turns to other tricks. She makes herself a mantle of seaweed, and, 'As the last touch to her mermaid's garb, Pearl took some eel-grass, and imitated, as best she could, on her own bosom . . . the letter A,—but freshly green instead of scarlet!' When Hester beholds her handiwork she says, 'My little Pearl, the green letter, on thy childish bosom, has no purport. But dost thou know, my child, what this letter means which thy mother is doomed to wear?' Pearl, with her preternatural intuition, answers 'Truly do I! It is for the same reason that the minister keeps his hand over his heart!' But Hester cannot bear to tell her what she seems already to know, and breaks off, saying, 'I wear it for the sake of its gold thread.'

This scene perhaps seems a digression which fails to advance our understanding of either Hester or Pearl. But in fact it comprises a metaphoric recapitulation and explanation of the nature of Hester's offense. Pearl's allegorical function brings into *The Scarlet Letter* the pagan values which Hawthorne had synthesized in 'The Maypole at Merry Mount.' But in *The Scarlet Letter* the amoral freedom of the green natural world is viewed with yet greater reservations than was true of his story, written fifteen years earlier. We have already noticed that the forest is described, in Hester's rendezvous with Dimmesdale, as 'wild, heathen Nature.' The child will not let her mother cast the scarlet letter aside because Pearl herself is emblem of a passion which partook of that same heathen, natural wildness. 'What we did had a consecration of its own,' Hester assures Arthur, but that consecration was not a Christian or a moral sanctity. It was an acknowledgment of the life force itself. Consequently Pearl is endowed with the morally undirected energies of life. 'The spell of life went forth from her ever creative spirit, and communicated itself to a thousand objects, as a torch kindles a flame wherever it may be applied.' This spell is the power of fecundity, and its derivative power, that of imagination. 'The unlikeliest materials—a stick, a bunch of rags, a flower—were the puppets of Pearl's witchcraft . . .'[4] These she brings to life, and she feels in herself kinship with life in every form. Although the forest is a place of dread and evil, the haunt of witches and of heathen Indian sorcerers, Pearl is at home among its creatures. It 'became the playmate of the lonely infant' and 'put on the kindest of moods to welcome her.' Squirrels fling their treasured nuts to Pearl, while even wolves and foxes take caresses from her hand. 'The mother-forest, and those wild things which it nourished, all recognized a kindred wildness in the human child.'

It was in this mother-forest that Hester had had her tryst with Dimmesdale, beyond human law and divine truth. Hester herself sees that 'The child could not be made amenable to rules. In giving her existence, a great law had been broken; and the result was a being whose elements were perhaps beautiful and brilliant, but all in disorder.'

What is lacking in Pearl of course is the imposition of that transcendent ordering principle which man, through grace, imposes upon Nature. Lacking this, she seems to the Puritans a 'demon offspring.' Mr. Wilson, the most humane among them, asks her, 'Art thou a Christian child, ha? Dost know thy catechism? Or art thou one of those naughty elfs or fairies, whom we thought to have left behind us, with other relics of Papistry, in merry old England?' Pearl is indeed an elf, a pre-Christian Nature-spirit in human form, whose soul must be made whole

[4] Compare the passage on imagination in 'The Custom House' chapter: 'Nothing is too small or too trifling to undergo this change [from materiality into things of intellect], and acquire dignity thereby. A child's shoe; the doll . . . the hobby-horse. . . .'

by submission to divinely ordered morality before it can be saved. Mistress Hibbins, the witch, is eager to attach Pearl to her legion, and tells her that her father is the Prince of the Air, just as she tells Dimmesdale to let her know when he goes again into the forest, for 'My good word will go far towards gaining any strange gentleman a fair reception from yonder potentate you wot of.' When Dimmesdale protests that he was only on his way to greet the Apostle Eliot,

> 'Ha, ha, ha!' cackled the old witch-lady. . . . 'Well, well, we must needs talk thus in the daytime! You carry it off like an old hand! But at midnight, and in the forest, we shall have other talk together!'

Dimmesdale, however, has not yet sold his soul to the devil, as had Young Goodman Brown—who was lawfully wedded at that. Dimmesdale's intuitive knowledge of the sin that sears all human hearts has made him more compassionate, not less so, and his sufferings result from his moral cowardice rather than from the presumptive sin of loving Hester. In the exposition of Dimmesdale's spiritual progress Mistress Hibbins plays a considerable role, though she remains a minor character. We find her present, for instance, on that midnight when Dimmesdale mounted the scaffold but could not bring himself publicly to confess his sin. He shrieks aloud, but no one awakes, or, if they did, 'the drowsy slumberers mistook the cry either for something frightful in a dream, or for the noises of witches . . . as they rode with Satan through the air.' Besides the family group (Hester, Pearl, and Chillingworth) there are but three observers of Dimmesdale's self-torment. One is Governor Bellingham, who comes to his window, startled by the cry. He is the surrogate of earthly power, the ranking representative of civil government. Dimmesdale could confess to him, but he does not do so. A second observer appears at the window of the same house—Mistress Hibbins, who is Governor Bellingham's sister. In historical fact one Mrs. Ann Hibbins, 'widow of one of the foremost men in

Boston and said to have been a sister of Governor Bellingham,' was executed for a witch in 1656.[5] This account fitted Hawthorne's schematic purposes perfectly, to have the figurehead of Earthly Power aligned by blood and residence with the Mistress of Darkness. The third passerby is the Reverend Mr. Wilson, who 'came freshly from the death-chamber of Governor Winthrop.' Thus Dimmesdale's abortive confession is made at the moment of the reception into Heaven of a Puritan saint. Wilson represents the power of Heavenly succour. These are the three realms of power in Puritan New England—civil, daimonic, and divine. Dimmesdale is thus given opportunities to ally himself with each, and allay or compound his guilt. But his isolation is so complete that none of these links with man, the devil, or God, can comfort him.

I would suggest that Mistress Hibbins's role as a witch should be taken as seriously in *The Scarlet Letter* as was the use of witchcraft in 'Young Goodman Brown.' Indeed, she brings into the moral universe of *The Scarlet Letter* all of the associations which are so fully developed in the earlier story. Like Young Goodman Brown, like Mr. Hooper, like Dimmesdale himself, she, who has experienced sin herself, has intuitive knowledge of the sinful nature of her fellow-mortals:

> Many a church-member saw I, walking behind the music, that has danced in the same measure with me, when Somebody was fiddler . . . But this minister! Couldst thou surely tell, Hester, whether he was the same man that encountered thee on the forest-path?

Hester, startled, protests that she knows nothing of this. But Mistress Hibbins takes the scarlet letter to be Hester's badge in her own sorority of sin:

> I know thee, Hester; for I behold the token. . . . But this minister! Let me tell thee, in thine ear! When the Black Man sees one of his own servants, signed and sealed, so shy of owning to the bond as is the Reverend Mr. Dimmesdale, he hath a way of order-

[5] John Hale, *A Modest Inquiry into the Nature of Witchcraft* (1702), reprinted in Burr, *Narratives*, p. 410, n. 1.

> ing matters so that the mark shall be disclosed in open daylight to the eyes of all the world!

Who could say that the demonic prophecy failed of fulfillment?

Mistress Hibbins had already set her cap for Hester's soul. Like a good witch she is always on the look-out for acolytes, and so she had whispered 'Hist! . . . wilt thou go with us to-night? There will be a merry company in the forest; and I well-nigh promised the Black Man that comely Hester Prynne should make one.' What saved Hester from this temptation, if such it would otherwise have been to her, was Mr. Wilson's Christian charity in granting her custody of Pearl. 'Had they taken her from me, I would willingly have gone with thee into the forest, and signed my name in the Black Man's book too, and that with mine own blood,' says Hester. As long as Hester is responsible for Pearl—who represents both the emblem of her sin and, as grace, the possibility of her own redemption, she will be proof against the blandishments of the Black Man's coven.

The salvation of Pearl depends upon Dimmesdale. Until he acknowledges himself her father she can have no human patrimony, and must remain a Nature-spirit, untouched by the redemptive order that was broken in her conception. For Hawthorne, Nature is amoral but not malign. Witchcraft is not the forest's nature; it comes into being when man repudiates God and chooses Satan. The forest, having no moral will, can shelter either the spirit of the Maypole or the self-damned coven of the Prince of Air. Hence Pearl, like the Maypole mummers, is not yet damned, because unfallen; but, like them, she is not yet wholly human either. Dimmesdale's confession wrenches her first kiss for him from Pearl, and her first tears. 'As her tears fell upon her father's cheek, they were the pledge that she would grow up amid human joy and sorrow, nor forever do battle with the world, but be a woman in it. Towards her mother, too, Pearl's errand as a messenger of anguish was all fulfilled.'

If Mistress Hibbins be the devil's servant, the Prince of Darkness has yet a closer liegeman in *The Scarlet Letter*. From his first appearance Roger Chillingworth is described in demonic terms. He steps forth from the forest accompanied by a heathen sachem, and later avows that he has learned more of his medical arts from 'a people well versed in the kindly properties of simples' than from the universities of Europe. Indeed, the townsfolk, who had at first welcomed him as Mr. Dimmesdale's companion and saviour, by the end of chapter IX have begun to suspect that his medicine was learned from those 'powerful enchanters' skilled 'in the black arts.' And many persons of 'sober sense and practical observation' note the change that has overtaken Chillingworth. 'Now there was something ugly and evil in his face. . . . According to the vulgar idea, the fire in his laboratory had been brought from the lower regions, and was fed with infernal fuel; and so, as might be expected, his visage was getting sooty with smoke.' Here again the superstition is offered half-mockingly; yet the image, which links Chillingworth with the base, demonic alter ego of the alchemist Aylmer in 'The Birthmark'—a monster stained with soot—is indeed appropriate to Chillingworth; like Aylmer himself, Chillingworth too is guilty of an unforgivable sin of intellect, and much less forgivably so. Hawthorne goes on to aver that 'it grew to be a widely diffused opinion, that the Reverend Arthur Dimmesdale, like many other personages of especial sanctity, in all ages of the Christian world, was haunted either by Satan himself, or Satan's emissary in the guise of old Roger Chillingworth. . . . The people looked, with an unshaken hope, to see the minister come forth out of the conflict, transfigured with the glory which he would unquestionably win.' Public opinion is now unanimous in reading Chillingworth's role aright, but at the beginning of that chapter it had concurred in seeing his presence in its obscure community in a different light: it was believed 'that Heaven had wrought an absolute miracle, by transporting an eminent Doctor of Physic, from a German university, bodily through the air, and setting him down at the door of Mr. Dimmesdale's study.' At the doctor's suggestion, Dimmesdale's friends arrange for them to lodge in the same house. Not until much later do the people recognize that their German doctor may well be a Faust. Yet in the end it is popular rumor and fireside tradition which does see the truth about Chillingworth. The force of popular belief is stronger, in the end, than even the force of religious law which branded Hester, for she long outlives the censure with which her letter was to have forever marked her. The same people who reviled her at the scaffold live to seek her counsel in their own trials.

Hawthorne rather heavily underscores Chillingworth's demonism in the eleventh chapter, calling him 'the Pitiless . . . the Unforgiving.' There it is made plain that Dimmesdale's sufferings are purgatorial, but that those of his leech have no cessation in prospect since he has broken both the natural ties that bind and the natural barriers that separate men. Chillingworth's demonism is closely associated with his metamorphic power: indeed, he is the only character in this book who holds that power. From the beginning he appears in disguise, hiding his true name and his relationship to Hester, as he will later mask his vengeful hatred of Dimmesdale. Neither the minister, on his way toward repentance, nor Hester, on hers toward stoical resignation and reintegration with society, can avail themselves of such slippery tricks. Dimmesdale's seeming purity wracks him with inward torture, while Hester is bound by Chillingworth's will, not her own, to conceal his relationship to her. The lovers' desperate plan of escaping from New England to assume new identities among the anonymous multitudes of London is stillborn, and not only because Roger would prevent it. Just as Hester realizes that she cannot flee, so is Dimmesdale drawn again and again to the scaffold, the scene of her public and his secret shame. They can struggle toward grace, they can know their own true identities, only in their own persons. And they are what their histories have made them be. But Chillingworth, like the hero of 'Wakefield,' like Ethan Brand, steps out of his place in the procession of life to try on new identities in the pursuit of the Unpardonable Sin. One would scarcely guess, from the fate of the metamorphic wizard, that the hero of Hawthorne's next romance would be a Yankee master of self-transformation.

10

Paradise Regained at Maule's Well

In *The House of the Seven Gables* Hawthorne would seem to have gone to some lengths not to emulate the taut economy of *The Scarlet Letter.* His tale is spread over six generations in time, his plot divagates into the destinies of ten characters instead of three, and there is no single controlling symbol like the letter to unify these dispersed materials. The manner, too, lacks the unification of tone of the earlier romance. There is the novelistic realism involved in presenting a social background more extensive than Hawthorne attempts elsewhere; there is also the machinery of Gothic romance, including an interpolated fable which recapitulates many of the themes of the work in which it is embedded.

Although its unity is flawed by the unassimilated presence of these several modes, and by the introduction of more materials than the fiction effectively uses, *The House of the Seven Gables* has nonetheless an almost-successful ethical consistency. Such a consistency was among the chief of Hawthorne's aims; in his preface he calls it 'the truth of the human heart.' In its evocation, he insists, the author 'has fairly a right' to choose or create his circumstances, including the prerogative 'to mingle the Marvellous' with the realistic elements of his scene. These are the responsibilities of the author of a romance, which, 'as a work of art, must rigidly subject itself to laws.' This is about as much as we get from Hawthorne of a direct aesthetic statement; since the structure of each of his romances is unique, it would appear that the laws to which he made himself subject were revealed in the process of composition. Each of his works is an experiment, an attempt to discover these laws.

Hawthorne presents his work as a romance, and his reason for distinguishing this form from the novel appears to have been defensive. He would prepare the reader to grant him license to escape the necessity of aiming 'at a very minute fidelity, not merely to the possible, but to the probable and ordinary course of man's experience.' Aiming instead at the revelation of universal truths, he must free himself from too-close subjection to circumstances, especially contemporary circumstances. For these he finds inimical to the imaginative idealization of experience. What he needed, then, were patterns of possible conflict whose working-out would demonstrate the truths of the heart. Hence his dependence upon both the mythical and the marvellous—the mythical for a substructure of thematic action, the marvellous for the concretization of detail. But *The House of the Seven Gables* is also a determinedly historical novel whose issues can be presented only in terms of the culture of a particular place. On this account the mythical and the marvellous elements of the romance have to be subsumed into the novelistic values of a probable reality. The fusion of techniques is incomplete, because the materials are by nature incompatible. On the ethical level, however, as I have said, Hawthorne achieved a near-success. Thematically, this near-success unwittingly expounds the failure of hopefulness.

The House of the Seven Gables is built on an implicit substructure of Puritan myth. On this is erected an historical reconstruction of folk belief in witchcraft as it varied over two centuries. This witchcraft—and the sins it represents—is superseded by the ebullient optimism of the contemporary Yankee character. Doubtless this is among the reasons for the book's great popularity among his contemporaries. Yet while *The House of the Seven Gables* reflects the spirit of popular culture, its avoidance of tragic fate goes against the grain of Hawthorne's own convictions. Not even the grace and shadowed charm of its style can mend this flaw in the conception of the book.

ONE

Maule's Well is the fountain that fouls Eden in the New World. In *The Scarlet Letter* Hawthorne had explored the themes of original sin, retribution, and redemption. In *The House of the Seven Gables* his version of the myth of the Fortunate Fall dramatizes expulsion from Eden and the visiting upon the sons of the sins of their fathers. There is a curse upon the house of Pyncheon, a curse well earned, which cannot be expiated or escaped until the inherited pattern of complicity and reduplication of the original sin is broken. Each generation has the chance to exercise free will in breaking the fateful pattern, but this happy ending to mankind's heritage of woe takes place only in contemporary New England. After two centuries of guilt and sorrow, the bloodlines of the wronged Maules and the blighted Pyncheons at last produce a generation of the new unfallen Americans whose advent Crèvecœur had so confidently announced.

Hawthorne draws with good effect upon the two chief traditions of early New England folklore in the working-out of his ambitiously conceived panorama. Providences and witch lore give him a sombre, chiaroscuro palette with which to depict the fate of his fallen, ambitious, worldly Pyncheons, who would presume to found a great house on the grave of a wronged man. To rescue both Pyncheons and Maules from an eternity of suffering he creates his most optimistic character. Holgrave is a representative man of the nineteenth century. Although actually a descendant of old Matthew Maule, the lineage of Hawthorne's daguerreotypist leads straight back to the Yankee—to Dominicus Pike, to Robin, come to a confident and happy end.

Holgrave's first forebear, Matthew Maule, had cleared 'an acre or two of earth . . . out of the primeval forest, to be his garden-ground and homestead.' Almost at once he is despoiled of his incipient Eden by Colonel Pyncheon, the type of the aggressive man of iron:

> The Puritan—so, at least, says chimney-corner tradition, which often preserves traits of character with marvellous fidelity—was bold, imperious, relentless, crafty; laying his purposes deep, and following them out with an inveteracy of pursuit that knew neither rest nor conscience; trampling on the weak, and, when essential to his ends, doing his utmost to beat down the strong.

Chimney-corner tradition, in this romance, speaks the ultimate truths of the heart. 'Ancient superstitions,' Hawthorne writes, 'after being steeped in human hearts and embodied in human breath . . . through a series of generations, become imbued with an effect of homely truth . . . By long transmission among household facts, they grow to look like them.' Thus folk belief is invoked as the voice of the heart's truth, whose revelations must be heeded in the conflict with the crafty and relentless Puritan. Hawthorne's men of iron have no hearts. Colonel Pyncheon is akin to Ethan Brand and Roger Chillingworth.

The Colonel not only dispossessed Maule from his plot, but took a zealous part in declaring Maule a wizard. The plebeian was hanged for witchcraft, while Colonel Pyncheon—like Cotton Mather at the execution of George Burroughs—'sat on horseback, grimly gazing at the scene.' Maule, who 'declared himself hunted to death for his spoil,' curses Pyncheon with his dying words: 'God will give him blood to drink!'

Colonel Pyncheon is in no way deterred by this curse from his plan of founding a dynasty. His holdings are enlarged by the grant of a vast tract of territory in Maine, 'more extensive than many a dukedom, or even a reigning prince's territory, on European soil.' But the title remained in some doubt, and in succeeding generations the land was 'partly cleared and occupied by actual settlers.' Their situation repeats that of Maule with regard to the Pyncheons' dubious claim to the original property. The first element in the Pyncheon birthright is an aggravation of the clan's inherent materialism, 'an absurd delusion of family importance' based on their expectation of claiming the dubious tract and 'ultimately forming a princedom for themselves.' The Pyncheons, then, are fated to play the painful role of the disinherited aristocrat. But they have other roles too, none happier.

Their second birthright is their inherited guilt. What shall they make of 'the awful query, whether each inheritor of the property—conscious of wrong, and failing to rectify it—did not commit anew the great guilt of his ancestor, and incur all its original responsibilities'?

The curse completes their inheritance. The first Pyncheon, building his mansion over the unquiet grave of Matthew Maule, gives the wizard's ghost 'a kind of privilege to haunt its new apartments.' At the opening of his house, Colonel Pyncheon has an apoplectic seizure, and dies with his own blood gurgling in his throat. In recent times the Pyncheons have endured 'the heaviest calamity that ever befell the race; no less than the violent death—for so it was adjudged—of one member of the family by the criminal act of another.' The victim was a repentant Pyncheon who, concluding that his ancestor had swindled and then murdered Maule, raised the question 'whether it were not imperative upon him, even at this late hour, to work restitution to Maule's posterity.' This Christian gentleman, naturally enough, was murdered by one of his kin. The crime was attributed to Clifford Pyncheon, whose sister Hepzibah now lives alone in the house while his cousin Judge Pyncheon flourishes downtown. Clifford languishes in jail until, midway in the book, he is returned, ruined in spirit, to the House of the Seven Gables. Now that the blood the Pyncheons drink is one another's, the Maules have disappeared from view. The curse combines the repetition of a Remarkable Judgment with the legend of Cain and Abel.

This chronicle of inherited guilt, reduplicated sin, and repeated retribution comprises the history of the House. Yet the setting, the actual land, continues to be paradisal in its attractiveness, as though the Pyncheon garden, with its bees 'plying their golden labor,' would become an Eden in truth, were its inhabitants worthy of such grace. It seems most paradisal to the characters most innocent—to Phoebe, the country cousin of the Pyncheons, and to Holgrave, who says to Phoebe, 'What a good world we live in! How good and beautiful! How young it is, too . . . the garden would every day be virgin soil, with the earth's first freshness in the flavor of its beans and squashes; and the house!—it would be like a bower in Eden, blossoming with the earliest roses that God ever made.' The penultimate chapter, in which Judge Pyncheon's death finally releases the remaining innocents from the curse, is called 'The Flower of Eden.' Phoebe, of course, is the flower, and is promptly grafted onto Holgrave's family tree. Not only does *The House of the Seven Gables* tell of man's long exile from Paradise, but it strongly hints that its American lovers will return there.

What credence we give to this conclusion depends in large part on our confidence in Holgrave as 'the representative of many compeers in his native land.' Holgrave's character, as I have said, is significantly rooted in the folk traditions of Yankee metamorphosis and optimism. But if the folklore of Yankee character contributes to the book's optimistic conclusion, the folklore of witchcraft and necromancy determines the difficulties which must first be overcome.

TWO

Witchcraft in *The House of the Seven Gables* begins in the season of Salem's horror. But as the Pyncheon story is an historical chronicle stretched over two centuries, the treatment of witchcraft changes with the changing times. Hawthorne shows scrupulous fidelity to both historical fact and oral tradition in recording the transformation from the Puritan to the contemporary version of folk belief. Just as the Puritan faith was relaxed and liberalized in the Unitarian and Transcendental periods, so too folk faith in witchcraft transformed itself to accord with the new spirit of the age. Yet Hawthorne manages to keep his modern version of witchcraft alive as a manifestation of active spiritual evil, even though he must turn his latter-day necromancer into a hypnotist. At the end, the last of the Maules, who by birthright should have inherited his ancestors' evil powers, renounces his opportunity to avenge again the wrongs done his line by the Pyncheons. Holgrave, as we have seen, marries Phoebe instead of bewitching her.

Is it often noticed that the original Maule was not a witch at all?[1] He was completely innocent, falsely accused by Colonel Pyncheon. Yet a curse from the lips of a dying man is ever an especially terrifying portent. Hawthorne describes Old Maule as 'one of the martyrs to that terrible delusion, which should teach us, among its other morals, that . . . those who take upon themselves to be leaders of the people, are fully liable to all the passionate error that has ever characterized the wildest mob.' At the same time, though, 'The mode of his death . . . blasted with strange horror the humble name . . . and made it seem almost a religious act to drive the plough over the little area of habita-

[1] Hawthorne's character is based upon an actual person, Thomas Maule, likewise a victim of Puritan bigotry. Thomas Maule was persecuted not for witchcraft but for being a Quaker. He was the author of a book, *Truth held forth,* which 'contained severe reflections on the Government for their treatment of his denomination, the Friends, and held up, that one of the judgments for such conduct was the witchcraft lately suppressed.' Mr. Curwin, who had served with John Hathorne as magistrate in the witch trials, confiscated Maule's books and committed him to prison—where he languished for eleven months before being released. This Maule was troublesome to the Puritans—in 1669, twenty-six years before his arrest, he was given ten stripes 'for saying, that Mr. Higginson preached lies, and that his instruction was "the doctrine of devils."' (Joseph B. Felt, *The Annals of Salem from Its First Settlement* [Salem, Mass., 1827], pp. 236, 323, 325, 379. Felt's book was one of Hawthorne's sources of Salem history.)

What makes this transformation of Quaker into witch especially interesting is his acknowledgment, in 'The Custom House,' and in 'Main Street,' of his first Colonial ancestor as a 'bitter persecutor, as witness the Quakers, who have remembered him in their histories.' This Hathorne was the father of the magistrate John Hathorne. Nathaniel expiated *his* sins against the Friends in the story 'The Gentle Boy.'

tion, and obliterate his place and memory from among men.' This is another alternative choice in which both the literal, rational statement and the superstitious one are true.

That is to say, although Matthew Maule was innocent when alive, both his ghost and his posterity become witches. They have been wronged, they have been invested by 'ancient superstitions . . . steeped in human hearts and embodied in human breath . . .' with the malignity of witchcraft. They seek revenge upon the Pyncheons, thus implicating themselves in that contagion of original sin which Colonel Pyncheon's pride and avarice began. Old Maule's curse is fulfilled as the Pyncheons of one generation after another are struck dead with a gurgle of blood in their throats. His son, Thomas Maule, a master carpenter, actually served Colonel Pyncheon as architect of the House of the Seven Gables. Not until much later, from Holgrave's interpolated fable of 'Alice Pyncheon,' do we learn of Thomas's revenge upon his father's persecutor. He secreted the title to the Maine estate behind the Colonel's portrait, denying the Pyncheons' posterity their hope of aristocratic preferment.

There are two later generations of Maules in the romance. One is Thomas Maule's son, named Matthew like his grandfather; the other is the contemporary Holgrave. We learn of Matthew's vengeful witchcraft from Holgrave's story. Among his many other accomplishments the latest Maule is a fiction-writer, and he reads his manuscript to Phoebe in the paradisal garden of the House of the Seven Gables. Thus the witchcraft in 'Alice Pyncheon' is presented as the literary exercise of a young man of the most advanced rationalistic ideas. Yet the fable presents Matthew's necromancy with the same seriousness that Hawthorne shows toward sortilege in Puritan times.

Even the witchcraft alleged of Old Maule showed the tradition in a state of decay, compared to its full rendering in 'Young Goodman Brown.' We hear nothing of covens or sexual orgies, nor, as in *The Scarlet Letter,* is there mention of the Black Man and the Devil's compact. Instead there is generalized dread, a sense of active malignity worked by supernatural means. Old Maule's spirit and his descendants earn their repute as witches through the exercise of personal vengeance, not through their search for the Unpardonable Sin. Now the common witch of New England folk tradition, as we have seen, is the malicious night-rider—a lone operator, not the Sweet Devil's covenanters whom we find in the Lancashire trials. Hawthorne, describing popular beliefs about the Maules, presents their evil prowess in this early passage:

> They were half believed to inherit mysterious attributes; the family eye was said to possess strange power. Among other good-for-nothing properties and privileges, one was especially assigned them, —of exercising an influence over other people's dreams. The Pyncheons, if all stories were true, haughtily as they bore themselves in the noon-day streets of their native town, were no better than bond-servants to these plebeian Maules, on entering the topsy-turvy commonwealth of sleep. Modern psychology, it may be, will endeavour to reduce these alleged necromancies within a system, instead of rejecting them as altogether fabulous.

The reduction of these necromancies to a system of modern psychology occurs in *The Blithedale Romance*. Here Hawthorne is content to identify the power of witchcraft with the malign possession of another's soul in 'the topsy-turvy commonwealth of sleep.' We remember his raising the possibility that Young Goodman Brown had merely fallen asleep and dreamed in the forest. This might have been true, but if so it would in no way have negated the truth of the story. The possession of a soul is both real and evil, whether in dreams or waking.

Some of the lore in Holgrave's tale parallels oral traditions reported in Whittier's *Supernaturalism of New England:* the unquiet ghost who protests the division of his estate, and the use of hypnotism to enter the world of spirits.[2] Matthew Maule has the Evil Eye, with its powers of 'blighting corn, and drying children into mummies with the heartburn.' In 1837 Hawthorne had

[2] Whittier, pp. 13-15, 51, 62.

read Sir Walter Scott's *Letters on Demonology and Witchcraft;* he may there have found the suggestion for his statement that what most influenced popular belief in Matthew Maule's wizardry was not even his Evil Eye but 'the suspicion of his holding heretical tenets in matters of religion and polity.[3]

In the story of 'Alice Pyncheon' the double drama of reduplicated guilt is played again in the third generation since the proud Colonel and the wizard Maule. Gervayse Pyncheon has lived abroad with his daughter; returning to the House of the Seven Gables, he finds that provincial manse too narrow to contain his ambitions of great estate. He is determined to prosecute the claim to the lands in Maine, and summons Matthew Maule the carpenter for an interview. There are persistent popular traditions of 'some mysterious connection and dependence, existing between the family of the Maules and these vast unrealized possessions of the Pyncheons.' Here Hawthorne cites folklore and providences: an old crone, dead now, had been used to say 'in her fireside talk, that miles and miles of the Pyncheon lands had been shoveled into Maule's grave.' Again, 'it was a by-word' that the missing deed 'would never be found, unless in the wizard's skeleton hand.' Gervayse Pyncheon's lawyers had even searched Old Maule's grave. 'Nothing was discovered, however, except that, unaccountably, the right hand of the skeleton was gone.'

All these, of course, are the traditions of time past. What now ensues is that Matthew Maule agrees to furnish the document, in return for two conditions: surrender of the grounds and the House; and 'the favor of a little talk with your fair daughter Alice.' So strong is Gervayse's desire to become Lord Pyncheon, the Earl of Waldo, that he consents to both.

Alice is so beautiful that 'her presence imparted an indescribable grace and faint witchery to the whole edifice.' Though haughty toward the menial, she finds Maule sexually attractive

[3] Scott, Letter VIII (London, 1830).

at first glance—a glance which 'the carpenter never forgave.' Her father begins to have misgivings:

> Had not [the wizard] bequeathed a legacy of hatred against the Pyncheons to this only grandson, who, as it appeared, was now about to exercise a subtile influence over the daughter of his enemy's house? Might not this influence be the same that was called witchcraft?

Alice, however, is confident 'that a lady, while true to herself,' can fear no one. Her father muses on the dowry which Matthew Maule will make possible—and on her marrying an English duke or German prince instead of a New England lawyer. 'The ambitious father almost consented, in his heart, that, if the devil's power were needed to the accomplishment of this great object, Maule might evoke him. Alice's own purity would be her safeguard.'

But there are evils against which purity is powerless. Maule puts Alice into a trance. 'She is mine!' he gloats, 'Mine, by the right of the strongest spirit!' He now uses the hypnotized girl to establish communication with the ghosts of old Matthew and Thomas Maule and Colonel Pyncheon. But this interview with the departed is frustrated by the revenant Maules, who prevent the Colonel's ghost from revealing the secret. 'It will never be allowed,' young Matthew tells Gervayse. 'The custody of this secret, that would so enrich his heirs, makes part of your grandfather's retribution. He must choke with it . . .' Gervayse Pyncheon tries to speak, 'but—what with fear and passion—could make only a gurgling murmur in his throat.'

Alice is now roused from her trance, but Matthew has not yet had his revenge upon her for her haughtiness. Henceforth she is 'Maule's slave.' 'A power that she little dreamed of had laid its grasp upon her maiden soul. A will . . . constrained her to do its grotesque and fantastic bidding.' Seated at his fireside, the carpenter commands her 'Alice, laugh!' or 'Alice, be sad!' or 'Alice, dance.' 'It seemed to be Maule's impulse, not to ruin Alice, nor to visit her with any black or gigantic mischief, which would have crowned her sorrows with the grace of tragedy, but to wreak a low, ungenerous scorn upon her. Thus all dignity of life was lost.' Her ultimate ignominy is to wait attendance on Maule's bride, a laborer's daughter. Returning homeward in the snow, she takes sick and dies. At her funeral Maule gnashes his teeth in frustration, for death has cheated him of his revenge.

As he finishes his tale Holgrave discovers that he has put Phoebe to sleep. Here is his chance—to repeat Matthew's invasion of Alice's soul. That he is competent to do so we already know, for in the preceding chapter

> he had been a public lecturer on Mesmerism, for which science (as he assured Phoebe, and, indeed, satisfactorily proved, by putting Chanticleer, who happened to be scratching near by, to sleep) he had very remarkable endowments.

But somehow, suffering has purified the bloodline of the Maules. Perhaps it is through his immersion in contemporary America, with its unlimited opportunities for personal development and advancement, that Holgrave has freed himself from the obsessive revenge which cursed his ancestors. At any rate he has that matchless probity and innocence which 'never violated the innermost man.' Holgrave repudiates his opportunity to repeat his ancestors' sin of vengeance. He is no longer a Puritan, nor a Puritan witch, but a New England Yankee.

THREE

Hawthorne rarely committed himself to the comic mode, yet surely, despite its dark details, *The House of the Seven Gables* has claims to be considered a comedic romance. This warrant lies in Holgrave's character, which redeems the history from what had hitherto been its seemingly predestined pattern of woe. Holgrave is the only hero in Hawthorne's major romances who has the positive power of self-transformation. Like the folk heroes of popular culture, young Holgrave is a master of metamorphosis.

Though not yet twenty-two, he has already been a country schoolmaster, a salesman, a political editor, a travelling peddler and dentist, a shipboard official and European tourist, and member of a Fourierist colony, as well as a lecturer on mesmerism. When we meet him 'his present phase' is a daguerreotypist, and Hawthorne underscores the point that 'amid all these personal vicissitudes, he had never lost his identity. . . . but had carried his conscience along with him.' This observation emphasizes what Hawthorne felt to be the inherent moral threat of the power of transformation. The buoyant optimism with which he tries to resolve the dilemma of this romance is supported by his conception of the bridegroom's character.

Sympathetic though Hawthorne's portrait is of this young evangel of the latest doctrines, the picture is yet tinged with ironical qualifications. 'He considered himself a thinker, and was certainly of a thoughtful turn, but, with his own path to discover, had perhaps hardly yet reached the point where an educated man begins to think.' This incipient philosopher demands, 'Shall we never, never get rid of this Past? It lies upon the Present like a giant's dead body. . . . We read in dead men's books! We laugh at dead men's jokes, and cry at dead men's pathos! We are sick of dead men's diseases, physical and moral, and . . . We worship the living Deity according to dead men's forms and creeds.' Here is popular exemplar of Emersonian self-reliance. His strictures against the past are all perfectly justified by the facts of his own situation, yet he is quite unwilling to acknowledge the ineluctability of its influence upon *his* life. His image of himself is again the popular conception of the unfallen, self-created man whose own will determines his destiny.

In his rejection of the past and in his immature philosophy of self-determined metamorphosis Holgrave is of course a foil to the aristocratic illusions of the declining Pyncheons. The contrast between their fortunes and their views of fate was for Hawthorne an inevitable one. Indeed, the opportunities afforded in an egalitarian society for changes in rank and status seemed to Hawthorne much more likely to lead to a fallen aristocracy than to the upward climb of the sober, industrious, and honest yeoman celebrated by Crèvecœur, Franklin, and the popular mythology of the day.[4] Holgrave and Dominicus Pike are the signal instances of Hawthorne's accepting the popular myth, the peddler in a rural, agrarian context, the daguerreotypist in a more complex society of commerce. Elsewhere Hawthorne characteristically turns the popular myth upside down. For him metamorphosis in a viable society has the obsessive implication of descent, degradation, decrepitude. His notebooks record many instances of social mobility downward,[5] and this is the common pattern of social change in his fiction.

[4] In this work Hawthorne views such a career as Franklin's—one wholly concerned with the outward display of good works and of apparent service to society—with much the same attitude that Melville showed in *Israel Potter*. Hawthorne presents Judge Pyncheon (in chapter 15) as almost a parody of Franklin, a confidence-man taken in by his own hypocrisies:

> 'We might say . . . that there was enough of splendid rubbish in his life to cover up and paralyze a more active and subtile conscience than the Judge was ever troubled with. The purity of his judicial character, while on the bench; the faithfulness of his public service in subsequent capacities; . . . his remarkable zeal as president of a Bible society; his unimpeachable integrity as treasurer of a widow's and orphan's fund; his benefits to horticulture, by producing two much-esteemed varieties of the pear, and to agriculture, through the agency of the famous Pyncheon bull; the cleanness of his moral deportment, for a great many years past; . . . his efforts in furtherance of the temperance cause; . . . the studied propriety of his dress and equipment; . . . the smile of a broad benevolence wherewith he made it a point to gladden the whole world,—what room could possibly be found for darker traits in a portrait made up of lineaments like these?'

The other side of Franklin's character appears in the genial folk-wisdom of simple Uncle Venner, whose maxims could be taken for Poor Richard's: 'Give no credit! Never take paper money! Look well to your change! . . . At your leisure hours, knit children's woollen socks and mittens! Brew your own yeast, and make your own ginger-beer!'

[5] The annals of Sir William Pepperill's and Governor Knox's families lead from the mansion to the poorhouse. Lawyer Haynes's fortunes decline from professional eminence to maimed penury. Hawthorne meets an unemployed naval officer, 'a man of splendid epaulets, and very aristocratical equipment and demeanor,' now 'without position, and changed into a brandy-burnt and rowdyish sort of personage.' At Parker's grog-shop he sees an 'elderly ragamuffin . . . who had been in decent circumstances . . . there is a sort

Since Hawthorne makes the reader aware of other influences on Holgrave's fortune than those the youth himself acknowledges, there is a special interest in his occupation as daguerreotypist. On the one hand his camera links him with all the magic portraits and mirrors in Hawthorne's Gothic repertoire. But on the other the daguerreotype signifies that Holgrave *deals* in representations of personal identity—the portraits of persons. And this links him with his author's prepossessive concern with identity and its vicissitudes in an egalitarian culture. The case histories of Hepzibah and Clifford Pyncheon show that sudden changes of wealth and status do not leave untouched the souls that suffer them. Holgrave's ebullient denials of any but the smiling possibilities of change make it seem unlikely that the ancestral curse in *The House of the Seven Gables* can be as readily exorcised as the contrivance of its plot maintains. Here is the basic flaw of Hawthorne's only full-length attempt at a happy ending. It contradicts his own fundamental conception of 'the truth of the human heart.'

of shadow or delusion of respectability about him; and sobriety too, and a kind of decency, in his groggy and red-nosed destitution.' (*American Notebooks,* ed. Stewart, pp. 94, 116, 22-3, 36-7, 255-6, 248.)

The fall of families in egalitarian New England was of course a pattern the Hawthornes themselves had experienced. Inheritance itself seemed no blessing to him: 'A young girl inherits a family grave-yard—that being all that remains of rich hereditary possessions'; 'To inherit a fortune—to inherit a misfortune.' See also the locofoco sentiments of his great-uncle Ebenezer Hathorne: 'the most arrant democracy . . . nobody ought to possess wealth longer than his own lifetime, and that it should return to the people.' (*American Notebooks,* pp. 99, 27.)

11

The Blithedale Romance:
May-Day in a Cold Arcadia

No wonder *The Blithedale Romance* is Hawthorne's least popular book. The story, although filled with memorable characters and vivid incidents, is unfolded through the perceptions of a narrator many readers have disliked and few have understood. A self-styled 'minor poet,' Miles Coverdale is wryly detached from his idealistic fellow-members of the Blithedale community. His gratuitous involvement in their affairs makes him appear a prying, snooping busybody. He cannot leave his friends alone, nor can he fall in love intensely enough with either them or their schemes of reform to warrant his continued meddling. Besides, Coverdale's way of telling their story is enough to try the patience of many a reader. Everything proceeds with an air of mystification, with such questions as these introduced and left to dangle unanswered until almost the end of the book: 'Zenobia's whole character and history; the true nature of her mysterious connection with Westervelt; her later purpose toward Hollingsworth, and, reciprocally, his in reference to her; and, finally, the degree in which Zenobia had been cognizant of the plot against Priscilla, and what, at last, had been the real object of that scheme.' Listing these queries in chapter 25, Coverdale says, 'On these points, as before, I was left to my own conjectures.' The reader has also been baffled by the identity of Old Moodie and the Veiled Lady. All semblance of orderly fictional development vanishes with the introduction of two fables told by characters other than the narrator but retold by him. Zenobia's story of 'The Silvery Veil' and Old Moodie's account of 'Fauntleroy,' although providing hints and answers to some of the foregoing perplexities, seem in form detachable short stories. It is therefore not surprising that until quite recently the main problems in interpreting this book appeared to be whether or not Hawthorne's Blithedale was a slander upon Brook Farm, or to what degree his Zenobia was based on Margaret Fuller.

In recent years, with the closer reading of the text, has come a growing awareness that this curious work may not be entirely a failure. Frank Davidson a decade ago pointed to one of its most important patterns of imagistic coherence when he observed that 'Almost everything in the romance . . . is partially hidden or totally obscured by a veiling medium or mask.'[1] The obscurity in fact is purposeful on Hawthorne's part, for one of his great subjects is objectified by the reader's bafflement. What is so obscure in *The Blithedale Romance* are the central truths of life: the individual's awareness of his own identity, of his true relation to others, and of the relation of human life to time and to Nature. In choosing a 'minor poet' for his narrator, Hawthorne adopts 'poetic' methods for the telling of his intricate fable. In Coverdale's narrative these themes are not only obscured but clarified as well. Far from being a failure, *The Blithedale Romance* is almost a great success. Behind the shadowy presentation is true clarity of design; the style of the book is taut, urbane, and resonant with the implications of its metaphors. The book is a *tour de force* of story-telling from a controlled point-of-view.[2] If we must qualify its 'great success' with

[1] 'Toward a Re-evaluation of *The Blithedale Romance*,' *New England Quarterly*, XXV (Sept. 1952), 374-83.

[2] There is a valuable discussion of this aspect in Frederick C. Crews, 'A New Reading of *The Blithedale Romance*,' *American Literature*, XXIX (May 1957), 147-70.

'almost,' this is because Hawthorne has made yet a new synthesis of novelistic realism and 'poetic' romance which, over a century later, still strikes us as experimental. He loses the advantages of working within an established form, but gains those that come from creating a form consonant with the complexity of his materials.

ONE

Hawthorne entitles one of his chapters 'A Modern Arcadia,' and references to Arcadia and Arcadian images striate the entire book. 'In a literature rich in pastoral idyls,' Richard Chase observes, '*The Blithedale Romance* is one of the few anti-pastorals.'[3] We may take this as a key to Hawthorne's symbolic method, for the book is by no means as impenetrable as I have been making it out to be.

The essential tensions in any pastoral work derive from the contrast between the 'pastoral idyl' and 'real life.' The pastoral genre invites a comparison between the actual—the corrupted realm of necessity—and a bucolic image of perfection. In any anti-pastoral these contrasts are likely to be more explicit than implied, and to work to the disadvantage of the claims of perfection made for the bucolic idyl. For surely the best way to attack the idea of pastoral is to subject it to the same scrutiny which we usually give to the life of the real world. This of course is what Hawthorne in his preface pleads with us *not* to do; but, as D. H. Lawrence says, we must save the tale from its teller. At any rate, we must save it from the teller's apology for having based a romance on his stay at Brook Farm.

Coverdale describes Blithedale's ideal as this:

> It was our purpose—a generous one, certainly, and absurd, no doubt, in full proportion with its generosity—to give up whatever we had heretofore attained, for the sake of showing mankind the

[3] *The American Novel and Its Tradition,* p. 85.

> example of a life governed by other than the false and cruel principles on which human society has all along been based.
>
> And first of all, we had divorced ourselves from pride, and were striving to supply its place with familiar love.

What is necessary to our reading of the book (as it is to Coverdale's understanding of his experience) is the realization that in Arcadia knowledge of self, of fellow-man, and of love proves if anything more difficult than in the 'real life' the communitarians would overthrow. If folklore is slighted, as it must be, in this urbane discourse among an intellectual elite, we find nonetheless that the ritualistic patterns defining the rhythms of Nature are strongly reaffirmed. But among Hawthorne's sophisticates the human rituals of masquerade, metamorphosis, and rebirth are not in consonance with the corresponding processes in Nature. The community that would supplant injustice with 'familiar love' can exist only by competition with the neighboring farmers. Their thoughts, supposed to soar from their labors upward towards the clouds, are in fact debased by the clods they hoe. As for 'familiar love,' the romances in this romance reveal the aborting of passion, the spoliation of love by the very pride they would root out, in the incapacity of the four principals simply to love one another. These important personal relationships are class relationships also, for Hawthorne has cunningly interwoven his characters' dreams of personal happiness with their Utopian dream of reform.

To many readers, though, all this has seemed too well-hidden by the vagaries of Coverdale's narration. Is the first chapter, for example, an irrelevance, introducing the mysterious Old Moodie as though he would figure for something in the plot, then abandoning him as Coverdale sets off for Blithedale? We are puzzled, too, at not learning the message which Moodie wanted Coverdale to deliver to Zenobia; the old man changes his mind for an obscure reason, a result of something Coverdale says, and withholds his message. This does seem a strange way to begin. Why these gratuitous mysteries?

Much later, when Coverdale returns to the city, the pattern furtively hinted at is revealed. We must bear in mind that for Hawthorne (and for Coverdale) the life of the city is the 'real life' in *The Blithedale Romance;* this point bears mention because the most fantastic episodes take place not at Blithedale but in town. At exactly midpoint in the romance Coverdale leaves the Arcadian community, having begun 'to lose sight of what kind of a world it was, among innumerable schemes of what it might or ought to be.' 'No sagacious man,' he adds, 'will long retain his sagacity if he live exclusively among reformers and progressive people, without periodically returning into the settled system of things, to correct himself by a new observation from that old standpoint.' Now, having placed himself once again in contact with reality, he learns that Zenobia, the opulent, luxurious, sexually awakened woman, is the former lover of Professor Westervelt, the lecture-hall quack. Zenobia is also the half-sister of Priscilla, although she knows neither this nor that Old Moodie is their father. Seeking out Old Moodie, Coverdale learns how the old man had, at a past time, been as wealthy as a prince, and as irresponsible. He had begotten a daughter, but having committed an unforgivable sin (apparently adultery), had, as it were, disappeared from life and taken a new name and a new wife. The former Fauntleroy becomes Old Moodie, living amidst the grinding penury of the modern city. The daughter of Old Moodie's poverty is Priscilla, the spindly, anemic sweatshop seamstress; among the communitarians she alone knows of her blood-connection to Zenobia. As Mrs. Leavis has said of this chapter, 'Hawthorne already in 1852 had anticipated Dos Passos' discovery of the Two Nations, symbolized at the end of *U.S.A.* in a neat parable but compared with Hawthorne's artistically barbarous.'[4]

Hawthorne's parable is yet more complex than I have indicated. For the message which Moodie declined to entrust to

[4] 'Hawthorne as Poet,' *Sewanee Review,* LIX (Summer 1951), 454.

Coverdale in chapter 1 had, it seems, to do with his knowledge that both of his daughters would be at Blithedale. Would Zenobia, the daughter of luxury, show sisterly compassion for Priscilla, the child of deprivation? There are yet further entangling coils in their relationship. As is strongly hinted from Zenobia's legend of 'The Silvery Veil' (chapter 13), Priscilla *is* the Veiled Lady (whose 'wonderful exhibition' Coverdale had witnessed just before coming to Blithedale), and the mesmeric master who violates her spirit is the same Professor Westervelt who has possessed her sister's body. Thus Zenobia is implicated in his exploitation of Priscilla. And both have come to Blithedale to escape him.

But Westervelt follows his women there. Coverdale, communing with Nature in his eyrie tree-house, describes the stranger's approach: a fashionable man-about-town, the modern incarnation of both the Black Man and 'the salvage man of antiquity, hirsute and cinctured with a leafy girdle.' In Westervelt we see the contemporary form of Young Goodman Brown's Devil, of Matthew Maule's hypnotic wizardry. Nowadays the evil which past ages discovered in the supernatural walks among us in the spiritual humbuggery of a mesmerist. Westervelt's depravity is total. He states his creed in chapter 23 (he has recaptured Priscilla and is exhibiting her in a village hall):

> He spoke of a new era that was dawning upon the world; an era that would link soul to soul, and the present life to what we call futurity, with a closeness that should finally convert both worlds into one great, mutually conscious brotherhood. . . .

This is truly a vicious parody of the idealism of Blithedale, spoken as the pitch of the Unpardonable Sinner who has violated the will of the pure Daughter of the Poor.

These are among the tangled webs of their past lives that the communitarians would so confidently abandon as they found Blithedale. None of them knows very much of these truths about his fellow-idealists; some do not yet know the truths about themselves. Coverdale alone, through his incessant prying conversation and peeping, uncovers the threads of connection between them.

By now it may be apparent that the obscurities in the narrative method are neither mere Gothic spiderwebbing nor, as is sometimes charged, the inept results of Hawthorne's inability to handle his realistic materials. The mystification exemplifies the true nature of the reality which the dreamers at Blithedale would idealize, the complexity of all that Blithedale assumes to be simple. The great point of the concealment of relationships until the second half of the book is that these intertwined, corrupted, and degrading life histories represent the reality which it is Blithedale's self-appointed mission to reform. But at Blithedale no one acknowledges their existence.

TWO

The name 'Blithedale' means 'Happy Valley.' The colony that bears it is a modern version of Merry Mount. As was true of Morton's jocund band, Coverdale's companions would free themselves from shackling toil and the dynasty of time. Whatever the season, they celebrate the year's rebirth: 'May-Day—I forget whether by Zenobia's sole decree, or by the unanimous vote of our Community—had been declared a movable festival.' But if Zenobia is the Queen of the May at Blithedale (and she is often described in regal images), there is no King. Indeed, Hollingsworth, the communitarian whom Zenobia loves, casts her aside for Priscilla; thus betrayed, proud Zenobia, a 'discrowned queen,' drowns herself. Nature does not condone such failures of the ritual marriage that celebrates her fecundity. Coverdale's story begins in a Spring snowstorm and ends in the Fall of the year, the time of dying. There is no harvest reported from the farm at Blithedale.

The mission of that colony, as we have seen, is to inaugurate the rebirth of society. The community's vision of life, Coverdale admits, is 'a generous one,' more generous indeed than that of the stale world they have left behind. But Blithedale's vision, like Merry Mount's, is incomplete. The communitarians see a life of perpetual rebirth and delight. In contrast to the Maypole story, however, Hawthorne now places the party of gloom and duty in the midst of his Arcadia. The opposition to Blithedale's dream of joy comes not only from the outside world but from the most powerful figure among the reformers themselves. Hollingsworth, the man of iron purpose, sees all human relationships only in terms of his single *idée fixe.* His dogmatic idealism, however, is a subversive force in Blithedale, since he has joined that colony really to recruit supporters for yet another scheme of reform—his own. Hollingsworth would have the rebirth of society begin by establishing a foundation for the reclamation of criminals. Coverdale can justly suggest that he begin this philanthropy by committing a crime himself; in the end this is what happens, as Hollingsworth, withholding his love from Zenobia, drives her to suicide. Although he marries Priscilla he remains the sole inmate of his own house for the correction of murderers. In *The Blithedale Romance* we see not Puritanism itself but the modern detritus of Puritanism, the impulse toward moral duty and gloom turned inward and compounded with stiff-necked pride. Hollingsworth represents much of the sour consequences of the Puritan past which Hawthorne deplored in 'Main Street': 'Such a life was sinister to the intellect, and sinister to the heart; especially when one generation had bequeathed its religious gloom and the counterfeit of its religious ardor, to the next.' The virtues of Governor Endicott's theocracy have not survived in contemporary Massachusetts. In a society without religion at the core of its experience, only Coverdale the artist may interpret life intelligibly, if he can.

At Blithedale, where life is ever being reborn, there is no provision made for death. When Zenobia's corpse is recovered—the scene is all grisly realism—her friends must rely on the conventional liturgy since Blithedale had not yet got around to reforming the funeral service. Blithedale, then, believes in the great American comic possibility, rebirth without death. With this myth it combines its own transcendental version of Puritan moral energy. In the very founding of the colony a total commitment to ideal laws is translated into a symbolic action.

Our acceptance of Blithedale's idealism must be qualified, however, not only by Coverdale's skeptical tone but also by his account of several other trials at achieving rebirth. These are individual attempts, more limited in scope than Blithedale's effort to reform the world. The first of these is a singular experience of his own. Having arrived in a blizzard, he takes sick and almost dies. It is the substitute May-Day, when the two women 'had been a Maying together,' on which Coverdale emerges:

> I was now on my legs again. My fit of illness had been an avenue between two existences; the low-arched and darksome doorway, through which I crept out of a life of old conventionalism, on my hands and knees, as it were, and gained admittance into the freer region that lay beyond. In this respect, it was like death. And as with death, too, it was good to have gone through it. Not otherwise could I have rid myself of a thousand follies, fripperies, prejudices, habits, and other such worldly dust as inevitably settles upon the crowd along the broad highway. . . .

The indolent, pleasure-loving city bachelor perishes—to become the Arcadian farmer who tends the pigs. 'Emerging into the genial sunshine, I half fancied that the labors of the brotherhood had already realized some of Fourier's predictions.' On this May-Day, 'In my new enthusiasm, man looked strong and stately, —and woman, O how beautiful!—and the earth a green garden, blossoming with many-colored delights. Thus Nature, whose laws I had broken in various artificial ways, comported herself towards me as a strict but loving mother. . . .' Coverdale's rebirth proves to be illusory, but we must not let his disenchanted telling of the story a dozen years afterwards obscure the important fact that he has won by suffering the right to feel reborn into a truer sense of union with Nature's laws.

The others in the colony, however, have not entered that 'low-arched and darksome doorway' through which Coverdale rid himself of 'follies, fripperies, prejudices.' And they have divorced the celebration of May-Day from the occasion in Nature which it is intended to hallow. The festival loses its function by becoming a 'movable' feast, for a May-Day which does not observe the return of life to the world after the near-death of winter is no May-Day at all, but a masquerade. As for Coverdale himself, his euphoric mood soon passes among those who would achieve rebirth without suffering.

In the city, too, non-reformers seek an easy rebirth. This Coverdale observes in the saloon, where topers gain a momentary sense of youthfulness. But this vanishes, leaving them torpid and morose. It is while under the reviving spell of a bottle of wine that Moodie reveals his history as Fauntleroy. This fable tells us that his second identity is a false rebirth, an inference proved by the catastrophe in Coverdale's romance. For it is the daughter of Fauntleroy who dies at Blithedale. Old Moodie cannot escape the wages of his life merely by changing his identity.

Here again the experience of one character is a paradigm of the whole. All at Blithedale are striving to do as Fauntleroy did in assuming new identities. Thus the theme of rebirth is joined with the theme of metamorphosis. But before we examine the consequences of their personal metamorphoses we must heed the colonists' collective intention. Their attempt to bring about the millennium is as dangerous to the stability of society as was the violent conspiracy against Major Molineux. In substituting the ideal of perfection for the necessary discipline of life the Blithedale colonists commit again the sin of Merry Mount. Their Eden is doomed even before they arrive to found it, for Nature does not smile on such abrupt upheavals of her established rhythms. Coverdale's departure from town implies the reluctance of Nature to propitiate millennial reforms:

> The snowfall, too, looked inexpressibly dreary . . . coming down through an atmosphere of city smoke, and alighting only to be moulded into the impress of somebody's patched boot or over-shoe. Thus the track of an old conventionalism was visible on what was freshest from the sky.

But the voyagers do not heed such portents; nor do they attend his next observation, that when

> our muffled hoof-tramps beat upon a desolate extent of country road, and were effaced by the unfettered blast as soon as stamped, then there was no better air to breathe. Air that had not been breathed once and again! air that had not been spoken into words of falsehood, formality, and error, like all the air of the dusky city!

Hidden from Coverdale himself, by his stock rhetoric of pastoral condemnation, are the truths that Nature uncorrupted by human society is *desolate,* and the imprint of human paths upon it is immediately excoriated by the elements. These things bode not well for the noble experiment of transforming man's relation to the world.

What Coverdale does not himself acknowledge his dreams reveal. 'Had I made a record of that [first] night's half-waking dreams . . . it would have anticipated several of the chief incidents of this narrative, including a dim shadow of its catastrophe. Staring up in bed, at length, I saw that the storm was past, and the moon was shining on the snowy landscape, which looked like a lifeless copy of the world in marble. . . . How cold an Arcadia was this!'

Coverdale's dream-image is an accurate vision of Blithedale. The price of pure idealism is the extinction of reality, as Poe acknowledged in 'To Helen,' transforming his beloved into a statue. Thoreau, in *Walden,* has a still closer analogue to Hawthorne's perception: 'Why is it that a bucket of water soon becomes putrid, but frozen remains sweet forever? It is commonly said that this is the difference between the affections and the intellect.' If we would have the affections we must be willing to risk mortality and the souring of its joys; eternal purity comes only in frozen buckets, and for Hawthorne, as for Thoreau, it is the intellect that ices the fresh waters of life. But Thoreau would half-prefer his water pure though rigid. Hawthorne, as we know, sees the icy intellect as perpetrator of the greatest sin. Hollingsworth is among his intellectual dogmatists who freeze the bonds of the affections (although at the end he is humbled almost to repentance). But Blithedale itself, trying to supply the place of pride 'with familiar love,' is similarly doomed by its rigid moral intellectualism. It fails to accommodate the human affections, and they wither there.

The imagery of marble and ice reappears at the end of the book, when the catastrophe dimly foreseen in Coverdale's first dream is about to occur. Returning from town to Blithedale, he finds his three friends together in the woods. But Coverdale has come just too late to hear Hollingsworth reject Zenobia for Priscilla. Her appearance was 'that of a queen . . . dethroned. . . . Zenobia looked like marble.' When, after a scene of passionate denunciations, she dismisses Coverdale, her hand is 'now cold as a veritable piece of snow.' In this scene the 'familiar love' that was to reign at Blithedale is frozen forever. Coverdale describes their tryst in terms Hawthorne has often used before:

> I saw in Hollingsworth all that an artist could desire for the grim portrait of a Puritan magistrate holding inquest of life and death in a case of witchcraft;—in Zenobia, the sorceress herself, not aged, wrinkled and decrepit, but fair enough to tempt Satan with a force reciprocal to his own;—and, in Priscilla, the pale victim, whose soul and body had been wasted by her spells.

As was true of Hawthorne's iron Puritans, Hollingsworth is frozen in his narrow conception of virtuous duty. His is the typically Puritan sin of intellectual pride, mistaking his own selfish purpose for the moral imperative of the universe.

In a romance so determinedly contemporary the sudden intrusion of this historical imagery may seem out of key. Yet these similitudes with witchcraft times are not merely 'atmospheric' elements of 'the Marvellous.' Coverdale had reappeared at Blithedale after witnessing Hollingsworth's triumph at the Village Hall. There Westervelt had exhibited 'The Veiled Lady,' but Priscilla is rescued from her degradation by the iron-willed former blacksmith. Approaching Blithedale, Coverdale feels a genuine affection for the place, an affection won by toil. In a fantasy reminiscent of Robin's dream in 'My Kinsman, Major Molineux,' Coverdale sees himself taking his accustomed place at the supper table. But the farmhouse is deserted, and Coverdale senses 'that some evil thing had befallen us, or was ready to befall.' While Miles had responded with the affection won by his work, his sometime companions are playing at 'A Masquerade' (so chapter 24 is titled). 'The wood . . . seemed as full of jollity as if Comus and his crew were holding their revels,' garbed as Indian, woodsman, Shaker, shepherds, pagan goddesses, and grim Puritans, 'allegoric figures from the Faerie Queen' and 'Moll Pitcher, the renowned old witch of Lynn.' Masquerade is the characteristic dress at Blithedale, as May-Day is the festival. And the Devil is fiddler. Much as the scene resembles Merry Mount, there are suggestions too of 'Young Goodman Brown.' The scene dissolves as the masquers recognize Coverdale: 'The whole fantastic rabble forthwith streamed off in pursuit of me, so that I was like a mad poet hunted by chimeras.' It is in his person as Dionysus fleeing from the Maenads that Coverdale stumbles upon his three friends, and to his eye they too seem actors in a masquerade.

We may now see that the main theme of abortive rebirth is dramatized through the pervasive rituals of masquerade and metamorphosis. As early as the third chapter Coverdale had observed,

> the presence of Zenobia caused our heroic enterprise to show like an illusion, a masquerade, a pastoral, a counterfeit Arcadia, in which

> we grown-up men and women were making a play-day of the years that were given us to live in. I tried to analyze this impression, but not with much success.

What makes this impression valid is that *all* of the characters are in one way or another wearing masks. Zenobia's very name is a pseudonym, 'a sort of mask in which she comes before the world . . . a contrivance, in short, like the white drapery of the Veiled Lady, only a little more transparent.' Priscilla is so concealed from us behind her veil that she has no character at all, only a presumptive innocence. Moodie's identity is not fully revealed by his story; his present activity—insinuating curious purses of Priscilla's manufacture into the notice of patrons at a meaty tavern—seems sinisterly couched in terms of sexual exploitation. Dr. Westervelt, appearing as the 'salvage man of antiquity,' as the hypnotic master of the Veiled Lady, as Zenobia's lover and as man-about-town, is a shifty portmanteau figure whose versatility in assuming these roles indicates his own lack of identity—just the opposite of Holgrave's moral consistency through vicissitudes of station. It is our sense of Westervelt's lack of personal identity which generalizes the sensual vulgarity and materialism for which he stands in the book. It is our sense that Westervelt's qualities are not his personal peculiarities (like his horrible gold-rimmed teeth) but, as his name suggests, aspects of the society which the Blithedale farmers are trying to transform, which gives his character weight. Yet all at Blithedale are vulnerable to his parody of their ideals, since they, like him, are portmanteau figures too. Each of the colonists, to dig new crops in Eden, has cast off his prior life like a worn-out cloak and becomes an Arcadian, tending the pigs, mixing the gruel, supervising the laundry. Their perpetual masquerade hides their true identities from one another.

THREE

What further complicates Coverdale's performance as tale-teller, besides the obscurity of his materials, is his sense of his own relation to the other characters. He sees his reportorial and interpretive role as necessarily compromising his moral scruples. Is he, after all, but a high-toned Peeping Tom?

> I had left duties unperformed. With the power, perhaps, to act in the place of destiny and avert misfortune from my friends, I had resigned them to their fate. That cold tendency, between instinct and intellect, which made me pry with speculative interest into other people's passions and impulses, appeared to have gone far towards unhumanizing my heart.

As Mr. Chase observes, these sentiments may be good morality but are hardly conducive to the practise of fiction, if the novel of manners be our end in view. But Coverdale's (and Hawthorne's) is specified as something other than this.

Although Coverdale appears to be telling the story of Blithedale, one of his actual subjects proves to be the revelation of his difficulties in dealing with his ostensible subjects. Because this is true, *The Blithedale Romance* stands at the head of that tradition, continued by Henry James, of stories about artists and their art. As a matter of fact it is Coverdale's own character which determines our perception of everything that he chooses to reveal to us. He is the camera-eye, and his lens is somewhat distorted by his own peculiarities. His obtuseness and timidity have troubled many readers who want to get the *real* story about Hollingsworth & Co. But there isn't any story except as Coverdale records it. He is the ironic, self-deprecatory nonhero of his own tale. Miles Coverdale is indeed one of the most interesting and fully revealed characters in American fiction, a mid-century original of the inhibited man of sensibility who appears again and again in the tales of Henry James, in *The Education of Henry Adams*, in T. S. Eliot's early poems.

In yet another way Hawthorne's romance anticipates later fiction. We can never be certain whether Miles Coverdale is reporting what he has actually seen and heard, or what he has dreamed. Parts of the book indeed seem to rely on, to create, a stream-of-consciousness narration. For instance, we have noted that midway in the tale Coverdale suddenly leaves Blithedale. 'I was beginning to lose the sense of what kind of a world it was, among innumerable schemes of what it might or ought to be.' This is all reasonable enough, but when he returns to town and looks out of his hotel window, 'I beheld—like a full-length-picture' in the window facing his own, 'no other than Zenobia.' Priscilla and Professor Westervelt complete the tableau. This is perhaps the most bizarre incident in the entire romance, although it reveals the answer to a lot of difficulties the reader may have stumbled over earlier. The narrative is so dreamlike here that we have the option of taking the whole scene as a hallucination of Coverdale's. What else would he have on his mind but the fates of his companions at Blithedale? It is indeed extraordinary that they should have chosen the very day of his absence to make their sole excursion to town. But wherever he goes, they are necessarily with him. Even the speech in which Zenobia passionately denounces him as a meddler and he realizes that her heart is set on Hollingsworth may well be the report of his imagination, his intuition, rather than of actuality.

In the preface Hawthorne speaks of his sojourn at Brook Farm 'as being certainly the most romantic episode of his own life,—essentially a day-dream, and yet a fact.' In his romance he has Miles Coverdale treat Blithedale as though it were both. The dream is not only the narrator's, but the ideals on which the colony is based. The facts are not only those of Coverdale's personal experiences but the relation to reality of the Blithedale community and of its members to one another. The facts and the dreams appear inextricably intertwined.

In one of his early tales Hawthorne has a humble woodcarver speak an important aesthetic principle: 'The figure lies within that block of oak, and it is my business to find it.' Miles Coverdale's 'business' is more difficult, for the material on which his art is practiced is not a block of oak in which Nature has secreted the form of a Naiad (as was true in 'Drowne's Wooden Image'). It is nothing less than society itself. Coverdale's art proves even harder to practice than Owen Warland's, for 'The Artist of the Beautiful' devoted himself to creating a single artifact imaging forth a natural form of perfection. In doing so he became at one with the object of his art, recapitulating in his own history the larval, pupal, and winged phases of the butterfly he made. But Coverdale's subject knows no such harmonious rhythms of growth. It is as chaotically disunified at the end of 'his' book as it was at the beginning. The only progress made is in Miles's and our comprehension of its complexities.

When he arrived at Blithedale Zenobia had praised his verses and hoped he would not abandon poetry for the sake of their new project. His reply—it sets the tone of ironic badinage between them—is, 'I hope, on the contrary, now to produce something that shall really deserve to be called poetry,—true, strong, natural, and sweet, as is the life which we are going to lead.' As their relationship becomes more complicated Zenobia taunts him with his penchant for prying into other people's troubles, as though to find themes for his own poems and ballads. To this extent her indictment is right—his vocation is to discover in society the true materials of his art, and to accomplish in art what Blithedale had mistakenly tried to perform in life, the creation of a romance. We never see Coverdale's poems—at the end of the book he professes to have given up verses—but we do not need to. *The Blithedale Romance* is his one great 'poem.'

PART III

Melville

'Why, ever since Adam, who has got to the meaning of this great allegory—the world?'

—Herman Melville, in
a letter to Hawthorne

'I try everything; I achieve what I can.'

—Ishmael

12

Loomings

ONE

'A sense of unspeakable security is in me this moment, on account of your having understood the book. I have written a wicked book, and feel spotless as the lamb.' How insecure Melville had been of finding a reader who would understand him we can only guess from his letter to Hawthorne, to whom he had dedicated *Moby-Dick.* He was, in fact, rather too intense for the reserved Hawthorne to return his 'ineffable socialities' in kind: 'Your heart beats in my ribs and mine in yours, and both in God's. . . . I feel that the Godhead is broken up like the bread at the Supper, and that we are the pieces.'[1] Next to going to sea at seventeen, meeting Hawthorne just as he started *Moby-Dick* was the luckiest event of Herman Melville's life. For the first time since he came ashore after his gams in the rigging with his sailor friend Jack Chase, Melville had found a man he could talk to. Shortly before his meeting Hawthorne in the summer of 1850, Melville had read, or re-read, Shakespeare. Already the author of five books himself, Melville chanced on the two greatest writers of the European and the American world at the moment when his imagination was most ready to be stirred by them. For *Moby-Dick* was the book that Melville

[1] *The Letters of Herman Melville,* ed. Merrell R. Davis and William H. Gilman (New Haven, 1960), p. 142.

was born to write; his earlier books are but a making-ready for it, his later ones a falling-off from its singular and forever after inaccessible achievement.

The two romancers, near neighbors in the Berkshires, met at a literary picnic given by Hawthorne's publisher, J. T. Fields. The picnic was held on the site of an Indian legend celebrated in Bryant's poem, 'Monument Mountain.' Melville pretended the cliff was a bowsprit, Hawthorne 'looked wildly about for the great Carbuncle,' Dr. Oliver Wendell Holmes complained of vertigo, and Cornelius Mathews read Bryant's poem. More seriously, Holmes upheld 'the superiority of Englishmen'—apparently in contemporary literature;—and 'Melville attacked him vigorously.' Within a week the editor Evert Duyckinck, who reported these details in a letter to his wife,[2] left for New York with the manuscript of Melville's article 'Hawthorne and His Mosses,' the notable result of the excursion on the mountain.

As though in rebuttal to Dr. Holmes, Melville offers Hawthorne as an American author worthy of comparison to Shakespeare. Although the tone of his essay is sometimes shrill and jingo ('let America first praise mediocrity even, in her children, before she praises . . . the best excellence in the children of any other land'), Melville clearly sees the profundity of Hawthorne's work. And he finds in Hawthorne the same qualities 'that make Shakespeare, Shakespeare'—'those occasional flashings-forth of the intuitive Truth in him . . . those short, quick probings at the very axis of reality.' For Melville sees the artist as the discoverer and revealer; his longest quotation from *Mosses from an Old Manse* is Hawthorne's description, in 'The Intelligence Office,' of the man who says 'I seek for Truth.' And Melville is stirred by the same 'blackness of darkness' in both authors. 'Through the mouths of the dark characters of Hamlet, Timon, Lear, and Iago, he craftily says, or sometimes insinuates the things which we feel to be so terrifically true that it were all

[2] Elinor Melville Metcalf, *Herman Melville, Cycle and Epicycle* (Cambridge, 1953), pp. 81-7.

but madness for any good man, in his own proper character, to utter, or even hint of them'—there is no closer hint as to Ahab's conception anywhere in Melville's writings. Charles Olson, in *Call Me Ishmael,* has shown Shakespeare's influence on Melville. Hawthorne's, though less direct, was no less important. Melville's borrowings of details for *Moby-Dick* from *Mosses*—the imagery of fire and demonism, for instance—are in fact of less moment than the assurance lent his own enterprise by Hawthorne's successful example. For beyond any specific debts to the older author is his demonstration, in fictions whose structural and metaphoric unity is unassailable, of how allegory may be the basis for symbolism, and thus be turned upon its own monistic assumption that all truth is foreknown, to become an instrument for the discovery of the truth that is yet unknown. Hawthorne's tales may well be the most significant literary influence upon Melville's development from the artistically inept allegorist of *Mardi* to the master of 'linked analogies' in *Moby-Dick.*

Melville's early life was subject to influences akin to those which moulded Hawthorne's mind. Although not a son of the Puritans, Melville was reared in the Dutch Reformed Church at Albany, then the most orthodox Protestant sect in the United States. His pious mother imposed upon her children a Calvinism as predestinatory and unforgiving as that of Hawthorne's colonial ancestors. Besides the kinship in their religious backgrounds, Melville was doubtless stirred by Hawthorne's uses of mythical and folk materials which already teemed in his own imagination. These results of his egregious readings and varied experiences were not as yet forged into functioning metaphors. Much as Melville worked up his fictions from other men's nonfiction—books on whaling, travel, the Bible, and Biblical commentaries like Pierre Bayle's, and works of classical mythology such as Ovid—he appears to have made little use of the sort of antiquarian collectanea that Hawthorne found so fruitful. He is known to have read several such works, but I cannot find direct evidence that he used them to such an extent as Hawthorne did, or needed to. He got his views of Yankee and frontier character from rubbing shoulders and hauling sheets with the living creatures. In gams on the main-top or the fo'castle he learned more than any antiquarian of the time could know not only of the native character but of that 'superstitiousness hereditary to all sailors'; for, as he says in *Moby-Dick*, whalemen are 'by all odds the most directly brought into contact with whatever is appallingly astonishing in the sea . . . they not only eye its greatest marvels, but, hand to jaw, give battle to them. . . . The whaleman is wrapped by influences all tending to make his fancy pregnant with many a mighty birth.'

Yet Melville's participation in shipside folklife was supplemented by eclectic readings, and we know him to have been unusually retentive of whatever in his readings contributed to his own imaginative life. Somewhere—perhaps in one of the theological works which were sold by Mrs. Melville after his death [3]—he learned enough about medieval witchcraft to put into Ahab's 'delirious' mouth the witches' heretical renunciation of God: 'Ego non baptizo te in nomine patris sed in nomine diaboli.' [4]

[3] Merton M. Sealts, Jr., 'Melville's Reading,' *Harvard Library Bulletin* II (1948), 142-3.

[4] Melville's notations on the flyleaf of the volume of Shakespeare containing *Lear, Othello,* and *Hamlet* give the formula in its traditional fulness: 'Ego non baptizo in nomine Patris et Filii et Spiritus Sancti—sed in nomine Diaboli.' As Charles Olson (who transcribed the entry) remarks, 'Of necessity, from Ahab's world, both Christ and the Holy Ghost are absent. . . . The conflict in Ahab's world is abrupt, more that between Satan and Jehovah, of the old dispensation than the new.' The rest of Melville's note is significant as showing his acquaintance with the two traditions of Black and White Magic: '—madness is indefinable—It & right reason extremes of one,—not the (black art) Goetic but Theurgic magic—seeks converse with the Intelligence, Power, the Angel.' As Olson points out, 'Goetic' refers not to Goethe and *Faust* (although they figure in Melville's conception of Ahab too), but 'its source is the Greek "goetos," meaning variously trickster, juggler and, as here, magician. . . . "Theurgic," in sharp contrast, is an accurate term for a kind of occult art of the Neoplatonists in which, through self-purification and sacred rites, the aid of the divine was evoked.' *Call Me Ishmael* (New York, 1947), pp. 52-6. Montagu Sommers, in *The History of Witchcraft and Demonology* (New York, 1926),

In a letter to Hawthorne, Melville called this 'the book's motto (the secret one).'[5]

Like the longer works of Hawthorne, *Moby-Dick* defies classification as a novel. Were we to read *Moby-Dick* without any preconceptions as to its genre we should find it possible to describe that work as an epic, as an allegorical fiction, as either a tragedy or a comic work (depending on whether we take Ahab or Ishmael as its hero). We could regard it also as a poem, to such a degree is its metaphoric coherence a part of its structure. To be sure, it is also a whaling story—it is this first of all. My point is simply that *Moby-Dick* is many things at once, and the amalgam, though at many points anticipated by Melville's earlier writings, is in fact original both with him and with *Moby-Dick*. Compared to Hawthorne's carefully blocked-out romances with their consistent tone and style, *Moby-Dick* is a great sprawling outpouring. But much as he learned from Hawthorne's example of how mythic, folklore, and metaphoric materials similar to his own might be used, and much as Hawthorne contributed to Melville's suddenly achieved command of symbolism through allegory and of the Gothic mode, the ground-rules for *Moby-Dick* are Melville's own.

TWO

We must begin with the whale. Eighteen years before *Moby-Dick*,

> A seaman in the coach told the story of an old sperm-whale which he called a white whale which was known for many years by the whalemen as Old Tom & who rushed upon the boats which attacked him & crushed the boats to small chips in his jaws, the men generally escaping by jumping overboard & being picked up. A vessel was fitted out in New Bedford, he said, to take him. And he was

cites seventeenth-century ecclesiasts who give substantially the same formula as Melville's for the renunciation of Christianity as necessary to 'a solemn and complete profession of Witchcraft' (p. 81).

[5] *The Letters of Herman Melville*, p. 137.

> finally taken somewhere off Payta head by the Winslow or the Essex.

What Emerson had heard in 1834 as anecdote—and left as one—would for Melville become the focal myth-making image of his imaginative life. It was to be the role of the dumb beast Old Tom, under the name Moby Dick, to unloose in Herman Melville the power to discover the 'linked analogies' which bind the universe together.

Here too Emerson had touched up Melville's riches before him. In 'The Poet,' Emerson had written—using a maritime image that caught Melville's eye—

> As the limestone of the continent consists of infinite masses of the shells of animalcules, so language is made up of images, or tropes, which now, in their secondary use, have long ceased to remind us of their poetic origin. But the poet names the thing because he sees it, or comes one step nearer to it than any other.

Melville marked the passage, 'This is admirable, as many other thoughts of Mr. Emerson's are.' Perhaps he did not see or hear Emerson's discourses on language and poetry until long after writing *Moby-Dick*—Melville read the passage above in 1862; by then he could recognize that his own practice proved the rightness of Emerson's aesthetic doctrine. For Melville had written, had *imagined* on like assumptions about the nature of the world and of the mind that perceives it. For him, too, the word is a sign of the natural fact, particular natural facts are symbols of particular spiritual facts, and nature is the symbol of spirit. But one must not cut short Melville's comment on Emerson begun above; he continues, 'His gross and astonishing errors & illusions spring from a self-conceit so intensely intellectual and calm that at first one hesitates to call it by its right name. Another species of Mr. Emerson's errors, or rather, blindness, proceeds from a defect in the region of the heart.' [6]

[6] Quoted in Jay Ledya, ed., *The Melville Log* (New York, 1951), p. 649 [March 22, 1862].

Melville enthusiastically endorses two-thirds of Emerson's transcendental creed: Ahab, in his aside to Starbuck at the quarter-deck, says,

> All visible objects, man, are but as pasteboard masks. But in each event—in the living act, the undoubted deed—there, some unknown but still reasoning thing puts forth the mouldings of its features from behind the unreasoning mask.

This much of Ahab's madness is divinest sense. But Ahab goes on to assert, 'If man will strike, strike through the mask! . . . Who's over me? Truth hath no confines.' Here he preaches a second Emersonian doctrine which Melville cannot accept: that identity of man with the godhead makes man a god. A third transcendental doctrine, however, is proved true in Ishmael's whole attempt to comprehend the mystery of existence. This is belief in the immediacy of revelation. Knowledge of the truth comes not at secondhand, from books and dogmas, but from experience itself. ('A whaleship was my Yale-College and my Harvard.') This truth may be discerned in the lives of the lowly and humble as well as among 'the proud gods and commodores of this earth':

> Thou shalt see it shining in the arm that wields a pick or drives a spike; that democratic dignity which, on all hands, radiates without end from God; Himself! The great God absolute! The centre and circumference of all democracy! His omnipresence, our divine equality! (Chap. 26.)

In Ahab, then, Melville creates a Shakespearean king; in Ishmael, a Whitman-like exemplar of 'our divine equality.' 'What of it, if some old hunks of a sea-captain orders me to get a broom and sweep down the decks?' asks Ishmael at the outset. 'What does that indignity amount to, weighed, I mean, in the scales of the New Testament?' Those scales we shall meet again, but here, this early in the book, Ishmael asks further, 'Who ain't a slave? Tell me that.' This question we may well remember when Ahab hisses 'Who's over me? Truth hath no confines.' The mask Ahab would strike through is pressed just as closely against Ishmael's eyes. The differences in their sight are inward, the inevitable results of their contrary relations to reality. In dramatizing their contrasts Melville dove deep into his own unconscious life and into the myths of mankind's collective experience. These he elaborated within a single simple framework, the literal, realistic, believable story of the whale-hunt. The framework is itself a lath that myths are made on, containing implicitly the archetypal motifs of the Hunt, the Quest, and the Initiation.

Taken literally—as of course it must first of all be taken—*Moby-Dick* is the greatest hunting story in American literature. Its underlying plot, however, is its least original feature. Tales of the chase are as old as the chase, and wherever modern cultures relive the predatory phase of human history tales like the ancient myths of the hunt are born again in actual deeds, in anecdotes, in folk tradition, in literature. On every American frontier where the larger mammals were found, folk anecdote celebrated both them and their mighty hunters. In New England the game was catamount; in the Cumberlands, Davy Crockett became prodigious among the bear; Mike Fink, the riverman, ran a moose ashore unarmed. But the only big-game hunter who participated in a corporate industry was the whaler. His hunt was especially fitted, above others, to become the subject of an epic which disclosed the national character.

Therefore the greatest blessing of Herman Melville's life was the chance or predestination which led him to sign aboard the Acushnet out of Nantucket and spend two years pursuing whales in the Pacific Ocean. In the course of that voyage around the world, Melville, oppressed by tyrannical officers and the seaman's bitter lot, jumped ship off the isle of Taipee. Hampered by an infected leg, he was for three weeks a prisoner of a Polynesian tribe, reputedly cannibals. Yet they treated him kindly, and his eyes beheld a sensuous celebration of life which would have appalled the strict communicants in the Dutch Reformed Church in Albany. These elements—the exhilaration of the chase, the titanism of the whale, the crippled leg, the primitive energies of life, and even cannibals—were to be fused together in the writing of *Moby-Dick.* These materials gripped Melville, in whose sensibility intuitive primitivism was a source of strength. He used them as though he were a modern-day scop, an epic-making bard as free as Homer to use ritual action, magic spells, and animism to invoke the primitive emotions of heroism, fear, and veneration of the hunted beast.

While these adventures contributed to his store of experience, much of Melville's material lay latent in American popular culture during the years when Andrew Jackson was in the White House, when Davy Crockett was in Congress. At lower levels of intensity than he himself would give the theme, scores of oral yarns and printed sketches celebrated the hunt of a marvelous beast. And two of these sketches, widely known in Melville's time, have a bearing on his masterpiece.

The hunting tale seemed a natural expression of the frontier spirit, and such journals as *The Spirit of the Times,* soliciting readers of the sporting class, specialized in them. By far the best was Thomas Bangs Thorpe's sketch, 'The Big Bear of Arkansas' (1841), often reprinted. In this tale a shaggy hunter boards a riverboat and tells of his exploits pursuing the biggest bear ever seen in the state with the richest soil and the hugest crops in the country. This beast is so preternaturally clever that the hunter must be endowed, not only with his considerable craft in bear-lore, but also with a gun that is 'a perfect epidemic among bear' and shoots by itself, at a warm scent. His dog, too, is a prodigy, with perfect knowledge of bear-nature. The huge quarry, however, eludes his every trick until at last, 'missing that bar took hold of my vitals, and I wasted away. . . . I would see that bar in every thing I did; *he hunted me.*' After dogged chases and humiliating failures he swears by an unretractable oath 'to catch that bar, go to Texas, or die.' Just before he sets out, though,

> what should I see, getting over my fence, but *the bar!* . . . stranger, he loomed up like *a black mist,* he seemed so large, and he walked right towards me. I raised myself, took deliberate aim, and fired. Instantly the varmint wheeled, gave a yell, and *walked through the fence* like a falling tree would through a cobweb. . . . by the time I reached him he was a corpse.

In this celebration of man's easy triumph over Nature, 'My private opinion is, that that bar was an *unhuntable bar, and died when his time come.*'

At sea, years before Melville sailed for the whaling ground in 1841, prodigious whales had gripped the imaginations of their hunters. In 1820 the whaler Essex was struck by an eighty-five-foot sperm and sunk; the crew, in two whaleboats, set out for South America, two thousand miles away. The tale of their horrible sufferings—the survivors had literally to eat one another—was written by Owen Chase, the mate, and became widely known. Melville sailed with Chase's son, and, on one occasion, saw the father when their ships held a gam 'within a few miles of the scene of the catastrophe.' The whale that rammed the Essex was but one of several who attacked their attackers. In 1804 there was New Zealand Tom, who mashed nine whaleboats to bits before being taken; probably it was he of whom the sailor who shared Emerson's coach told a plain unvarnished tale. Such adventures found their way into magazines as nautical analogues to the frontier hunting yarns.[7] In 1839 the prolific magazine writer, J. N. Reynolds, published in the *Knickerbocker Magazine* a lively fifteen-page sketch about 'Mocha Dick: Or the White Whale of the Pacific.' It is entirely probable that this yarn (later reprinted as the title sketch of a book) was seen by the author of *Moby-Dick, Or, The Whale.*[8] The conjecture is given

[7] The Essex story was briefly retold as the final climax of a sketch, 'The Story of the Whale,' in *Harper's New Monthly Magazine* for March 1856; although *Moby-Dick* by *Harper's* contributor Melville had appeared four years earlier, the sketch did not mention it.

[8] See Luther S. Mansfield and Howard P. Vincent, eds., *Moby-Dick* (New York, 1952), pp. 691-3, 720-21. These editors suggest that 'legends of the great White Whale . . . [Melville] must have collected in gams with other

support by the interesting parallels between the sketch and the romance. Moby Dick appeared to Ishmael as 'one grand hooded phantom, like a snow hill in the air'; the captain of the Penguin in Reynolds's tale had described Mocha Dick as 'white as a snow-drift,' 'white as wool,' 'white as the surf around him.' This captain, to prove his valor, had once managed to 'leap from the "cuddy" to the back of the fish, sheet his lance home, and return on board in safety.' Melville writes of a similar act of bravado, with a different outcome: 'one captain . . . had dashed at the whale, as an Arkansas duellist at his foe, blindly seeking with a six inch blade to reach the fathom-deep life of the whale. That captain was Ahab.' Moby Dick's ferocity when attacked and peaceful aspect otherwise are paralleled earlier in the report of Mocha Dick:

> Though naturally fierce, it was not customary with Dick, while unmolested, to betray a malicious disposition. On the contrary, he would sometimes pass quietly round a vessel, and occasionally swim lazily and harmlessly among the boats. . . . But . . . his foes would swear they saw a lurking deviltry in the long, careless sweep of his flukes.

Moby Dick, too, bore 'a back serried with irons, and from fifty to a hundred yards of line trailing in his wake.' Mocha turns on attacking whaleboats, jaws agape or tail a-swinging. There are further points of resemblance in the action. The captain of the Penguin, like him of the Pequod, sights the whale before it is seen by the lookout on the masthead. These and many other details are doubtless taken by both authors from actual experience;

ships.' And Melville wrote in a letter of 27 June 1850 that his book was 'founded upon certain wild legends in the Southern Sperm Whale Fisheries, and illustrated with the author's own personal experience, of two years or more, as a harpooner.' The book containing Reynolds's *Mocha Dick* appeared in a publisher's series of which Melville is known to have owned another volume, Schiller's *The Ghost-Seer*, reported by Sealts as item no. 438a in 'Melville's Reading,' *Harvard Library Bulletin*, III (1949), 417, and 'Supplementary List,' ibid. VI (1952), 245. It is unlikely that Melville, seeing *Mocha Dick* advertised in *The Ghost-Seer*, would not have made a point of reading a work on a subject so much at the center of his own imagination.

yet Reynolds does anticipate Melville. In one respect, however, Reynolds's tale is signally different from *Moby-Dick:* the captain of the Penguin triumphs and Mocha Dick is killed.

Fables such as these characterize the form in which American popular culture accepted and transformed the traditional myth of the Huntsman as culture-hero. The quarry, endowed by superstition with magical powers, personifies Nature, against which the American hunter sees himself in a combative relationship. His efforts are exacted not so much to rid his people of the beast that scourges them as to demonstrate his own mighty prowess and indomitable strength. Whether he relies solely on his own magnificent skills, as does the hunter of Mocha Dick, or, as in 'The Big Bear,' these are humorously enhanced with magic aids, there is no doubt of his easy triumph over Nature. Melville appropriated this crude fable and, in giving the Hunt epical dimensions, made his romance both more sophisticated and more primitive than its brief analogues in popular literature.

13

Myth, Magic, and Metaphor in Moby-Dick

ONE

'There are some enterprises in which a careful disorderliness is the true method,' Melville writes, and his curious phrase suggests the delicate balance he had to maintain between the multitudinous metaphors that poured forth from his imagination and the prefiguration which had to be applied to their arrangement. Melville, as Constance Rourke suggested, 'used the familiar method of the legend-maker, drawing an accumulation of whaling lore from many sources, much of it from New England, some of it hearsay, some from books, including stories of the adventures of other ships encountered at sea, or further tales suggested by episodes within the main sequence of his story.' [1] Among those who have observed the fact, Matthiessen has said it best: 'In his effort to endow the whaling industry with a mythology befitting a fundamental activity of man in his struggle to subdue nature, [Melville] came into possession of the primitive energies latent in words.' [2]

Although there are dim prefigurations in his earlier romances of what he was to do in *Moby-Dick,* he found his mature purpose and the means of fulfilling it in the process of writing his greatest book. Consequently we cannot trace with exactness, as

[1] *American Humor,* p. 194. Melville's debt to extant whaling literature is exhaustively traced in Howard P. Vincent, *The Trying-Out of Moby-Dick* (Boston & New York, 1949).

[2] *American Renaissance,* p. 423.

we could with Hawthorne, the gradual evolution of his mythical themes. They seem to leap fully formed from his mind. We may observe, however, that he draws together the mythical patterns of several cultures and of several levels within his own culture: the primitive ritual, the Greek myth, the Biblical legend, the folklore of supernatural dread and wonder (common to both the Old World and the New), and the specifically American folk traditions of comic glorification, of Yankee and frontier character. And in the 'careful disorderliness' which is 'the true method' of *Moby-Dick* these themes from myth, folklore, and ritual are ranged in a series of dialectical contrasts which dramatize and unify the several controlling tensions of the work.

Among these tensions the chief are those between the two examples of the hero. The contrary commitments of Ahab and Ishmael are dramatized in large part by their respective allegiances to certain heroes of Old World myth and of New World folklore. The narrative of the hunt we have seen to embody the seminal myth of a divinely endowed hero who in hand-to-hand combat rids his people of the evil monster that was their scourge. Ahab appears to belong in the company in which Ishmael jocularly enrolls himself: among Perseus, Theseus, and Saint George. (Ishmael maintains that Cetus, the Medusa, and the dragon, being sea-creatures, were necessarily whales.) But Ahab in fact differs from these prototypical figures in being a false culture-hero, pursuing a private grievance (rather than a divine behest) at the expense of the mankind in his crew. He is more properly a Faust who has sold his soul to the devil (who is aboard as Fedallah the fire-worshipper). A Faust who commands and enchants his followers becomes, as Ahab does, a Satan, a sorcerer, an Antichrist.

The lowly sailor, contrarily, is humanely adaptable and receptive to experience. Ishmael's style, the doubly comic and fearful cast of his imagination, and his metamorphic career all relate him to the qualities of the American folk character. His own involvement in the adventure he records takes the unsought but intrinsic form of initiation and rebirth. Indeed, for all aboard the Pequod the voyage is one of search and discovery, the search for the ultimate truth of experience. But each seeker can make only those discoveries his own character has preordained as possible for him. Ishmael's initiation is revealed through the pattern of the hunt whose object becomes known only when the crew is welded to their mad commander's purpose by the magical rites which Ahab as Antichrist performs on the quarter-deck. Then 'Ahab's crazy quest seemed mine.' But Ishmael discovers a deeper magic, a more potent source of supernatural energy, and dissolves this specious bond of Ahab's with a counter-ritual of his own. The brotherhood of violence to which Ahab bound him proves to be the self-destructive moral nihilism of selfhood uncontrolled. Freed by his discovery, in 'A Squeeze of the Hand,' of the organic unity of man with fellow-man, Ishmael wins his right to be the 'sole survivor' of the final catastrophe. Cast up by the sea, he is saved by the coffin prepared for his boon companion, Queequeg the cannibal, to whom the bonds of human love had bound him closest.

Opposed to the legend of the mighty hero are other mythical patterns in *Moby-Dick* which dramatize the contraries to Ahab's aggression against the inscrutable forces in the universe. The Hunter may be not only an aggressor but a Seeker, a seeker after truth. Opposed to Ahab's power and defiance is love. But love, to be an effective counter-principle, must find its proper object; should love turn inward, rather than embrace the 'Not-Me,' it becomes its own opposite, the wish for death. One of the manifestations of love in *Moby-Dick* occurs in versions of the myth of Narcissus, who, falling in love with his own image, destroys himself. In the Narcissus myth, which Melville invokes in the very first chapter (and often again), the hunter becomes both a seeker and a solipsist. Yet it is the power of love alone, an outward-reaching love, that can overcome the wished-for death, as Ishmael but not Ahab learns.

When the hunt is for a whale who seems to embody divine

power, when the Hunters and Seekers are also Rebels against divinity or candidates for repentance and redemption, it is inevitable that the Biblical legend of Jonah govern much of the metaphor and the action. In fact Melville introduces this myth into the narrative early too, taking from the Book of Jonah the text for Father Mapple's sermon. That Christian sermon states the ethical standards against which the fates of Ahab, Ishmael, and the rest are subsequently measured. Part of their fate is to relive aspects of Jonah's rebellion against God's Word, his incarceration in the whale, his being cast forth, and his redemption. Only Ishmael can reenact the entire myth; for the others, to each is given his own portion of Jonah's suffering, wisdom, and glory.

These then are the executive metaphors from mythology and folklore which give the book much of its inner coherence. The opposing claims of aggression and passivity, of hostility and acceptance, of defiance and of submission to the 'Divine Inert,' are consistently proposed and elaborated by these masterful myth-symbols. The interstices of the action are braced by the enactment of rituals. Among the most important are the 'marriage' of Ishmael and Queequeg, the cannibal's worship of his idol, Father Mapple's sermon and the cook's, Ahab's black mass on the quarter-deck, Ishmael's cleansing of his soul in the spermaceti, and the final annihilating catastrophe. The work is yet almost everywhere saved from becoming what Melville shunned as 'a hideous and intolerable allegory' by his insistence upon tangible fact: the reality of an actual ship and live whales, of a particular captain and his crew, and the documentation which makes *Moby-Dick* a guide to all of the operations of the whaling industry.

TWO

Folk humor and fear of the supernatural are linked in tandem throughout *Moby-Dick*. Melville uses these two veins of folk tradition early in his presentation of Ishmael. The narrator introduces himself as the familiar hero of a thousand jokes and yarns whose way of looking at things is half the time that of the Yankee raconteur, leaping without warning from reportage of the most actual fact to the most exaggerated metaphors of tall talk and folktale. Metamorphosis is the key to his nature, a metamorphosis like that of Hawthorne's Holgrave, for through all vicissitudes Ishmael's essential self remains untrammelled. And what vicissitudes! This narrator of the great hunt is both a 'sub-sub librarian' who has 'swum through libraries' and a 'simple sailor, right before the mast' who has 'sailed through oceans.' He has been stonecutter, schoolteacher, and in the course of his own tale, becomes both bumpkin dupe and Yankee trickster, both sweeper of decks and hero among heroes, a philosopher who climbs to the masthead with Plato, Spinoza, and the Stoics in his head, and a boon companion to a cannibal. He is by turns a poet steeped in the rhythms and images of Shakespeare, and a folk raconteur whose speech leaps with the hyperboles of native humor or delves into the deepest mysteries and terrors half revealed through folk beliefs and wonders. As Richard Chase perceptively observes,

> The soliloquist of *Moby-Dick* speaks in the style required by the basic relation between fact and fantasy in American folk art. . . . The book is a monologue told through a mask, Ishmael; the mask is an abstraction from the full richness of American folk experience—it is the consciousness of that experience. The outward voice speaks more often and more explicitly; it describes objectively and states facts; it gives us the whole science of whaling and tells the story. Combining subtly with the inner voice of fantasy, it creates the larger metaphors and the allegory and the hundreds of incidental supporting figures of speech.[3]

Ishmael's metamorphoses are also expressed in another way than his changing vocations, a way more directly functional to his thematic role. He is capable, as Ahab is not, of experiencing the wildest ranges of emotion. In the first part of the narrative—until the Pequod sets sail—there is a regular, wave-like alterna-

[3] *Herman Melville, A Critical Study* (New York, 1949), p. 73.

tion in Ishmael's feelings, veering between boisterous comedy and sheerest terror. Arriving in New Bedford, Ishmael is a green country lad, fit game at the Spouter Inn for the practical joke of the landlord, ominously named Coffin. With many a wink and grimace the landlord assigns him to share a bed with another lodger, who, appearing in the middle of the night, proves to be a tattooed cannibal carrying human heads for sale! Ishmael is *really* scared, but reasonably decides 'better sleep with a sober cannibal than a drunken Christian,' and by morning he and Queequeg are sleeping cozily. The tone of terror dissipates into laughter as Ishmael tells tall tales of how 'New Bedford fathers . . . give whales for dowers to their daughters, and portion off their nieces with a few porpoises apiece. . . . Elsewhere match that bloom of theirs, ye cannot, save in Salem, where they tell me the young girls breathe such musk, their sailor sweethearts smell them miles off shore, as though they were drawing nigh the odorous Moluccas instead of the Puritanic sands.' Immediately thereafter Ishmael and Queequeg, now boon friends, go to the seamen's chapel and read the dolorous gravestones of those drowned at sea. The somber tone continues—'Yes, the world's a ship on its passage out, and not a voyage complete; and the pulpit is its prow'—through Father Mapple's sermon on Jonah. The mood changes again as we hear tall-tale encomia of Nantucket's barrenness; and yet again as these become heroic celebrations of the Nantucket whaleman's enterprise. 'He lives on the sea as prairie cocks on the prairie. . . . under his very pillow rush herds of walruses and whales.'

Now the bumpkin Ishmael reverses his role, and, in Mrs. Hussey's Try Pots restaurant, becomes the trickster, cadging the proprietress for *both* clam chowder and cod. Ishmael ebulliently bubbles forth more tall tales—'There was a fishy flavor to the milk . . . I saw Hosea's brindled cow feeding on fish . . . with each foot in a cod's decapitated head, looking very slip-shod, I assure ye.' This is followed by the serious decision to ship out on the Pequod, 'A noble craft, but somehow a most melancholy!'

His ill-omened description of the ship is interrupted by the laconic comedy of Yankee character. This time the butt is Captain Peleg, a stereotype of the pinchpurse Quaker:

> 'Is this the Captain of the Pequod?' said I, advancing to the door of the tent.
>
> 'Supposing it be the captain of the Pequod, what dost thou want of him?' he demanded.

The other Quaker owner, Bildad, more penurious still, amusingly tries to reduce Ishmael's wages. Lacing the comic argument are obscurely foreboding references to Ahab, the captain who will sail the ship. These are reinforced by the weird ravings of one Elijah who tries to prevent Ishmael's sailing with fearful hints as to Ahab's past crimes and the fulfillment of dark prophecies.

Thus if Ishmael shows his Yankee adaptability and humor half the time, the other half he reveals the American's engagement with terror in Nature and with dread and wonder in the supernatural world. His flux between comedy and dread tells us many things, among which the chief may be that all experience is multiple and the distinctions between laughter, wonder, and woe are more shifting than either the tragedian or the rationalist would be likely to acknowledge. Ahab, for one, is signally unlike Ishmael in that he scorns all omens that contradict his unassailable will, and he has no sense of humor. His tragic destiny has blasted almost all of his 'humanities,' and in the ameliorating leaven of laughter he adamantly will not share.

Ahab's mighty monism is constantly called into question by both the comic and the superstitious imagination in *Moby-Dick*, for these two modes of perception see the same visible objects that Ahab sees but render them in metaphors his will cannot accept. Those of comedy are, for Melville, apt to be the appearances alternative to reality which a skeptical, tolerant mind perceives. While the metaphors of superstition may be as monistic in meaning as Ahab's own, the faith that produced them—having dwelled in many human hearts—has the authority of humanity's collective spiritual judgment to stiffen its readings of doom and dread.

Ishmael is the self, Ahab the anti-self. The democratic folk-hero discovers the redemptive principle which alone can save him from the death-wish that drove him in the first place to choose a sea voyage as 'a substitute for pistol and ball.' But the titan captain, 'lord and commander of this world,' is caught within the iron-forged rails on which his own soul runs toward doom. The ultimate, unintelligible energy of the universe, which so appalled Goethe's Faust that he had to turn away and beseech the lesser power of Lucifer, cannot terrify Ahab or turn his unappeasable aggression aside: 'Oh! thou clear spirit of clear fire . . . I now know that thy right worship is defiance.' This maimed, maddened, predestinated old man is not only Captain of the Pequod; he becomes also the objectification of those very impulses in his own soul that Ishmael had fled to sea to escape. Ahab is the inescapable human wish for death, forged in daimonic proportions, inevitably ennobled by the superhuman energy of his commitment to anarchic, Satanic, mind-pulverizing power.

In the fusion of elements that Melville welded into Ahab's person there is the ultimate daredeviltry of the frontier folk hero defying Nature herself in his upleaping rhetoric of self-glorification. With the 'Arkansas duellist,' who in his insane fury of self-assertion would stab a whale with a bowie knife, American popular culture contributes a memorable metaphor to Ahab's extremity of Romantic egoism. As was true even in Irving's 'Legend of Sleepy Hollow,' the frontier character is basically anarchic while the Yankee—whether drawn in satire or in sympathy—represents the values of man in society.[4]

[4] Frontier character is more fully developed in the mates. Both Stubb and Flask exhibit the frontiersman's traditional braggadocio and reckless daring; Stubb shows also his shrewdness (in his deceptions of foreign whaling captains he resembles Davy Crockett outwitting Easterners), while Flask, especially, is gifted with a Mike Fink vein of gratuitous cruelty, as in his cast-

But where the American hero's characteristics are paramount in Ishmael, Ahab's main features are imaged from the great religions, legends, and rituals of the Old World: from the sinful king of the Old Testament whose name he bears, from the Fallen Angel of the Christian Heaven, from apostate gods of heathen faiths, from demigods and heroes of antiquity, from the magician Faustus and those primitive shamans who seize supernatural powers for their own purposes. The very pattern of his experience heavily suggests his superhuman stature. His wound, his long brooding seclusion in the cabin, his emergence on the high seas to reveal his purposed vengeance, the rites by which he binds the crew to his will, the mysterious prophecies attending his advent and his fate,—all link him with those culture-heroes or gods who suffer, retire from society to seek divine enlightenment, and return to lead their peoples in accordance with their newly acquired vision. Melville's text is sprinkled with comparisons of Ahab to Perseus, Prometheus, Hercules; as we have observed, he is unlike these demi-deities in that his motive is anarchic rather than culturally sanctioned and he becomes the victim of his prey. Indeed, in each case Ahab's resemblance to his prototypes proves to be an inversion of their cultural roles. Thus Ahab as Prometheus creates not fire as a civilizing instrument; he worships fire as the destructive element and creates the very vulture that gnaws his own bowels. Again, in the scene with the carpenter Ahab envisages Prometheus not as the suffering civilizing gift-bringer but as a mechanician who creates an automaton with a quarter-acre of brains, no heart, and a skylight on top of his head instead of outward-seeing eyes.

Ahab is named for the king of Israel who 'did evil in the sight of the Lord above all that were before him' and went into battle at the behest of false prophets. Melville envisages the Biblical Ahab as a prototype of the Antichrist and renders his whaling

ing a harpoon into the festered sore of a sick whale. A more favorable portrait of Western character is Steelkilt, the sea-going Erie Canaller, who is hero of 'The Town-Ho's Story.'

captain accordingly. His Ahab casts off for his voyage of vengeance on Christmas Day. His first appearance before the crew suggests a heretic at an *auto-da-fé*, 'a man cut away from the stake,' and he wears 'a crucifixion in his face.' Asleep, his palms bear the stigmata of nails—but the nails are his own. Again his resemblances to a deity are inversions suggesting his opposite role. All this had been hinted by Elijah, the crazy prophet of the Nantucket wharfs:

> What did they *tell* you about him? . . . Nothing about that thing that happened to him off Cape Horn, long ago, when he lay like dead for three days and nights; nothing about that deadly skrimmage with the Spaniard afore the altar in Santa? . . . Nothing about the silver calabash he spat into? And nothing about his losing his leg last voyage, according to the prophecy?

Even Captain Peleg, the literal-minded Quaker, says 'Ahab's been in colleges as well as 'mong the cannibals; been used to deeper wonders than the waves; fixed his fiery lance in mightier, stranger foes than whales.'

In the Bible, Ahab 'went and served Baal, and worshipped him'; Melville's Ahab invokes the 'spirit of clear fire whom on these seas I as Persian once did worship, till in the sacramental act so burned by thee, that to this hour I bear the scar.' His ship is named for a heathen Indian tribe extirpated by the Puritans; his only shipmates of earlier voyages are the three pagan harpooners, who alone with him have seen the white whale. As Henry Murray suggests, 'Captain Ahab, incarnation of the Adversary . . . has summoned the various religions of the East to combat the one dominant religion of the West . . . He and his followers, Starbuck excepted, represent the horde of primitive drives, values, beliefs, and practices which the Hebraic-Christian religionists rejected and excluded, and by threats, punishments, and inquisitions forced into the unconscious mind of Western man.'[5] Ahab is 'a grand ungodly, god-like man,' an incarnation

[5] 'In Nomine Diaboli,' *New England Quarterly*, XXIV (Dec. 1951), 443.

of godlike potentialities and ungodly purposes; a Satan whose shadow is lengthened by that of Fedallah, his fire-worshipping familiar and false prophet. Fedallah, the most allegorical figure in the cast, embodies Ahab's deepest, most anarchic desires for vengeance and annihilation. He is comparable to both Mephistopheles and the evil angel in *Faust*, the 'good angel' in *Moby-Dick* being Pip.

As was true of Faust, Ahab first masters scientific knowledge (he is an expert oceanographer, studying charts, currents, winds, and the feeding habits of whales), but then rejects rationality (smashing his quadrant) to rely upon supernatural power. He transcends Faust in the uses he makes of magic: not for the trivial ends of self-gratification but literally to spellbind the mankind of his crew against the malice in the universe that has injured *him*. Acting simultaneously as sorcerer, Satan, and the Antichrist, Ahab 'possessed their souls' by 'evil magic' exercised in rituals that parody the Christian sacraments. He enslaves his men with a black mass; he dedicates his own weapon with a blasphemous baptism; he appears to command the elements by black sorcery, and he stands on the kneeling Fedallah to worship again the 'sacred spirit of clear fire' that has seared him.

Ahab's black mass on the quarter-deck (chapter 36) at once divulges the hitherto hidden purpose of his quest and establishes his unequivocal control over all of the men. Setting the tableau with the ritualistic skill of a cultist priest, Ahab first welds their voices in the whalers' traditional communal chant:

> 'What do ye do when ye see a whale, men?'
> 'Sing out for him!' . . .
> 'And what do ye next, men?'
> 'Lower away and after him!'
> 'And what tune is it ye pull to, men?'
> 'A dead whale or a stove boat!'

Next he rivets their excited attention upon himself, commanding the mate Starbuck to fetch him a hammer, while he promises a gold doubloon to the man aboard who first sights the white whale. He nails the gold to the mast; the harpooners, his 'three pagan kinsmen,' query him about the white whale they alone have seen. Starbuck asks, 'Was it not Moby Dick that took off thy leg?'

> Aye, aye! and I'll chase him . . . round perdition's flames before I give him up. And this is what ye have shipped for, men! to chase that white whale. . . . What say ye, men, will ye splice hands on it now?

Starbuck alone resists him—'Vengeance on a dumb brute! that simply smote thee from blindest instinct! Madness!' But Ahab draws the mate aside and divulges the depths of his own nihilism:

> I see in him outrageous strength, with an inscrutable malice sinewing it. That inscrutable thing is chiefly what I hate; and be the white whale agent, or be the white whale principal, I will wreak that hate upon him. Talk not to me of blasphemy, man; I'd strike the sun if it insulted me.

Then passing round the grog that sanctifies their spliced handclasp, Ahab calls on his pagan harpooners, his 'braves,' to reverse the hollow harpoon irons. Using these as chalices, they take 'the fiery waters.' As Ahab gazed at the crew, their 'wild eyes met his, as the bloodshot eyes of the prairie wolves meet the eye of their leader, ere he rushes on at their head in the trail of the bison; but, alas! only to fall into the hidden snare of the Indian.' This sudden infusion of Indian imagery is triply effective here, suggesting not only the barbarous Sioux of the prairies, but also (as elsewhere in Hawthorne and Melville) the Indians as Satan's tribesmen; and not least, the 'hidden snare of the Indian' as Fedallah's yet undisclosed prophecy of Ahab's death by hempen rope.

Ahab intensifies his role as Black Priest by a blasphemous consecration of his own harpoon (chapter 113). He himself blows the fire and welds the iron; the barb he cools in 'the true death-temper,' the blood of his three pagan lancers. '"Ego non baptizo te in nomine patris, sed in nomine diaboli," deliriously howled Ahab.' Ahab embraces the 'speechless, placeless power' of the corposants which burn from the three masts 'like three gigantic wax tapers before an altar.' He must mingle his flesh with that supernal power—'Hand me those mainmast links there; I would fain feel this pulse, and let mine beat against it.' At this moment he casts away whatever binds him still to mankind: 'Thou art my fiery father; my sweet mother, I know not. . . .' By this irrevocable act Ahab rejects forever his feminine, creative, organic, loving inheritance of humankind, and cries, 'Here again with haughty agony, I read my sire.' Possessed now by machine-like, inhuman power, he can play sorcerer and seemingly control the very elements, proving himself 'lord over the level lodestone yet' when the electric storm reverses the compass needle (Ahab's manner of controlling the needle was, fittingly, reported two centuries earlier in Increase Mather's *Remarkable Providences.*[6]) Aboard the Pequod, 'As for the men . . . their fear of Ahab was greater than their fear of Fate.'

Everywhere Ahab is attended by the dark omens and providences appropriate to his demonic role. Like Moby Dick himself, he is rendered mighty and fearful by superstition. Ahab's nature and his doom are deeply *felt* by the primitives of the crew, whose intuitive perceptions the more 'civilized' American characters—Yankee mates and land-bound Quaker captains—lack. For instance, at Ahab's advent, Ishmael describes the 'slender rod-like mark, lividly whitish,' that threaded 'its way from among his grey hairs and continuing right down one side of his tawny scorched face and neck . . . disappeared in his clothing.' Ishmael adds, 'By some tacit consent, throughout the voyage little

[6] (London, 1890), preface [unpaged] and pp. 63-5, 73-7. Melville seems to have drawn for this material upon W. J. Scoresby's *Journal of a Voyage to the Northern Whale Fishery* (1823); cited by Mansfield and Vincent, *Moby-Dick*, pp. 823-4. He might have encountered it also in Book II, chapter 2 ('Concerning the Loadstone') of Sir Thomas Browne's *Vulgar Errors*, which Melville had borrowed by 1848 and bought in 1849 (Sealts, nos. 89-90).

or no allusion was made to it, especially by the mates,' whom he has just described as 'Every one of them Americans.' But the primitives immediately interpret Ahab's scar with the intuitional conviction of folk belief. A Gay Head Indian, oldest man aboard, 'superstitiously asserted that not till he was forty years old did Ahab become that way branded . . . in an elemental strife at sea. . . . Yet this wild hint seemed inferentially negatived by . . . a grey Manxman' whom 'old sea-traditions . . . popularly invested' with 'preternatural powers' and who avows the scar to be 'a birth-mark on him from crown to sole.' These conjectures parallel Hawthorne's 'formula of alternative possibilities'; although neither is completely valid, both are largely true, and each is truer than the rational censoring of all mention of the scar. The first thing the primitives notice about Ahab is that he is *a marked man.*

He, of course, like his Biblical namesake, is contemptuous of all omens sent to deter his purpose. Starbuck, the conventional Christian, can read the supernal meaning written by the finger of fire on Ahab's harpoon (chapter 109): 'God, God is against thee, old man, forebear.' But even in the three-day chase of Moby Dick Ahab scorns all omens. 'If the gods think to speak outright to man, they will honorably speak outright; not shake their heads, and give an old wives' darkling hint.—Begone!' Evil omens seem to Ahab 'not so much predictions from without as verifications of the foregoing things within' his own soul.

THREE

The opposed ethical commitments of Ishmael and Ahab thus result from splitting the personality of man. (There are yet further 'splits'—in a sense, the totality of human possibility is represented in *Moby-Dick* by the sum of the individual reactions to experience of the members of the crew, each of whom is endowed to excess with a particular trait or humor. This conjecture will become clearer in the discussion of the doubloon chapter.)

Just as the sermon of Father Mapple remains in the background as the 'scales of the New Testament' on which their respective souls are weighed, so the white whale swims ever in the foreground as the impetus to thought and action by which we continually compare the double heroes of this book. In presenting Moby Dick, Melville faced original problems in literary strategy whose solutions contributed both to his narrative method and to his effective dramatization of the dialectic between Ahab and Ishmael. For the most momentous difference between them is in their conception of the great whale that prepossesses both their imaginations.

Moby Dick, too, is heralded by portents, superstitions, omens of dread and apparitions of beauty, images which enchant and appall us at the same time. Long before the great white whale himself is seen, the entire crew beholds the spirit-spout (chapter 51):

> It was while gliding through these latter waters that one serene and moonlight night, when all the waves rolled by like scrolls of silver . . . a silvery jet was seen far in advance of the white bubbles at the bow. Lit up by the moon, it looked celestial; seemed some plumed and glittering god uprising from the sea. Fedallah first descried this jet.

With the cry 'There she blows!' the boats are lowered and the jet pursued—but it vanished and 'was seen no more than night.' As the whaleboats set off, the ship 'rushed along, as if two antagonistic influences were struggling in her—one to mount direct to heaven, the other to drive yawingly to some horizontal goal.' And in Ahab, too, 'you would have thought . . . two different things were warring. While his one live leg made lively echoes along the deck, every stroke of his dead limb sounded like a coffin-tap. On life and death this old man walked.' Night after night the spirit-spout was seen.

> Nor with the immemorial superstition of their race, and in accordance with the preternaturalness, as it seemed, which in so many things invested the Pequod, were there wanting some of the sea-

> men who swore that whenever and wherever descried; at however remote times, or in however far apart latitudes and longitudes, that unnearable spout was cast by one self-same whale; and that whale, Moby Dick. For a time, there reigned, too, a sense of peculiar dread at this flitting apparition, as if it were treacherously beckoning us on and on, in order that the monster might turn round upon us, and rend us at last in the remotest and most savage seas.

This chapter occasioned a comment from Mrs. Hawthorne, the reply to which gave us Melville's only statement of his aesthetic intentions:

> Your allusion to the Spirit Spout first showed to me that there was a subtle significance in that thing—but I did not, in that case, mean it. I had some vague idea while writing it, that the whole book was susceptible of an allegorical construction, & also that parts of it were—but the speciality of many of the particular subordinate allegories were first revealed to me after reading Mr. Hawthorne's letter, which, without citing any particular examples, yet intimated the part-&-parcel allegoricalness of the whole.[7]

Leaving aside his disclaimer of conscious intent (could he have been so ingenuously unaware of the pattern the 'linked analogies' of his metaphors had made?), we yet must face the problem of 'allegoricalness.' Were Melville writing with our critical vocabulary at his disposal he might be more prone to say 'symbolism' than 'allegory.' Yet his very 'symbolism,' like Hawthorne's, evolves from the most intense insistence upon allegory in order to deprive allegory of its monistic authority. Ahab has the most allegorical mind of any character in American fiction. To him the white whale represents 'all the subtle demonisms of life and thought; all evil.' But as he tells us this, Ishmael calls his captain 'crazy Ahab.' And the only other character as certain as Ahab is of the white whale's meaning is indeed crazy—Gabriel, the mad prophet aboard the Jeroboam. To him, Moby Dick is 'no less a being than the Shaker God incarnate'—a rigid, sterile, unmerciful God, just like the evil power that Ahab hates.

[7] *The Letters of Herman Melville,* p. 146.

Ahab's tragedy results from his forcing upon the protean multiplicity of experience his single iron purpose of vengeful woe. Ahab must be defeated because he is his own enemy; he has implacably placed himself in an untenable relation to reality. Yet to recognize this is not to deny that allegories may be found in nature. Although Ahab is unlegged, dismasted, battered, and drowned by the allegorism of the ego that would defy the gods, Moby Dick swims through allegorical seas and the book abounds with supernatural omens and portents, all fulfilled. These are nothing if not allegories.

A few paragraphs later in 'The Spirit-Spout' chapter, the Pequod runs into troubled seas.

> . . . thick in our rear flew the inscrutable sea-ravens. And every morning, perched on our stays, rows of these birds were seen; and . . . obstinately clung to the hemp, as though they deemed our ship some drifting, uninhabited craft; a thing appointed to desolation, and therefore fit roosting-place for their homeless selves. And heaved and heaved, still unresistingly heaved the black sea, as if its vast tides were a conscience; and the great mundane soul were in anguish and remorse for the long sin and suffering it had bred.

This passage, as Howard Vincent suggests, echoes Coleridge's *Rime of the Ancient Mariner;* the use of spectral ship, haunted ocean, and death omens serve Melville similarly. Such beliefs as these serve to knit into one indissoluble chain of 'linked analogies' the actions of man and the reactions of the natural world. What links man and nature by these supernatural ties but the omnipresence of the same spirit in both?

But Ishmael, too, is driven beyond himself to 'grasp the ungraspable phantom of life' in the deep seas where it lies hidden. The opening chapter tells us that

> in the wild conceits that swayed me to my purpose, two and two there floated into my inmost soul, endless processions of the whale, and, mid most of them all, one grand hooded phantom, like a snow hill in the air.

For Ahab there are no whales in the sea but Moby Dick; he hunts others grudgingly, merely to keep up the semblance of normal life with his restless crew, and he wastes no words in gams with captains who have no news of Moby Dick, what though their ships have passed through armadas of other sperm. Ishmael, on the other hand, throughout conceives of Moby Dick as the whale of whales, larger, more beautiful, more fearsome, more powerful than others, but of their kind and species, and alive with the life that lives in them. His phrase 'two and two' describing the whales' procession in the passage above, recalls Genesis 7:9, 'They went in two and two unto Noah into the ark, the male and the female, as God had commanded Noah.' Thus Moby Dick first appears to Ishmael's mind amongst the mating couples; later, in 'The Grand Armada' (chapter 87) Ishmael, seeing the coupling whales, asks, 'who could tell whether, in that congregated caravan, Moby Dick himself might not be temporarily swimming.' For Ishmael Moby Dick *is* Nature, concentrated in a single unfeatured visage. And the superstitions about that 'grand hooded phantom' represent, for Ishmael, the immanence of spirit in the material forms that it creates. This being so, then all that Ishmael observes, thinks, or feels of all whales pertains in some measure to his thoughts and feelings regarding Moby Dick.

In this light we may approach Ishmael's comical reclassification of whales (chapter 32), the first of many chapters of cetological lore which some readers find an impediment to the narrative. Ishmael, it will be recalled, rejects the structural classifications of the explorer Scoresby and the biologist Linnaeus, and divides whales instead 'according to magnitude' into 'Books (subdivisible into chapters),' a scheme appropriate enough from a former 'Sub-Sub-Librarian.' Ishmael's basis for his enterprise is a very Emersonian assertion of the superiority of first-hand experience over book-learning: 'I have had to do with whales with these visible hands; I am in earnest.' His rejection of Linnaeus is sanctioned by 'my friends Simeon Macy and Charley

Coffin, of Nantucket,' who 'profanely hinted' that the scientist's reasons 'were humbug.' Abetted by these folk companions, Ishmael offers his Folio System as a long-bow compounded in the exaggerative spirit of the tall tale; it is based on what the senses perceive and what the imagination makes thereof. Thus Ishmael denies that either rationalism or science can tell us the truth about the whale.

The tall-tale mode continues as he quotes Charles Coffin on the use the Narwhale makes of his horn—breaking the Polar ice. Ishmael tops this with another—the Narwhale's horn is 'convenient . . . for a folder in reading pamphlets.' Then he reaches back from present tall tale to the legends of antiquity: 'He is certainly a curious example of the Unicornism to be found in almost every kingdom of animated nature,' and relates how the horn was anciently 'the great antidote against poison.' The basic argument against science, however, is this: 'I take the good old-fashioned ground that the whale is a fish, and call upon holy Jonah to back me.'

At the chapter's end Ishmael must avow that the mystery escapes even his sportive imagination:

> I now leave my cetological System standing thus unfinished, even as the great Cathedral of Cologne was left, with the cranes still standing upon the top of the uncompleted tower. For small erections may be finished by their first architects; grand ones, true ones, ever leave the copestone to posterity. God keep me from ever completing anything. This whole book is but a draught—nay, but the draught of a draught.

Here Melville links Ishmael's imaginative play with the writing of his book, while the tower image suggests that Ishmael's story is written in the same spirit in which the great cathedral was built. In a truly reverent work of human hands, the copestone must be left 'to posterity,' since, as Father Mapple in his sermon on 'holy Jonah' had asked, 'What is man that he should live out the lifetime of his God?' Not even the artist's imagination, then, can tell us the truths about the whale which science is unable to discern. In chapters 55-57 we get a disquisition 'Of the Monstrous Pictures of Whales,' and learn that 'the great Leviathan is that one creature in the world which must remain unpainted to the last.' Again it is only experience, neither science nor art, which can bring man to the truth. 'There is no earthly way of finding out precisely what the whale really looks like' save 'by going a whaling yourself; but by so doing, you run no small risk of being eternally stove and sunk by him. Wherefore, it seems to me you had best not be too fastidious in your curiosity touching this Leviathan.' But Ishmael, though he knows the danger, cannot turn back.

FOUR

Ishmael's motives actually are more complex than Ahab's vengeance. When he finds himself following funerals and pausing before coffin warehouses, instead of suicide he takes to the sea. In the book's first paragraph the double aspect of water is already apparent: in the ocean Ishmael seeks an immersion in the infinite which is a substitute for death itself. Yet immersion will return him to life reborn. Indeed, in the end it is a coffin that buoys him on the ocean. But now at the beginning Ishmael muses on water—'There is magic in it,' he says, turning at once from magic to myth:

> Why did the old Persians hold the sea holy? Why did the Greeks give it a separate deity, and own brother of Jove? Surely all this is not without meaning. And still deeper the meaning of that story of Narcissus, who because he could not grasp the tormenting, mild image he saw in the fountain, plunged into it and was drowned. But that same image, we ourselves see in all rivers and oceans. It is the image of the ungraspable phantom of life; and this is the key to it all.

That key slides surely but slowly into the lock upon the mystery of the universe.

Melville's knowledge of Narcissus came from Book III of

Ovid's *Metamorphoses*, where Tiresias had prophesied of the youth, 'If e'er he knows himself, he surely dies'; and this fate comes to him after he spurns the love of Echo and tries to merge with his own reflected image in the pool. The Narcissus image this early in *Moby-Dick* puts into play a cluster of related concepts, subsequently expanded. Narcissus is first of all a seeker; but he is also a solipsist and self-lover. In each respect he is the prototype of all in *Moby-Dick* who seek 'that same image . . . in all rivers and oceans.'

The Narcissus image recurs potently again just before the quarter-deck ritual, when Ishmael, aloft on the masthead, is

> lulled into such an opium-like listlessness of vacant, unconscious reverie . . . by the blending cadence of waves with thoughts, that at last he loses his identity; takes the mystic ocean at his feet for the visible image of that deep, blue, bottomless soul, pervading mankind and nature; . . . every dimly-discovered, uprising fin of some undiscernible form, seems to him the embodiment of those elusive thoughts that only people the soul by continually flitting through it. . . .
>
> There is no life in thee, now, except that rocking life imparted by a gentle rolling ship; by her, borrowed from the sea; by the sea, from the inscrutable tides of God. But while this sleep, this dream is on ye, move your foot or hand an inch; slip your hold at all; and your identity comes back in horror. Over Descartian vortices you hover. And perhaps at mid-day, in the fairest weather, with one half-throttled shriek you drop through that transparent air into the summer sea, no more to rise for ever. Heed it well, ye Pantheists!

Such was the fate of Bulkington, the perfect shipmate with tragic wisdom in his eyes—'Up from the spray of thy ocean-perishing—straight up, leaps thy apotheosis!' And of Pip, the little black boy abandoned in the illimitable sea. But Ishmael, poised over the vortex, retreats from this immersion in the universe which results in the loss of self. Ahab, we shall see, on the first day of the chase looks down into the sea at exactly the same vision, here described so lullingly, there with terrifying malignity.

The triple function of Narcissus is enacted again in the ritualistic examination by the ship's company of that doubloon which Ahab had nailed to the mast (chapter 99). This coin, we are reminded, the superstitious sailors had 'set apart and sanctified' as 'the white whale's talisman.' Eight principal characters in turn step forward to regard it. Each sees 'the image of the ungraspable phantom of life,' and reads it in the light of his own character. The doubloon, as the metaphoric double of the whale, operates here in a way similar to Pearl's relationship to the scarlet letter. This is a pivotal point of the narrative, for we have seen how inscrutable is the truth of the whale, undefined by either science or art and rendered bafflingly both comical and portentous by folk traditions. Here, instead of a monster which threatens to stave in the observer who would approach him, we have as his surrogate a simple coin with a readily comprehended design:

> On its round border it bore the letters, REPUBLICA DEL ECUADOR: QUITO. So this bright coin came from a country planted in the middle of the world, and beneath the great equator, and named after it; and it had been cast midway up the Andes, in the unwaning clime that knows no autumn. Zoned by those letters you saw the likeness of three Andes' summits; from one a flame; a tower on another; on the third a crowing cock; while arching over all was a segment of the partitioned zodiac, the signs all marked with their usual cabalistics, and the keystone sun entering the equinoctial point at Libra.

Ahab finds 'something ever egotistical in mountain-tops and towers. . . . The firm tower, that is Ahab; the volcano, that is Ahab; the courageous, the undaunted, and victorious fowl, that, too, is Ahab; all are Ahab; and this round globe is but the image of the rounder globe, which, like a magician's glass, to each and every man in turn but mirrors back his own mysterious self.' Succeeding interpreters verify Ahab's view of a universal Narcissistic solipsism. Starbuck, the good Christian who lacks the will to rebel, thinks he sees 'the Trinity, in some faint earthly symbol,' but he fears to probe it. Stubb makes a mock-almanac of the zodiac, tracing man's life as a joke, according to his own morally slothful, rationalistic optimism. Flask, crassly materialistic, calculates the doubloon's worth at 960 cigars. The next three observers are primitives among the crew. The superstitious old Manxman, recalling astrology learned from 'the old witch in Copenhagen,' portends unspecified disaster for the ship. Queequeg finds analogies between the zodiac and his own tattooed body. Fedallah bows to the sun.

These views of the doubloon are presented in concentric rings of vision. Ahab, Starbuck, Flask, Manxman, and Queequeg know only their own versions. But Stubb sees—and reports—all who follow him. Last comes Pip, seeing all who preceded him. 'Here's the ship's navel, this doubloon here, and they are all on fire to unscrew it. But unscrew your navel, and what's the consequence?' Only Ishmael's vision encompasses all the others. Ishmael, reporting them all, adds nothing himself—except that the whole of *Moby-Dick* is Ishmael's contemplation of the whole. 'I look, you look, he looks; we look, ye look, they look,' Pip had crowed, emphasizing the multiple appearances of the single reality, the 'ungraspable phantom of life.' The doubloon chapter splits the observer into eight pairs of eyes, representing, in a crude reduction, will, faith, accommodation, greed,—here we leave the white race for more intuitive members of mankind—fear (the Manxman), power (Fedallah), and Pip's gibberish which transcends human wisdom. But I have left out Queequeg from this roster; his reading of the doubloon deserves closer attention.

Stubb watched in surprise as Queequeg compared his tattooings to the zodiac, and the doubloon's symbols to his body: 'Thinks the sun is in the thigh. . . . By Jove, he's found something there in the vicinity of his thigh—I guess it's Sagittarius, or the Archer.' What Queequeg finds of course is sexuality, his creative power, imaged on the doubloon as both the sun and the Archer, the source of energy and himself as harpooner. But the doubloon after all replaces the white whale in the scheme of things. What Queequeg recognizes, then, is the identity of his own sexual vitality with the supernal potency of Moby Dick. This is his intuitive acknowledgment that fertility is sacred. If we each enact Narcissus's fate, then lucky is he whose 'own mysterious self' plunges deepest into the depths of truth in the vortex. Queequeg, bound to Ishmael by a ritualized comradely marriage, stands, in the geometry of the soul this scene devises, for a Narcissus finding his Echo: the copulative, conjugal capacities of human love. From these capacities Ahab's will, like his symbolically castrating wound, debars him. Ishmael, who alone encompasses the composite vision of the others, is the whole man, more so even than his loving Queequeg. The cannibal-bedmate is that part of Ishmael's own primeval self which asserts his love of life, as Ahab objectifies his primordial urge toward suicide.

When at last the final chase begins, it becomes a dreamlike repetition of key motifs.[8] Ahab, peering into the depths of the sea, beholds precisely what Ishmael had seen from the masthead. But Ahab's 'own mysterious self' is no Platonist dreamer lulled by the sea. 'He profoundly saw a white living spot no bigger than a white weasel, with wonderful celerity uprising, and magnifying as it rose, till . . . The glittering mouth yawned beneath the boat like an open-doored marble tomb.' The ungraspable phantom of life reveals the image of its beholder: Ahab's violent destructive will projects upon Moby Dick the image of his own vengeance. In the vortex Ahab, like Narcissus, seeks and finds himself, and dies.

FIVE

In the world of *Moby-Dick* nothing exists without its opposite and no vision which fails to encompass both poles of every contrast can embrace the truth. The qualities Melville dramatized

[8] Ahab of course wins his own doubloon by sighting Moby Dick himself; he offers it again, wins it again, and loses his leg (the ivory one) again.

through the Narcissus myth are necessarily in tension with their opposites, and those qualities inhere in another legendary nexus of images: the Jonah story. This theme is early introduced by Father Mapple's sermon in chapter 9. When Narcissus as Seeker leans toward 'the mild image in the fountain,' Jonah as Rebel tries to flee by water from the command of God. Where Narcissus proves a solipsist, the rebel Jonah at last acknowledges the God beyond himself. In consequence Jonah is not, like Narcissus, a suicide, but is reborn, literally resurrected from his death inside the whale. These experiences of Jonah's prove to be prototypes of several adventures suffered not only by Ishmael and Ahab but also by the harpooners Tashtego and Queequeg and by the demented cabin-boy Pip.

It is essential that we recognize these not only as Biblical parallels but also as the enactments of the ritual significance of the Jonah story itself. That story, as William Simpson demonstrated in 1899 in *The Jonah Legend* is in fact the account of an initiation in which the candidate for admission to divine knowledge at first ceremonially rebels against submission to the divine behest, the 'Not-Me'; then undergoes a symbolic mock-death in the whale's belly (actually, a vault below the floor of the temple[9]); and emerges reborn into the cult or priesthood.

Melville, writing half a century earlier, yet had access to the evidence the theologian would, with the help of Frazer's anthropology, systematize into his ritual interpretation. Drawing on both Pierre Bayle's *Historical and Critical Dictionary* and John Kitto's recently issued *Cyclopedia of Biblical Literature,* Melville found the very rationalistic hypotheses which Simpson would use to support his contention that the Biblical Jonah legend was in fact a late variant of an ancient initiation ritual. Melville's two sources take opposite views of the same evidence (it is probable that for his articles on 'Jonah' and 'Whale' Kitto drew on Bayle, disputing the Frenchman's skepticism). Mel-

[9] In the prefatory 'Etymology' Melville cites as one origin of the word *whale* the Danish *hvalt,* 'arched or vaulted.'

ville mined whole paragraphs from both, sportively adopting the rationalizations of the legend which the Frenchman proposed and which the pious encyclopedist had been at pains to discredit.[10]

Melville, however, can make the descent into the whale just as literal as it seems in the Book of Jonah, as he does when Tashtego falls into the severed head of a dead sperm. Or he can describe the Pequod in similes suggesting the ship itself as a whale: 'A cannibal of a craft'—as though she would swallow her crew—'tricking herself forth in the chased bones of her enemies,' her bulwarks 'garnished like one continuous jaw, with the long sharp teeth of the sperm whale,' and her tiller 'carved from the long narrow jaw of her hereditary foe.' The similitude is already established in Father Mapple's text: 'Beneath the ship's water-line, Jonah feels the heralding presentiment of that stifling

[10] Melville's debt to Bayle is exhaustively treated by Millicent L. Bell, 'Pierre Bayle and *Moby-Dick*,' *PMLA*, LXVI (Sept. 1951), 626-36; Mansfield and Vincent cite the parallels to Kitto on pp. 778, 780-81 of their edition of *Moby-Dick*. Both commentators allege, as Melville does in ch. 82, that Jonah sailed from Jaffa, where a pagan temple for ages displayed the bones of a whale claimed to be those of the dragon slain by Perseus. In ch. 83, 'Jonah Historically Regarded,' Melville slightly paraphrases the following suppositions given by Kitto, proposing them as tenable, despite Kitto's evident disdain:

'Now, if the text be literally taken, the transaction is plainly miraculous . . . and if it be allegorical, as some, we think, erroneously assume, then, whether the prophet was saved by means of a kind of boat called *dagh* [the Hebrew word for whale, which Melville prints in 'Etymology'], or it be a mystical account of initiation where the neophyte was detained three days in an ark or boat, figuratively denominated a fish, or Celtic *avanc;* and it assuredly would be derogating from the high divinity of the prophet's mission, to convert the event into a mere escape, by boat, into a pagan legend such as Hercules, Bacchus, Jamsheed, and other deified heroes of remotest antiquity, are fabled to have undergone, and which all the ancient mysteries, including the Druidical, symbolized.'

Kitto similarly dismisses the proposal, which Melville quotes approvingly that 'Jonah, when thrown into the sea, was taken up by a ship having a large fish for a figure-head,' and the hypothesis that Jonah was saved 'by a life-preserver.' This is doubtless the hint for Ishmael's eventual deliverance by means of Queequeg's unused coffin, which the cannibal had offered (in ch. 126) as a life buoy for the crew.

hour, when the whale shall hold him in the smallest of his bowels' wards.'

The conventional Christian interpretation of Jonah proposes his 'death' and resurrection after three days in the whale as a prefiguration of Christ's rising. Melville consistently presents Ahab, his Antichrist, in the guise of an unrepentant Jonah. Ahab's disobedience of God's commands foredooms the voyage;[11] his aggressive will, we recognize, is in flight from truth rather than possessing it. His godless purpose provokes the elements themselves at the Pequod's first pursuit of a whale. As the boat crew strike the whale, the storm strikes them; the ship looms through the mist and the frightened men cast themselves into the sea. But where Jonah confessed his apostasy and the crew threw him overboard, Ahab's 'confession' on the quarter-deck puts his entire crew in league with him. The Antichrist is at this stage an Anti-Jonah, welcoming the catastrophe his own mad pride had created. Father Mapple had warned, 'Delight—top-gallant delight is to him, who acknowledges no law or lord, but the Lord his God, and is only a patriot to heaven.' This delight Ahab can never know, who blindly refuses to disobey himself. But Ahab meets his end as though it were a triumph; although he dies, Moby Dick has proved to be the 'outrageous strength, with an inscrutable malice sinewing it; whether agent or principal,' which Ahab hates; in death Ahab merges at last with the uncontrollable power he pressed his pulse against when the corposants blazed above him. Even some part of Jonah's delight is his after all: 'And eternal delight and deliciousness will be his, who coming to lay him down, can say with his final breath—O Father!—Known to me chiefly by Thy rod—mortal or immortal, here I die.' For the Hebraic-Calvinistic God of the Nantucket sailors' Bethel *is*, in the end, patristic, unknowable power. Compounded

[11] In his earlier assault against God's command (on the previous voyage) the whale had given him warning of God's will by *swallowing only his leg*. Ahab is maddened rather than forewarned.

of heretical apostasies though Ahab's woe-reaping monism may be, he is yet on his own terms triumphant in defeat, acknowledging the justice of his dreadful punishment. But Ahab's terms are those of the sterile, regressive, annihilation-seeking solipsist. Having made himself into a destructive machine, he must perish without hope of resurrection.

Ishmael's original disobedience would consist in the 'damp, drizzly November in his soul,' the denial of life that brought him, too, to the Pequod's wharf. (The sketch of the blacksmith, chapter 112, suggests that this death-wish is a universal motive.) Ishmael had said, 'The world's a ship on its passage out.' He was in the boat that chased the first whale in the storm, and, when the Pequod loomed out of the mist he too leapt into the sea. 'Saved' by the ship, the Pequod for him becomes the whale it so curiously resembles. When it sinks, he is cast forth as Jonah was spewed from the mouth of the fish.

Although Ishmael more completely than the rest enacts Jonah's initiatory ritual, he does so in the presence not of Jonah's God but of Job's. Jonah's God, as Matthew 12:40 tells us, becomes God the Merciful Father of Jesus: 'For as Jonas was three days and three nights in the heart of the earth.' And the next verse prophesies that 'The men of Nineveh shall rise in Judgment with this generation, and shall condemn it: because they repented at the preaching of Jonas.' When we compare Father Mapple's sermon to the Book of Jonah we are struck by Melville's suppression of the sequel to Jonah's deliverance from the whale; his Jonah does not propose to God vengeance against the sinners of Nineveh, nor is he chastened by the parable of the gourd, illustrating God's infinite mercy.

The fifth 'Extract' is especially significant: 'In that day, the Lord with his sore, and great, and strong sword, shall punish Leviathan the piercing serpent, even Leviathan that crooked serpent, and he shall slay the dragon that is in the sea' [Isa. 21:1]. Here is Biblical support for both Ishmael's contention that whalemen are the culture-heroes of antiquity and for Ahab's contention of his self-appointed destiny. It is of course the fatality of Ahab's hubris that he sees himself as the lordly avenger slaying the tangible shape of evil. But Ishmael, just after the quarter-deck, declares Ahab (in chapter 41) to be an 'ungodly old man, chasing with curses a Job's whale round the world.' After Ishmael has endured the annihilation Ahab willed, he begins his epilogue with the words of Job's messengers of destruction: 'And I only am escaped alone to tell thee.'

But who is 'thee,' and what message is Ishmael alone escaped to tell? He survives to preach to *us*, his Nineveh, as Father Mapple had said of Jonah who 'did the Almighty's bidding. And what was that, shipmates? To preach the Truth to the face of Falsehood! That was it!'

Yet Ishmael's 'Truth' is neither the submission of Jonah to God's will nor the still more Christian humility Father Mapple proposed as 'top-gallant delight.' How far Melville was from accepting the 'Divine Inert' as his guide to this world is apparent from the contrast between Ishmael and Pip. For Pip's actions parallel Jonah's being cast away and Christ's resurrection, but at the cost of his accommodation to any life in this world. In a chapter titled 'The Castaway' we learn how little Pip on his first whale chase had leapt in terror into the sea and was abandoned as Stubb pursued the whale. 'The intense concentration of self in the middle of such a heartless immensity, my God! who can tell it?' When saved by the ship,

> the little negro went about the deck an idiot . . . The sea had jeeringly kept his finite body up, but drowned the infinite of his soul. Not drowned entirely, though. Rather carried down alive to wondrous depths where strange shapes of the unwarped primal world glided to and fro before his passive eyes. . . . He saw God's foot upon the treadle of the loom, and spoke it; and therefore his shipmates called him mad. So man's insanity is heaven's sense.

Pip's resurrection is entirely spiritual—his very name, Pip for Pippin, suggests Matt. 13:38, 'the good seed are the children of the kingdom.' Losing his earthly senses, he participates in glory.

In his gibberish he plays Fool to Ahab's Lear; in his sanctity, Good Angel to Ahab's Faust. Unheeded, Pip yet brings the New Testament God of Mercy and Transfiguration before the mind that conceives only of the Old Testament God of Wrath, vengeance, and destruction. 'Hands off that holiness!' Ahab cries, acknowledging the godliness in Pip that he has inverted and denied in himself. Ishmael may have Pip's transcendent glory in mind when he says, at the end of 'The Castaway,' 'In the sequel of the narrative it will then be seen what like abandonment befell myself.' Pip is in glory already; Ishmael, saved like Jonah from the whale, has yet to endure his span of life with the knowledge of God won at last by all his senses from experience of that whale. And the whale, as he had said, was 'a Job's whale.'

Tashtego's deliverance was more literally Jonah-like, since his peril was to fall into the head of a whale. Where Pip is spiritually 'saved,' the redemption of Tashtego is emphatically physical. Queequeg leaps overboard, knife in hand, cuts his way into the now sinking head, and by dint of 'agile obstetrics,' rescues Tashtego 'in the good old way, head-first,' in 'a running delivery.' This is but one of Queequeg's several acknowledgments of the divine law of love which makes him, at life's risk, assume responsibility for his fellow-man—first a bumpkin on a New Bedford schooner, later Ishmael himself; and, in the end, Queequeg proffers the coffin prepared for his sickness as a life-preserver with thirty life-lines, for the entire crew. Tashtego's rebirth from the whale keeps the Jonah imagery afloat in mid-passage, but it is focussed throughout on Ahab's rebellion and Ishmael's survival. Queequeg is the agent both of Tashtego's delivery and of Ishmael's. A closer look at the cannibal's part in these rituals may help us discern more precisely what qualifies Ishmael to outlive the annihilation which Ahab brings to all his shipmates.

SIX

Following the chain of images that link Queequeg to Ishmael, Ishmael to cannibals, cannibalism to Nature, and Nature to Moby Dick, we can best begin with the coffin–life buoy. When Queequeg willed his own recovery from sickness, he passed his convalescence carving on the wooden box the very designs tattooed on his own skin. These he had found analogous to the zodiacal signs on the doubloon.

> This tattooing had been the work of a departed prophet and seer of his island, who, by those hieroglyphic marks, had written out on his body a complete theory of the heavens and the earth, and a mystical treatise on the art of attaining truth.

Thus in Queequeg the human body is a holy writ, and the text, could he read it, would reveal truth of the sort Narcissus sought and Jonah suffered for. But 'these mysteries were . . . destined in the end to moulder away with the living parchment whereon they were inscribed, and so be unsolved to the last.' Yet not quite unsolved. For although Ishmael does not finally formulate the mystery he has experienced, his experience is the knowledge, his knowledge *is* the experience. And Queequeg with his 'mystical treatise' plays a pivotal role in saving Ishmael from becoming like Ahab an irredeemable 'isolato.'

Awaking in the Spouter Inn, himself and the cannibal 'a cosy, loving pair,' Ishmael finds 'I began to be sensible of strange feelings. I felt a melting in me. No more my splintered heart and maddened hand were turned against the wolfish world. This soothing savage had redeemed it.' There follows the ritual of their 'marriage,' 'meaning, in his country's phrase, that we were bosom friends.'[12]

Queequeg's tattooing at first had affrighted Ishmael, as it had Landlord Coffin and other civilized Christians who behold it. Civilization recoils at savagery. But by morning Ishmael acknowl-

[12] Queequeg's country 'is not down on any map; true places never are.'

edges Queequeg 'For all his tattooings . . . on the whole a clean, comely looking cannibal. . . . a human being just as I am.' Much later in the book we find that Ishmael himself is tattooed: in 'A Bower in the Arsacides' he once beheld a chapel made in the vine-hung skeleton of a whale, where 'Life folded Death; Death trellised Life,' and on his right arm he had tattooed the dimensions of that skeleton. No doubt Ishmael, too, could have found similitudes to his own hieroglyphs on the zodiac-rimmed doubloon.

By taking a cannibal for his bosom friend Ishmael acknowledges that part of himself which finds its identity in Queequeg: the unfallen Adam characterized by instinctual grace, sensuous beauty, and the primordial energies affirming life and love. These analogies linked to Queequeg show forth the conflict between pagan and Christian values in contexts much different from Ahab's allegiances to heathen gods and apostate sinners. In and around Queequeg cluster value-laden images not only of cannibalism opposing Christianity but of primitivism versus civilization, of intuition versus willed purpose. The son of a cannibal king, Queequeg had 'a profound desire to learn among Christians the arts to make his people . . . still better than they were.' Ishmael, for his part, thinks 'I'll try a pagan friend . . . since Christian kindness has proved but hollow.' It is Queequeg who proves the better soul than the Christians around him. In fact he learns nothing from them but their capacities for evil; pure to the end, he is not even contaminated by knowledge of their sin. Ishmael on the other hand learns everything from Queequeg of the unfallen man that Queequeg is, that Ishmael himself longs to but cannot be. He will not be ready to receive the mercy of survival after 'just punishment' until he knows the Queequeg as well as he knows the Ahab within him.

The Ishmael-Queequeg relationship, it is plain, makes peculiar demands upon the reader's participation. We must be willing to follow Melville from 'Better sleep with a sober cannibal than a drunken Christian' to 'I found Queequeg's arm thrown over me in the most loving and affectionate manner. You had almost thought I had been his wife.' This latter image is shortly developed into the marriage ritual mentioned above. It is worth noting what comes between 'You had almost thought I had been his wife' (chapter 4) and 'henceforth we were married'; 'he would gladly die for me, if need be' (chapter 10). What intervenes is a typically Ishmaelite sequence of alternating terror, comedy, and awe. On waking under Queequeg's arm, Ishmael recalls a childhood nightmare of entrapment and possession by a menacing Other; this is followed by Yankee fun about a bumpkin dandy's sea-faring costume and the tall tales of New Bedford dowries and Salem sweethearts; then Father Mapple's sermon. Queequeg's marriage-rite, which promises his dying for his bosom friend, comes between that sermon and the propitiation, by both, of Queequeg's god, the little black idol Yojo. 'Thus, then, in our hearts' honeymoon, lay I and Queequeg—a cosy, loving pair.'

This extraordinary relationship is the fantasy of one whom the psychologist Henry A. Murray has called 'a profoundly creative man in whose androgynic personality masculine and feminine components are integrally blended.' Doubtless Melville's duality resulted both from his own familial relations and from 'the Hebraic-Christian, American Calvinistic tradition . . . which conceived of a deity in whose eyes Eros was depravity.'[13] Queequeg, prefigured by *Typee, Omoo,* and *Mardi,* is the final elixir of Melville's own awakening—among the unfallen, indolent, sybaritic, occasionally man-eating Polynesians—to the erotic impulse as the source of life-giving energy. In *Moby-Dick,* as in most of Melville's work, one cannot but be struck by the absence of women; here the repression of femininity, and its recrudescence in the passive aspects both of male characters (Ish-

[13] 'In Nomine Diaboli,' p. 447.

mael, Pip) and of the white whale, is dreamlike.[14] Some of the difficulties Melville had in envisaging the man's sexual role are more than hinted at in Ishmael's dream. Once, as a child, on the afternoon of the longest day of the year, his 'stepmother' had found him trying to crawl up a chimney; she had dragged him out 'by the legs,' and sent him off to bed, supperless. 'I lay there dismally calculating that sixteen hours must elapse before I could hope for a resurrection.' At last he fell into 'a troubled nightmare of a doze,' from which he awoke to find

> the before sun-lit room was now wrapped in outer darkness. Instantly I felt a shock running through all my frame . . . a supernatural hand seemed placed in mine. My arm hung over the counterpane, and the nameless, unimaginable, silent form or phantom, to which the hand belonged, seemed closely seated by my bedside. For what seemed ages piled on ages, I lay there, frozen, with the most awful fears, not daring to drag away my hand; yet ever thinking that if I could but stir it one single inch, the horrid spell would be broken.

Except for absence of 'the awful fear,' Ishmael's feelings are 'very similar' when he found 'Queequeg's pagan arm thrown round me.' For though Ishmael tried to 'unlock his bridegroom clasp . . . he still hugged me tightly, as though naught but death should part us twain.'

Connected with the dream-transformation of sexual penetration, such intense associations of guilt, parental punishment, unspeakable terror, imaged death and resurrection might have completely inhibited the narrator's expression of Eros. Certainly this is the case with Ahab, whose dismemberment is, dream-like, reduplicated in chapter 106 in terms that make unequivocal his symbolic emasculation. ('By some unknown, and seemingly inexplicable, unimaginable casualty, his ivory limb . . . had stake-wise smitten, and all but pierced his groin.') Ishmael es-

[14] Yet Job gives Melville warrant for making Moby Dick both masculine and feminine: 'Hath the rain a father? or who hath begotten the drops of the dew? Out of whose womb came the ice? and the hoary frost of the heaven, who hath gendered it?' [28:28-9].

capes Ahab's fate, finding, as Arvin says, an ethical rather than sterile dependence upon his fellow-man. Within the patterns of *Moby-Dick* what justifies Ishmael's ritual of affiliation with Queequeg is its symbolic representation of the whole soul giving allegiance to its own unfallen creative energy.

That this is specifically Ishmael's chief claim for salvation is made dramatically clear when he universalizes the original marriage ritual in 'A Squeeze of the Hand.' Ishmael, we recall, like the rest of the crew, had been bound by Ahab's evil rites on the quarter-deck. Then 'Ahab's crazy quest seemed mine.' Before he can be saved from the just punishment of that quest Ishmael must dissociate himself from Ahab's purpose. And this will require a yet more powerful ritual of his own.

The scene is carefully prepared for by passing again through Ishmael's consciousness the alternating emotions of comic trickery (Stubb's outwitting a French whaler to capture an ambergris-laden whale), wonder (Ishmael's meditation on St. Paul, 'we are sown in dishonor, but raised in glory'), terror and transfiguration (Pip's story). Now Ishmael and his shipmates must squeeze the lumpy ambergris into clear fluid.

> As I snuffed up that uncontaminated aroma. . . . I forgot all about our horrible oath; in that inexpressible sperm, I washed my hands and my heart of it. . . .
>
> I squeezed that sperm till I myself almost melted into it . . . till a strange sort of insanity came over me; and I found myself unquittingly squeezing my co-laborers' hands in it, mistaking their hands for the gentle globules. . . . Come; let us squeeze hands all round; nay, let us all squeeze ourselves into each other; let us squeeze ourselves universally into the very milk and sperm of kindness.

The universal squeezing of mankind's hands, all immersed in this richly sexual imagery, dissolves Ahab's 'What say ye, men, will ye splice hands on it?' It affirms and extends Ishmael's bantering defense, against Captain Peleg when he and Queequeg signed aboard, of the cannibal's membership in 'the great and everlasting First Congregation of this whole worshipping world,' in which 'we all join hands.'

Yet Queequeg must die for Ishmael to live, as in his marriage vow the savage had sworn to do. For Melville is too profound a soul to settle his battle against the modern world by regression into that 'insular Tahiti' which lies 'in the soul of man . . . full of peace and joy'; Melville must acknowledge too that his paradise is 'encompassed round by all the horrors of the half known life. God keep thee! Push not off from that isle, thou canst never return.' It is most apposite, therefore, that his unfallen character be not merely a savage, but a *cannibal.* Though natural goodness makes this cannibal a purer soul in his savagery than any Christian in his civilization, his state of nature is yet spiritually incomplete. And ambiguously fraught with dangers of its own.

> Long exile from Christendom and civilization inevitably restores a man to that condition in which God placed him, *i.e.* what is called savagery. Your true whale-hunter is as much a savage as an Iroquois. I myself am a savage; owning no allegiance but to the King of the Cannibals; and ready at any moment to rebel against him. (Chapter 57)

The instinctual self, then, is the source both of Eros and of anarchy. To separate oneself from it, as Ahab tries to do, inevitably leads to the dehumanization of the ego. The unfallen cannibal within us must be 'married' and assimilated; it cannot be escaped.

It cannot be escaped because the energy it holds—both fecund and anarchic—is an intrinsic part of Nature. Here are 'the horrors of the half known life.' These are made known, in the chapter called 'The Shark Massacre,' as the 'horrible vulturism of earth, from which not the mightiest whale is free.' Stubb has killed a whale and must have the cook prepare him a steak for supper. This bluff, thoughtless mate has a streak of Mike Fink's humor in him, and bullies the cook into preaching a sermon to the sharks who are 'mingling their mumblings with his own mastications.' The old Negro's reluctant sermon is comic in the frontier fashion, but it reiterates without parody the ethical view of Father Mapple. That the cook preaches to sharks is, however, of some moment:

> 'Your woraciousness, fellow-critters, I don't blame ye so much for; dat is natur, and can't be helped; but to gobern dat wicked natur, dat is de pint. You is sharks, sartin; but if you gobern de shark in you, why den you be angel; for all angel is not'ing more dan de shark well goberned. . . . Don't be tearin' de blubber out your neighbour's mout. . . . de brigness of de mout is not to swallar wid, but to bite off de blubber for de small fry ob sharks, dat can't get into de scrouge to help demselves.'
>
> 'Well done, old Fleece!' cried Stubb, 'that's Christianity.'

SEVEN

Father Mapple's Christianity is meaningless in a world of sharks. Only Pip, whose soul did not know the savagery necessary to the true whaler, the mortal man, can attain the selflessness of the Sermon on the Mount. The only other practising Christian on the Pequod is the first mate, Starbuck. And he is described at the outset as suffering 'the incompetence of mere unaided virtue or right-mindedness.' Although physically no coward, the mate 'cannot withstand those more terrific, because more spiritual terrors, which sometimes menace you from the concentrating brow of an enraged and mighty man.' Living by his own code of Christian charity, he yet fails in what Ishmael presents to us as a higher law: active rebellion against active evil. Starbuck alone has the temporal authority, intelligence, and moral perception to overthrow Ahab's wicked tyranny and thus save all the crew. But he lacks the power to meet power with power. His unfulfilled duties are made plain by the interpolated fable of 'The Town-Ho's Story' in which a subordinate's rebellion against a tyrannous mate is given divine sanction—by Moby Dick.

Nature does not accommodate or condone the failure to meet amoral force with force, what though power itself corrupt. Nature, God's own creation, is not pure, but sharkish, vulturish, cannibalistic, horrible. And Ishmael, as we have seen, knows himself a cannibal, ever ready to rebel against even his savage king. Christianity as Melville knew it was unequal to the needs his faith must fulfill. On one side it led to the repression of Eros, the worship of force, to Ahab's emasculation of humanity; on the other, to Starbuck's ineffectual passivity or to the superhuman acceptance of the Divine Inert—Pip's mindless purity, which proves effeminate, passive, deathlike.

What faith Melville proposes through Ishmael's initiation is of course determined by the nature of his God. In the rituals of non-Christian worship and in the entire constellation of legends, superstitions, and beliefs about the whale we may find at last the lineaments of Deity in *Moby-Dick.* To find his God, his father, had been Ahab's quest; his method he foretold in saying 'All visible objects, man, are but as pasteboard masks. . . . If man will strike, strike through the mask!' Ahab's violence, projecting itself through the mask of appearances, never doubts that anything but itself lurks there: Narcissus as avenger.

But once, Ishmael does see what lies behind the pasteboard mask. In his bedchamber at the Spouter Inn was 'a papered fireboard representing a man striking a whale.' Queequeg's first act on entering—before he even knows that Ishmael is in the room—is to remove this paper screen, and, there between the sooty firedogs, *he himself puts the image of his own god.* The pasteboard mask conceals nothing that man has not put there.

Queequeg's idol is a black figurine named Yojo, who later counsels the cannibal to let Ishmael choose the ship of their adventure. After they have heard Father Mapple preach, Ishmael, by now 'married' to his friend, 'must turn idolator,' kindle Yojo's fire, and salaam to the pagan deity. What I take all this to mean is that the source of redemptive love is, for Melville, a divinity pre-Christian[15] and pre-rational. (This is why Queequeg invokes Yojo before being aware of Ishmael's presence.) But Yojo, the pagan love-god, is not the creator of the universe. The white whale seems as close as we can come to touching that power and awful beauty.

Yet neither is Moby Dick God; he is God's whale—and Job's whale. Ahab mistook God's power for God's essence, and heaped on that white hump 'the intangible malignity which has been from the beginning . . . all the subtle demonisms of life and thought.' To Ishmael, however, the most terrifying aspect of the whale's whiteness is 'a colorless all-color of atheism,' the ever-present possibility of cosmic nothingness, in which 'the palsied universe lies before us a leper.' All of Ishmael's explorations of the attempts made in art, science, folklore, and myth to define the whale are a contradictory labyrinth of suppositions which only his own experience can verify. And that experience proves the white whale unknowable to the last. If, then, we cannot know God's greatest handiwork, how can we know the God that made him?

On this reef many an interpreter of *Moby-Dick* has foundered. It seems hard to resist Ahab's incantatory power and not agree with him, that the white whale is indeed the immanent God of this work, even though one reject Ahab's definition of His nature. But Moby Dick is no more the God of *Moby-Dick* than Leviathan is the God of the Book of Job. The inscrutable whale, titanic in power, lovely in motion, ubiquitous in space, immortal in time, is the ultimate demonstration and absolute convincement of all anarchic, individualistic, egotistical, human doubt that

[15] Yojo is the same color as the whale's phallus and as that priapic idol which Queen Maachah worshipped and Asa, her son, destroyed and 'burnt for an adomination at the brook of Kedron, as darkly set forth in the fifteenth chapter of the first book of Kings' (ch. 95; cf. I Kings 15:13). Melville surely invented this obscure comparison (the Bible does not even darkly hint at the color of the Queen's idol) because at the very place where Asa burnt the phallic image, Judas betrayed Jesus (John 18:1-5). Christianity and the sensual Eros are mutually exclusive in *Moby-Dick*.

there is a God beyond the powers of man to plumb. Melville's God lies beyond even the Gospel truths. He is Job's God, not Jonah's prefiguration of Christ's rising. That is why Ishmael ends his tale with the words of the messengers of calamity.

It is hard to unmingle the knowledge of God's essence from the knowledge of His power. Ahab must grasp the chain-link to feel the living lightning against his own pulse, power participating in power. Ishmael, too, touches the will of deity by an act which the linked analogies of his metaphoric mind makes analogous to the will of godhead. This act is the weaving of the sword-mat (chapter 47). Just before the first whale was sighted, Ishmael and Queequeg together wove a mat to protect their boat. Ishmael's own hand was the shuttle; Queequeg drove a wooden 'sword' between the threads to straighten the woof. Ishmael elaborates this scene in the manner of a Puritan preacher, making an extended conceit from homely images of common labor; as he speaks here of the most urgent philosophic problem of the book, a rather long quotation must be introduced:

> . . . it seemed as if this were the Loom of Time, and I myself were a shuttle mechanically weaving and weaving away at the Fates. There lay the fixed threads of the warp subject to but one single, ever returning, unchanging vibration, and that vibration merely enough to admit of the crosswise interblending of other threads with its own. This warp seemed necessity; and here, thought I, with my own hand I ply my own shuttle and weave my own destiny into these unalterable threads. Meanwhile, Queequeg's impulsive, indifferent sword, sometimes hitting the woof slantingly, or crookedly, or strongly, or weakly, as the case might be; and by this difference in the concluding blow producing a corresponding contrast in the final aspect of the completed fabric; this savage's sword, thought I, which thus finally shapes and fashions both warp and woof; this easy, indifferent sword must be chance—aye, chance, free will, and necessity—no wise incompatible—all inter-weavingly working together. The straight warp of necessity, not to be swerved from its ultimate course—its every alternating vibration, indeed, only tending to that; free will still free to ply her shuttle between given threads; and chance, though restrained in its play within the right

> lines of necessity, and sidewise in its motions directed by free will, though thus prescribed to by both, chance by turns rules either, and has the last featuring blow at events.

At the savage lookout's first cry 'There she blows!' 'the ball of free will dropped from my hand.'

Ishmael's quest from the beginning is to seek out and read the pattern of the loom. The opening chapter is called 'Loomings'; the pun on 'weavings' and the nautical term for the coming into view of something hidden below the horizon is but the first hint of Ishmael's comedic acceptance of what Father Mapple's hymn calls the 'terrible' and the 'joyful' in his earthly life. The weaving image (though somewhat contrived in the sword-mat passage) itself represents both the creative and dynamic elements in Ishmael's view of the cosmos. The loom is still a-weaving, the pattern ever emergent, never complete. Such a view is directly antithetical to Ahab's rigid and mechanical conception of his destiny: 'This whole act's immutably decreed. . . . I am the Fates' lieutenant.' Ishmael's loom metaphor knots together the clusters of images involving lines, ropes, and shrouds, realistically present on a sailing-ship but imaginatively made to ply the loom of Fate on which each thread adds its color and direction to the grand design. 'What depths of the soul Jonah's deep sea-line sound!' preached Father Mapple; 'Shipmates, it is a two-stranded lesson.' The strands of life and of death appear in later lines, especially 'the magical, sometimes horrible whale-line.' 'All men live enveloped in whale-lines. All men are born with halters round their necks.' This is the line that tossed Pip overboard, entangled Fedallah, slew Ahab. Complementary to this death-line is the life-line, the 'monkey-rope' that ties seamen together. 'So that for better or for worse, we two, for the time, were wedded; and should poor Queequeg sink to rise no more, then both usage and honor demanded that instead of cutting the cord, it should drag me down in its wake. So, then, an elongated Siamese ligature united us.' The life-line is at once a love-link, a death-line, and an umbilicus. These cords are intermingled again as the harpooner's line tangles with the trailing umbilicus of new-born whale cubs. Love and death are imaged together when Ishmael regards the whale-line in its tub as 'a prodigious wedding-cake to present to the whales.' Even the weather contributes to the loomed design as 'mingling threads of life are woven by warp and woof; calm crossed by storm, a storm for every calm. . . . Where lies the final harbor, whence we unmoor no more?'

That final harbor is as hidden from mortal navigators as the 'insular Tahiti' of unfallen delight, once pushed off from never to be found again. Yet Pip has moored there. For when afloat on the terrifying sea 'He saw God's foot upon the treadle of the loom, and spoke it. . . . So man's insanity is heaven's sense; and wandering from all mortal reason, man comes at last to that celestial thought, which, to reason, is absurd and frantic; and weal or woe, feels then uncompromised, indifferent as his God.' [16]

Indifferent, that is, to mortal weal or woe; these are no concern of the God who set down 'WHALING VOYAGE BY ONE ISHMAEL' in 'the grand programme of Providence that was drawn up a long time ago.' For that God—Ishmael's God—is himself creative power, subsuming all the fragmentary deities men erect in his partial image: Ahab's and Fedallah's destructive Force, Queequeg's all-fructifying love, Pip's and Bulkington's Christian Absolute, the Divine Inert. Transcending the sum of these is the ever-emergent God of Life and Death, revealing Himself through Nature, the Work that he creates. Moby Dick, the greatest of his handiwork, is the principle of Godhead *in* Nature. This God does not allow (as Richard Chase among others reminds us) either a tragic or a Christian resolution of man's fate; Melville's view does indeed resemble at some points Spinoza's

[16] Ahab saw *his* pattern too, 'when God's burning finger [was] laid upon the ship; when His "Mene, Mene, Tekel Upharsin" [was] woven into the shrouds and cordage.' Then Ahab embraced the corposants, as though to knot the design against the unravelling of chance.

(as Newton Arvin has suggested),[17] that man's happiness consists in knowing his true place in nature. Far more deeply than the literary naturalists of the end of his century, he comprehends in the cosmos a God of energy whose moral laws, if they exist, transcend all human divination. Yet Melville's God of Force is not like Zola's or Dreiser's or Crane's, Himself a mere machine; in *Moby-Dick* that view is Ahab's blindness. Melville posits not immutable mechanical law but the universal vitality of Nature, embracing death as preludial to rebirth. In this he comes close to Whitman, though Melville cannot rest as easily as Whitman did with the facile and unstable resolution of all dilemmas proposed in 'Song of Myself.'

As close as Melville comes to a resolution in *Moby-Dick* is in a chapter few critics have noticed, 'A Bower of the Arsacides.' Here the images of the white whale and the weaver-god come together in Ishmael's mind, and here too is the image of the machine—indeed, a modern industrial factory. Such images define the limits on Ahab's will, for his 'path . . . is laid with iron rails, whereon [his] soul is grooved to run'; but here Ishmael sees the mechanical in its right relation to cosmic truth. These images of whale, weaver, and machine occur in Ishmael's mind as he recalls a previous voyage when he visited the island where a whale's white skeleton forms a chapel decked with vines. This is a context independent both of Ahab, his own crippling death-wish, and of Queequeg, his own regressive infantilism.

> The industrious earth beneath was as a weaver's loom, with a gorgeous carpet on it, whereof the ground-vine tendrils formed the warp and woof, and the living flowers the figures. . . . Through the lacings of the leaves, the great sun seemed a flying shuttle weaving the unwearied verdure. Oh, busy weaver!—pause!—one word!—whither flows the fabric? what palace may it deck? wherefore all these ceaseless toilings? Speak, weaver!—stay thy hand!—

[17] Chase, *The American Novel and Its Traditions,* p. 107; Arvin, *Herman Melville* (New York, 1950), p. 190.

> but one single word with thee! Nay—the shuttle flies—the figures float from forth the loom; the freshet-rushing carpet for ever slides away. The weaver-god, he weaves; and by that weaving is he deafened, that he hears no mortal voice; and by that humming, we, too, who look on the loom are deafened; and only when we escape it shall we hear the thousand voices that speak through it. For even so it is in all material factories. The spoken words that are inaudible among the flying spindles; those same words are plainly heard without the walls, bursting from the opened casements. . . . Ah, mortal! then, be heedful; for so, in all this din of the great world's loom, thy subtlest thinkings may be overheard afar.
>
> Now, amid the green, life-restless loom of that Arsacidean wood, the great, white, worshipped skeleton lay lounging—a gigantic idler. Yet . . . the mighty idler seemed the cunning weaver; himself all woven over with the vines . . . but himself a skeleton. Life folded Death; Death trellised Life; the grim god wived with youthful Life, and begat him curly-headed glories.

Here process is mechanical; in the mortal activity of becoming, the Word is drowned.[18] That activity is only the effect, not the Source, of divine energy. The skeleton whale—white—'*seemed* the cunning weaver'—for on this island as well as on the Pequod's ocean (and in Job) we can come no nearer to the Source than to behold the greatest of His works. It is the loom of this whale's dead bones, interwoven with life, that Ishmael measured with a ball of twine and tattooed upon his own right arm.

How then can we stand beyond the walls of the factory to hear the Word that its mechanical humming drowns? How fathom the pattern in the endless fabric of Life and Death? One way is amply plain—by stepping outside of the world of process, we, with the death of our human senses, may behold the grand design. But Ishmael at last will be redeemed from such a Re-

[18] The priests of this temple are mechanicians and dogmatists. They have rigged the skeleton with an artificial smoke-jet, reducing the mystery of life-in-death to a machine; they try to stop Ishmael from measuring 'this our god,' but when he asks them for the measurements 'a fierce contest rose among them, concerning feet and inches; they cracked each other's sconces with their yardsticks.' Only Ishmael, free from all dogmas, can conclude his 'own admeasurements.'

demption. He wills himself to *live*. And what truth he has survived to tell us we may find written on the whale's brow, 'pleated with riddles.' These are unriddled on the whale's talisman, the doubloon.

On that coin 'the keystone sun' came through the zodiac at 'the equinoctial point of Libra,' the scales. And the coin was made in Ecuador, 'a country planted in the middle of the world,' named for the equator, and was minted 'in the unwaning clime that knows no autumn.' None of these visible facts had been *felt* by any of the doubloon's beholders; each save Pip sought the phantom of life and grasped only 'his own mysterious self.' Pip, already at the Resurrection, is beyond the doubloon's gift of wisdom, which Ishmael alone receives.

The scales of Libra are no doubt those 'scales of the New Testament' by which Ishmael weighed his mortal lot at the beginning and found it tolerable. What is important here is that at *their* point in the heavens the 'keystone sun' enters the universe. But the conception of balance is not only transcendent; represented by the pagan zodiac, the geographic equator, and the physical reality of that 'unwaning clime' halfway up the Andes, the idea necessarily extends to *that wholeness which is comprised of both the halves:* both hemispheres, both peaks and valleys, both winter and summer, both hot and cold—both love and death, highest good and deepest evil, mortality and immortality. Unlike Starbuck's *mediocritas,* this balanced, doubled vision encompasses all extremes and thereby asserts its absolute stability. It is godlike. To attain it and survive, Ishmael must drown his Ahab and his Queequeg. But first he must have acknowledged them.

Like the builders of the Cathedral of Cologne, Melville leaves the true copestone of *Moby-Dick* to posterity. Had he imposed perfect form upon his partial vision of the truth he sought, he would have falsified his own achievement. This is an intrinsic principle of Melville's aesthetic. Yet in *Moby-Dick* the incandescence of the metaphoric linkage we have observed does project successfully the unification of experience. It does this by creating autonomously the world within which its own meanings are true. This world is braced and pinioned by the primitive sanctions and mythic values, the supernatural forces and ritualistic acts that we have traced. And yet, as distant as such materials would seem to be from the workaday life of Melville's time, in *Moby-Dick* he elaborates almost all of the levels of experience, as well as of mythic feeling and metaphoric thought, which might typify his culture and his time. From savagery to spindle-factories, from Old Testament Calvinism to the game-cocks of the frontier, from demonology to capitalism, the imagery of American life on every level sinews the entire book. Melville's view of life is doubtless a less catholic view than we find in Dante, or in his favorite author Shakespeare, or in Cervantes. Yet his is the greatest work by an American imagination for the same reasons that theirs are the greatest works of European Christendom. *Moby-Dick* most profoundly expresses the aspirations and the limitations of the culture as well as the individual genius that produced it. And that culture has, thus far, given us fewer tragic heroes and transcendent Christians than individualists alienated from their pasts, striving to discover those 'humanities' which yet bind them to 'the magnetic circle of mankind.'

14

The Confidence-Man: His Masquerade

'Strike through the mask!'
—Ahab

ONE

After *Moby-Dick*, Melville, like Ishmael, managed to survive. Such a survival demanded the Stoic virtues; romantic heroism he had abjured, and the affirmative primitive energies of Eros and Momus were henceforth blighted. In *Moby-Dick* the inner conflicts of the individual and the outer conflicts between the soul and its environment had been magnificently fused. His next two major efforts tried to deal with these problems singly. Emerging from the involuted ambiguities of *Pierre*, Melville turned from that too-personal narrative to one last attempt at a panoramic view of society. Every reader of *The Confidence-Man* is struck by the diminution of the scale of character and action. The confidence man himself deprecates the mode of the book: 'Irony is so unjust; never could abide irony; something Satanic about irony. God defend me from Irony, and Satire, his bosom friend.' Now there is no mighty hero, no world-mastering whale, no tattooed savages. The great hunters of *Moby-Dick* are replaced, in irony and satire, by these lesser breeds:

> Natives of all sorts, and foreigners; men of business and men of pleasure; parlor-men and backwoodsmen; farm-hunters and fame-hunters; heiress-hunters, gold-hunters, buffalo-hunters, bee-hunters,

happiness-hunters, truth-hunters, and still keener hunters after all these hunters.

Melville's main interest is in the last-named hunters. The only Ishmael we can find aboard the riverboat Fidèle is a frontiersman—a truth-hunter—who, despite his truculent independence and strong mind, is nonetheless duped, as are all the other hunters, by the confidence man.

The balanced encompassing of all the antinomies of experience, which saved Ishmael in *Moby-Dick*, had not proved possible for Herman Melville in life. 'Lord, when shall we be done with growing?' Melville had written Hawthorne just after finishing *The Whale;* 'As long as we have anything more to do, we have done nothing. So, now, let us add Moby Dick to our blessings, and step from that. Leviathan is not the biggest fish;—I have heard of Krakens.' But this ebullience could not last. Hawthorne gives this account of Melville's state of mind five years later, just after writing *The Confidence-Man:*

> Melville, as he always does, began to reason of Providence and futurity, and of everything that lies beyond human ken, and informed me that he had 'pretty much made up his mind to be annihilated'; but still he does not seem to rest in that anticipation; and, I think, will never rest until he gets hold of a definite belief. It is strange how he persists—and has persisted ever since I knew him, and probably long before—in wandering to-and-fro over these deserts, as dismal and monotonous as the sand hills amid which we were sitting. He can neither believe, nor be comfortable in his unbelief; and he is too honest and courageous not to try to do one or the other.[1]

In *The Confidence-Man* Melville wanders to-and-fro over the deserts of an American world in which humane values are impossible and divine laws remain shrouded in mysteries impene-

[1] Melville to Hawthorne, 17 November 1851; Hawthorne, *The English Notebooks* (20 November 1856), ed. Randall Stewart (New York & London, 1941), pp. 432-3. Hawthorne was then American Consul in Liverpool. Melville, on the verge of a nervous breakdown, had sailed to England for his health.

trable to anyone aboard his 'ship of fools.' This is a despairing book, a bitter book, a work of Byzantine ingenuity. It is as though Melville, denied Ishmael's godlike power to grasp the farthest limits of life, tries, and tries, and tries to spin out of the knotted web of severely limited experience the furtive pattern of truth. In *The Confidence-Man* experience *is* severely limited—to the operations of a swindler on a riverboat, playing, it would seem, for low cash stakes. But each of his diddles demands 'full confidence' of his dupe, and each is a 'type' of the Fall of Man.

Despairing though it be, *The Confidence-Man* has a wry gusto that carries the reader over its vertiginous argument. Stylistically it is distinguished, and marks a radical departure from both the high rhetoric and the comic palaver of *Moby-Dick.* This style has a new satiric edge, sharpened by images as unexpected as they are apt:

> The miser, a lean old man, whose flesh seemed salted codfish. . . . His cheek lay upon an old white moleskin coat, rolled under his head like a wizened apple upon a grimy snowbank.

And there is a new rhythm, whose involutions, even in descriptive passages, dramatize the serpentine twistings of reason proposed by the confidence man:

> Goneril was young, in person lithe and straight. . . . Upon the whole, aided by the resources of the toilet, her appearance at distance was such, that some might have thought her, if anything, rather beautiful, though of a style of beauty rather peculiar and cactus-like.

What is given is taken away; what is removed, lingers. All is equivocal here.

The literary, philosophical, and cultural materials in this book are fused in so enigmatic a fashion that its interpreters have differed as to what the book is really about. Richard Chase, to whose study of Melville in 1949 we owe the discovery of its importance, called *The Confidence-Man* Melville's 'second-best book.' He sees it as a work of social criticism, drawing on mythical prototypes for satirical intensity. John Schroeder soon rejected Chase's thesis; he reads *The Confidence-Man* as a religious allegory, proving debts to Hawthorne's 'Celestial Railroad' and to *Pilgrim's Progress.* And Elizabeth Foster, uncovering still other sources for her critical edition, finds the book to be a tightly organized satire on optimism in its successive historical forms: the Shaftesbury position, the utilitarians, the Deists' faith in Nature, and transcendentalism. Nor are the critics agreed as to the form of the book, although there seems general opinion that it is fiction, and a novel—whether satirical, allegorical, symbolist, or tractarian.[2]

TWO

Melville's *Confidence-Man,* like Hawthorne's *Blithedale Romance,* is the attempt of a romancer to deal directly with the surfaces of contemporary life while presenting allegorically an ironic criticism of its depths. As was true of Hawthorne's book, the form of Melville's has a baffling intricacy which results both from the complex purposes of the author and from his attempt to assimilate hitherto unmingled literary methods and materials. To judge *The Confidence-Man* we must first understand it; to understand it we must not only read it with the close attention that its style demands, but also we must follow Melville's furtive hints as to the sources, models, and analogues in his mind as he wrote it. Otherwise we may judge the book by standards inappropriate to its achievements. We are about to deal with the confidence man, and, as he himself tells us the true book says, 'An enemy speaketh sweetly with his lips.' We may easily be misled. (His warning, it appears, is only apocryphal, not Gospel.) We may in fact be taken in by the confidence man.

Although Mr. Chase called this work 'a book of folklore' and

[2] Chase, *Herman Melville,* pp. 185-209; Schroeder, 'Sources and Symbols for Melville's *Confidence-Man,*' *PMLA,* LXVI (June 1951), 363-80: Foster, 'Introduction' to *The Confidence-Man* (New York, 1954).

proposed its central character as a portmanteau figure combining attributes of native heroes (Brother Jonathan, Uncle Sam, the Yankee) with those of the heroes of world-historical myths (Christ, Orpheus, Prometheus), later critics have neither verified nor extended his position. Yet Melville in this book transformed in a radical way several of the dominant themes from folklore and myth which Hawthorne had used before him and which he himself had used in *Moby-Dick*. There is witchcraft in *The Confidence-Man,* and demonology. There are the folklore themes of transformation in an egalitarian society, and the contrasting of regional stereotypes; the dominant tension between characters (as well as ideas) pits images of the East against those of the West. The confidence man is, among other things, an amalgam of America's popular comic figures: the sly, dupe-bilking Yankee and the frontier sharper. Indeed, the riverboat swindler himself was by 1856 a standard addition to the rogues' gallery of American picaresque lore. In this book he embodies these regional characteristics and tries to fleece persons who embody others—not only the shaggy frontiersman but a Yankee peddler who sits for a savage caricature of what Melville took to be Emerson's fatal shortcomings. There are rituals, too, in *The Confidence-Man.* How else can we regard the recapitulations of Orpheus' descent into hell, the parody of Prometheus' fire-bringing in the con man's extinguishing of the Light of the World? For that matter, as the entire action occurs on All Fools' Day, each episode is a ritual of intensification of the theme of the book, as well as a ritual of initiation for each of the dupes, who trades 'full confidence' for the consequences of the Temptation.

What disguises does this confidence man wear in his Masquerade? First (and most ambiguously), a Mute in cream-colors boards the ship, displays mottoes on charity from I Corinthians, begs alms, is abused by some passengers, and goes to sleep. We do not see him again but next observe one Black Guinea, a crippled Negro beggar who lists eight 'ge'mman' who can vouch for his character; a minister sets out to find these, but no matter, when he returns the beggar is gone. As the boat stops at wharves and landings various personages debark or enter. Most of Black Guinea's references do appear in turn: a Man with a Weed; an agent of the Seminole Widow and Orphan Asylum; the President of the Black Rapids Coal Company. This last becomes before our eyes an Herb-Doctor, peddling Omni-Balsamic Reinvigorator below decks and Samaritan Pain Dissuader in the cabin. Again, he is the Happy Bone Setter. He too would seem to step ashore, and is succeeded by a man from the Philosophical Intelligence Office (an agency that hires out boys). As Man with the Weed he had hinted to a businessman passenger of quick profits to be made in Black Rapids stocks; as Herb-Doctor he spreads word that an officer of that company is on the boat; later, he clandestinely sells the shares. These masquerades take up the first half of the book. A variety of dupes accede, sometimes reluctantly, to the confidence man's pleas, and contribute to his begging, his Indian Orphanage, his Universal Easy Chair, his proposal for The World's Charity ('Missions I would quicken with the Wall Street Spirit'). The Naturopath's herbs find customers—misers are especially vulnerable. Sometimes the con man tells stories to his dupes, or they repeat yarns he has told earlier, or they tell tales of their own. We learn of the cruel wife Goneril, of the Happy Soldier in the Tombs, and, later, tales of Colonel Moredock the Indian-hater, of Charlemont the Gentleman-Madman, and of China Aster who was ruined by requesting a loan. These fictitious characters are discussed: was Goneril cruel or justified? can Moredock's character be believed? In every case the con man's views prevail.

In the latter half of the book the confidence man appears in a bizarre get-up made from the national costumes of every country. This Cosmopolitan, 'a true citizen of the world,' is involved with several hard-headed and unappealing characters in close arguments on confidence, money-lending, and friendship. At last he descends into the hold of the boat, cheats the barber, and, blowing out the 'solar lamp' in the cabin, leads a senile old man away into the darkness.

One can see why the reviewer in the *Literary Gazette* complained of 'an uncomfortable sensation of dizziness in the head.' Nor could he accept *The Confidence-Man* as a novel, 'unless a novel means forty-five conversations . . . conducted by personages who might pass for the errata of creation.' We may prepare the way for a better understanding and judgment of this curious book by first determining to which genre of writing it belongs.

There is no gainsaying Mr. Schroeder's proofs of its relation to 'The Celestial Railroad' and *Pilgrim's Progress.* Like those religious allegories this is a journey narrative, although Melville is anything but specific, in their fashion, as to who is going where. Doubtless he substituted a riverboat for Hawthorne's railroad and followed out, in his allusive, inferential way, the voyage of those aboard, whom he calls 'that pilgrim species, man.' Mr. Schroeder says that these references 'locate the events geographically and spiritually'; the world of the book is 'a great Vanity Fair, situated on an allegorical steamboat which, presumably sailing for New Orleans (on the symbolic level, for the New Jerusalem of nineteenth-century optimistic and liberal theology), is inclining its course dangerously toward the pits of the Black Rapids Coal Company.' These observations point up a major theme, as do Miss Foster's on Melville's systematic philosophical satire. But neither suffices to explain the form of the work, or its milieu, or the original conception of its characters.

Hawthorne's influence upon the structure of *The Confidence-Man* goes beyond the borrowings from 'The Celestial Railroad.' In his review of *Mosses from an Old Manse,* Melville seems extravagant in his praise of such bare-boned allegories as 'Earth's Holocaust' and 'The Intelligence Office.' In the first of these, millennial reformers, deciding to burn the world's ills, commit to the bonfire first emblems of rank and privilege, then liquor, tobacco, and the instruments of war and capital punishment. In the end, 'as the final sacrifice of human error' the Bible itself is thrown on the fire. Hawthorne's moral is not left to inference—'man's agelong endeavor for perfection had served only to render him the mockery of the evil principle.' Until he purify the heart 'wherein existed the original wrong of which the crime and misery of this outward world were merely types,' all reform is duplicity. Both in theme and structure this sketch anticipates *The Confidence-Man,* as does 'The Intelligence Office,' which Melville praised as 'a wondrous symbolism of the secret workings of men's souls.' No doubt his Philosophical Intelligence Office has affinities here; more generally, these sketches, like others of Hawthorne's discursive and unfictional allegories, provided examples of fictions in which the governing action consists of discussions between a central character and a series of interlocutors. Hawthorne frequently used an allegorical personification to whom a number of representative characters make comments, or an allegorical conception (such as Truth, or Ambition) by which they are measured. This is the structure Melville could find in 'The Great Carbuncle,' 'Fancy's Show Box,' 'The Ambitious Guest,' 'The Seven Vagabonds,' and 'Chippings with a Chisel' in *Twice-Told Tales;* and, in *Mosses,* 'The Procession of Life,' 'The Hall of Fantasy,' and 'A Virtuoso's Collection.' In his doubloon chapter of *Moby-Dick* (written just after 'Hawthorne and His Mosses') Melville had already adopted the Hawthornian technique of having multiple observers comment on the same object. In *The Confidence-Man* he reversed the technique, with a single masquerader approaching diverse and typical characters to discuss his ever-present theme.

The digressive, argumentative, nondramatic quality of *The Confidence-Man* derives also from the picaresque romance. The book has affinities with *Don Quixote,* mentioned in chapter 44. As is often true of Melville, the resemblances are more often inverted than direct. In both books we have a pilgrimage toward ostensible truth. But where Don Quixote knows perfectly well who he is and what values he acts by, in the confidence man's world there are no values and identity is a mystery in a maze of appearances. The con man enters in a parody of Christ's 'advent'; he confuses every moral issue he touches, dissuading well-meaning persons from the instinctual truth of their hearts' wisdom; he quotes Scripture to lead men away from God, if there is a God; he himself leads them into darkness. Of all the characters he meets or is told about, only the Indian-hater has the steadfastness of soul to withstand his sweet voice, yet his impassioned misanthropy severs his human bonds. Where Don Quixote acts from the belief that man is better than he is, that the ideal is in the real, the con man treats man as knaves treat fools, as horses oats. In the one book we see life through the eyes of a saint, in the other through those of a devil.

As is true in *Don Quixote,* we find interpolated fables introduced as extensions of themes already discussed by the characters in the main story. These fables are actually more credible than the disputatious webs that surround them. In chapter 33 Melville says as much, and offers a view of 'reality' in fiction we would do well to ponder. 'In books of fiction, [readers] look not only for more entertainment, but, at bottom, even for more reality, than real life itself can show. Thus, though they want novelty, they want nature too; but nature unfettered, exhilarated, in effect transformed. . . . It is with fiction as with religion: it should present another world, and yet one to which we feel the tie.'

In *Pierre,* Melville had specifically rejected the 'realistic' novel. There he charged such works with falsification of reality, attacking 'their false, inverted attempts at systematizing eternally unsystematizable elements; their audacious, intermeddling impotency in trying to unravel, and spread out, and classify, the more thin than gossamer threads which make up the complex web of life.' For 'human life,' he writes, 'partakes of the unravellable inscrutableness of God.' This same idea recurs early in *The Confidence-Man,* as he claims that human nature, 'like the divine nature . . . is past finding out' (chapter 14). As in *The Blithedale Romance,* the convoluted opacity of presentation

—even to the sentence structure with its skeins of qualifying adjectivals—is meant to insist upon the very difficulties which the author hopes to resolve. But where Hawthorne satirized his blithe critics of society from the rock of his own political and cultural conservatism, Melville can find no orthodoxy to protect mankind from the sophistries of his spiritual swindler.

He repeatedly refers to the con man as 'an original.' The curious phrase is parsed in the penultimate chapter:

> The original character, essentially such, is like a revolving Drummond light, raying away from itself all round it—everything is lit by it, everything starts up to it (mark how it is with Hamlet), so that, in certain minds, there follows upon the adequate conception of such a character, an effect, in its way, akin to that which in Genesis attends upon the beginning of things.

The reality Melville creates in this book, then, is to be a transfiguration of nature, in which an 'original character' sheds the light of its originality upon a world created after its own image. Here is the clue to the wry energy that sinews a book whose philosophy drives all hope to the wall. Ishmael's emergent creativity, his salvation through participation in God's loomings, is still available to Melville. This is true even though the pattern of the weaver-god is farther than ever from human sight; true although the 'original character' is not God, but the Adversary. But creativity emergent from this premise can hardly, as with Ishmael's, be a kind of salvation.

The form of Melville's story and the rhythms of its development are determined not so much by characters in action as by the dialectical development of ideas. Lacking the dramatic incidents of *Don Quixote, The Confidence-Man* yet resembles that work in its intricate shiftings of the points of view from which reality and appearances are investigated. Perhaps the clandestine analogue and probable model for Melville is the Platonic dialogue, in which the search for truth proceeds through query and reply. As is true in Plato, when Melville reaches the limits of rational (or sophistical) discourse he introduces parables.

These, like the Platonic myths, dramatize depths of experience beyond the capacity of the rational premises of the argument to define. But the place of truth-loving, steadfast Socrates is taken by the obscurantist, slippery confidence man.

THREE

This 'original character' appears in the mercantile and philanthropic guises characteristic of American life. Therefore his diabolic nature is hardly visible—not at all so to most of his dupes, and only by inference to us. If we note that Black Guinea used 'an old coal sifter of a tambourine,' that the Herb-Doctor debarks at a bluff called 'the Devil's Joke,' that the descent of Black Rapids Coal stock is described in a paraphrase of Satan's first speech in Hell in *Paradise Lost;* if we recall that the stock swindler tried also to sell shares in 'the New Jerusalem . . . the first settlement was by two fugitives who had swum over naked from the opposite shore'—if we notice these details we are wiser than anyone aboard the Fidèle. Only Pitch the truculent frontiersman thinks 'analogically . . . the insinuator's undulating flunkyisms dovetail with those of the flunky beast that windeth his way on his belly.' His next interlocutor is the Cosmopolitan who speaks of 'our Fair' and proclaims himself 'a taster of races; in all his vintages smacking my lips over this racy creature, man'—traditionally the favorite entrée of the Devil. 'When I think of Pocahontas, I am ready to love Indians,' says the Cosmopolitan, hearing of the Indian-hater; Melville treats the Indians in the fashion of Puritan allegory. The Cosmopolitan, smoking a cigar, uses for an ashtray a pottery globe of Indian manufacture—an apple of Sodom.

Where did Melville get this stunningly 'adequate conception of such a character'? Again we find a clue in 'Hawthorne and His Mosses'—the paradigm of a world of masqueraders in league with the devil in 'Young Goodman Brown.' This tale Melville had found 'deep as Dante.' He cannot forbear to quote Young

Goodman's despairing cry, '"Faith! Faith!" as if bewildered wretches were seeking her all through the wilderness.' (Goodman is the name the con man gives as Cosmopolitan, his most dangerous disguise.[3]) And in his review of Hawthorne, Melville acknowledged that

> this great power of blackness in him derives its force from its appeals to that Calvinistic sense of Innate Depravity and Original Sin, from whose visitations, in some shape or other, no deeply thinking mind is always and wholly free.

'In some shape or other,' Innate Depravity would manifest itself in modern man; Melville finds it in the same insidious sophistries of liberal optimism that Hawthorne had allegorized in 'Earth's Holocaust' and 'The Celestial Railroad,' and in the moral sloth of those who are taken in by such false gospels masquerading as the true.

But Melville's sense of contemporary America as a Devil's Masquerade comes not only from his own bitterness and from Hawthorne's witchcraft story. He was by this time familiar too with one of Hawthorne's major sources and Irving's before him—the *Magnalia Christi Americana* of Cotton Mather. The *Magnalia* had just been reprinted in 1853, and it is plain that Melville read at least the chapters on wonders and witchcraft. His story 'The Lightning-Rod Man' appeared in *Harper's* in 1854; a phrase in the very first sentence—'the Acroceraunian hills'—can allude only to '*Ceraunius.* Relating remarkables done by thunder,' the title of a chapter in *Magnalia* (VI, 3). The title character of this tale is a preliminary sketch for the con man. He sells a mechanical safety device to protect man against the 'supernal bolt.'

In 1856, the year he wrote *The Confidence-Man,* Melville published another story that draws on Mather. In 'The Apple-Tree Table' we enter a musty garret to find the old table with 'one hoofed foot, like that of the Evil One,' bearing 'a mouldy old

[3] Miss Foster suggests also that Melville named the steamboat Fidèle after Hawthorne's Faith. Op. cit. p. 291.

book in the middle—Cotton Mather's *Magnalia.*' The subtitle of this fine story ('Or, Original Spiritual Manifestations') tells us what Mather is doing in that garret, which is a fairly obvious symbol of the author's head. The *Magnalia* stands as a fearful emblem of spiritual life—a counter-symbol to the hope of resurrection signified by the bug that emerges alive after a 150-year sleep in the dead wood of the table.

> The truth was, that though . . . Cotton Mather had but amused me, upon this particular night he terrified me. . . . What possible motive could such a man have to deceive? His style had all the plainness and unpoetic boldness of truth. In the most straightforward way, he laid before me detailed accounts of New England witchcraft, each important item corroborated by respectable townsfolk, and, of not a few of the most surprising, he himself had been eye-witness.

Some of 'The Wonders of the Invisible World' which Mather himself saw are told in the chapter on 'Wolves in sheeps cloathing: Or, an history of several impostors, pretending to be ministers remarkably detected in the churches of New-England.' Not the least interesting of these was one who 'came on board the vessel under some concealment, not professing, nor supposed for to be a minister, but rather a mendicant, until they had sailed many leagues. . . . His plausible delivery presently enchanted abundance of honest people, who thought all was gold that glittered.'[4] Melville's impostor would come aboard as a beggar, and later turn into a whole cotillion of honey-tongued 'metaphysical scamps.'

In the May issue of *Putnam's* appeared not only 'The Apple-Tree Table' but an unsigned article on 'The Spirits in 1692, And What They Did at Salem.' The republication of the *Magnalia* had made witchcraft once again a current topic of discourse in advanced circles, and not only among descendants of the Salem

[4] *Magnalia Christi Americana,* Book VI, chap. 7; Bk. VII, chap. 5. Mather provides a rogues' gallery of such impostures and adduces 35 pages of witchcraft cases.

judges. Melville could have read in this rehash of the materials Hawthorne had been making stories of for twenty years that 'the prevailing religious opinion of New England was strongly committed to the importance of the devil and his agents; and his power, by many was believed to be equal, if not superior, to that of God.'

Melville, then, had immersed himself in Hawthorne's and Mather's witchcraft writings just as he was about to begin *The Confidence-Man.*[5] He neither followed his friend in reconstructing Puritan superstition, nor repeated the primitive witchcraft beliefs of his own Manxman and Dansker in *Moby-Dick.* Instead he completely modernized the *Magnalia,* translating the folk and theological significance of witchcraft into believable contemporary terms. His confidence man is what Cotton Mather, with his belief in the devil's wiles, would have asserted, had that divine been alive in 1856. Although such treatments of the witchcraft delusion as the *Putnam's* article expressed only revulsion for Mather's vengefulness and egomania, Melville's attitude toward his nineteenth-century world—toward American life—is pretty much in agreement with Mather's direst fears two centuries earlier. Melville is in fact more despairing than the Puritan, for

[5] His reading the *Magnalia* at this time doubtless reinforced the conception of Satan with which he had been long familiar in one of his favorite books, Sir Thomas Browne's *Vulgar Errors (Pseudodoxia Epidemica).* He had acquired Browne's *Works* in 1848 or 1849 and drew on them often in *Moby-Dick.* In Book I, chapter x, Melville had read:

> 'Besides the infirmities of human nature, the seed of error within ourselves, and the several ways of delusion from each other, there is an invisible agent, the secret promoter without us, whose activity is undiscerned, and plays in the dark upon us: and that is the first contriver of error, and professed opposer of truth, the devil. . . . To attempt a particular of all his wiles, is too bold an arithmetic for man. . . . How strangely he possesseth us with errors may clearly be observed, deluding us into contradictory and inconsistent falsities; whilst he would make us believe,—That there is no God—that there are many—that he himself is God—that he is less than angels and men—that he is nothing at all. . . . Thus he endeavours to entangle truth; and, when he cannot possibly destroy its substance, he cunningly confounds its apprehensions—that from the inconsistent and contrary determinations thereof, consectary impieties and hopeful confusions may arise.'

his book gives us the comfort of neither an enlightened witch-finder nor an orthodox faith. Ministers as well as miscreants are numbered among his devil's dupes. Satan is at large on the Fidèle, and, except for the frontiersman who resists twice but is yet taken, no one who retains his 'humanities' is proof against his inexplicable cunning.

FOUR

A further demonstration of Melville's originality is his rendering of the American life with which his devilish con man makes such sport. Melville adapts to his own satiric uses a setting and two types of character long familiar in popular culture, where they inevitably appeared affirmatively in comic stories.

The riverboat setting, while it may have been suggested by Melville's youthful trip to Illinois, would seem to owe much to the fictional sketches of Thomas Bangs Thorpe. At the same time it anticipates Mark Twain's *Life on the Mississippi;* but Melville is doubtless truer to reality in his attention to the unsavory characters aboard—an aspect of 'Old Times on the Mississippi' which rather slipped Mark Twain's nostalgic mind. Even were Melville unfamiliar with Thorpe's 'The Big Bear of Arkansas,' he doubtless read that writer's 'Remembrances of the Mississippi' in *Harper's New Monthly,* to which he subscribed. Thorpe's sketch appeared in December 1855, in the issue following Melville's own story, 'Jimmy Rose,' just before he began *The Confidence-Man.* Here, as in 'The Big Bear,' the passengers are described as a microcosm of the nation's peoples, and the river in terms suggesting Melville's description of 'the Mississippi itself, which, uniting the streams of the most distant and opposite zones, pours them along, helter-skelter, in one cosmopolitan and confident tide.'

The cosmopolitan confidence man is thus an emblem of the national character, but, like the water of the river, he is made up of its parts. The consistent pattern behind both his masquerade and his clashes with his dupes is the interplay of native regional types. During the first half of the book the con man plays the Yankee peddler to perfection. In fact this role allows him to sidle among the throng in the native image most familiar to them, and most like his own nature. As stock peddler and medicine-doctor he wears Sam Slick's mask, but in philanthropic roles the disguise is that of Johnny Appleseed, the Civilizer in homespun.

Yet, as Mr. Chase points out, the native image is cunningly intermingled with hints and glints of older heroic figures. Intimations of Christ, Orpheus, and Prometheus appear in such inverted forms as to suggest that the con man is an Antichrist, a mock-Orpheus, a false Prometheus. There are omens of his double-dealing nature in the opening chapter. When the mute in cream-colors appears, 'It was plain that he was, in the extremest sense of the word, a stranger.' Boarding the Fidèle, he passes

> a placard nigh the captain's office, offering a reward for the capture of a mysterious imposter, supposed to have recently arrived from the East, quite an original genius in his vocation, as would appear, though wherein his originality consisted was not clearly given; but what purported to be a careful description of his person followed.

The crowd, greedy for the captor's reward, on tiptoe reads the placard, while pickpockets work them over and hawkers sell pennydreadful lives of frontier desperadoes, all dead now; 'which would seem cause for unalloyed gratulation, and is such to all except those who think that in new countries, where the wolves are killed off, the foxes increase.' We are moving into Simon Suggs's territory, whose thought that 'IT IS GOOD TO BE SHIFTY IN A NEW COUNTRY' had appeared a decade earlier.

The mute then traces on his placard the words of St. Paul, 'Charity thinketh no evil . . . Charity suffereth long and is kind . . .' Accordingly, some readers take this fellow to be a Christ figure; his buffeting by the crowd (who don't object to the barber's sign, 'NO TRUST') indicates the fate of Christ's message in this world. More likely, he *is* the confidence man himself, a mock-Christ, devilishly quoting Scripture to his purpose. What can be on that placard of 'a mysterious imposter . . . from the East' but a description of his own person? In the first of his many masks he walks scot-free through the crowd. He is never what he seems. His parody of Christ's suffering among thieves is a sabotage of Christ's heroism: this 'lamb-like' mute lays him down to sleep. Color symbolism also allies the mute with the confidence man. Here he is white; next he is Black Guinea with a coal sifter. Then he is the Man with a Weed, in gray with a mourning band. Later, as Cosmopolitan, he is a sartorial rainbow, suggesting the 'colorless all-color of atheism from which we shrink' in 'The Whiteness of the Whale.'

The East he arrives from is inferentially not only Bethlehem but the American East, traditional home-base of guile and wile. Like the Yankee peddler, the con man is itinerant, crafty, an inveterate prying busybody and thimblerigger. He never gives up; every man has his fatal weakness—be it his vices of greed or gullibility or cynicism, or, better still, his virtues of philanthropy or idealism. The con man will undo him one way if another won't work, and, like the venal peddler, take a virtuoso's delight in his own mendacity.

Here is one of his more obvious Yankee bargains: A consumptive miser (from whom he has already bilked $100) objects to the price of the Omni-Balsamic Reinvigorator:

> 'Well, if two dollars a box seems too much, take a dozen boxes at twenty dollars, and that will be getting four boxes for nothing; and you need use none but those four, the rest you can retail out at a premium, and so cure your cough, and make money by it. . . . Cash down. Can fill an order in a day or two. Here now,' producing a box; 'pure herbs.'

The price is as spurious as the arithmetic (he had just sold three boxes at fifty cents apiece). His line of reasoning is the same as that peddler of brooms whose clean sweep in Providence we observed in chapter three.

Melville had often used the traits of Yankee guile, sly trickery, hoaxing, and swift repartee, but never before for satire so disenchanted. Except for Dr. Benjamin Franklin in *Israel Potter* (the most extended forerunner of the 'original genius' in this later book), his Yankee tricksters had not been lacking in their 'humanities.' The first such character in Melville's work is Dr. Long Ghost in *Omoo,* whose practical jokes are not judged adversely since the narrator, in his beachcomber phase, is not far removed from Long Ghost's attitude towards authority. Ishmael had his trickster side, while Stubb 'diddles' the French whaler of the precious ambergris by a ruse worthy of any Yankee. In fact their sense of humor, displayed in such jolly hoaxes, makes these sometime rascals appealing in our eyes.

Israel Potter himself is, as Chase maintains, closely modelled on the Yankee of popular lore. He is by turns farmer, bateauxman, surveyor in the wilderness, hunter, peddler, sailor, harpooner on a Nantucket whaler, Revolutionary soldier, and prisoner of war. Escaping from a prison ship to the English shore, he must live a masquerade in earnest now and becomes a royal gardener at the very palace of King George. Then as courier for the Continental underground he is dispatched to Paris with messages in the heel of his boot; he delivers these to Franklin and meets both John Paul Jones and Ethan Allen before the war's end finds him destitute in the London slums. The rest of his 'Fifty Years of Exile' is a testament of sorrows, concluded by his return to his birthplace to find a stranger plowing over 'a little heap of ruinous burnt masonry.' In Israel Potter we see the Yankee character at its best—upright, manly, opposing first a tyrant father, then a tyrant king; outwitting the enemy in the latter's own gardens, besting even Dr. Franklin—yet defeated by life in the end.

Israel Potter is clearly transitional between *Moby-Dick* and *The Confidence-Man,* and nowhere is this more evident than in the treatment of Yankee character. For if Israel Potter is manly and resourceful, he is hardly shrewd; Melville separates these two aspects of Yankeeism. Franklin is a 'household Plato' dressed in 'a conjuror's robe,' full of complacent saws and prudent counsel; too prudent to be incorrupt. (This conception of Franklin is Melville's own, for Franklin is barely mentioned in Potter's autobiography which Melville used as his source.) On the other hand, Ethan Allen is a stirring portrait of the idealized American character. Melville takes an unusual view of the half-legendary leader of the Green Mountain Boys of Vermont:

> Allen seems to have been a curious combination of a Hercules, a Joe Miller, a Bayard, and a Tom Hyer. . . . Though born in New England, he exhibited no trace of her character. He was frank, bluff, companionable as a Pagan, convivial, a Roman, hearty as a harvest. His spirit was essentially Western, for the Western spirit is, or will yet be (for no other is, or can be), the true American one.

Ethan Allen seems the fulfillment of that creative promise hinted at in *Moby-Dick* in the mysterious character of Bulkington, 'full six feet in height . . . chest like a coffer-dam . . . one of those tall mountaineers from the Alleghenian Ridge in Virginia.' Perhaps it is significant that in *Israel Potter* we see Ethan Allen only in chains.

In *The Confidence-Man* the shift of sympathy away from Yankee character toward the Westerner is complete. We see this in the only two characters who claim our sympathies as heroes do: Pitch the frontiersman and Colonel Moredock the Indian-hater. The most savage caricature in the book is of a 'practical poet' of Yankee cuteness—the con man's hardest touch.

But first, the frontiersman. At midpoint in the book the herb-doctor meets 'a rather eccentric person':

> sporting a shaggy spencer of the cloth called bear's-skin; a high-peaked cap of raccoon-skin . . . raw-hide leggings; grim stubble chin; and to end, a double-barrelled gun in his hand—a Missouri bachelor, a Hoosier gentleman, of Spartan leisure and fortune, and equally Spartan manners and sentiments; and, as the sequel may show, not less acquainted, in a Spartan way of his own, with philosophy and books, than with woodcraft and rifles.

This Ring-Tailed Roarer with the Stoic philosophers under his coonskin cap—a backwoods Ishmael—challenges the con man:

> 'Nature is the grand cure. But who froze to death my teamster on the prairie? And who made an idiot of Peter the Wild Boy?' . . .
>
> 'Did I hear something about herbs and herb-doctors?' here said a flute-like voice, advancing. . . . 'If I caught your words aright, you would seem to have little confidence in nature; which, really, in my way of thinking, looks like carrying the spirit of distrust pretty far.'
>
> 'And who of my sublime species may you be?' turning short round upon him, clicking his rifle-lock. . . .
>
> 'One who has confidence in nature, and confidence in man, with some little modest confidence in himself.'

The double-dealer would seem to have met his match. Typically, the confidence man dismisses the woodsman's knowledge as 'drollery,' and carefully shifts the topic away from his home ground. Seizing a chance remark about the innate bad character of the boys on the bachelor's plantation, the con man asks if he will replace them with a machine, since 'Philanthropic scruples, doubtless, forbid your going as far as New Orleans for slaves?' At this moral cant the Missourian snaps, 'You are an abolitionist, ain't you?'

> 'As to that, I cannot so readily answer. If, by abolitionist you mean a zealot, I am none; but if you mean a man, who, being a man, feels for all men, slaves included, and by any lawful act, opposed to nobody's interest, and therefore rousing nobody's enmity, would willingly abolish suffering (supposing it, in its degree, to exist), from among mankind, irrespective of color, then am I what you say.'
>
> 'Picked and prudent sentiments [replies the Missourian]. You are the moderate man, the invaluable understrapper of the wicked man. You, the moderate man, may be used for wrong, but are useless for right.'

The bachelor has proved a harder nut than the herb-doctor foresaw. The latter retires with condescending remarks about the eccentric influence of the wilderness on human feelings.

At this point the backwoodsman has won the first victory of

any passenger over the confidence man. We see him as an Ethan Allen-like image of the West. No longer does Melville envisage 'a most imperial and archangelical image of that unfallen western world,' as in *Moby-Dick;* the Western character now is tested and tempered in adversity, aware of the evil in the world, and on perpetual guard against it.

But the Devil is not so easily vanquished. Soon after the herb-doctor debarks, the Missourian is accosted by another stranger, a grovelling, obsequious agent of the Philosophical Intelligence Office. The talk turns to boys, and the con man now reverses his former position that the bachelor should replace them with a machine. He begs to differ with the conviction that those thirty-five boys, like all boys, were rascals. The bachelor rebuffs him yet again: 'My name is Pitch; I stick to what I say.' But let it not be said that the boy is father to the man; the man *succeeds* the boy as the butterfly the worm. But, Pitch maintains, 'The butterfly is the caterpillar in a gaudy cloak, stripped of which there lies the impostor's long spindle of a body, pretty much worm-shaped as before.' This should draw blood, for the grovelling con man is himself the worm, and in his next recrudescence, as Cosmopolitan in a gaudy cloak, he becomes the butterfly of the analogy. Pitch is already half-aware of what none of the others had suspected—that his interlocutor is a masquerader playing many roles.

Pitch, then, has both the hard-won wisdom of experience and the determination not to be trapped by the confidence man. To maintain this defensive posture he must resemble 'Bruin in a hollow trunk,' abjuring the 'human' feelings of geniality on which the confidence man trades. There is the real danger in Pitch's attitude that, as the herb-doctor said, 'since, for your purpose, you will have neither man nor boy, bond nor free, truly, then, some sort of machine for you is all there is left.' Pitch may go too far in his misanthropy. Perceiving the innate depravity of human character, he claims 'cider-mill, mowing-machine, corn-husker . . . doing good all their lives long . . . the only practical Christians I know.' Truth itself, he says, is 'like a threshing-machine.' These may be said in only half-earnest, yet such remarks portend two developments. One is the defeat of the frontiersman by the con man. To withstand him, Pitch would need to give himself completely over to mechanism. But he yet has his humanities, and these are his undoing. The other is the appearance, in the tale of Moredock, of a Western character who *has* become machine-like in his truculent opposition to evil.

Pitch is undone when the con man appeals to his vanity and his latent kindliness. 'Ah, sir, permit me—when I behold you . . . thus eccentrically clothed in the skins of wild beasts, I cannot but conclude that the equally grim and unsuitable habit of your mind is likewise but an eccentric assumption, having no basis in your genuine soul, no more than in nature herself.' The first sign of 'a little softening' is all the con man needs to wheedle three dollars and a pledge of confidence in the boy to be sent, sight unseen, in two weeks. Then the Intelligence Officer debarks—at a 'grotesque bluff' called the Devil's Joke. At the rail, Pitch ponders his experience.

> He revolves, but cannot comprehend, the operation still less the operator. Was the man a trickster, it must be more for the love than the lucre. Two or three dirty dollars the motive to so many nice wiles?

It is only then that he thinks of the serpent who tempted Eve. At that moment he is cordially greeted by yet another stranger with a voice 'sweet as a seraph's.'

The Cosmopolitan, although maintaining that 'Life is a picnic *en costume*,' has no success in turning Coonskins into a friend. Pitch now knows him for what he is: despite genialities, he sees 'Diogenes masquerading as a cosmopolitan.' The latter admonishes him: 'To you, an Ishmael, disguising in sportiveness my intent, I came ambassador from the human race, charged with the assurance that for your mislike they bore no answering grudge, but sought to conciliate accord between you and them.' Pitch, however, is now confirmed in misanthropy, and Melville leaves him 'to the solitude he held so sapient.' He is indeed an Ishmael, the 'wild man [whose] hand will be against every man and every man's hand against him.' Unlike the Ishmael of Genesis, however, this frontiersman is curiously cast in a reversal of the Westerner's usual role. Possessing ethical vision without power, he is a paradigm of the ironic role of the intellectual humanist in a philistine culture.

Pitch is now succeeded by an unsavory stranger who, far from rebuffing the ambassador from the human race, comes forward to meet him 'with the bluff *abord* of the west.' This is Charles Arnold Noble, with a hint of treachery in his middle name: sly and venal, the Western promise rotted from within, he is soon the con man's pal, seeming to believe in what the cosmopolitan seems to believe. Together they uphold geniality (while trying to get each other drunk), uplift, progress, and free-and-easies. The cosmopolitan now calls himself Frank Goodman, and Charlie, having overheard Frank's last exchange with 'Coonskins,' is reminded of the misanthropy of Moredock, the Indian-hater. But Frank finds it unthinkable that anyone should hate Indians. 'I admire Indians . . . finest of primitive races.' Charlie sees that he must explain the 'Metaphysics of Indian-hating' to make Moredock's career comprehensible, and he begins by describing, as though to an Easterner who had never seen one, what a backwoodsman is.

> The backwoodsman is a lonely man. He is a thoughtful man. He is a man strong and unsophisticated. Impulsive, he is what some might call unprincipled. . . . self-reliance, to the degree of standing by his own judgment, though it stand alone. Not that he deems himself infallible . . . but he thinks that nature destines such sagacity as she has given him, as she destines it to the 'possum. . . . As with the 'possum, instincts prevail with the backwoodsman over precepts. Like the 'possum, the backwoodsman presents the spectacle of a creature dwelling exclusively among the works of God, yet these, truth must confess, breed little in him of the godly mind. Small bowing and scraping is his, further than when with bent

> knee he points his rifle, or picks its flint. . . . The sight of smoke ten miles off is provocation to one more remove from man, one step deeper into nature. Is it that he feels that whatever man may be, man is not the universe? . . . Be that how it will, the backwoodsman is not without some fineness to his nature. Hairy Orson as he looks, . . . beneath the bristles lurks the fur.
>
> Though held in a sort a barbarian, the backwoodsman would seem to America what Alexander was to Asia—captain in the vanguard of conquering civilization.

This is of course a portrait of Pitch, raised to a higher power of heroic idealization. Yet in Charlie's story there is already an ominous portent as to Moredock's character. In a world where God's works are godless, what is the fate of the captain of civilization's vanguard who follows his natural instincts to become indistinguishable from the beasts of the wilderness? Melville seems to be saying that, though man is damned, he is more damned in isolation from his fellows than when he acknowledges his humanity. Moredock is an ambiguous case. After Indians slaughter his family he becomes the slave of his unquenchable passion for revenge. Yet he 'demonstrates something curious . . . namely, that all Indian-haters have at bottom loving hearts . . . No cold husband or colder father . . . He could be very convivial; told a good story . . . with nobody, Indians excepted, otherwise than courteous in a manly fashion; a moccasined gentleman, admired and loved.' No doubt Mr. Schroeder is right in presenting the Indians in this tale as devils, as confidence men. Yet Moredock is not, as Schroeder maintains, the ultimate hero of this book. Nor does the opposite view—Roy Harvey Pearce's—acknowledge sufficiently Moredock's human complexity. 'The Indian-hater,' Mr. Pearce suggests, 'can see nothing but the dark side of life [in which] he loses sight of his human self. The issue of blind confidence and blind hatred is in the end identical.'[6] But this won't do; Moredock retains his human self, *except with Indians;* and his tragedy is that, still strongly feeling his 'hu-

[6] Schroeder, p. 379; Pearce, 'Melville's Indian-Hater: A Note on the Meaning of The Confidence-Man,' *PMLA*, LXVII (Dec. 1952), 942-8.

manities,' to follow instinctual vengeance—even against red devils —requires that he secede from the human community. He is urged to become the Governor of Illinois: to civilize the district as its chief of state. But how could he 'enter into friendly treaties with Indian tribes'? His monomaniacal passion resembles Ahab's, though his enemy is more unequivocally the Adversary than was the whale. Commitment to revenge leads Moredock not to Ahab's self-destruction but into the sterile, mechanical defeat of all his human promise. What 'The Metaphysics of Indian-Hating' tells us is that the hero dedicated to extirpating evil must be a lonely isolato. He cannot be a leader of men.

The con man professes not to get the point. 'If the man of hate, how could John Moredock be also the man of love?' For Frank there is no such thing as the conflict between the threat and the promise of the Western character—between Mike Fink the retrograde barbarian avenger and Davy Crockett, 'Captain in the vanguard of conquering civilization.' The confidence man has a contrary metaphysics of his own. For the unfathomable complexity of human nature he substitutes his false synthesis of simplicity; for the true wild rhythms of nature, which Westerners well know, he substitutes avowals of regularity and kindliness. Frank Goodman eulogizes the press as 'defender of the faith in the final triumph of truth over error . . . machinery over nature, and the good man over the bad.'

Charlie, telling the tale to show man's complexity to Frank, in the end agrees that man is simple. He is therefore unprepared when Frank tests his own avowals of friendship by requesting a loan of fifty dollars. Charlie indignantly spurns him, as 'Out of old materials sprang a new creature. Cadmus glided into the snake.' In short, Charlie, who has done the devil's office, becomes a human version of the confidence man. But that won't do for Frank, who is a taster, not of devils, but of *man*. With a magic ritual he *enchants* Charlie back to his 'best shape,' laying down a circle of ten coins 'with the air of a necromancer' and 'a solemn murmur of cabalistical words.' Now that Charlie is human again,

Frank is about to renew his request for a loan. Already defeated (for the con man has by now tasted him), Charlie pleads a headache, and retires.

There are coils within the coils of logic in this book, as Melville tries to strike through, or peel away, the masks that hide the truth. And he finds, time and again, that the masks conceal yet other masks. Where then does identity ultimately reveal itself? Charlie's place is taken by yet another stranger in whose person 'shrewdness and mythiness' were 'strangely jumbled . . . he seemed a kind of cross between a Yankee peddler and a Tartar priest, though it seemed as if, at a pinch, the first would not in all probability play second fiddle to the last.' Having shown us Western character in Pitch as manly but fallible, in Moredock as heroic but doomed, and in Charlie Noble as corrupt and invidious, Melville now turns to the Westerner's opposite as a final foil for the confidence man. And that opposite is in this book what it was in popular culture: the Yankee peddler.

The description of Mark Winsome as half peddler, half Tartar priest certainly resembles Lowell's set piece on the Yankee character in *The Biglow Papers*—and the same author's double-edged view of Emerson in *A Fable for Critics.* It recalls also a comment of Melville's on the Concord sage—'this Plato who talks through his nose.' Mark Winsome is his caricature of Emerson, and it would seem that Melville, though spurning orthodoxy himself, was of the same mind as the Reverend Andrews Norton, who, on hearing Emerson's Divinity School Address, had called his transcendental gospel 'the latest form of infidelity.' Perhaps that is why his cosmopolitan devil, upholding the Emersonian idea of the incompatibility of beauty with evil, not only proposes 'confidence in the latent benignity of that beautiful creature, the rattle-snake,' but 'all but seemed the creature he described.' His words echo Milton's when Satan appears before Eve. Expressing this doctrine, the devil reveals his identity. But Winsome is no more concerned to be consistent than is Emerson himself, and rejects the proposal. His mystical air is replaced by 'an expression of keen Yankee cuteness' as he obscurely argues the cosmopolitan into a 'labyrinth.' Winsome, chill and icy in aspect, soon proclaims the spiritual superiority of death to life, and calls in a disciple to take his place and demonstrate his cold philosophy in action.

The disciple Egbert is not so much a smack at Thoreau (as has been maintained) as Melville's caricature of the Emersonian man. Even shrewder-looking than his Master, Egbert is 'a practical poet in the West India trade . . . if mysticism, as a lesson, ever came his way, he might, with the characteristic knack of a true New Englander, turn even so profitless a thing to some profitable account.' The action he proposes is to debate with Frank Goodman the compatibility of friendship with the lending of money. They take up Frank's discussion where it broke off with Charlie Noble. Now Egbert *assumes the identity* of 'Charlie.' In a savage hit at Emerson's 'Friendship,' Egbert as 'Charlie' tells Frank (who assumes the role of 'Frank') the fable of China Aster, a tart little allegory on the bloodless ethic of Yankee cuteness. For China Aster was ruined by confidence and a friendly loan.

The tale shows us also the fate of the Promethean creative spirit in a world where the confidence man sets the tone of social intercourse. For China Aster, whose name suggests the Star of the Orient and thus hints at Christ, is allegorically presented also as the Promethean spirit in American life. He is 'a young candlemaker . . . whose trade would seem a kind of subordinate branch of that parent craft and mystery of the hosts of heaven, to be the means, effectively or otherwise, of shedding some light through the darkness of a planet benighted. But he made little money by the business.' His friend Orchis, winning money in a lottery, insists on lending him money so that he may 'hold up the pure spermaceti to the world.' The name of Orchis suggests not only the superfluous luxury of the tropical plant (by contrast, the china aster is a common field flower), but also its origin in the Greek word for testicle. Orchis is the confidence man in yet another masquerade. For he is 'a shoemaker; one whose calling it is to defend the understandings of men from naked contact with the substance of things.' He urges the Promethean spirit to abandon the austerities which dedication to his 'mystery' demands, and live in ease and sensuality. China Aster, doomed by his inability to withstand temptation, is ruined in a corrupt world by his virtues too. His honesty is incompatible with success, while confidence is incompatible with his mission of making candles to enlighten a benighted world. And 'the root of all was a friendly loan.'

When Frank persists in asking a loan, Egbert terminates the 'social and intellectual' phase of their acquaintance, for 'If you turn beggar, then, for the honor of noble friendship, I turn stranger.' His Yankee ethic makes friendship an ideal which cannot be sullied by the claims of compassion. Scornfully turning, the cosmopolitan leaves Egbert 'at a loss to determine where exactly the fictitious character had been dropped, and the real one, if any, resumed.' In this practical poet of Yankee cuteness who upholds death over life, mind over heart, the ideal over the possible, and the self over the ties of compassion, the confidence man at last has met his match. For how can the Devil catch a creature who *has no soul?* Who, then, is Egbert, and who Winsome? The philosopher himself had asked Frank, 'What are you? What am I? Nobody knows who anybody is.' And introducing his disciple he had said, 'I wish you, Egbert, to know this brother stranger.' It was the mute who entered 'in the extremest sense of the word, a stranger.' The Mystical Philosopher and his Practical Disciple are 'brother strangers' with the confidence man. Their faith in heartless self-reliance complements his in indiscriminate confidence. His makes no room in the moral universe for evil, theirs leaves none for good. They show that 'defect in the region of the heart' which Melville found so repelling in Emerson's philosophy.

Sophisticated as is the intellectual background of these tortuous arguments, Melville has leavened both sets of confidence men with the common yeast of traditional Yankee character. He found that character seemingly genial, and frigid; ingratiating, and repelling; dealing in abstract ideals, and in shrewd cutpurse bargains. The traditional type of the Yankee peddler gave Melville the master masks in his confidence man's masquerade.

FIVE

His failure to diddle Egbert does not cast down the Cosmopolitan. A fellow-devil is not his lawful prey; blithely, he goes below decks to finish his work among mankind. The last chapter has occasioned some strange readings of the book. Its final sentence—'Something further may follow of this Masquerade'—leads many critics to assert either that the book as it stands is unfinished (Melville, the argument runs, was so tired out that he quit in the middle of the book and sent an incomplete manuscript off to the printer), or that a sequel is promised, but never was written. The error of such readings may not be obvious, but wrong indeed they are. The chapter is called 'The Cosmopolitan Increases in Seriousness,' a title which indicates that his masquerade is coming to a close. Let us be serious too; like the old man he meets in the cabin, let us have before us a Bible.

That cabin is curiously described. Many men sleep in berths ranged on the walls; a 'solar lamp' swings from the center ceiling. Other lamps hang nearby, 'barren planets, which had either gone out from exhaustion, or been extinguished by such occupants of berths as the light annoyed, or who wanted to sleep, not see.' The setting is clearly an emblem of the end of a universe in which man is too tired to grope any longer toward moral choices. All of China Aster's little candles are dark now. The one solar lamp has a

> shade of ground glass . . . all round fancifully variegated, in transparency, with the image of a horned altar, from which flames rose, alternate with the figure of a robed man, his head encircled by a halo.

This iconography is certainly allegorical. But we don't as yet know what to make of it; nor does the old man even notice the fanciful images on the lampshade. He is poring over the Book, with a look of 'hale greenness in winter.' His aspect suggests the beatitude of Simeon beholding the Master of Faith, and one who goes heavenward 'untainted by the world, because ignorant of it.' These and other hints suggest that the old man, the ultimate dupe in this Masquerade, is America grown old in ignorance of evil—a senile Captain Delano. The cosmopolitan, seeing him read the Bible, genially assures him, 'You *have* good news there, sir—the very best of good news.' From a curtained berth a voice objects, 'Too good to be true.' The cosmopolitan then professes 'a disturbing doubt' concerning the Book. Despite his good opinion of man, he has been told that it is written, 'Believe not his many words—an enemy speaketh sweetly with his lips . . . With much communication he will tempt thee.' The curtained sleeper interjects, 'Who's that describing the confidence-man?' But the innocent old man sets the con man's doubts at rest; the passage came not from the true book but merely the Apocrypha, so it need not be heeded.[7] 'What's that about the Apocalypse?' cries the voice from the berth—we by now suspect the curtained sleeper to be a voice from the dead, 'seeing visions,' as the cosmopolitan says. The old man now proposes that 'to distrust the creature, is a kind of distrusting the Creator.' Since the old fellow had 'a countenance like that which imagination ascribes to good Simeon' (who beheld the boy Jesus and acknowledged the Christ), we may take a special interest in the sudden appearance of a young boy at the cabin table. Can this oldster possibly have the spiritual perceptivity of the saint he seems to resemble?

[7] The confidence man even *misquotes* the Apocrypha. 'This Son of Sirach even says . . . "Take heed of thy friends," not, observe, thy seeming friends, thy hypocritical friends, thy false friends, but thy *friends*, thy real friends—that is to say, not the truest friend in the world is to be implicitly trusted.' But the verse following the con man's quotation reads, 'A faithful friend is a strong defense and he that hath found such a one hath found a treasure' (Ecclesiasticus: 6.13).

Not that the boy is the Christ; he is a peddler, dressed in fluttering red and yellow rags 'like the pointed flames in the robes of a victim in *auto-da-fé*.' From his grimy face sloe-eyes gleamed 'like lustrous sparks from fresh coal.' He offers door-locks and money-belts; despite the old man's trust of his fellow-creatures, the young peddler sells him one of each, throwing in as bonus a Counterfeit Detector. The lad seems in cahoots with the cosmopolitan, but the old man does not catch his wink, nor suspect anything at all. Now that the oldster has armed himself against untrustworthy fellows, the con man reminds him of his earlier assertion that such distrust 'would imply distrust of the Creator.' The old man is confused; unknowingly he has sold his soul to the young devil. Besides, his new counterfeit detector is untrustworthy too—so complicated are the instructions. Completely bamboozled, when he whimpers for a life preserver he accepts what the con man hands him—a tin chamber pot—and takes his proffered arm.

> 'Ah, my way now,' cried the old man . . . 'where lies my way to my state-room?'
>
> 'I have indifferent eyes, and will show you; but, first, for the good of all lungs, let me extinguish this lamp.'
>
> The next moment, the waning light expired, and with it the waning flames of the horned altar, and the waning halo round the robed man's brow; while in the darkness which ensued, the cosmopolitan kindly led the old man away. Something further may follow of this Masquerade.

The awakened voice who asked about the Apocalypse suggests the locus of unstated meaning in this icon. After the seventh seal was opened, John 'heard a voice from the four horns of the altar which is before God.' This announced the destruction of a third part of mankind by fire, smoke, and brimstone, 'And the rest of the men which were not killed by these plagues yet repented not of the work of their hands, that they should not worship devils' (Rev. 9:13-21). The robed and haloed figure on the lampshade is of course Saint John, who, like the altar of God, wanes into darkness as the confidence man extinguishes the Light. What 'may follow of this Masquerade' is no sequel Herman Melville would write; the consequences of man's traduction aboard the Fidèle will be revealed in Hell on Judgment Day.

SIX

One leaves this book feeling as Huck Finn did about one of its sources, *Pilgrim's Progress*—'The statements was interesting, but tough.' As a work of fiction *The Confidence-Man* is clearly a desperate experiment; its partial success—the satiric power of individual episodes and characters—was won at the cost of a larger failure. This is the failure of form. Melville had led himself into a maze of nondramatizable speculation to which none of the traditions he could make use of were fitted to give adequate form. His method of uniting ideas with action, as R. P. Blackmur long ago made clear,[8] is largely 'putative'; this is especially so in *The Confidence-Man.* He attempts allegory without a superstructure of belief, and dialectic without the possibility of resolution. The traditions of native character, so effectively humanized in *Moby-Dick,* here are separated into the Westerner's independence, pushed to the point of self-damning isolation; and Yankee guile without a saving grace, pushed to the point of demonic inhumanity. A book of brilliant fragments, its method of development is too like a charade in which the clues are perversely half-concealed, or incomplete. When we do track down Melville's clues to their sources, there is an awry ambiguousness in applying them to the allegories we hope they will illuminate. In the last chapter, for instance, why is the old man reading the Bible unaware of the icons on the source of light? The con man misquotes Apocrypha to make the oldster infer that if what is apocryphal is not to be believed, then the

[8] In *The Expense of Greatness* (New York, 1940).

opposite of the Apocrypha is Gospel. But if Gospel is 'too good to be true,' does it matter whether the old man is ignorant of the world's evil? Won't he be duped anyway, as was the experienced frontiersman? This is a book without hope; yet Pitch in his wounded wisdom, and Moredock, ennobled by the passion that damns him, remain as testimonies to Melville's creative humanism beset by all the enemies of the contemporary world.

Allegory in *The Confidence-Man* is transmuted into arcane insinuations of reversals of meaning. The ironic vigor of the style is itself reversed by the unrelenting Timonism which condemns all mankind to founder on the 'grotesque bluff' of the Devil's Joke. Melville is still worrying Satan's wager with the Lord, in Job; this time there is no Job's whale in view, and no Job. The Devil's Orphic voice from the machine wins all.

As Roy Fuller has said, 'It is as though in *Gulliver's Travels* Swift had left out Gulliver . . . the eighteenth-century reasonable man has disappeared. In the mid-nineteenth-century world of America . . . so runs Melville's inexorable logic and terrible honesty—there can be no person outside the struggle capable of making a valid moral judgment of it.'[9] Yet the presence of the reasonable man, the center of judgment, is the very basis of satire, a mode whose reason for being is to expose human folly to moral correction. The ambiguity of Melville's position is plain in his use of the Christian ethic to condemn a world in which that ethic is clearly inoperable. That ethic is too good to be true, but none other is good enough.

Flawed though it is, *The Confidence-Man* demands comparison with those great picaresque satiric romances whose scope is as ambitious as its own: not only *Gulliver's Travels*, but *Don Quixote*, *Gargantua and Pantagruel*, and *Candide*. Melville in fact goes beyond them, and beyond Hawthorne's experiments, too, in using the romancer's imaginative freedom for intellectual rather than psychological analysis. Although he satirizes many

[9] Introduction to *The Confidence-Man* (London, 1948), p. xi.

follies his viewpoint is less satiric than ironical. And irony is the uncomforted refuge of perception without power. The great European satires are works of comic imagination based on the affirmation of man's ideals; Melville's, though their equal in indignation, attacks not only human institutions and human folly, but, as they never do, human nature itself.

Melville's life spanned the century in which the community of Christendom was irreparably broken into chaos. His progress from blithe good humor through the extremities of romantic egoism to the despairing ironies of *The Confidence-Man* marked both a personal tragedy and the experience of his culture. It was shared by Hawthorne, in whom increasing confusion destroyed the sources of his creative powers. And it is still more clearly exampled in Mark Twain. He suffered as deeply as Melville but, by suppressing *What is Man?* until after his own death, tried to protect himself from the public consequences of his realization that God had abdicated from the universe. That book and *The Mysterious Stranger* seem the naïve fantasies of a village atheist, compared with Melville's merciless apocalypse published sixty years earlier.

After *The Confidence-Man* Melville seemed to have little choice but to follow the fate of the character in his story 'Bartleby,' and, facing the blank wall, 'prefer not to' write any further stories. Like the Scrivener in the Dead Letter Office, Melville spent most of his remaining thirty-five years as an obscure customs inspector on a New York wharf and took no part in the literary life of his country. His great work had been done, but in the era that Mark Twain called 'The Gilded Age'—and characterized in Colonel Sellers, who is both dupe and confidence man—nobody heeded Herman Melville. That generation sought a literary hero more congenial than moody Melville with his demonic Ahab and sardonic cosmopolitan. In the platform funnyman who regaled audiences with frontier humor and found no fault with President Grant, post-Civil War America thought to behold its avatar. How much his contemporaries overvalued

Mark Twain's lesser talents, how little they understood the depths of his genius, our own generation has sufficiently acknowledged. We can see better than they how closely Mark Twain's greatest work draws on traditions similar to Melville's. The imaginations of both are deeply stirred by the lore of omens and witchcraft, and both respond to the bracing tensions of native character and humor. The conflicts between native and stranger, between truth and deception, between reality and appearance, characteristic of the popular imagination, are intensified both in Melville's romances and *Adventures of Huckleberry Finn.* The signal difference in their handlings of these materials is in their conceptions of an 'original character.' Although Twain saw perhaps as clearly as Melville the depravity of 'the damned human race' who line his Mississippi's shores, he made his hero not only moral, and a human being, but triumphant. In doing so he remained true to the ebullient optimism of the folk traditions which contributed to his view of the American world.

PART IV

Mark Twain

'That book was made by Mr. Mark Twain, and he told the truth, mainly. There was things which he stretched, but mainly he told the truth . . . with some stretchers, as I said before.'

—Huck.

'Let me make the superstitions of a nation and I care not who makes its laws or its songs either.'

—'Pudd'nhead Wilson's New Calendar'

15

Black Magic—and White—
in Huckleberry Finn

ONE

The most universal book to have come out of the United States of America begins with this preamble:

> NOTICE
>
> Persons attempting to find a motive in this narrative will be prosecuted; persons attempting to find a moral in it will be banished; persons attempting to find a plot in it will be shot.

What a way to begin: 'No Trespassing!' This, of course, is only the first of the innumerable jokes, pranks, disguises, tricks, deceptions, ruses, and verbal extravagances that make *Adventures of Huckleberry Finn* a book that has won the world's heart. At the start Mark Twain establishes its tone of frontier humor. His preamble is nailed to a stake, and it posts the limits of his claim, and of ours, on the golden lode of his own remembered boyhood on the Mississippi.

But why such caution behind his bumptious fooling?

What a way to begin a book. Think, for instance, of the 'Author's Prologue' to *Gargantua,* exactly three and a half centuries earlier. Rabelais began by comparing his book to the Sileni of old, 'little boxes . . . painted on the outside with wanton toyish figures . . . and other such counterfeited pictures, at pleasure, to excite people unto laughter.' But within those caskets lay 'many rich and fine drugs . . . balm, ambergreese, amonomon

. . . and other things of great price.' And he goes on to speak of Socrates, for whose outer appearance 'you would not have given the peel of an onion . . . always laughing, tippling, and merry, carousing to everyone, with continual gibes and jeers, the better by those means to conceal his divine knowledge.'

Divine knowledge, of course, is not a commodity much in demand in the world, and those who find it burdening their souls are often hard-pressed to put a good face on the matter. The faces of Silenus, god of mirth, are as good a disguise as any.

Even Rabelais, in his mock-monkery fashion, drives a stake against the scholiasts, just as Mark Twain would do. If you believe, he says, that 'Homer, whilst he was couching his Iliads and Odysses, had any thought upon those allegories' which the critics have 'squeezed out of him,' you may as well take the gospel sacraments to be written by Ovid. Now Mark Twain could be just as bookish, as well as just as truly comic, as Rabelais, but in posting his 'Notice' he intuitively chose the vernacular way of warning off the critics who would squeeze the juice of allegorical lemons from a work which he had freshened with the juices of life. To divine knowledge he makes no claims. Yet what can explain his cautious parrying of critical exegesis but that he well knew the motive, the moral, and the plot of his own book—he had recognized the divine knowledge that came to him when he finally plumbed the images of his deepest recollection—and this he did not want abstracted from the only form in which it could retain the fullness of its truth: *Adventures of Huckleberry Finn.*

Despite his 'Notice,' scholars, annotators, and critics have poached all over Mark's place. Indeed, in the past generation there has been an unparalleled exploration of motive, moral, and plot in *Huckleberry Finn.* As regards the plot, many readers have taken Mark Twain literally, or at least assumed that the book has no more intrinsic a plot than the picaresque pattern of a journey imposes. Certainly their contention was strengthened by Bernard DeVoto's publication in *Mark Twain at Work* of the author's plan for a concluding episode—mercifully never carried out—which involved Huck, Jim, and Tom's encountering an escaped circus elephant in the Louisiana bayous. The ending that he actually did give the book—Tom Sawyer's burlesque liberation of the already-freed slave—has been much criticized as disastrously out of key with the fundamental themes of the rest of the story. Yet T. S. Eliot and Lionel Trilling have found this ending satisfactory; other recent critics have contended the contrary against them as well as against Mark Twain.

As for the first two clauses in the author's 'Notice,' both motive and moral have been scrutinized with Geiger-counter sensitivity by critics of a dozen different persuasions. Where some find the theme of the book to be the search for freedom, another proposes the 'theme of appearance versus reality.' J. M. Cox suggests initiation and rebirth as its besetting theme, while Philip Young discovers that 'an excessive exposure to violence and death' have produced 'an ideal symbol' for dying, namely, a 'supremely effortless flight into a dark and silent unknown.' Yet again 'death and rebirth' and 'Huck's journey in search of a father' are urged by K. S. Lynn as themes, while R. W. Frantz terms Huck 'a creature of fear.' As for motive, the ingenious Leslie Fiedler reads the book as a wish-fulfillment of homosexual miscegenation. On the other hand Mr. Trilling has made a definitive case for 'Huck's intense and even complex moral quality.'[1]

[1] T. S. Eliot, 'Introduction' to *Adventures of Huckleberry Finn* (London, 1950); Lionel Trilling, 'Huckleberry Finn,' *The Liberal Imagination* (New York, 1951), pp. 104-17; William Van O'Connor, 'Why Huckleberry Finn Is Not the Great American Novel,' *College English,* XVII (Oct. 1955), 6-10; Leo Marx, 'Mr. Eliot, Mr. Trilling, and Huckleberry Finn, *American Scholar,* XXII (Autumn 1953), 423-40; Lauriat Lane, Jr., 'Why *Huckleberry Finn* Is a Great World Novel.' *College English,* XVII (Oct. 1955), 1-5; James M. Cox, 'Remarks on the Sad Initiation of Huckleberry Finn,' *Sewanee Review,* LXII (Summer 1954), 389-405; Philip Young, *Ernest Hemingway* (New York, 1952), chap. 6; Kenneth S. Lynn, 'Huck and Jim,' Yale Review, XLVII (Spring 1958), 421-31; Ray W. Frantz, 'The Role of Folklore in *Huckleberry Finn,' American Literature,* XXVIII (Nov. 1956), 314-27; Leslie Fiedler, 'Come Back to the Raft, Huck, Honey!' *An End to Innocence* (Boston, 1955), pp. 142-57.

Mark Twain should have known better; in Academe, as in Missouri, a notice without a sheriff proves utterly unavailing. This chapter is itself yet another act of trespass. An assortment of critical readings such as those just enumerated suggests that if the disguises Mark Twain painted upon his Sileni have been baffling in their variety, there is yet indeed a divine knowledge concealed within them. Although each of these essays is helpful in noting valuable themes and structures of the book, a most important pattern has not been sufficiently explored. This is the pattern of relationships in *Huckleberry Finn* between the human and the divine.

Mr. Eliot and Mr. Trilling agree in their readings that the River is a god, presiding over the action, its divinity everywhere implied though nowhere stated outright. But there is a more explicit supernaturalism in this book. Or, more properly, there is an exemplification and a testing of three attitudes toward the imaginative fulfillment of life, and these are largely indicated in supernatural terms. Each typifies the moral nature of those who profess it. Two of these imaginary supernatural worlds prove morally inadequate; the third—which pays homage to the river god—gives dignity to human life.

These attitudes, so compellingly dramatized by Mark Twain, are the conventional piety of the villagers; the irrelevant escape of the romantic imagination (as played by Tom Sawyer and an assorted adult cast of rapscallions and Southern gentlemen); and the world of supernatural omens which Jim, the runaway slave, best understands. Huck Finn is the sorcerer's apprentice. The superstitious imagination recognizes evil as a dynamic force; it acknowledges death. It is truer to the moral demands of life than is either the smug piety of Christian conformity or the avoidance of choice by escaping to fantasy and romance.

Bernard DeVoto has made it impossible for us to miss Mark Twain's indebtedness to Negro superstitions. Yet their significance in *Huckleberry Finn* has not adequately been shown. Jim's and Huck's beliefs in witches, ghosts, and omens are not merely authentic touches of local color; they are of signal importance in the thematic development of the book and in the growth toward maturity of its principal characters. When understood as a commentary upon and criticism of the two conventional traditions of white society in reconciling the moral sense with the realities of life on the Mississippi, this folklore of the supernatural becomes a structural element essential to the work of art.

In working out the conflicts between the three otherworlds and their human representatives in *Huckleberry Finn* I hope to do full justice to the character of Jim. Insufficient notice has been taken of the ways in which Jim, as well as Huck, grows to maturity and assumes a man's full obligations. Some of the most important evidence of his development is given us in his role as seer and shaman, interpreter of the dark secrets of nature which the white folks in the church deny, secrets which Tom Sawyer and all the other romanticists along the Mississippi cannot discover.

These three commitments of the imagination allow Mark Twain to explore the possibilities of establishing sympathetic relations between man and nature and between man and man. The local conditions of Huck Finn's world are those of the sleepy village of 'St. Petersburg'—or, to be more accurate biographically, of Hannibal, Missouri, the riverfront town where young Sam Clemens grew up, played with the outcast boy Tom Blankenship (the original of Huck), and listened to the Negroes speak of ghosts and omens. His best two books of boyhood create this river hamlet for us; several of the themes of *Huckleberry Finn* have their beginnings in *The Adventures of Tom Sawyer.* We should consider both books in order to explore the three otherworlds of Hannibal.

TWO

In his old age, Mark Twain remembered,

> My school days began when I was four years and a half old. . . . I was sent to Mrs. Horr's school and I remember my first day in that little log house with perfect clearness, after these sixty-five years. . . . Mrs. Horr was a New England lady of middle age with New England ways and principles, and she always opened school with a prayer and a chapter from the New Testament . . . she dwelt upon the text, 'Ask and ye shall receive,' and said that whosoever prayed for a thing with earnestness and strong desire need not doubt that his prayer would be answered.[2]

Mrs. Horr's confident Christianity is the faith of Tom's Aunt Polly, of Miss Watson and the teachers in the Sunday and the District Schools; it is the faith of Mary and Sid Sawyer. In Sunday school, had Tom been able to remember the Sermon on the Mount, he would have received a blue ticket for each two verses. 'Ten blue tickets equalled a red one, and could be exchanged for it; ten red tickets equalled a yellow one; for ten yellow tickets the superintendent gave a plainly bound Bible (worth forty cents in those easy times) to the pupil.' Tom cannot remember a single verse, yet he wins the Bible—by swapping lickrish, fishhooks, and marbles for tickets of all colors. Like a Yankee trader, Tom gets something for nothing. It was for nothing, too, because he simply traded back the truck he had collected for his noblesse in allowing the other boys to whitewash his fence. Tom's winning the Bible is deftly humorous, yet the episode is at the same time Mark Twain's oblique criticism of the values for which the church and Sunday school stand. The formalistic piety of the adult world is meaningless to Tom; he applies their own materialistic standards against the sham his elders have made of religious values. We are told also of a German boy in the village who had won five Bibles by reciting 3000 verses without stop-

[2] Bernard DeVoto, ed., *Mark Twain in Eruption* (New York, 1940), p. 107.

ping. Alas, he lost his wits and 'was little better than an idiot from that day forth,' a dire judgment upon his mentors who had subjected a boy's spirit to so unnatural an imprisonment in the name of virtue.

In *Huckleberry Finn* the institutionalized smugness of the adult world is still more scathingly attacked. Here too the values for which formal Christianity stands are in the end seen to be the opposites of the virtues professed by the pious. Miss Watson, like the original Mrs. Horr in Hannibal, is in her own eyes and those of the village a very temple of Christian virtue. It is she whose attempts to cultivate young Huckleberry prove so onerous that he soon reconciles himself to living for a time with Pap. Her faith is summed up in the formula of prayer: 'She told me to pray every day, and whatever I asked for I would get it.' But this faith does not stand the tests by which Huck measures everything he meets: it won't work. He tries prayer. 'Once I got a fish-line, but no hooks. It warn't any good to me without hooks. . . . I says to myself, if a body can get anything they pray for, why don't Deacon Winn get back the money he lost on pork? . . . Why can't Miss Watson fat up? No, says I to myself, there ain't nothing in it.' As it was for Tom in Sunday school, this sort of religion is meaningless because it has no vital connection to the actual urgencies of his life. The point is made again in caricature when Huck and the Grangerfords go to church. 'The men took their guns along, so did Buck, and kept them between their knees or stood them handy against the wall. The Shepherdsons done the same. It was pretty ornery preaching—all about brotherly love, and such-like tiresomeness; but everybody said it was a good sermon.' That night Sophia Grangerford elopes with young Harney Shepherdson, and by morning the river is stained with feuders' blood. Meanwhile the pigs have wandered into the House of God, because the floor is so cool in the summer heat. 'If you notice,' says Huck, 'most folks don't go to church only when they've got to; but a hog is different.'

Again and again Mark Twain returns to the inefficacy of formal religion. When Huck and Jim escape the shooting of the feud they are soon joined by the King and the Duke, and it isn't long before the King is at still another religious service—this time, an evangelical prayer meeting. The King stands up to testify: he's got the light, he'll reform and give up being a pirate in the Indian Ocean. He'll return to the haunts of his crimes and convert his former crews. The crowd, hysterical with joy, takes up a collection and the King makes off with $87.75 plus a three-gallon jug of whiskey he lifts along the way. The religion of ecstasy is no more proof against hypocrisy than the faith of conformity had been against corruption. We remember that one of the acts which made Huck and Jim's voyage necessary was Miss Watson's decision to sell Jim down the river; her Christian principles were susceptible to an offer of eight hundred dollars for a human life.

Discussing the thematic unity of *Huckleberry Finn*, Edgar Branch suggests that the book be read as a struggle between two views of Christian providence.[3] One is Miss Watson's; the other is that of the Widow Douglas, who counselled Huck that 'the thing a body could get by praying for it was "spiritual gifts" . . . I must help other people and do everything I could for other people, and look out for them all the time, and never think about myself. . . . I couldn't see no advantage to it—except for the other people; so at last I reckoned I wouldn't worry about it any more, but just let it go.' Her counsel, of course, actually does define Huck's moral attitude, and the Widow and Mary Jane Wilkes are among the rare company who may be compared to Huck and Jim in goodness. But while Mr. Branch's thesis has much to recommend it, it is notable that this 'spiritual gift' the Widow urges Huck to seek is something he already has; it comes to him and to Jim without the machinery of prayer,

[3] Edgar Branch, 'The Two Providences in *Huckleberry Finn*,' *College English*, XI (Jan. 1950), 188-95

and she and Mary Jane have it as a result of their inner natures, not as a product of their Christian belief. The spiritual gift is natural goodness.

THREE

The second kind of imagination in *Huckleberry Finn* is the romantic escape from the commonplace into the faraway and long ago by which Tom Sawyer makes life in his humdrum hamlet a series of adventurous surprises. Tom, who could remember neither verses from the Bible nor the simple lessons of the district school, has got down by heart a prodigious amount of courtly ritual, chivalric practice, details concerning the incarceration of noble prisoners and the proper techniques by which they languish for thirty years and at last laboriously escape.

This imaginary baggage of Tom's—we think at once of *Don Quixote,* a book Tom has read—includes magic as well as ritual and romance. After Our Gang swears its Dark Oath, the boys played robber for a month. 'Then,' says Huck, 'I resigned. All the boys did. We hadn't robbed nobody, hadn't killed any people, but only just pretended.' According to Tom, turnips and hogs stolen from farmers' carts were 'julery' and ingots, but Huck 'Couldn't see no profit in it.' Ambuscading the A-rabs appealed to Huck, who wanted to see the camels and elephants, but the caravan proved to be only a Sunday school picnic. Tom is scornful of Huck's skepticism. 'He said it was all done by enchantment. . . . we had enemies which he called magicians, and they had turned the whole thing into an infant Sunday-school, just out of spite.' These magicians have supernatural agents who, when summoned by rubbing a magic lamp or ring, will obey any command. If a magician tells them 'to build a palace forty miles long out of diamonds and fill it full of chewing gum, or whatever you want, they've got to do it.' But Huck thinks they're 'a pack of flatheads' for not keeping the palace themselves. He responds to Tom's bookish genies just as he had to Miss Watson's prayers—it is hardly accidental that both occur in the same chapter. Both prayers and genies get you what you ask for. Huck tests these selfish faiths by common sense and finds them wanting.

Everywhere in *Huckleberry Finn,* Huck has this commonsensical pragmatic approach to such problems as how to escape from Pap, how to protect Jim, how to free him from the jail on Uncle Silas's farm. Huck always has the *right* attitude, yet he usually thinks Tom could do better what he himself does superlatively well. When Tom does reappear at the end of the book, Huck defers to him and allows him to put Jim through a series of preposterous inconveniences. This ambivalence and humility toward his own prowess is an irony which makes all the more apparent Huck's superiority. His is not merely a practical superiority, but a moral eminence.

The relation of each character to Jim is the key to his nature. For Jim is in fact the moral touchstone of the book. As a slave, Jim has no status in society; and society assumes that he has no human dignity. As a fugitive Jim is in the most vulnerable position possible. Only those who neither have malice in themselves nor countenance evil in others will resist the impulse to harm him or to see him harmed. Tom, of course, is acquainted with Jim of old, and *means* him no harm. Yet when Tom first sees Jim asleep, in chapter 2, he 'wanted to tie Jim to the tree for fun'; when Tom arrives at Uncle Silas's place and finds Jim chained to a bed in the barn, he perpetrates unnecessary miseries upon his old friend simply to quench his own thirst for excitement. What is worse, Tom does this knowing all the while that Miss Watson had repented and freed Jim in her will before she died. Tom fills Jim's cell with snakes and spiders, makes him chisel inscriptions on a grindstone, keeps him in chains, and gets the whole neighborhood so stirred up that, when he does at last let Jim escape, he and Jim and Huck are chased into a swamp by an angry posse of armed vigilantes. All were glad to escape, 'but Tom was gladdest of all because he had a bullet in the calf of his leg.' Tom is a sensation-seeker who makes no moral choices in imposing his imaginary world of romance upon the commonplace world of harsh reality.

But the real world demands moral choices, and when Tom insists on gratifying his longings for the strange, the exotic, the dangerous, at whatever cost to his friends, we realize that he is not only selfish but perhaps, concealed from us by his boyish charm, he is cruel too. In *Tom Sawyer* there is a revealing scene which foreshadows the famous one in *Huckleberry Finn* in which Huck tricks Jim in the fog and, in begging Jim's forgiveness afterwards, assumes responsibility toward him. Tom had similarly tricked Aunt Polly by pretending to be dead; coming home by night to find her grieving for him, he had stolen away again and not left the birchbark note that would have reassured her that he lived. Thus Tom had the exquisite opportunity to attend his own funeral. But that was not so much fun for Aunt Polly. 'You didn't think! Child, you never think . . .' she upbraids him later. Tom says he is sorry, but he is in no way changed by his repentance as Huck will be by his. In defense of Tom, however, one remembers his magnanimity toward Becky when they are lost in the cave. Yet his conduct there was prescribed by the chivalric code: one is supposed to be noble toward pretty girls in distress. How one acts toward aged aunts or freed slaves was not prescribed, and Tom got all the thrills he could at their expense.

In *Huckleberry Finn*, other characters in their maturity express some of the imaginative qualities which make Tom in his boyhood seem such a winningly mischievous lad. When we, with Huck, fall in among the Grangerfords, we cannot help but think how they and Tom would have liked one another. (They do have a son named Tom!) These Grangerfords bow to each other at breakfast and drink to the health of their parents; they apologize to little Huck for the indignity of searching his pockets, and they have more culture than Huck believed could exist under one roof. The Grangerfords make a morality of manners, but their chivalric rituals, we come to learn, are a thin veneer over their essential barbarism. Their sense of honor is worthy but limited; they do not understand what it is to which they give their loyalty. In pursuing an endless revenge for a grievance none can remember, they live by the law of the feral wilderness. Their feud is an American *Oresteia,* a tragedy in which Apollo and Athene, the gods of light and wisdom, do not appear, and the Furies are never appeased. Despite their strong sense of honor, their estimable loyalty to kin, there is no room in their universe for love: the sermon on Christian charity moved them not, and the love of Harney and Sophia brings death, not conciliation, to their kin. This grim episode is partly Mark Twain's reaction to the aristocratic pretensions of the Old South (pretensions his own family shared); some of its fascination is that he shows us so much in the Grangerfords that we wish to admire. But insofar as they act out in the realm of moral choices the romantic notions of Tom Sawyer's daydreams, they indict themselves and their culture for their lack of forgiveness, their failure to love.

Tom's daydreams are also acted out by adults at the opposite end of the social scale. It is curious how closely the King and Duke's stock-in-trade of shifty disguises parallels Tom's dreams of glory memorized from old romances. Tom was always concerning himself about captive or outcast nobles; they turn up as the dispossessed Duke of Bilgewater and the lamented Dauphin of France. Tom was forever acting parts, and, as Mr. Eliot reminds us, he always needed an audience; they are professional thespians—The Great David Garrick of Drury Lane and Edmund Kean. Tom's favorite sop to self-pity in *Tom Sawyer* was to imagine himself a pirate; but the only pirate we see is the King at the camp meeting, acting again. We remember, too, that Tom had tried to ambuscade the A-rabs; now, when the Duke wants to keep Jim from being recognized by slave-hunters, 'He dressed Jim up in King Lear's outfit . . . and painted Jim's face and hands and ears and neck all over a dead, dull, solid blue, like a man that's been drowned nine days. Blamed if he warn't the horriblest-looking outrage I ever see. Then the duke took and wrote out a sign on a shingle so: *Sick Arab—but harmless when not out of his head.*'

They resemble Tom grown up in their shrewdness too, for he was the lad who got his fence whitewashed by a ruse, and the parallel between the King's camp-meeting trick and Tom's winning the Bible is plain. These two strains in Tom—his shrewdness and self-pitying romanticism—are run to seed in them. When we see them betray Huck's trust and sell Jim for forty dollars, we may not be surprised to find Tom himself capable of toying with Jim's freedom.[4]

FOUR

The third imaginary realm is the world of superstition, a world we enter as soon as we meet Huckleberry Finn. As DeVoto observes, 'On page 64 of *Tom Sawyer,* Huckleberry Finn wanders into immortality swinging a dead cat.' Huck and his cat symbolize freedom to Tom, who meets them on a Monday morning between his bondage at church the day before and his approaching incarceration in the district school. That dead cat also represents the lure of an unknown and forbidden world of spirits, omens, and dark powers, a world which attracts Tom not only by its Gothicism and horror but because, unlike his romantic escapades, this imaginary realm succeeds in transcending reality

[4] Parallels between the two rascals and Tom are so frequent that one must remark another still: at the very end, when Tom reveals that Jim had been free all along, he pays him a salary of *forty dollars* for having been such a good prisoner. Much earlier, when Huck shields Jim from capture for the first time, he pretends to slave-hunters on the river that Jim is his father, sick with smallpox, and asks their aid. They refuse to help him, but assuage their guilt by floating $40 in gold pieces on bits of board down to Huck, who shares the money with Jim. All three payments are guilt-money for the betrayal of loyalties. Tom's payment comes last and its meaning is signified by the preceding incidents.

by rendering life itself in mythic terms. The boys exchange cures for warts; yet try as he will, Tom can never really enter Huck's world. When he tries to recover by incantation all the marbles he ever lost, Tom's charm is bound to fail, for the first allegiance of his imagination—as we have seen—lies elsewhere. Besides, he is after all a village boy, nephew of the respectable Aunt Polly, brother of the model prig Sid Sawyer; Tom shares their status, and to him Huck is a 'romantic outcast.' Therefore Tom will never share Huck's secret wisdom—or his freedom.

The association of these superstitions in Mark Twain's mind with freedom from restraint is reiterated in the first chapter of *Huckleberry Finn.* This time it is Huck who sweats through the lessons, about Moses and 'the Bulrushers.' At last the widow 'let it out that Moses had been dead a considerable long time; so then I didn't care no more about him, because I don't take no stock in dead people.' Huck is then lectured on going to Heaven by Miss Watson; this is so depressing that by nighttime 'I felt so lonesome I most wished I was dead.'

> The stars were shining, and the leaves rustled in the woods ever so mournful; and I heard an owl, away off, who-whooing about somebody that was dead, and a whippowill and a dog crying about somebody that was going to die; and the wind was trying to whisper something to me, and I couldn't make out what it was, and so it made the cold shivers run over me. Then away out in the woods I heard that kind of a sound that a ghost makes when it wants to tell about something that's on its mind and can't make itself understood, and so can't rest easy in its grave, and has to go about that way every night grieving. I got so downhearted and scared I did wish I had some company. Pretty soon a spider went crawling up my shoulder, and I flipped it off and it lit in the candle; and before I could budge it was all shriveled up. I didn't need anybody to tell me that that was an awful bad sign and would fetch me some bad luck, so I was scared and most shook the clothes off of me. I got up and turned around in my tracks three times and crossed my breast every time; and then I tied up a little lock of my hair with a thread to keep witches away. But I hadn't no confidence.

Freedom from the restraints of civilization, yes; but such freedom has its dangers too. For Huck, the omens are an acknowledgment of the fact of death. 'I didn't take no stock in dead people' applies to the dead lessons in Bible or school, not to these immanent realities. These portents are an admission of evil as a positive force in the natural world. His exorcisms attempt to control the operation of malevolent powers. But while he knows far more about such things than Tom does, Huck is still a mere disciple. The magus is Nigger Jim.

But when we first meet him, Jim is a slave. His superstitions, like the hagiolatry of the ignorant peasants in *The Innocents Abroad,* are the manacles upon his soul. Mark Twain dramatizes his bondage by the quality of his beliefs. Far from controlling nature, Jim in slavery is helpless before the dark powers, a gullible prey to every chance or accident which befalls him. This is made humorously manifest in chapter 2, when Tom and Huck find Jim snoozing on the widow's kitchen steps. Tom hangs his hat on a branch and leaves a five-cent piece on the table. 'Afterward Jim said the witches bewitched him and put him in a trance, and rode him all over the state, and then set him down under the trees again, and hung his hat on a limb to show who done it.' Other slaves come from miles around to hear Jim's expanding account of this marvel. It gives him status! But he is more than ever enslaved to his fears; and a week later Miss Watson decides to sell him down the river to a more arduous bondage. That is a fear he cannot transform into personal distinction through the artistic control of a tall tale. Jim runs away to Jackson's Island.

On the island he lives in terror of capture. Huck, having escaped from Pap, is there before him. Still the fearful, haunt-ridden man-child, Jim takes Huck for a ghost and drops to his knees, imploring, 'Doan' hurt me—don't! I hain't ever done no harm to a ghos'. I alwuz liked dead people, en done all I could for 'em. You go en git in de river ag'in, wah you b'longs.' But once he learns in earnest that Huck is alive, Jim realizes that he himself is free. The mighty river rises and the two move camp to a womb-like cavern. Animals take refuge in the trees, and 'they got so tame, on account of being hungry, that you could paddle right up and put your hand on them if you wanted to; but not the snakes and turtles.' This is an uneasy Eden, menaced by the implacable flooding river.

Now that he is free in this ambiguous paradise the nature of Jim's superstitious beliefs undergoes a change. We hear no more of ghosts and witches. Instead, Jim instructs Huck in the lore of weather, in the omens of luck, in the talismans of death. 'Jim knowed all kinds of signs.' Seeing young birds skip along means rain; catching one brings death. You must tell the bees when their owner dies or they will weaken and perish. Death is never far from the superstitious imagination. Jim goes on—don't shake the tablecloth after sundown, or count the things you cook for dinner, or look at the moon over your left shoulder—these bring bad luck. 'It looked to me like all the signs was about bad luck, and so I asked him if there warn't any good-luck signs. He says: "Mighty few—an' *dey* ain't no use to a body. What you want to know when good luck's a-comin' for? Want to keep it off?"' Luck is the folk concept of what the Greeks called Fate, the Anglo-Saxons, Wyrd. There is a stoical wisdom in Jim's resignation before it which makes a manly contrast to the psalm-singing optimism of Miss Watson and the revivalists, and to Tom's romantic evasions of reality.

Soon after they see the young birds flying, sure enough, it rains: a huge, frightening storm that reasserts the dominance of nature over man. The river rises, and as was foretold in so many of their omens, the House of Death floats by. When Jim's omens come true he is no more a gullible supplicant to witches. He is a magus now, a magician in sympathetic converse with the spirits that govern—often by malice or caprice—the world of things and men.

As soon as Jim begins to feel his freedom, his attitude toward

Huck develops. One of the grand ironies of this book is that while it seems to show Huck protecting Jim, Jim is also taking care of Huck all along. Jim's folk wisdom saved Huck from the storm; Jim builds the wigwam on the raft. 'I'd see him standing my watch on top of his'n, 'stead of calling me, so I could go on sleeping.' Just after the storm, when the House of Death floats by, it is Jim who goes aboard first, sees the corpse, and won't let Huck behold it. Huck boyishly salvages an old straw hat, a Barlow knife, 'a ratty old bedquilt. . . . And so, take it all around, we made a good haul.' These squalid remnants, we discover much later, constitute Huck's patrimony from Pap, the father whose savagery he fled. So terrible was the self-destructive anarchic energy of Pap that Huck had to simulate self-destruction to escape him. But now it is Jim who comprehends the degradation of Pap's death and protects Huck from that cruel knowledge. Jim is now free to take the place that Pap was never worthy to hold as Huck's spiritual father. When Jim and Huck shove off from the House of Death their odyssey begins. Jim can now act as Huck's father, and Huck's first act is to protect him, as a son might do.

Because of this filial relationship, Huck cannot play tricks on Jim as he could on Tom or Ben Rogers. This he discovers when he kills a rattler and coils it in Jim's bed. Jim had warned him, 'it was the worst bad luck in the world to touch a snake-skin.' The dead snake's mate coils round it and bites poor Jim. But Jim has a folk cure—eating the snake's flesh roasted, tying the rattles around his wrist, and drinking whiskey. Just as his omens come true, his cures cure. Again we see Jim as medicine man, free to control—within mortal limits—his universe.

Another aspect of Jim's shamanistic role is his power to interpret oracles and dreams. Here, too, when in slavery this attribute parodies itself because Jim then held pretensions without power. He had a hairball from the fourth stomach of an ox with which he 'used to do magic.' Huck consults him after seeing Pap's footprints in the snow, to learn what Pap would do. Accepting

Huck's counterfeit quarter, Jim reels off a counterfeit prophecy, concluding, 'You wants to keep 'way fum de water as much as you kin.' But when Huck returns to his room, 'there sat Pap—his own self!' and the only escape from Pap is to flee by water. Jim's next oracular occasion comes when he and Huck find each other after being separated by the fog. Huck, as a joke, convinces Jim that they had been together on the raft all the time; Jim must have dreamed their separation. So Jim 'said he must start in and 'terpret it, for it was sent for a warning.' Towheads and currents stand for men who will aid or hinder them; their cries were warnings of trouble ahead, but all would work out well in the end. Then Huck points to the leaves, the rubbish, the smashed oar. Jim ponders:

> What do they stan' for? I's gwyne to tell you. When I got all wore out wid work, en wid de callin' for you, en went to sleep, my heart wuz mos' broke bekase you wuz los', en I didn' k'yer no mo' what become er me en de raf'. En when I wake up en fine you back ag'in, all safe en soun', de tears come, en I could 'a' got down on my knees en kiss yo' foot, I's so thankful. En all you wuz thinkin' 'bout wuz how you could make a fool uv ole Jim wid a lie. Dat truck dah is *trash;* en trash is what people is dat puts dirt on de head er dey fren's en makes 'em ashamed.

This speech, so moving in its avowal of dignity, combines Jim's attempt at magical interpretation (which is in fact accurate) with the realism that underlies it, and with his staunch adherence to the code of simple decencies by which good men must live. It is indeed the first major turning-point of the romance. It reinforces the lesson of the snakeskin: Huck now realizes that he is bound to Jim by ties too strong for mischievous trifling, ties so strong that he must break the strongest mores of the society he was raised in to acknowledge them. 'It was fifteen minutes before I could work myself up to go and humble myself to a nigger; but I done it, and I warn't ever sorry for it afterward, neither.'

Now that Huck has learned how he and Jim are inseparable,

circumstances at once thrust them apart. In the next chapter their raft is run over by a paddlewheeler; when Huck gets ashore and sings out for Jim he finds himself alone. This, he thinks, is what comes of handling that snakeskin. He is taken in by the Grangerfords and does not find Jim again until after the shooting. Then the Duke and Dauphin come aboard. From this point on Jim and Huck are never again alone together, and Jim does not act as magus again. His powers have their mysterious source in the river, partaking of its inscrutable might. For if the river is a god, Jim is its priest. The river god is indifferent to humanity; he runs on, uncontaminated by the evils along his shores, asserting now and then in storms and floods which sweep the House of Death downstream his dominance and power over 'the damned human race.' Only when Jim is alone with Huck on the river island or drifting on the current is he so free from the corruption of civilization that he can partake of the river god's dark power. Jim responds on a primitive level to that power, through which he can interpret the signs that are older than Christianity.

But now he is on the sidelines while Huck observes the Duke and King play out their grasping roles. After their failure to filch Mary Jane Wilkes' patrimony, the King sells Jim to Tom Sawyer's Uncle Silas. Huck sets out to find him. Suddenly aware of his guilt in having aided a runaway slave, Huck wrestles again with his conscience. In a memorable climax to his discovery of his own natural goodness, Huck dares to defy the codes of Miss Watson's church and of Tom Sawyer's village by stealing Jim out of slavery again: 'All right, then, I'll go to hell.'

There are witches again on Uncle Silas's farm, for this is slave territory. Silas's slave, Nat, wears wool in his hair to ward them away, thinks he is bewitched when Tom tells him he is, knows this is true when a pack of hounds leap into Jim's cell through the escape hole the boys had Jim dig beneath the bed. But Jim knows better. Although manacled while Nat has the run of the place, Jim is spiritually free. Now that he has experienced the freedom of life on the raft, life in accord with the rhythms of nature, mere chains will not reduce him to subjection again. As Tom knows, he is legally free anyway. But Jim does not know this; his fortitude during his imprisonment is one of the signs of his moral stature.

Jim's stature is made manifest at the end of the book when, having suffered such needless discomfitures at Tom's hands, he voluntarily gives himself up in the swamp to help the doctor nurse back to health the boy who had plagued him. Then, brought back to the farm as he knew he would be—in chains, suffering the abuse of an angry mob, in momentary danger of lynching—Jim refuses to recognize Huck in the crowd lest he involve this other, truer friend in his own misfortunes. Jim's loyalty is so great that he is willing to sacrifice his freedom for his young friends' sakes. His selflessness is truly noble, a far cry from the chuckle-headedness of the slave who was ridden all over the country by witches when Tom Sawyer lifted his hat.

FIVE

During the decade when critical opinion at last recognized the inherent dignity of Jim, *Adventures of Huckleberry Finn,* in response to strong pressure from the N.A.A.C.P., was removed from the high school curriculum in our largest city.[5] The most eloquent statement of the objections of a Negro reader to Mark Twain's characterization of Jim is that of the novelist Ralph Ellison:

> Writing at a time when the blackfaced minstrel was still popular, and shortly after a war which left even the abolitionists weary of those problems associated with the Negro, Twain fitted Jim into the outlines of the minstrel tradition, and it is from behind this stereotype mask that we see Jim's dignity and human capacity—and Twain's complexity—emerge. Yet it is his source in this same tradition which creates that ambivalence between his identification

[5] New York *Times,* Sept. 12, 1957, pp. 1-2.

> as an adult and parent and his 'boyish' naivete, and which by contrast makes Huck, with his street-sparrow sophistication, seem more adult. . . . Jim's friendship for Huck comes across as that of a boy for another boy rather than as the friendship of an adult for a junior; thus there is implicit in it not only a violation of the manners sanctioned by society for relations between Negroes and whites, there is a violation of our conception of adult maleness.[6]

Speaking of the blackfaced minstrel, the 'smart-man-playing-dumb,' Mr. Ellison remarks that his role grows 'out of the white American's manichean fascination with the symbolism of blackness and whiteness.' This color symbolism is openly appropriated in *Huckleberry Finn;* it is used in full awareness of its ironies. We remember Pap's first appearance in the book—his face 'was white . . . a white to make a body's flesh crawl—a tree-toad white, a fishbelly white'; he it is who out of pride of color would secede from the government because it permits 'a free nigger from Ohio—a mulatter, most as white as a white man,' to vote. This early in the book the falsity of the manichean color symbolism is dramatized.

But there is no gainsaying Mr. Ellison that when Jim analyzes the stock market, or asks 'Was Sollerman Wise?' or kowtows to the bogus royalty or endures his torturous liberation for Tom's amusement he is indeed akin to the Mr. Bones of minstrel fame. I hope to have shown, however, that this is what he begins as, what he emerges from. Jim plays his comic role in slavery, when he bears the status society or Tom imposes upon him; not when he lives in his intrinsic human dignity, alone on the raft with Huck.

If Jim emerges from the degradation of slavery to become as much a man as Mark Twain could make him be, we must remember that Jim's growth marks a progress in Twain's spiritual maturity too. 'In my school days I had no aversion to slavery. I was not aware that there was anything wrong with it. No one arraigned it in my hearing . . . the local pulpit taught us that

[6] 'The Negro Writer in America: An Exchange,' *Partisan Review* XXV (Spring 1958), 215-16.

God approved it, that it was a holy thing.'[7] In 1855 Sam Clemens wrote home to his mother that a nigger had a better chance than a white man of getting ahead in New York. Mark Twain began with all the stereotypes of racial character in his mind, the stereotypes that he as well as Jim outgrows.

It is clear that supernatural folklore plays an important part in Twain's handling of Jim. Since this lore is used to differentiate Jim from the white characters, there remains the question of Mark Twain's accuracy in assigning folk belief to the black man.[8] In the preface to *Tom Sawyer*, Mark Twain makes explicit his assumption about the provenience of folk beliefs: 'The odd superstitions touched upon were all prevalent among children and slaves in the West at the period of this story—that is to say, thirty or forty years ago' (1835-45). In both books the only whites who are superstitious are either young boys or riffraff like Pap—the two categories of white folks who might have picked up the lore of the slave quarter. The only 'white' superstition in *Huckleberry Finn*, attributed to the villagers in general, is belief in the power of bread and quicksilver to discover a drowned corpse.[9] More typical of the attitude of white characters toward superstition is the derision of the raftsmen when their companion tells the ghost story of the murderer pursued by the corpse of his slain child floating in a barrel beside the raft.[10] Twain's usual assumption is that white persons of any

[7] *Mark Twain's Autobiography*, ed. Albert Biglow Paine (New York, 1924), p. 101.

[8] 'Regarding the feelings, emotions, and the spiritual life of the Negro the average white man knows little,' writes Newbell Niles Puckett in his magisterial *Folk Beliefs of the Southern Negro* (Chapel Hill, 1926), vii. 'Should some weird, archaic, Negro doctrine be brought to his attention he almost invariably considers it a "relic of African heathenism," though in four cases out of five it is a European dogma from which only centuries of patient education could wean even his own ancestors.'

[9] The identical belief is reported by Harry Middleton Hyatt in *Folklore from Adams County Illinois* (New York, 1935), a region on the opposite shore of river above Hannibal; item no. 10283.

[10] I follow Bernard De Voto (*The Portable Mark Twain*) in considering this episode, usually printed as chapter 3 of *Life on the Mississippi*, an integral part of the book for which it was originally written.

status higher than trash like Pap have little knowledge of, and no belief in, superstition.[11]

Mark Twain's memory played him wrong. All but one of the beliefs in witch-lore and in omens he used in *Huckleberry Finn* prove to be of European rather than African origin and to have been held widely among the whites as well as among the Negroes of the region. The witch who is warded off by tying one's hair with threads and who rides her victims by night is an old familiar European folk figure:

> This is that very Mab
> That plaits the manes of horses in the night

whom Mercutio described in *Romeo and Juliet* (I, iv, 88-9). Jim's fear of snakeskins, his belief that one must tell the bees of their keeper's death, his conviction that counting the things you cook for supper, or shaking the tablecloth after sundown, or speaking of the dead, or seeing the moon over your left shoulder all bring bad luck, and that a hairy chest means he's 'gwine be rich'—all these were known among the white folk of the Mississippi valley.[12] Only his divination with a hairball from the stomach of an ox is a Negro belief of voodoo origin.

Why, then, does Mark Twain make such a point of having only Negroes, children, and riffraff as the bearers of folk superstitions in the re-created world of his childhood? *Huckleberry Finn* was written while Twain lived among the insurance magnates, the manufacturing millionaires, and the wealthy literati of the Nook Farm colony in Hartford, Connecticut. It had been many years since he had lived in a superstitious frontier community, and in his own not-too-reliable memory this folklore became associated with the slaves he had known in his boyhood. The original of Jim, he writes in his *Autobiography*, was '"Uncle

[11] Pap wears a cross of nails in the heel of his boot as a charm against the devil.

[12] I have traced in detail the European origins and white provenience of these beliefs in 'Jim's Magic: Black or White?' *American Literature*, XXXII (March 1960), 47-54.

Dan'l," a middle-aged slave' on the farm of Mrs. Clemens' brother John Quarles. 'I can see the white and black children grouped around the hearth' of the slave's kitchen, 'and I can hear Uncle Dan'l telling the immortal tales which Uncle Remus Harris was to gather into his book and charm the world with.' [13] On such nights Dan'l's favorite encore was no animal fable but—as Twain wrote it down years later, in 1881, for Joel Chandler Harris's benefit—'De Woman wid de Gold'n Arm,' [14] a ghost story widely collected by folklorists since. In those days, 'every old woman' was an herb doctor; in Hannibal and Florida the young Sam Clemens knew also old Aunt Hannah, so old she had talked with Moses, who tied threads in her hair against witches. A subtle emotional complex binds together *superstition* : *slaves* : *boyhood freedom* in Mark Twain's mind. These three aspects of his experience had occurred most vividly together, and he seems, in his greatest book, not to have thought of any one of them without invoking both of the others. There is, then, no invidious intention behind his characterizing Jim by the superstitions common to both races.

I hope in the foregoing pages to have cleared Mark Twain of the imputation that 'the humor of those scenes of superstition . . . illustrate the ridiculous inadequacy and picturesque inventiveness of the fearful human responses to the powers of evil,' for such an interpretation—it is that of Francis Brownell [15] —would put all of Jim's folk beliefs in the service of the degrading minstrel characterization to which Mr. Ellison objects. The minstrel stereotype, as we have seen, was the only possible starting-point for a white author attempting to deal with Negro character a century ago. How else could young Sam Clemens have known a Negro in the Missouri of the 1840's except as the

[13] *Autobiography*, pp. 100, 112.

[14] *Mark Twain to Uncle Remus*, ed. Thomas H. English (Atlanta, 1953), pp. 11-13. Mark Twain gives another version of the tale in 'How to Tell a Story.'

[15] 'The Role of Jim in *Huckleberry Finn*,' *Boston Univ. Studies in English*, I (1955), 81.

little white boy on familiar terms with his uncle's household retainer? The measure of Mark Twain's human understanding—Mr. Ellison calls it his complexity—is evident when we compare Jim to the famous Negro character in the writings of Mark Twain's friend, Joel Chandler Harris, remembering that Sam Clemens was in real life to 'Uncle' Dan'l as the little boy in Harris's books is to Uncle Remus. The Georgia author's Negro fablist never ceases to be the minstrel in blackface. The poetic irony in the Uncle Remus books is one of which Harris was probably unaware: the Negro's human dignity survives the minstrel mask not in Uncle Remus's character but in the satirical stories he tells the white boy. That many of these were thinly veiled avowals of the Negro's pride and dignity and refusal to submit his spirit to the unjust yoke of custom would not seem to have occurred to Joel Chandler Harris, whose conscious literary strategy was to palliate Northern antagonism of the South by idealizing ante-bellum plantation life.[16] But Mark Twain tries to make Jim stride out of his scapegoat minstrel's role to stand before us in the dignity of his own manhood. It is true that Mark Twain's triumph here is incomplete: despite the skillful gradation of folk belief and other indications of Jim's emergent stature, what does come through for many readers is, as Mr. Ellison remarks, Jim's boy-to-boy relationship with Huck, 'a violation of our conception of adult maleness.' We remember that Mark Twain himself admired Uncle Remus extravagantly, and much as he means for us to admire Jim—much as he admires Jim himself—the portrait, though drawn in deepest sympathy, is yet seen from the outside. The closest that Mark Twain gets to Jim's soul, and the furthest from the stereotyped minstrel mask, is the ethical coherence with which the author's manipulation of folk superstitions allows him to endow the slave. In both his emergence toward manhood

[16] This is a point I have discussed in some detail in a review of *Joel Chandler Harris—Folklorist* by Stella Brewer Brookes, in *Midwest Folklore,* I (Summer 1951), 133-8. See also John Stafford, 'Patterns of Meaning in *Nights with Uncle Remus,' American Literature,* XVIII (May 1946), 89-108.

through the exercise of his freedom and in his supernatural power as interpreter of the oracles of nature, Jim comes to be the hero of his own magic. The test and proof of natural goodness, which raises Jim and Huck above religious hypocrisy and selfish romanticism, is its transforming power upon him. The fear-ridden slave becomes in the end a source of moral energy. The shifting of Jim's shape is reversed at the end, as he sinks back from his heroism to become the bewildered freed darky of reconstruction days, grateful to the young white boss for that guilt-payment of forty dollars. (It did bring true his only good luck omen: a hairy breast and arms meant that he's 'gwineter be rich . . . signs is signs!') For Jim has status now, a status imposed by society, not, as was his moral eminence, determined by his inner nature. And it is status of which Huck is now afraid; for at the end he is preparing to flee again, this time to 'light out for the territory ahead of the rest. . . . Aunt Sally she's going to adopt and sivilize me, and I can't stand it. I been there before.' For Huck, '*there*' means the stasis of being a part of society. His voyage, like Jim's, was a quest for freedom too; after their idyll and their ordeals, both find only the equivocal freedom of status at the end of their odyssey. The pattern of action in this double quest depended upon their freedom of movement—of both spatial movement and social mobility. Freedom to die in each identity, freedom to be reborn anew in another—this pattern of action is the theme of the next chapter.

16

Huckleberry Finn: His Masquerade

ONE

It is often noted that the very first chapter of *Huckleberry Finn* introduces suggestions of the classical pattern of the death and rebirth of the hero. That chapter is titled 'Moses Among the Bulrushers,' and the flotation or immersion of Moses, his discovery, and his subsequent assumption of a new identity appear to be re-enacted by Huck himself. When he escapes from Pap his ruse involves a mimetic death; he then escapes by water to Jackson's Island. Again, each time Huck is accosted on the raft, or steals ashore, or when the raft is run over by a steamboat, he emerges from the baptismal river to assume a new identity. But is this pattern actually comparable to the rebirth of the mythical hero, or to his assumption, after initiation, of a new identity?

Huck's character seems rather to remain true to the American folk concept of the metamorphic hero. He changes his identities without altering the character which it is their function to conceal behind the comic masquerade of American folklore. He is not initiated into any sacred knowledge through his metamorphoses. That initiation comes to him through his relationship with Jim, and his identity with respect to Jim is constant. Indeed, it is his only constant identity in all of his *Adventures*.

Huck's other identities are disguises of two kinds, those which he assumes of his own volition and those which are thrust upon him. The selves which he is obliged to wear include the civilized village boy adopted by the Widow Douglas; the romantic outlaw of Tom Sawyer's gang; the valley (valet) of the Duke and King —a prop to their masquerade as the Wilks brothers returned from England and their plot to steal Mary Jane's inheritance; and his role as Tom Sawyer which Aunt Sally Phelps puts upon him at the end. In none of these guises is Huck either free or happy.

The other roles are those Huck himself assumes. If he was Jim's pupil in the superstition line, here he is his own master. Huck makes up whole life histories as quickly as his tongue can tell them. He puts ashore at a cabin dressed as a girl, name of Sarah Williams.

> No'm, I ain't hungry. I was so hungry I had to stop two miles below here at a farm; so I ain't hungry no more. It's what made me so late. My mother's down sick, and out of money and everything, and I come to tell my uncle Abner Moore. He lives at the upper end of the town, she says. . . .

But the farm woman unmasks him by testing the way he threads a needle and holds a lump of lead in his lap. 'So I said it wouldn't be no use to try to play it any longer, and I would just make a clean breast . . . Then I told her my father and mother was dead, and the law had bound me out to a mean old farmer . . .' Under the new alias of George Peters, Huck makes his getaway from the wily Mrs. Judith Loftus.

After escaping with Jim from the wrecked steamer Walter Scott, Huck assumes yet another mask. 'There ain't no telling but I might become a murderer myself yet,' he muses, for no role is beyond possibility's pale for him. This fact gives him sympathy for even the undeserving, and so he dons a new identity to inveigle the ferryman to rescue the three murderers marooned aboard the wreck. He soon has to become something else in a hurry when the nigger-hunters approach the raft. In a moment the mask is on him again, and out comes a full-blown tale of pap and mam and Mary-Ann all sick with—Huck never *says* it's the smallpox, but he manipulates grown men with all of Sam

Slick's knowledge of 'human natur and soft soder.' Bobbing up from the waters after a riverboat runs down the raft, Huck finds his next identity as George Jackson while the Grangerfords frisk his pockets. As he escapes from the feud, he and Jim are overtaken by the Duke and Dauphin. Again it is Huck's sympathy for the underdog that makes him heed when 'they sung out and begged me to save their lives.' He lets them come aboard but soon has to explain why he hid the raft, ran it by night, and whether Jim was a runaway. 'Goodness sakes! would a runaway nigger run *south?*' asks Huck:

> My folks was living in Pike County, in Missouri, where I was born [these phrases and pauses are of course time-fillers, till Huck can fit a good yarn together], and they all died off but me and pa and my brother Ike. . . . a steamboat run over the forrard corner of the raft one night, and we all went overboard and dove under the wheel; Jim and me come up, all right, but pa was drunk, and Ike was only four years old . . . Well, for the next day or two we had considerable trouble, because people was always coming out in skiffs and trying to take Jim away from me, saying they believed he was a runaway nigger. We don't run daytimes no more now; nights they don't bother us.

All of Huck's freely chosen commitments to one face or another of his varied masquerade are given with the ultimate end of protecting Jim and himself from the world.

Huck finds the perfect fulfillment of self only after his escape from Pap; the pages between that escape and his discovery of Jim's campfire on Jackson's Island are the most idyllic in the book. Here is Huck, before most of his adventures have begun, in perfect accord with the natural world around him and the natural boy within. But the reality-principle reasserts itself by involving him with his fellow-man. With Jim he must assume responsibility and give love. Then he will receive Jim's love and solicitude in return. But in almost all of the episodes that follow, the idealized realization of their relationship is frustrated, impinged upon, almost destroyed. (For instance, the idyllic tone is resumed—for the last time—just after the feud; but then the

Duke and Dauphin come aboard, and Huck has no occasion to speak so lyrically again.) It is society which threatens the fulfillment of the individual—straight transcendentalist doctrine as lived on the frontier. In each of his metamorphoses, which Huck assumes only as a means of defense, he is momentarily free. But this freedom is immediately circumscribed by the curiosity, self-interest, or malice of the people whose intrusion upon his and Jim's solitude had led him to don the face of the mask.

Huck's powers of transformation are not, however, illimitably protean. There are some selves which he cannot wear save at his peril. Whenever he tries to be like Tom Sawyer, the results are fraught with danger. The snakeskin trick reminds us of the pranks Tom played. Huck's boarding the Walter Scott was sheer folly, yet he makes Jim climb aboard with the taunt, 'Do you reckon Tom Sawyer would ever go by this thing?' When he tries to outwit the bogus royalty during their nasty masquerade as the Wilkes brothers, 'I reckoned Tom Sawyer couldn't 'a' done it no neater himself'; but Huck's plan, although as complicated as any Tom might have drawn, is completely forestalled by the unforeseen arrival of the *real* Wilkes brothers. 'This was the most awful trouble and most dangersome I ever was in.' Yet Huck's elaborate plan had, after all, the aim of exposing the fraud and returning their fortune to the Wilkes girls. If he adopted Tom's style, it was for his own good ends, and this failure is not at all comparable to Huck's inability to carry out the role the King and Duke had assigned him in the furtherance of their designs. When Lawyer Bell holds inquest at the tavern, Huck, the master of the long bow, is at once exposed. 'Set down, my boy . . . I reckon you ain't used to lying, it don't seem to come handy; what you want is practice. You do it pretty awkward.' At that kind of lie Huck doesn't have the knack; whatever 'stretchers' he spins on his own, he cannot go against the goodness of his nature. Not even in prayer, as he discovers in chapter 31. The King has sold Jim and Huck figures Jim would be better off being a slave back home. 'I was trying to make my mouth *say* I would do the right thing and the clean thing, and go and write that nigger's owner and tell where he was; but deep down in me I knowed it was a lie, and He knowed it. You can't pray a lie—I found that out.' Huck writes the letter to Miss Watson, but he still can't pray. At last he decides to steal Jim out of slavery again. '"All right, then, I'll go to hell"—and tore it up.'

Huck's masquerade is his only defense against the treacherous world, and only twice does he 'resk the truth' instead of wearing it. With astonishment he discovers the truth to be safer than stretchers when he reveals the Duke and King's fraud to Mary Jane. Even then he doesn't tell the whole truth, for his secret is Jim, in hiding. Once more he is *about* to tell the truth—tell who he really is—when he arrives at the Phelps plantation to try to reclaim Jim. But the Phelpses are expecting someone, and just as Huck opens his mouth to confess his identity, Uncle Silas calls him 'Tom Sawyer.' From here until the final page Huck is Tom and Tom, when he arrives, is Sid: rather a painful downgrading of both. That Mark Twain did not lose sight of Huck's superior values in the concluding farce is explicit enough on the pages (chapters 40-41) where Huck leaves Tom, wounded in the swamp, to fetch the doctor. Tom's parting instructions are a farandole of mystification—blindfold the doctor, cross his palm with gold, etc., for 'It's the way they do.' As always, Tom's mind runs in the rococo grooves of romantic convention. But Huck tells the doctor a plausible tale of going hunting with his brother who 'must 'a' kicked his gun in his dream, for it went off and shot him in the leg.'

> 'How'd you say he got shot?'
> 'He had a dream,' I says, 'and it shot him.'

Tom's dream of course is more than half of Mark Twain's view of reality; Huck's view of reality is the far better half of Mark Twain's dream. These are the compelling reasons why Tom and his intricate deceptions of everybody—including Huck—must reappear at the end of the book. This is how the reader is made to awake from the dream of Huck's continuing escapes in his perfect innocence from the nightmares of entrapment which ever threaten to enclose him. Tom, and Tom's family, are the world of convention, respectability, and status from which Huck had fled in the beginning. Huck had been keen enough and innocent enough to avoid the threats to his identity of the retrograde Pap, of the avaricious slave-hunters, of the feuders with their courtly savagery and the lynch mob with its cowardly passions. He could even survive among the rapacious Duke and King, and pity them in their disaster. But among these Phelpses and Sawyers, among these genteel people of good intentions but artificial impulses, there is only one defense. And that is to flee again.

TWO

Huck's problem, then, is at the end what it had been all along: how to preserve his essential self. And which of his identities is his identity? In Emerson's terms, the 'Me' is inviolable, untouched by the masquerades which it must devise to arm itself against the 'not-Me.' This reminds us again of Hawthorne's Holgrave, who could move through so many vicissitudes without affecting the inner man or compromising his conscience. Both Mark Twain and, in that case, Hawthorne, apprehended that the metamorphic hero of folk culture would need the bonds of affection and of passion to humanize him. Hawthorne tried to give his Holgrave the tie of love, but we cannot take very seriously his feelings for Phoebe Pyncheon. Twain, however, endowed his metamorphic Huck with yet a stronger tie: brotherhood.

This bond has often been the closest relationship conceivable in the American imagination. Doubtless it is our residual puritanism which has made the power of sexual love less a force in our literature than the power of comradeship. Leslie Fiedler makes the most sensational statement of something approximating this thesis; he goes on to propose a 'myth' of the infantile, immaculate, homoerotic love of a white and a colored man as the passionate theme of *Huckleberry Finn*, the Leatherstocking tales and *Moby-Dick*. Seriously to entertain the notion of this as a major strand of American literature is surely to distort the cultural significance of the ties between Huck and Jim, Leatherstocking and Chingachgook, Ishmael and Queequeg. The two themes they actually exemplify are primitivism and egalitarianism.

Among the ideals of the American Enlightenment, when the outlines of our culture were drawn with so firm a hand, romantic love would seem to have had little place. Egalitarianism, however, appears early as the basis of our national character. It is written into our eighteenth-century political documents, and, as Crèvecœur observed even before those documents were drafted, it is in the spirit of our institutions and of our colonial laws. In a nation which has what Mr. Ellison calls 'the white American's manichean fascination' with color, isn't the ideal expression of equality an absolute commitment to a member of another race—just because such a relationship is in reality so difficult to entertain? Huck's relation to Jim deepens toward both perfect equality and toward filial love. In perfect equality there cannot be even the superiority of the older generation to the younger, the deference of child to parent. Hence Mr. Ellison's objections to Jim's character as a contradiction of our conception of adult maleness. Since Mark Twain couldn't make Huck a grown-up he had to make Jim seem Huck's buddy, and so he seems to the boy who tells the tale. To the perceptive reader, however, Jim's dignity is the reality which Huck respects.

In the last century the nonwhite races could seem living examples of still other doctrines deeply rooted in the American mind. As a Noble Savage the Negro, the Indian or Polynesian proved the sublimity of the natural man. He demonstrated the purity of life under the unobstructed influence of Nature, and so exposed in all its corruption the effects of civilization. Even when Jim wears the minstrel mask he does so in pastoral satire upon the society which relegated him to the lowly roles of clown and seer.

For the white Southerner the contemplation of the Negro raises a special problem with respect to his understanding of himself. His sense of personal identity cannot be dissociated from his relation to the Negro, whom his own society has disfranchised from all of the promises of American life. Since identity can have significance only as an expression of responsibility, Huck, alone on Jackson's Island, cannot yet know who he really is. He cannot learn this until Jim's fate is actually linked to his fate, in his hands. That a boy on the tattered fringe of white society should still have to conquer such vestigial pride of race, should have to try to 'pray a lie' and determine to go to hell to be true to his inner nature, is Mark Twain's harshest judgment upon the culture of the South. In this book Huck proves worthy of both Jim and of his own inner nature. Jim, for his part, proves worthy of Huck and of his own innate nobility too.

Yet at the same time that Huck moves toward self-knowledge, in another sense which we have seen his *Adventures* are a circle. Not only does Tom's world of learned pretense and romantic artifice close Huck's odyssey, but the final role in which Huck is cast duplicates the very first. Society has at last caught up with the fugitive Huckleberry. It has followed him clear down the river past Cairo and the lost dream of absolute freedom, of complete equality, of perfect comradeship. His only defense now is what it had been before—to 'light out for the territory ahead of the rest.' This seems to promise further escapes and further adventures, yet Mark Twain could not envisage Huck grown up save as sinking back into the moral sloth of Pap, like Crèvecœur's frontiersman. Thus Huck's *Adventures* both are and are not contained within the aesthetic form in which they are cast. Awakened from Huck's lost dream by Tom's romanticism, we must return to the reality of a world like that of Tom and Aunt Polly and the Phelpses. But Huck's dream has by now become ours, and never again can we accept our fate—being 'sivilized'—without the poignant awareness of how much of our soul's innocence and freedom we, like Huck, must surrender if we are to live in a world that others have made.

Retrospect:
Reality as Fable

Retrospect: Reality as Fable

The core of the American experience has been a radical search for identity by attempting to free ourselves from old forms, old orders, old hierarchies of rank and belief, to discover the emergent man. Our culture has traditionally proposed as the basis for its new, indigenous forms the innate sanctity of the individual—his natural goodness, his 'divine equality.' Therefore the romance, as Hawthorne, Melville, and Mark Twain envisaged it, proved a form of art peculiarly consonant with the bias of our culture. Their inward vision and their concern with archetypal individual experience (as with Robin, Coverdale, Ishmael, and Huck) objectify these 'real' values of American life.

Our romance writers have all taken the role of the artist to be the discoverer and revealer of truth. Rarely seeking that truth in contemporary reality, they found it disguised in the past of their ancestors or in their own childhoods or in symbol-freighted voyages abstracted from the economic and political life of their time. When they do treat social problems it is usually at a distance in time which makes the problems seem remote and 'unreal' to the contemporary reader. Such may be the effect of Hawthorne's concentration on Puritan days to demonstrate that sin of pride for which contemporary examples were not lacking, and of Mark Twain's resolution of the moral problem of slavery in 1885—a quarter-century too late to exert any political influence on the issue. At that, the center of consciousness in *Huckleberry Finn* is a boy. Among these books *The Blithedale Romance* is the only one in which contemporary social and political problems are dealt with directly and rendered by the sensibility of an adult. Yet Hawthorne places Miles Coverdale on the periphery of life, making him an observer and interpreter rather than an active participant. In using current social doctrines and realistic materials Hawthorne's concern is primarily aesthetic rather than political, as his hero's profession as 'minor poet' and the tautly controlled style of the book attest. On the whole, Hawthorne, Melville, and Twain do not present their characters 'as embedded in a total reality, political, social, and economic, which is concrete and constantly evolving.' The reality they render is more generalized than that proposed by Auerbach as the basis of realism.[1] Their romances reflect the isolation of the individual, his rebellion against authority and tradition, his solitary confrontation of primal forces, his consequent need to discover or redefine his own identity. Archetypal patterns derived from myth and folklore and ritual, enacted in both individual and communal experience, provide structures for their explorations of these themes.

In form and spirit, as well as in content, the romance proved peculiarly adaptable to the needs of these authors. The absence of classical precepts governing its structure offered freedom to the writer who would develop his forms empirically from his materials. The form itself remains indeterminate, picaresque, enveloping interpolated tales. The romance tends to absorb or become pastoral idyl, satire, or representational novel, yet it retains its distinctive character. The traditions immediately antecedent to the American romance were, as we have seen, allegorical, Gothic, and transcendental. In these works allegory was transformed into symbolism; the Gothic mode (despite its melodrama) assumed a seriousness unusual elsewhere by virtue of the communal values represented in supernatural folklore; and the transcendental aesthetic gave the whole work metaphoric consistency. In narrative method the romance tends to employ metaphor as a

[1] Eric Auerbach, *Mimesis* (New York, 1957), p. 408.

structural device. While the novel can get along in its absence, the romance cannot do without this unifying use of metaphor. Ernst Cassirer has shown the psychological identity of the metaphoric nature of language with the myth-making capacities of mind; in the American romance these two means for revealing the inherent forms of experience are readily linked, reinforcing each other at each juncture.

The unity these romances achieve is thus largely determined by both their 'poetic' and their 'mythic' dimensions. The romance is 'poetic' in its use of the radical powers of self-discovery of the metaphor-making mind. It is 'mythic' in appropriating from myth and folklore the patterns in which the archetypal themes of journey, quest, and initiation can best be organized. Since the romance is committed, as a form, neither to a tragic, a Christian, nor a comic resolution of its dilemmas, it was favored as an instrument for the discovery of meaning. Our authors, inheriting a disused Protestant orthodoxy, could not reconcile the absolute claims of faith with the moral ambiguities of life; tragic *hubris* to them exemplified the Romantic ego in its anarchy. Neither the tragic nor the Christian resolution appeared true to the life they knew. Comedy served them better with its implicit humanism, its tolerance of opposites, and its intrinsic offering of a masquerade in which the pursuit of truth may be clandestinely conducted. Insofar as they were concerned with the realistic aspects of culture they found such reality dramatized in the conflicts between indigenous and inherited values in American life. These tensions between their New and Old World heritages they envisaged most powerfully in re-creations of American folk characters and the legendary heroes of the past.

In tracing the shared debts of our romancers to these traditions it becomes clear that they do have common commitments to themes implicit in our national experience. Whether they treat native character in accordance with the vulgar optimism of popular comedy, or use comic stereotypes to explore in irony or satire the discrepancies between native self-assertion and what Melville called 'the blackness of darkness' within us, these authors responded to the same elements in American life and together contribute to a significant tradition. Our recognition of these concerns they share should alter somewhat our sense of where the continuities lie in American literature. It is quite true that if we divide our writers into 'Palefaces' and 'Redskins,' as Philip Rahv has suggestively proposed, we will think of Hawthorne taking tea with Oliver Wendell Holmes and Henry James, while Melville and Twain seek their dark-skinned camerados near Whitman's campfire in the wilderness. In assessing the traditions in our literature—as in defining its themes—I find pluralism more accurate than any prescriptive insistence upon mutually exclusive alternatives. Hawthorne, then, still wearing his undoubted pallor, can join the creators of Ishmael and Huck on the grounds he actually shares with them. His involvement with the themes they later drew upon, his pioneering development of forms they later used, indicate the profundity of his own mythmaking mind and the degree to which his sensibility, like theirs, was stirred by images of the subconscious primitive energies of fecundity and creation. Hawthorne's pallor comes from seclusion in the library. In the witchcraft documents and the pages of antiquarians he found his images akin to those that came to Melville and Twain not only from eclectic readings but from their own experiences in folk life. Yet even while we think of Hawthorne as a redskin indoors we must recall his own exposure to the folk life of a New England village with its population of Yankee characters and its local traditions of comic folktales, omens, and prophecies.

The traditions and themes these romancers share go beyond their responses to folk character and to folk-cherished images of the creative sources of life which Christianity and rationalism had repressed into the subconscious. In their sensibilities we see the conflict between pagan energy and Christian ethics, between primitivism and civilization, between free will and determinism, between optimism and despair. All of these dialectical conflicts may be subsumed in their exploration of the opposing claims of democracy and traditional order. The romancers all responded deeply to the promise of egalitarian freedom, a promise as indeterminate as it was all-encompassing. The free man in the free society would have to create his own order anew from the chaos out of which he had emerged; and that chaos seemed all the more threatening because it was largely by his own will that the established order of the social and the supernatural world had been destroyed. Yet the inherited order was itself an intolerable threat to the existence and self-knowledge of the individual, representing stasis, rigidity, the defeat of every force save inertia. In working out the destinies of such representative heroes as Robin Molineux, Hester, Holgrave, Miles Coverdale, Ishmael, Israel Potter, Pitch, and Huck Finn, our romancers made synoptic metaphors drawn from the folk traditions and the world-historical myths. Their imaginations placed these heroes in the crucial American experience: rebellion. They recognized that in his uncompromised rebellion the individual declares his independence from family, from social class, from church and God, from history.

Therefore in these romances the individual is defined not, as in the novels of Dickens, Flaubert, or Tolstoy, by his complex interrelationships with others who represent various social classes and their values. Instead he is defined by his relations to characters representing the contending forces in his own psyche or the alternative commitments of belief, value, and action available to him. The most significant relationships in the American romance, are those between the representative hero and characters who embody unfallen innocence or innate corruption, primitive purity or civilized guilt, intellectual isolation or passionate community. Consequently the characters in the romance tend to reflect the allegorical bias of their origins and are seldom drawn with the inclusive roundedness and realism of those in novels of society. Yet they give the reader a sense of their own urgency and their function in the narrative is at once morally and emotionally valid. They constitute the *archai* of the world they move in, and by their archetypicality they move us too.

The structure of the romances we have examined seems amenable to no single set of rules or preconceptions. As the work of the romancer has been the discovery of identity and of meaning, so his means have been empirical and experimental. The combinations our authors have made of mythic patterns, folklore themes, ritual actions, and observed social conditions proved capable of encompassing both the 'real' and the 'marvellous,' of moving from the natural to the supernatural, of dealing with the imagined past and the observed present in terms of comparable intensity. The language they have used has varied from Hawthorne's formal diction of public discourse to Twain's mastery of the vernacular; Melville in *Moby-Dick* not only combines Jacobean rhetoric with journalese, Yankee drawl, and frontier tall talk, but proves a word-coiner of astonishing poetic power. Yet it is incontestable that each of our authors has suffered from these very advantages of flexibility and freedom. For who can tell how much of his creative energy had to be expended on the continual invention of adequate forms, perhaps at the expense of works that might have come into being had the chief problem been merely how to write within a given tradition? Much as Hawthorne could learn from Irving, and Melville from Hawthorne, and Twain from all his predecessors, each still had to assimilate the materials for each of his books anew. We recall that Twain's solution in *Huckleberry Finn* was arrived at seemingly subconsciously, after an interruption of eight years when he was midway through the story and could not complete it. The difficulties in the composition of these romances testify to the unavoidable problems in the American sensibility which it is their authors' self-sought obligation to define.

American novelists after Mark Twain developed their form in a less parochial atmosphere than had prevailed before the Civil War. Howells set out to emulate the Russian novelists in the closeness of his study of modern society and the range of his observation of classes. James, who mastered Flaubertian precision in style, conceived of his work novelistically, as the imitation of reality, while yet retaining the imaginative license of the romance in his ghostly tales and in his often Gothic plots. By the century's turn, however, with the introduction of literary naturalism, the native themes and tensions explored by the romance writers were abandoned for the tracing and retracing of the unequal struggle between impersonal social forces and the slum-blighted human integers they oppressed, such as Crane's Maggie, Dreiser's Carrie and Clyde Griffiths, Farrell's Studs. In the realistic novel, folk characters degenerated to the dimensions of Howells's Bartley Hubbard in *A Modern Instance,* a Sam Slick adrift in the city, or the book-peddler who disappears after a hundred pages in Dos Passos's *U.S.A.*, where he had seemed a curious survival from an earlier condition of society.

Yet the sensibility informing the romance has not been outmoded, nor is it likely to disappear as an active force on the American imagination. As we pass mid-century the work of William Faulkner looms as the most sustained achievement in American fiction since Henry James. And although Faulkner has practised many genres of fiction and has based his work more firmly on the documentation of social reality than any other major novelist of our time, his continuing affinity with the romance-novels we have examined is strong and clear. Their themes are his themes; the folklore that leavens their characters lives anew in his; the mythic patterns as antique as time that braced their experiences are the bulwarks still of his vision of the tensions between individual responsibility and the heritage of his culture. The forms and themes of the American romance are present too, in the work of authors younger than Faulkner—Saul Bellow, Ralph Ellison, and others. Their achievements, taken together, suggest that the romance tradition, coupled in our time with a more immediate social documentation than Hawthorne, Melville, or Twain allowed themselves, will long continue as a shaping force in American fiction.

Index